IRISH POLITICAL ECONOMY

IRISH POLITICAL ECONOMY

Edited by
Tom Boylan and Tadhg Foley

Volume II

Value and Distribution

R Routledge
Taylor & Francis Group

LONDON AND NEW YORK

First published 2003
by Routledge
11 New Fetter Lane, London EC4P 4EE

Simultaneously published in the USA and Canada
by Routledge
29 West 35th Street, New York, NY 10001

Routledge is an imprint of the Taylor & Francis Group

Editorial matter and selection © 2003 Tom Boylan and Tadhg Foley;
individual owners retain copyright in their own material

Typeset in Times by RefineCatch Limited, Bungay, Suffolk
Printed and bound in Great Britain by
TJ International Ltd, Padstow, Cornwall

British Library Cataloguing in Publication Data
A catalogue record for this book is available from the British Library

Library of Congress Cataloging in Publication Data
A catalog record for this book has been requested

ISBN 0–415–14736–0 (Set)
ISBN 0–415–14738–7 (Volume II)

Publisher's Note
References within each chapter are as they appear in the original
complete work

CONTENTS

v

CONTENTS

INTRODUCTION TO VOLUME II

The period from the passing of the Corn Laws in 1816 to their repeal in 1846 has been described, in terms of economic theory, as 'the Age of Ricardo',[1] beginning with Ricardo's own *Principles of Political Economy and Taxation* (1817) and ending with John Stuart Mill's *Principles of Political Economy* (1848). Ricardo dominated economic discourse in the early nineteenth century, in the words of one commentator, burning 'deep scars on to the Classical-economic consciousness'.[2] However, a dominant Ricardian orthodoxy in any strict sense did not emerge. The early century was too intellectually turbulent for that to occur, riven as it was by social, political, and ideological conflicts. The foundations of political economy, both methodologically and substantively, were still insecure. Ricardo's centrality was based on the schematic structure of his contribution, the potency of his analysis, and the implications of his conclusions. As a result, most writers, particularly those of the first half of the century, had to locate their own contributions in relation to Ricardo, whether they accepted, rejected, modified, or indeed misrepresented his contribution. Three groups of writers within the British classical school have been identified: the Ricardians, the Ricardian socialists, and the anti-Ricardians. In Ireland all three variants of Ricardianism were represented by such writers as Cairnes, Thompson, and Longfield, in the area of value and distribution theory.

With regard to value theory, the historiography of Irish political economy has been dominated by the contribution of Mountifort Longfield, which received belated recognition as a progenitor of the subjective theory of value in the work of Seligman and Smith.[3] Building on this work, R.D. Collison Black extended this analysis to include a number of the early Whately Professors who, he argued, constituted a 'school' of subjective value theorists who anticipated by thirty years the marginalist revolution of the 1870s.[4] While the idea of a Dublin 'school' was a challenging one, it was perhaps an overstatement of the case. It is, however, certain that a number of Longfield's immediate successors did subscribe to, and provided insights into, the role of the subject in the theory of value. These developments may be traced largely to the influence of the founder of the chair, Richard Whately.

1

Whately himself was a product of British anti-Ricardianism. The use by socialists of Ricardo's theory of value and distribution generated an ideological hostility to his search for an absolute measure of value based on a labour theory of value. This group included Samuel Bailey, a strident critic of Ricardo who, in his *A Critical Dissertation on the Nature, Measure and Causes of Value* (1825), rejected the Ricardian idea of 'absolute value' in place of a concept of value which, based on exchange, gave rise only to a concept of 'relative value'. In addition, Bailey suggested that value was subjectively perceived and consequently it denoted only an effect produced in the mind of the economic agent. Mention should be made here of Robert Torrens, an Irishman who, three years prior to Bailey, also rejected Ricardo's labour theory of value immediately following its publication in Ricardo's *Principles*. In his *Essay on the Production of Wealth* (1822), Torrens developed his own theory of value which rejected Ricardo's attempt to establish an absolute theory, and argued instead that value was basically exchange value based on the costs of production, which included not just the capital to sustain production, but also the 'capital' used to pay labour, which was the basis for its designation as a 'capital theory of value'.[5] Other writers in the 'anti-Ricardian' tradition included Samuel Read whose *An Inquiry into the Natural Grounds of Right to Vendible Property of Wealth* (1829) and George Poulett Scrope whose *Principles of Political Economy* (1833), articulated an explicit anti-Ricardian stance, while William Foster Lloyd made a valuable contribution to the role of utility in the theory of demand, in his publication *A Lecture on the Notion of Value* (1834).

In an Irish context, by virtue of his influence on Whately, Nassau Senior was one of the most influential anti-Ricardian political economists.[6] Senior, who had held the first Drummond Professorship of Political Economy at Oxford, and who was succeeded by Whately before his departure for Dublin, rejected a number of the central tenets of Ricardo's economics, including the labour theory of value and the Malthusian population theory. In the domain of value theory, Senior attempted to reconcile two divergent strands of thought, the Ricardian and the subjectivist theorists, particularly those of Say in France and Bailey in England.[7] This led Senior to argue that value depended on the conditions of both supply and demand, analysing supply in terms of its limitations on the satisfaction of demand, and demand in terms of the utility of the goods demanded. Senior also came close to identifying the principle of diminishing marginal utility, but failed, as others had, to connect this to the demand curve. For Senior, a good had value if it had utility, was transferable, and was limited in supply. Value in exchange depended on the causes that limited the supply of commodities and those that conferred utility on the demand side. Value in exchange was also the only meaningful concept of value for Whately, a view that he held with deep conviction in opposition to the labour theory of value. Whately went so far as to propose that political economy should be renamed 'catallactics', or the science of exchange. While Whately's own writings contributed little to the substantive content of the theoretical corpus of political economy, he was more concerned with clarifying the conditions of the possibility of the discipline, or a particular version of political economy, a version that was deeply anti-Ricardian in character and strongly influenced by Senior's position on many issues. Given Whately's interest and involvement in the appointment procedures to the professorship that he established, it would have been surprising if the first incumbent turned out to be a Ricardian.

Four members of the Dublin School of subjective value theory are included in Volume II of this anthology. Two excerpts from Longfield's *Lectures on Political Economy* (1834) reflect the style and originality of his contribution and his disagreement with the Ricardian theory of value and distribution. He approached these topics primarily as a pricing problem, in which a theory of value, based on market prices and determined by supply and demand was located at the centre of the analysis, which was then applied to the pricing of the factor inputs. The early chapters of *Lectures* were devoted to, among other things, addressing objections to the discipline and offering a general defence of it, along with extended definitions of wealth and value. It is in the sixth and later lectures that Longfield's original contributions occurred. In this treatment of value in Lecture VI Longfield discarded his earlier preoccupations with labour as a measure of value and proceeded to develop an impressive theory of price determination. The influence of cost on market price through changes in supply was not neglected, but was no longer central to the analysis. The main emphasis was placed on demand, where Longfield introduced the concept of a demand schedule, where market demand was conceived as a ranking of individual demands according to their intensity, where 'the market price is measured by that demand, which being of the least intensity, yet leads to actual purchases' (vol. 2, p. 28). Longfield thus reverted to the concept of the individual's demand schedule as composed of 'several demands of different degrees of intensity'. This is now accepted as a seminal statement, foreshadowing the principle of marginal utility that was to find its formal and more complete articulation, in the 1870s, by the leaders of the neo-classical marginalist revolution.

Longfield's immediate successor, Isaac Butt, who held the Whately Chair from 1836 to 1841, is generally included as a member of the Dublin School, though his inclusion, while defensible, is less compelling. Butt certainly thought highly of Longfield and in the area of distribution theory attempted to combine the utility approach of Say and Senior with particular elements of Longfield's theory of distribution.[8] With respect to value theory and the theory of market prices, Butt relied almost exclusively on Say's analysis, noting that all market prices were 'regulated by nothing else than . . . utility and scarcity' (vol II, pp. 16–18). Butt made no attempt to elaborate on these comments nor to link this theory of value with Longfield's supply and demand theory of price determination. Butt's insights into utility with respect to value and market price were derived from sources other than Longfield, and in the course of his published writings Butt did not anywhere mention Longfield's theory of price based on supply and demand.

James Anthony Lawson, the third holder of the Whately Chair from 1841 to 1846, published his *Five Lectures on Political Economy* in 1844, which unfortunately did not include the section, referred to by Lawson in which 'the nature and production of value' was addressed. All that is available of his contribution to the theory of value is contained in an Appendix to this work, which is included in Volume II. There is no doubt about Lawson's commitment to the subjective theory of value and his contribution, though tantalizingly brief, was clear and lucidly expounded. Lawson was one of the first to argue that utility, and only utility, regulated market force. It was a proposition always true, and of universal application

> *that the exchangeable value of all artides depends upon their utility,* that is, upon their power to gratify the wants and wishes of man . . . Every other principle, which has been assigned as the regulating cause of exchangeable value, is of partial and limited application, and subject to many restrictions of exceptions.
>
> (vol. 2, p. 38)

This represents Lawson's view of both the cost-of-production and the supply-and-demand theories of value. For Lawson, both theories offered only partial explanations of how price was determined, since utility was the only determinant of price. Lawson proceeded to examine both of these 'partial explanations' and, in the course of his analysis of supply and demand, he clearly identified the principle of diminishing utility while, in his discussion of the cost-of-production theory, he perceptively argued that 'value is only made to coincide with cost of production *through the medium of a change in supply*, and when this cannot be brought about, there is no such coincidence and no tendency to it' (vol. 2, p. 39). It is hard to disagree with Black's comment that the 'quality of such passages . . . makes it a matter for regret that we have not access to Lawson's main work on value, and that he did not devote himself more thoroughly to economic theory'.[9] Had Lawson devoted himself 'more thoroughly' to theoretical issues, one can only speculate as to the extent that he would have surpassed Longfield's formidable contributions and have emerged as the intellectual leader of the 'Dublin School' of subjective theorists.

The contribution included here by William Neilson Hancock is from his only work on theoretical economics, his *Introductory Lecture on Political Economy* (1849) which is both interesting and perceptive with respect to the theory of value. Hancock, who succeeded Lawson in the Whately chair in 1846, was concerned with a central ambiguity in the use of the word 'value', which made it synonymous with cost. Hancock, however, pointed to the fact that the word price was 'fortunately free from all ambiguity' and always meant the 'exchangeable value of a commodity, estimated in the money of the country' where the exchange took place. He then proposed 'to substitute observations into the variations in price for observations into variations in value' (vol. 2, p. 45). Hancock proceeded to analyse different types of changes in price, or what he called 'intrinsic and extrinsic changes in prices', the intrinsic he described as price changes arising from 'changes from the side of things', and called this the theory of prices, while the extrinsic arose from 'changes from the side of money', and this he called the theory of money. In developing this theory of prices, he introduced his concept of 'degree of desirability', which is reminiscent of, thought different in substance from, Longfield's 'intensity of demand'.[10] Hancock went on to examine the relative contributions of both the supply and demand factors, and in the course of this analysis he clearly perceived and argued for viewing the returns to the factor inputs as a unified pricing problem. This recalls Longfield's framework, which may be the basis for the comment that Hancock's *Introductory Lecture on Political Economy*, 'provides one of the most interesting discussions of value theory given by any member of this group of Dublin economists, a discussion particularly noteworthy for its unusual anticipations of modern views'.[11]

William Edward Hearn's *Plutology: Or the Theory of the Efforts to Satisfy Human Wants* (1863) is a significant document in the debate on the subjective theory of value. Hearn was an undergraduate at Trinity College Dublin between 1842 and 1847, when Lawson was Professor of Political Economy and Longfield was Regius Professor of Feudal and English Law. Shortly after graduation he was appointed the first Professor of the Greek Language in Queen's College Galway in 1849, a position he held until 1854 when he was appointed the first Professor of Modern History and Literature, Political Economy and Logic at the University of Melbourne, thereby becoming Australia's first professor of economics.[12] In 1851 he published the *Cassell Prize Essay on the Condition of Ireland* and 'On Cottier Rents', a paper which he read before the Dublin Statistical Society.

The excerpts included here on value theory are from his later and best-known work, *Plutology*. The first, 'Of Human Wants', presented a taxonomy of the different kinds and degrees of human wants. *Plutology*, according to Jevons was 'both in soundness and originality the most advanced treatise on political economy which has appeared, and it should be familiar to every student of the science'.[13] Marshall also commented favourably on *Plutology*, being impressed with its general organizational structure and in particular its emphasis on human wants as the motive force in stimulating the development of industry.[14] In the second excerpt from *Plutology* included here, 'On Exchange', Hearn provided an interesting analysis of how demand could modify the impact of changes in the costs of production, arguably extending

Longfield's contribution on this topic. For Hearn, there were two types of commodities on offer, those he deemed absolutely essential or 'necessities' and those that were dispensable or what he termed 'superfluities'. Hearn's analysis focused on why an increase in the cost of production of those two categories of commodities would have a different effect on their final selling prices. In the case of 'necessities', a rise in their cost would raise their final price to the full extent, while in the case of 'superfluities a rise in their cost would cause some buyers to decrease or cease their purchases of the product and, as a result, the market price would rise by less than the full increase in their costs of production. For Hearn, therefore, the costs of production for particular categories of goods was modified by the 'character of demand', thus providing a rationale for the primacy of demand over costs of production theories of value. Clearly Hearn had not forgotten what he must have heard at lectures as an undergraduate at Trinity College Dublin in the 1840s.

The Ricardian tradition in value theory was reasserted by Cairnes, who remained a life-long adherent of the cost-of-production approach, though he differed from, and provided a more nuanced version of, Ricardo's original formulation. A contemporary and close personal friend of Mill (who had presented, in Book III, Chapter VI, of his *Principles*, one of the most succinct accounts of the cost of production theory of value), Cairnes was very influenced by Mill's analysis, though he produced a more complicated version of a theory of value than his mentor. In the extract, 'Normal Value', from *Some Leading Principles of Political Economy Newly Expanded* (1874), included in Volume II, Cairnes ostensibly provided a cost-of-production theory of value. But it was clear that 'normal value' was not to be identified just with cost of production, which Cairnes regarded as an identity, but that cost should mean real cost or sacrifice. Cairnes thereby extended the interpretation of cost of production, and in the course of his analysis he made the creative move of applying Mill's proposition of the determination of international values by reciprocal demand in the case of factor immobility between countries to the internal economy of a country. In the case of the latter situation, the existence of internal factor immobility gave rise to arguably Cairnes's most original application of the concept of non-competing groups.[15] Cairnes was the most celebrated Irish academic economist in the nineteenth century who advocated and defended the Ricardo–Mill approach and, as the sixth holder of the Whately chair between 1856 and 1860, he broke the continuity of the Dublin School.

The attempt by Cairnes's successor, Arthur Heuston, to synthesize, in his *Principles of Value in Exchange, Explained in Simple and Comprehensive Formulae* (1864), the 'two different theories of value' that had emerged in Irish academic circles is hardly surprising. In essence, Heuston emphasized the role of demand factors in the short-run, while supply factors were considered dominant in the long run. For Heuston, the longer-run factors, based on cost of production, were the more significant, with utility playing a minor

6

role. One can find resonances of various authors in Heuston's contribution, including Mill, Cairnes, and Hancock. Heuston's synthesis, while laudable, lacked anything approaching the intellectual sweep or analytical detail that characterized Marshall's magisterial *Principles* some twenty-five years later, which was the major attempt at the end of the nineteenth century to forge a similar synthesis of theoretical approaches to economic theory.

If value theory was primarily the preserve of the academic economists, in contrast, people who had no formal connection with academic institutions produced some of the most significant writings on distribution theory. The most noteworthy of these was William Thompson (1775–1833), who inherited the family estate in County Cork following his father's death in 1814. From an early age Thompson was impressed with, and quickly embraced, the ideals of the French Revolution, developing an interest in formulating the ideals of an alternative economic system based on the rights of the primary producer. Robert Owen was a major influence on Thompson who emerged as the most original and analytical thinker of the Owenite movement. Later this group became identified as the Ricardian socialists, and Thompson was Ireland's representative of this group.

The Ricardian socialists had direct links to the British classical school, drawing primarily on Ricardo's analysis. They accepted the labour theory of value and, in combination with their particular interpretation of the natural law theory of property ownership, they forged a stringent critique of the status and position of the primary producer within the existing social forma-tion. Building on Locke's arguments that labour was the source of value, they constructed a model of a 'natural' society, which they used to evaluate existing social arrangements, which they considered to be 'artificial'. This criticism arose from the fact that, while accepting Locke's views about pri-vate property, based on the natural right of individuals to possess the pro-duce of their own labour, they rejected the arguments that aimed at justifying a specific historical social situation with its particular distribution of social wealth and buttressed by a theory of political and social consensus. The Ricardian socialists rejected the idea that the emerging capitalist system pos-sessed the fundamental characteristics of their articulated 'natural' system, a view which was in direct conflict with that of many of the major theorists of the eighteenth century, including Adam Smith who ascribed a natural law basis to the new 'commercial' society. The Ricardian socialists, in contrast, regarded it as an 'artificial system', which subverted a fundamental principle of natural law, the rights of the primary producers to own the product of their labour.

Unique among this group, Thompson was committed to what was the most important intellectual influence on his thinking, the doctrine of Benthamite utilitarianism. Thompson was a personal friend of Bentham, an admirer of his educational reforms, and it has been claimed that Thompson's originality as a thinker consisted in his appropriation of the greatest happiness principle as a basis for fundamental social reform.[16] While radical utilitarianism provided him with a critical component of his rationale for social reform, it was Thompson's adoption of Owen's system of mutual co-operation, as a model of social organization, that alone could deliver to individual primary producers the fruits of their labour.

Thompson's arguments were presented in what was almost certainly the most substantial and original text of Owenite economic analysis, the *Inquiry into the Principles of the Distribution of Wealth Most Conducive to Human Happiness* (1824). Thompson's *Inquiry* is a work of magnificent intellectual scope and challenging analysis, the early portions of which provide an invaluable perspective on the nature and scope of political economy. Thompson rejected the polar positions of those he called 'intellectual speculators', who viewed human beings as creatures of reason only and who neglected or ignored the material dimension in economic and social progress, and the 'mechanical speculators', who perceived people merely as machines, devoted exclusively to the acquisition of wealth. Thompson saw political economists as subscribing, with few exceptions, to the second view. Thompson rejected both views and argued that human needs had to be recognized as both mental and physical, and must be viewed within a complex web of fragile and changing motivations, which included not only self-interest but also the need for the sympathy of others. It was only within this perspective, if properly understood and adopted, that the objects of study of political economy could be properly appreciated.

In his early writings, Thompson accepted that the aim of political economy was to discover the 'natural laws' of the distribution of wealth, along with the analysis of the implications of different models of distribution, including their economic, political, and moral effects. The central issue for Thompson, invoking Bentham, was how to reconcile equality with security, or how 'to reconcile just distribution with continued production'. For Thompson this solution was the discovery of the natural laws of distribution, which would provide security for all instead of only for the few. Security for Thompson meant the motivation that stimulated the production of wealth; without such security no natural motivations for productive activity existed. Within the framework of utilitarianism, however, the only rational motive to wealth creation of any sort, was the expansion of the means of happiness. Combining the arguments that wealth was created only by labour, with the aim of ensuring the maximum incentive to produce wealth in the first place through the choice of the correct distributional mechanisms, led Thompson to the conclusion that the best stimulus to production was to ensure 'security' in the use of the products of labour by those who produced them. Thompson's larger aim in the *Inquiry* was to discover which of three economic systems of organization would achieve this delicate balance between security of motivation and equality of distribution. The three systems were: labour by 'force or compulsion direct or indirect', labour by 'unrestricted individual competition', and labour by 'mutual co-operation. In the course of the *Inquiry*, Thompson produced, as the centre piece of his theory of distribution, an elaborate analysis which provided a rationale for returning the total produce of labour to the labourer. This was based on an utilitarian calculus along with a perceptive and complex analysis of the necessary conditions for the long-term production of wealth, which included a model of social organization based on Owen's system of mutual co-operation. Thompson's *Inquiry* must stand as one of the most impressive productions of Irish political economy in the nineteenth century, and of social philosophy in general, a point that was not lost on Marx, even if Thompson's fellow Irish were less than enthusiastic in their acknowledgement of his work.

The Ricardian tradition in general, and as part of the classical doctrine of political economy, continued to be represented in the works of Irish economists in the domain of distribution theory. Cairnes's 'The Rate of Wages' demonstrated his unswerving adherence to the classical doctrine of the wages-fund and the Mathusian principles of population and their impact on wages. The wages-fund doctrine was at the core of the classic theory of wages, representing a refinement of the so-called 'iron law of wages', which was seldom offered as the explanation of wage rate determination. Cairnes was unique in maintaining his defence of the wages-fund doctrine, even after Mill had abandoned it following its repudiation by Longe and Thornton.[17] An interesting historical summary of the doctrine is provided by William D. McDonnell, in his Whately Memorial Prize Essay for 1887. A more discursive treatment in the Ricardian tradition is provided by Posnett in his *The Ricardian Theory of Rent* (1884), which is primarily motivated by a number of methodological considerations concerning the historical relativity of certain economic concepts. The inclusion of these items under distribution theory is not based on their claim to our attention as major contributions to this particular domain of economic theory; rather they represent an interest in wider issues concerning the temporal and spatial relativity of concepts, the limitations of universal theorizing, and the specificity of Irish circumstances.

In contrast with these contributions, however, the manner in which conventional economics was to evolve, and the emergence of neo-classical economics as the dominant paradigm by the end of the century, has rescued Longfield from his 'neglected' status to that of a theoretical pioneer in the realm of distribution theory. If the classical economists found the unifying principle for their theories of distribution in the concept of cost of production on the supply side, then Longfield could be said to have discovered his unifying principle of factor pricing in his supply and demand analysis, with his innovative emphasis on the demand side. Longfield essentially unified the conceptual basis of factor pricing, and therefore distribution, by attempting to relate each of the three distributive shares, rent, profit, and interest to the supply and demand theory of price that he developed in the earlier chapters of his *Lectures on Political Economy*. Longfield's approach bears something of an asymmetrical relation with his classical contemporaries, in that this use of a fixed supply assumption in the development of his theory of price inhibited him from pursuing a more satisfactory analysis of the determinants affecting the supply of the factors of production, particularly labour and capital. The classical authors, neglecting demand, paid more attention to what affected the supply of the factors of production. The originality of Longfield's analysis, however, was its uniform emphasis on the role of demand in the price determination of both commodities and resources. More particularly, his identification of the role of marginal demand in the commodity market and marginal productivity in the factor market, a framework now familiar to every student of economics, justifies Longfield's claim as one of the leading progenitors of the neo-classical marginal theory of commodity and factor pricing, even though his achievements had to await almost seventy years before formal recognition was accorded to them.[18]

Longfield's work on distribution theory, though not recognized in his own lifetime within British academic circles, was not totally neglected in Ireland. The contributions of Butt, Vance, and Hearn included in this anthology represent different attempts to extend Longfield's framework of analysis. Butt's indebtedness to Longfield is contained in his *Rent, Profits and Labour: A Lecture* (1838), where he attempted to forge a connection between Say's utility approach and Longfield's method in his theory of profit.[19] Butt identified the essential insight of Longfield's approach that, crucial to the determination of its price, was the importance of applying a unit of whatever resource in its marginal use. This led Butt to conclude that the classical distinction between the theories of rent, profit, and wages were unsatisfactory and obscured the underlying general principles involved. These could be reduced to the proposition that factors of production were remunerated in relation to the utility they created in their least efficient, that is marginal employment. Moss has argued that Butt's *Rent, Profits and Labour*, 'represents one of the earliest attempts to work out a marginal utility theory of imputation', but, as in Longfield's case, this contribution went totally unnoticed by succeeding generations of economists.[20]

In 1848, Robert Vance read a paper to the Dublin Statistical Society entitled 'On the English and Irish Analyses of Wages and Profits'. Notwithstanding the somewhat provocative title, the paper was in fact a pointed criticism of the unjustified neglect of Longfield's writings on distribution theory in both Ireland and Britain. Vance admitted at the outset that his was a recently acquired interest in political economy, but he was appalled to discover that Longfield's novel contribution was ignored in Britain. McCulloch came in for a particular stinging criticism in this regard. Vance identified the two major differences between the two analyses as follows. First, English writers treated wages before profits and therefore based their analysis of profits upon that of wages. The Irish analysis, that of Longfield, did the precise opposite: it treated profits before wages, and based its analysis of wages upon that of profits. Second, British writers saw wages as commodity wages, while the Irish analysis saw wages as money wages. Vance went on to argue that Longfield had produced a consistent theory of profits and wages by making wages the 'residual' in contrast with the conventional approach, and by carrying out the whole analysis in money terms. This was contrasted with the Ricardian system where, Vance claimed, a number of confusions were rampant which undermined the analysis. Senior had attempted to address the problem, but succeeded only, according to Vance, in perpetuating the confusions by continuing to work in real terms rather than money terms. Vance concluded that Longfield's contribution was clearly superior in its clarity and coherence to what was on offer by British writers and attention to it would provide 'more readily a scientific knowledge of the subject' (vol. 2, p. 191).

In 1851, not long after Vance's contribution to the Dublin Statistical Society, Hearn presented one of his earliest offerings in political economy to the same society, his paper 'On Cottier Rents'. What is of particular interest in the paper is that, in addition to incorporating certain ideas of Longfield's productivity theory of distribution, it is addressed to the specific conditions prevailing in Ireland at this time. In contrast to Longfield's analysis of distribution, which was in principle applicable to an advanced society such as Britain, Hearn's paper was most decidedly an Irish paper, born out of Irish circumstances. Prior to its presentation, Hearn had written the *Cassell Prize Essay on the Condition of Ireland* (1851). Here he identified the principal economic problem as the absence of industry in Ireland, which meant that the main source of employment was restricted to the limited supply of cultivatable land. The theoretical implications of this situation were the main focus of his paper.

The main argument in Hearn's paper was that the differential theory of rent would have to be modified when applied to a predominantly agricultural economy such as Ireland. Hearn started conventionally, stating that land, being limited in supply, the payment of rent was going to be largely dependent on the demand for land. In Hearn's terminology, the rent offered for any specific piece of land would be determined by the 'intensity of the effectual demand' for that particular farm. Hearn demonstrated that the intensity of demand for land could be measured by the 'exact difference between its productiveness and the ordinary productiveness of the application of capital' (vol. 2, p. 192). By the ordinary productiveness of the application of capital, Hearn meant the alternative employment of capital and labour in the industrial sector. Depending on the relative rates of return, Hearn concluded that, as a general principle, rent was determined 'by the difference between the produce of the monopolized agent and the price of unassisted industry' (vol. 2, p. 192).

Hearn next considered the case of an agricultural economy, stating that where 'there is no field beyond the land for the employment of capital, the case will be very different' (vol. 2, p. 193). In the absence of an industrial sector, capital had no alternative source of employment. He distinguished between the impact on farmers' and cottier's rents arising from these circumstances. In the case of farmers, where cultivation was for profit, the landlords could increase rents up to the point where farmers were left with 'the ordinary rate of profit'. In the case of cottiers, however, where cultivation was for 'actual subsistence', the landlords could increase rents up to the point where cottiers were left only with the 'ordinary rate of wages'. In the Irish circumstances of the time, where cottiers dominated, the absence of employment opportunities in industry intensified competition for employment in agriculture. This competition, Hearn argued, drove rents higher and thereby lowered the 'ordinary rate of wages' even further, driving the agricultural economy towards subsistence levels of production. Based on this analysis, Hearn identified a vicious circle of poverty creation, which he applied to the Irish circumstances of the time: the forced lowering of the wage rate undermined the possibility of any economic development, while the absence of employment opportunities outside of agriculture generated a contrived demand for a limited supply of land, leading to further increases in rents and even lower level of wages. Hearn's short paper, which drew on a number of the analytical insights contained in Longfield's *Lectures on Political Economy*, was one of the most perceptive analyses of Irish circumstances produced by any Irish political economist in the nineteenth century.

Notes

1 Ernesto Screpanti, and Stefano Zamagni, *An Outline of the History of Economic Thought* (Oxford, 1995), p. 73.
2 D.P. O'Brien, *The Classical Economists* (Oxford, 1975), p. 45.
3 R.A. Seligman, 'On Some Neglected British Economists – I', *Economic Journal*, 13(1903), pp. 335–63; J.G. Smith, 'Some Nineteenth-Century Irish Economists', *Economica*, ns 2(1935), pp. 20–32.
4 R.D. Collison Black, 'Trinity College, Dublin, and the Theory of Value, 1832–1863', *Economica*, ns 12 (1945), pp. 140–8.
5 O'Brien, *The Classical Economists*, p. 91.
6 See S. Leon Levy, *Nassau W. Senior 1790–1864* (Newton Abbot, 1970).
7 Roger Backhouse, *A History of Modern Economic Analysis* (Oxford, 1985), p. 38.
8 Laurence S. Moss, 'Isaac Butt and the Early Development of the Marginal Utility Theory of Imputation', *History of Political Economy*, 5(1973), pp. 317–38.
9 Black, 'Trinity College, Dublin, and the Theory of Value', p. 144.
10 Laurence S. Moss, 'Mountifort Longfield's Supply-and-Demand Theory of Price and Its Place in the Development of British Economic Theory', *History of Political Economy*, 6(1974), p. 430.
11 Black, 'Trinity College, Dublin, and the Theory of Value', p. 145.
12 Thomas A. Boylan and Timothy P. Foley, 'Cairnes, Hearn and Bastable: The Contribution of Queen's College, Galway to Economic Thought', in Diarmuid Ó Cearbhaill (ed.), *Galway: Town and Gown 1484–1984* (Dublin, 1984), p. 186.
13 W.S. Jevons, *The Coal Question* (London, 1865), p. 126.

14 Alfred Marshall, *Principles of Economics: An Introductory Volume*, 8th ed. (London, 1961), p. 77.
15 Joseph A. Schumpeter, *History of Economic Analysis* (London, 1954), pp. 605–7.
16 Thomas Duddy, *A History of Irish Thought* (London & New York, 2002), pp. 226–32.
17 R.D. Collison Black, 'Economic Studies at Trinity College, Dublin – I', *Hermathena*, no. LXX, 1947, p. 77.
18 Laurence S. Moss, *Mountifort Longfield: Ireland's First Professor of Political Economy* (Illinois, 1976), pp. 108–26.
19 Moss, 'Isaac Butt and the Early Development of the Marginal Utility Theory of Imputation', pp. 317–18.
20 Ibid., p. 337.

Disclaimer

The Publishers have made every effort to contact authors/copyright holders of works reprinted in *Irish Political Economy*. This has not been possible in every case, however, and we would welcome correspondence from those individuals/companies who we have been unable to trace.

Part 1

VALUE THEORY

17

LECTURES ON POLITICAL ECONOMY

Lectures III and VI

Mountifort Longfield

Source: Mountifort Longfield: *Lectures on Political Economy*, Dublin: William Curry, Jun. & Co.; London: Longman, 1834, pp. 42–63, 108–15.

Lecture III

GENTLEMEN,—Having attempted to explain what value is, and how it may be measured, I shall proceed to call your attention to the circumstances which gave rise to its existence, and by their variations influence and regulate its amount. I felt it necessary to occupy some of your time in endeavouring to prove that labour, although frequently a useful and convenient measure of value, is not on that account to be considered the only real one. It is a convenient measure because it admits of being directly compared with all important commodities, but the arguments employed to prove it the only real measure are I think entirely inconsistent with every notion that we are accustomed to entertain of the meaning of the term value. The common argument is thus briefly stated by Mr M'Culloch, in his Principles of Political-Economy, page 297: "But however the same quantity of labour may be laid out, and whatever may be its produce, it unavoidably occasions the *same sacrifice* to those by whom it is performed; and hence it is plain that the products of equal quantities of labour or of toil and trouble must, how much soever they may differ in magnitude, always be of precisely the same real value." Now real value in this proposition can have no reference to its utility or exchangeable powers. The proposition, if true, is a trifling one, obtained by a mere comparison of the definition with the thing defined.

Labour is sometimes defended as the best measure of value, as being thought the most invariable one in different ages or countries; but even this is a proposition assumed upon very slender foundations. A man whose annual income 400 years ago amounted to a certain quantity of gold or silver

17

bullion, would indeed possess a different share of the luxuries, conveniences, and necessaries of life from that of the man who enjoyed the same income, measured in the same manner, in the present day. But equally different would be the shares possessed by two men, one of the present age and one who lived 400 years ago, if their incomes were equal, when measured by the quantities of labour they could command or purchase. The same quantity of labour will not, in different ages or countries, produce or purchase the same amount of the luxuries, comforts, or necessaries of life. Labour therefore is not a "real," in the sense of being an invariable, measure of value. Indeed it is utterly impossible that there can exist any invariable measure of value as long as the prices of different commodities vary in relation to each other.

To investigate with success the circumstances which regulate value, we must consider what it is that gives rise to exchanges. However useful, or even necessary to the subsistence of man, any commodity may be, there is a limit to the quantity of it which any individual can consume, and the love or necessity of variety will induce him to part with all that he possesses beyond a certain share, if by parting with it he can procure any thing which can contribute more to his enjoyments. And by a wise provision of nature, the more indispensable any commodity is to human subsistence or happiness, the more strict and absolute is the limit within which our consumption of it is confined. The most natural and most urgent of our appetites are those which can be the soonest and most certainly satisfied. Those which in their extent are the most insatiable, can be repressed or denied without any diminution to our happiness. By this provision the riches of the wealthy are prevented from interfering with the maintenance of the poor. The richest individual, whatever quantity of corn or other food he may possess or be able to purchase, is not able to consume more than the poor man. His wealth may enable him to command the labour of the poor, but he cannot himself consume the provisions intended by Providence for their subsistence, since the energy with which nature rejects all beyond a certain quantity is always proportional to the importunity with which she demands that portion. And the nature and reason of man leading him to exchanges, he will dispose of that surplus which he cannot use himself to some one who in exchange for it can give him something that may contribute to his enjoyment. Its power of serving others will not induce him to keep it, although it may enable him to procure a higher price for it from some one who can use it.

Thus in an exchange there must be two persons and at least two things concerned; that portion of any commodity which any one possesses and does not intend to consume is called the supply; the disposition to give something in exchange for it may be called the demand. An exchange of equivalents is advantageous to both parties, since each procures by means of it something which he considers to be of more use to himself, under his circumstances, than the article which he parts with.

The rules which regulate the relative values of commodities are simple, and may be considered as the consequence of this general law, which is not subject to many exceptions—namely, that every person is desirous to get as much as he can for the goods of which he disposes. This leads every man to buy as cheap, and to sell as dear as he can. The law of mutual competition does the rest.

In all civilized societies, goods are exchanged for money or sold, by those who dispose of the supply to the consumer, and are procured in exchange for money, by those who require them. It is with money that all commodities are compared by those who deal in them, as it is on their money prices that their profit or loss depends; if the seller demands more than a certain sum for his goods, others will undersell him, finding it more to their advantage to dispose of their goods, though at a lower price, than to retain them in their possession unsold; and in this manner, mutual competition will compel the former to sell his goods at a more reasonable price. But this reduction evidently has its limits; if the cheapness is such as to increase the number of buyers to an amount more than sufficient to take off the whole supply, the mutual competition of buyers, each anxious to procure an article, of which, on the supposition there is not enough for all, will increase the price to the highest sum that is consistent with the entire supply being disposed of. Thus there is a certain sum to which the market price of any article has a constant tendency to conform itself; namely, that price which will exactly adjust the supply to the effective demand. The entire supply could not be disposed of at a higher price, some share should remain unsold, to the injury of the person in whose hands it is left. Every seller is anxious that this loss should not fall upon himself, and thus mutual competition will lower the price of the commodity. In the same manner, the competition among the buyers will prevent the price from sinking too low; and the seller will have no inducement to reduce the price of his goods below the highest price which is consistent with his disposing of his entire stock.

Besides this adjustment between the supply and the demand, the cost of production or natural value of any commodity always exercises a very considerable influence upon its price. The cost of production regulates the supply, and keeps it pretty nearly in that proportion to the demand which may produce a conformity between the exchangeable and the natural value. In some articles this tendency of the market price to conform to the cost of production is so strong, that a difference between them can only be produced by a very considerable and accidental disproportion between the demand and the supply. If the cost of production or natural value of an article is ten shillings, that may be considered the price at which the article is offered by the manufacturer to the public; but if more persons are willing to purchase the article at that price than the quantity on sale can supply, some of them, rather than want the article, will offer a little more, and the competition among the buyers will raise the article to such a price that the supply will become equal to the effective demand—that is, to the demand of those who are willing to give for it the increased price to which it is raised. This equality between the effective demand and the supply is in such case produced, not by an increase of the supply, but by a diminution of the effective demand consequent upon an increase of price, which will prevent some from consuming such quantities of it as they would otherwise have been able to procure. This increase of price will be in proportion to the deficiency of the supply as compared with the demand, and to the inconvenience or difficulty of remaining without the article for any period, or of procuring a substitute for it, and to the length of time required to produce an additional supply. The producer gains an advantage by this increase of price, and the public sustains an inconvenience, some by being compelled to dispense with the use of an article of comfort or convenience, and others by being obliged to pay a higher price for it. But this advantage gained by the producer will never lead him to keep the market inadequately supplied. For when such a deficiency occurs, the profit derived from it by each individual producer is in proportion to the quantity he has to dispose of. In other words, the profit which he derives from this public inconvenience is exactly proportional to the exertions he has made to prevent it from taking place. On the other hand, if the quantity of the article to be sold is more than sufficient to supply all those who are willing to pay the natural price for it, the competition among the sellers, each being unwilling that the portion belonging to himself should remain unsold, will sink the price until the supply becomes equal to the effective demand, that is, to the demand of those who are willing to pay the reduced price for it. In this case the equality between the demand and the supply is produced not by diminishing the supply, but by the increased demand consequent upon a diminution of price. This diminution of price will be in proportion to the excess of supply as compared with the demand, to the strictness of the limits within which man's consumption of the article is confined, to the necessity under which the producers are of disposing of it within a limited period, to the expense or difficulty of keeping and storing it without injury, and to the length of time required to produce the next supply. In this manner, by a rise or fall in price the supply is always kept in a due proportion to the demand.

In manufactured goods the tendency of the exchangeable value or price to conform to the natural value is very strong, and a considerable disproportion between the demand and supply will frequently exercise little if any influence over the price. If the supply is for a short time in excess, the retailers may abate a little of their usual profits, but they will not readily sell their goods at an absolute loss. If the article is one the demand for which arises rather from necessity than from fluctuating fashion, they will find it more to their advantage to retain a part of their stock unsold, than to sell it at a lower price than that which they will have to pay to the manufacturer for the succeeding stock. In the same manner the manufacturer, when he finds a difficulty in disposing of his goods, will keep some of them rather than sell them at a lower price than it will cost him to replace them by manufacturing. In this manner a temporary derangement of the usual proportion between the demand and the supply is prevented from exercising any considerable influence over the price of manufactured articles, and any such derangement can be only temporary, as manufacturers will not continue to produce goods which they are unable to dispose of, or can only dispose of at a loss. This prevents any considerable fall of price; and a great increase of price cannot take place, since the consumer can in general wait until a new supply comes in. Thus in manufactures the cost of production exercises a double influence over the market price, both by producing an equality between the *average* supply and demand, and by preventing any temporary derangement of this equality from producing any considerable increase or diminution of price. It is in raw materials, and especially in food, that the greatest variations of price are found to occur. Here, in particular, all those circumstances concur which will cause a deficiency in the supply to produce the greatest effect upon the price. The use of the article cannot be dispensed with, and any considerable reduction in the consumption of it cannot take place without much inconvenience and distress; and from the nature of the seasons a new supply cannot be raised within the country until the expiration of nearly a year; and all are willing to undergo some privations in order to obtain as nearly as possible their usual supply of food. The farmers, by selling the usual proportion of their total produce, are unable to keep the markets fully supplied. The competition among the buyers has its usual effects in raising prices, the existence of the scarcity becomes generally known, and as the farmers and dealers are aware that a new supply will not be obtained until the succeeding harvest, even the high prices do not tempt them to dispose of all their stock immediately. Many of them keep it back, waiting for still higher prices. These high prices have the effect of preventing waste or improvident consumption, and compelling many persons who cannot afford to pay them, to diminish something from their ordinary consumption of food, at the expense of some inconvenience and distress. Much suffering is endured through the country, and appeals are naturally made to the charity of the benevolent, and in some instances the interposition of the legislature is demanded in aid of the suffering poor. I shall here call your attention to some obvious and certain principles, that may be of no slight practical importance in directing either public or private charity upon such occasions. I hope, however, that the necessity for their exercise may be very far distant from the present time; and the present price of corn does not seem to indicate a scarcity. When an increase of price is produced by a scarcity of provisions, the markets are not upon that account altogether empty, nor does any very considerable deficiency appear in their daily supply. An ordinary observer would not remark a deficiency amounting to as much even as one fifth of the ordinary quantity in the market, although such a deficiency would occasion a very considerable increase of price. Every person sees that there is enough there for himself, though he does not reflect that there may not be enough for the wants of all.

But as he sees more than he wants himself, and is prevented from obtaining it only by the high prices, he is not unnaturally led to complain more of the price than of the scarcity. In reality, however, high prices in such cases have the most beneficial effect in mitigating the evil consequences of a scarcity, and preventing an absolute famine from resulting towards the end of the season. They provide effectually that the reduction in the usual consumption shall be spread equally over the entire year. They do not much diminish the entire portion to be consumed by any one person or family, they only cause that portion to be given in the manner and at the times most beneficial to the consumer. To take an instance, suppose the crop of the ordinary food used in any country, as potatos in Ireland, was to fall short in some year one-sixth of the usual consumption. If this scarcity did not indicate and in some measure correct itself by an increase of price, the whole stock of provisions destined for the supply of the year would be exhausted in ten months, and for the remaining two months a scene of misery and famine beyond description would ensue. But this in fact does not take place, for prices do rise and cause an immediate diminution in the ordinary daily consumption, so that the existing stores hold out until the season for an arrival of a new supply. Undoubtedly some distress is endured during this interval, from the want felt by many of the poor of a proper quantity of food; but this distress is necessarily incident to a diminished supply, and would be incalculably increased instead of being diminished, if human legislation should attempt to regulate the prices. High prices effect the two great objects to be desired in such a case. First, they secure a provident and equable consumption of provisions during the year, instead of allowing the whole to be wasted or consumed before the year is over; and next they secure that the entire store shall be brought to market, and thus distributed for consumption within the year, and that no part of the stores in existence shall be held over from the present year when they are wanted, to the next year, when plenty may make them comparatively useless; since no one will keep his goods from the market when prices are high, to preserve them for a period of comparative plenty and cheapness. In such a year poverty is not the cause of famine or scarcity, which is in no respect to be attributed to the inequality of possessions. If all the provisions in the country were placed in a common stock, and every man allowed to take thereof freely as much as he desired to consume, they would shortly be exhausted. The same effect would take place, although not quite so speedily, if every person had money to purchase as much as he wanted; and if all the farmers and possessors of food were through benevolence to sell provisions at the accustomed prices, the poor would not be thereby relieved. The root of the distress would be left untouched. At such moderate prices the stock in the country would be insufficient to meet the demand of all who were willing to pay for it; and one of two things should happen, either that the supply of the day would be exhausted before some were able to procure any food; or if the daily supply was kept up to its usual fulness, the supply of the year would be exhausted before the next harvest came in. Dearness is therefore a salutary effect of scarcity. It mitigates the calamity by making it be felt early as an inconvenience, instead of allowing the scarcity to be concealed until a total irremediable famine should ensue. But when prices reach a certain height, an opinion frequently arises among the sufferers that it is not caused by a scarcity, and they forget that this increase of price was early apprehended and predicted. They suppose that there are provisions enough, but that the distress is caused by the insatiable rapacity of the possessors. Unwilling to admit the existence of any distress for which they cannot find somebody to blame, they flatter themselves with hopes that an appeal to the wisdom or humanity of those who govern them may be successful in rescuing them from the horror of famine. As it is difficult to argue with a starving population, they have generally succeeded in obtaining laws against engrossing, amassing, or forestalling provisions, and thus they remove the imaginary, and aggravate the real cause of their distress. This leads me to mention a very injudicious and injurious species of charity which is frequently practised upon such occasions. Persons of more benevolence than judgment purchase quantities of the ordinary food of the country, and sell them again to the poor at half price. The few observations I have made will shew that of all kinds of engrossing, this is the most mischievous, and that no regrating or forestalling is so injurious as this species, invented by mistaken benevolence, of buying dear and selling cheap in times of scarcity. It induces the farmers and dealers to send their stock more speedily to market, and it enables the poorer people to dispense with that harsh but necessary abstinence which alone can prevent the provisions from being entirely consumed long before a new supply can be obtained. Whenever this mode of charity is adopted, prices will necessarily rise on account of the increasing scarcity caused by such a premature and improvident consumption, and will generally arrive to such a height that even the reduced rates at which provisions are distributed by the charitable will be equal to the prices at which they would have been sold if charity had not led to any interference. This evil, caused by injudicious benevolence, could never be detected by experience. The increased prices would naturally be attributed to the scarcity which confessedly prevailed at the beginning of the season, and originally led to this interference. And the authors of this charitable scheme would even applaud its success, since on each particular day they would see the poor getting provisions at half the market price of that day, and would not consider that those very high market prices were principally caused by that charity which diminished the supply by causing an early consumption of it. This then is one of those numerous cases where what is called experience is in fact rash although disguised hypothesis, and where "theory" is extensive experience, enlightened and directed by common sense and reasoning.

Ought nothing then be done in times of scarcity to relieve the poor and mitigate their sufferings. Undoubtedly much may be done if it is judiciously attempted, if we direct our efforts to increasing the supply instead of accelerating the consumption of provisions. In this country especially, such assistance can be most easily afforded without importation. Potatos, it is well known, form the ordinary food of the labouring population. If there is a deficient supply of these, some distress and inconvenience must be felt. This evil will fall lightest if the supply is entirely consumed within the year, instead of part being held over until the next year, when it may not be so much wanted; and if the supply is equally distributed during that period, instead of too great a portion being consumed at the commencement of the season. Both these advantages we have seen are secured by the natural rise of prices, and nothing can be done by private charity or public legislation towards securing a better distribution of the existing supply. But much may be effected in the way of increasing the supply, or at least of diminishing the competition for it. Let those who can afford it abstain in such times from the use of potatos, or of animals fed on such food, and let them, if practicable, give a supply of bread at cheap prices to the poor. If this is done, the price of the staple food of the country will diminish instead of increasing as the season advances, and the scarcity will gradually diminish.

I fear I may be considered as having dwelt too long upon this subject, and I shall therefore leave it for the present, and conclude with some remarks upon the effects which regrating, forestalling, and other forms of speculation have upon price. Among the triumphs of Political-Economy, the victory it has obtained over the prejudices which so long existed against regrating and forestalling ought to be enumerated. Indeed so complete has been the victory that many of my auditors may perhaps not understand the meaning of those words, expressive of practices of which our ancestors entertained so great a terror. They signified by those words the buying up of goods to sell again in the same market. E. Spenser thus speaks in a passage you may see cited in Johnson's Dictionary, under the title 'REGRATING.' "Neither should they buy corn unless it were to make malt thereof. For by such engrossing and regrating, the dearth that commonly reigneth in England hath been caused." Our common law punished this offence of regrating or forestalling with the heaviest penalties, in the form of fines, imprisonment, and forfeiture. And our law books thus speak of it as "a kind of huckstry by which victuals are made dearer, for every seller will gain something, which must of necessity enhance the price." These prejudices against regrating, though supported by such a plausible argument, have disappeared before the voice of sense and reason. Part of the fallacy of this reasoning of our common law arises from a misapprehension of the source of the profits of retailers, which have often been supposed to be an injury to the consumer, whereas it is the price which he voluntarily pays for the advantage, which but for the existence of such a class he should give up, viz. the power of buying commodities, when, and in such quantities as he wants them. Indeed the few remarks which I have made on the manner in which the cost of production influences the market price of articles, may shew that the price never can be encreased in order to pay wages or profits to men who unnecessarily and uselessly concern themselves in the sale or production of the article. The dealer does not sell higher than he buys, on account of that being necessary to his profit, but he buys when he foresees that the market is likely to rise, and he gains a profit according to the prudence and correctness of his speculation. If he sells at a profit, that very circumstance shews that the markets were better supplied at the time he bought than at the time he sold; and as he is not exempted from the general rule of being obliged to buy and sell at the current price, his dealings do not add any thing to the price of the commodity. They merely alter the time in which it is offered to the consumer, and transfer it from a period at which the comparatively low prices shew that provisions are comparatively plentiful, to a period when the comparatively high prices indicate a comparative scarcity. Neither can their proceedings occasion a dearth, since they do not diminish the entire stock of provisions within the kingdom, and are so far from causing waste that they prevent waste and premature consumption of the food. The more judicious are their speculations, the more benefit the public derives from them. And there is very little danger that any excess in speculation, such as their keeping their goods too long on hands, can be of any serious injury to the country. The care which the dealers will take of their own interests will be a sufficient protection to the public. Their information on the subject is generally pretty correct, as their success depends upon it, and their interests are identical with that of the community. The common interest of both is that the store of provisions within the country should be uniformly or equably consumed during the period which it is destined to supply. That this is the interest of the public is sufficiently evident. And it can be easily proved that the dealer best effects his object by acting as if he had this result in view. If more is brought to market during any time than the proportion due to that period, it follows evidently that less must be brought at some other time. Prices must therefore be higher in the latter than the former period, and therefore the speculator, by purchasing at the former and selling at the latter period, will consult his own interest in buying cheap and selling dear, and that of the public by withdrawing provisions from the market when they are comparatively plentiful, and offering them again to the public when times of greater scarcity come on; and if by excess in speculation he kept the markets for a short time inadequately supplied, that is, with less than that period's fair proportion of the provisions destined to supply the year, the remainder of the year would on that account be better supplied, and the dealer would suffer by not having sold his goods when he could have obtained for them a higher price than will be given for the rest of the year. Such excess of speculation cannot continue so long as to do any serious injury to the public, since the dealer would soon be warned of his miscalculation by the gradually decreasing prices. A dealer soon learns to know what effects his speculations and purchases have upon the market price, and if the dearness is in part caused by his purchases, he knows that it will not continue, and he will cease to buy or to hoard what he forsees he must at a future period sell at a loss. Even a trifling rise of price would not be sufficient to secure him a fair profit on his capital, and an indemnity against the casualties of trade. The risk to the public is rather that he will not speculate enough. Even if he is guilty of an excess of speculation by keeping his provisions a little too long from the market, the injury thence resulting would not be so great as it would certainly be deemed in such a case. As long as those stores remained undisposed of in his possession, the public would think that the prices on each day were enhanced by his misconduct, by the excess of the market price above the price which provisions would sell at if all his stores, or at least a proper proportion of them, were on that day sent to market. But this is not the case. If his stores were sent to market they would cause a reduction of prices until they were disposed of, but after that period, whether they were sold and consumed or hoarded for future sale, can have no effect upon the market prices, unless so far as the knowledge that they are hoarded may have an effect in reducing the market price by dispelling the fears of famine.

This is not the only instance nor the only trade in which we shall find this close connexion between the interest of the individual and that of the community; and in general it may be remarked that the interest of the individual will lead him to adopt a course of conduct more consonant to the public good than even to that of the particular class or order to which he belongs. Having premised these few observations on the circumstances by which price is regulated, I shall call your attention to the circumstances which occasion some classes of labourers to obtain a higher rate of wages than other classes; but as the subject is of some importance, I must defer it until the next time I have the honor of addressing you here.

Lecture VI

GENTLEMEN,—Before I enter upon the subject to which I intend to call your attention this Term, I wish to recal to your minds, or to recapitulate a few of the principles which I have already attempted to establish. I defined, then, the utility of any article to be its power of satisfying the wants or wishes of mankind, either directly or indirectly; and by its value I wished you to understand its power of being exchanged for other articles. Of course therefore any thing that may be made the subject of an exchange, may be made use of as a measure of value. However, although a commodity may be a real measure, it may not be a convenient one; there may not exist ready means of comparing its value with that of other commodities. "In ruder ages, when men's wishes were confined to men's wants, the exchange of one commodity for another may have been sufficient to serve their purpose. It mattered not to them that one had cost double the time and labour of the other. Time and labour were

26

to them no further valueable than as they served to obtain what satisfied their simple desires. Like children, their wishes did not extend beyond the present moment. As civilization, and with it, foresight, advanced, men having more wishes to indulge, became more chary of their time and labour. Each commodity then acquired a value which required some measured independent of the passing desire of the moment. Money was then resorted to." And as in the ordinary transactions of life, exchanges are generally effected through the intervention of money, it is therefore in general made use of as a measure of value: and for most purposes it is a most convenient measure, although at different times the value of money may sustain very considerable variations. There is no more ready mode of conveying a definite idea of the value of any article, than by mentioning its value as measured in money; that is, by saying how much money it will cost to obtain it in exchange.

But as most of the commodities in which the wealth of a country consists are produced by labour, political-economists make use of it as a measure of value. It is not however, more than money, to be considered a peculiarly real measure of value, either as being of itself always of the same value, or as always demanding from the labourer the same sacrifice of ease and time. Still labour is the most convenient measure of value, because of its share in producing goods, or as it were purchasing them at the great mart of nature. It may be considered as the price which nature exacts from man for all the commodities of value which she furnishes for his use, and therefore the value of labour can be readily compared with that of other commodities; and it is a convenient measure to compare the values of those commodities with each other, For this purpose, however, that labour only must be regarded, which is expended in the most judicious and economical manner that the times and circumstances admit of.

In relation to value I also observed, that the value of every article depends upon the demand and the supply, and that indirectly the cost of production of any commodity, as well as its utility, has an effect upon its price. The cost of production, by its influence-upon the supply, since men will not produce commodities unless with the reasonable expectation of selling them for more than the cost of producing them. And the utility has some effect, although not so easily calculated, since it is to its utility, in the more extended sense of the word, that the demand is to be entirely attributed.

The price is regulated by the demand and the supply, and will be such a sum as is sufficient to produce an equality between the supply and the effectual demand. I mean by effectual demand, such a demand as actually leads to the purchase or consumption of the article.

I shall this Term attempt to investigate the laws which distribute wealth among the different orders of society; but before I enter upon the subject, I think it expedient to make a few remarks upon the nature of demand, and its influence upon price and value. The measure of the intensity of any person's demand for any commodity is the amount which he would be willing and able to give for it, rather than remain without it, or forego the gratification which it is calculated to afford him. On this we may observe, in the first place, that there may exist a demand not sufficiently intense to exercise any influence upon price. Thus the demand or desire of very indigent persons for rich and costly articles of dress or furniture, equipages, jewellery, &c. does not affect their price, since such demanders cannot possibly effect a purchase, even if the prices experienced a considerable reduction. Still a demand may affect prices, although it be not sufficiently intense to lead to an actual purchase. Of this an example is, the demand of those who will not purchase at the existing prices, but who would come into the market and purchase, if a slight reduction should take place. Such a demand always does exist, and has an effect in keeping up prices, exactly similar to the bidding at an auction of the person whose bidding is next in amount to that of the actual purchaser. Ordinary sales are similar to sales by auction in this, that the seller tries to sell as dearly, and the buyer to buy as cheaply as possible; the difference only consists in the form and mode of ascertaining the greatest prices which the seller can require, without injudiciously diminishing the extent of his sales.

But it is to be remarked, that there may be, and that in fact there generally is, an excess of intensity of demand, which exercises no perceptible influence upon the prices of commodities. This is the demand of those who, if necessary, would pay more than the existing prices, but who do not, because the state of the market enables them to procure the same commodities, or more desirable substitutes, more cheaply. Thus the high prices to which provisions rise in times of scarcity, prove the existence of a latent intensity of demand, which is only called into action by the scarcity which renders it impossible to purchase provisions at the usual cheap rate: the intense demand always exists, though it may not be apparent. But in some cases the demand itself is created by a scarcity, or other peculiar circumstances; as, when we read of a besieged city being reduced to such distress for want of provisions, that a dead rat was sold for a considerable sum. Such a case might happen again, and yet such a possibility would scarcely justify us in saying that in ordinary times there existed even a latent demand for such food.

For provisions and other articles of greater or less necessity, the intensity of demand among different persons varies according to the sacrifices of other objects which they can conveniently afford to make; and yet all will effect their purchases at the same rate, viz. at the market prices, and this rate is determined by the sum which will create an equality between the effectual demand and the supply. Now if the price is attempted to be raised one degree beyond this sum, the demanders, who by the change will cease to be purchasers, must be those the intensity of whose demand was precisely measured by the former price. Before the change was made, the demand, which was less intense, did not lead to a purchase, and after the change is made, the demand, which is more intense, will lead to a purchase still. Thus the market price is measured by that demand, which being of the least intensity, yet leads to actual purchases. If the existing supply is more than sufficient to satisfy all the demand equal or superior to a certain degree of intensity, prices will fall, to accommodate themselves to a less intense demand.

But the intensity of demand varies not only in different places, and among different individuals, but in many cases the same person may be said to have in himself several demands of different degrees of intensity. Of this there is a very palpable example, when provisions, owing to their scarcity or abundance, sustain a change of price. When they rise, a diminution of consumption is the effect. But the manner in which this diminution of consumption takes place usually, is not by the total abstinence of some from food, while the rest consume their accustomed portions. On the contrary, all continue to eat, as they must, or else cease to exist; but none except those whose wealth renders them indifferent to the price of their food, consume as much as usual. With every decrease of the total supply within the country, a corresponding diminution in the consumption of the great mass of individuals must take place. But the proximate cause of this diminution in the consumption of each individual, is the rise of prices which the scarcity produces. Now that portion which any person ceases to consume in consequence of a rise of prices, or that additional portion which he would consume if prices should fall, is that for which the intensity of his demand is less than the high price which prevents him from purchasing it, and is exactly equal to the low price which would induce him to consume it. On the other hand, for that portion which, notwithstanding the high prices, he continues to consume, he must have had a demand, the intensity of which was at least equal to those high prices which did not prevent him from purchasing it. Carry on this train of reasoning in your minds through successive degrees of scarcity and consequent high prices, and you will come to the conclusion, that each individual contains as it were within himself, a series of demands of successively increasing degrees of intensity; that the lowest degree of this series which at any time leads to a purchase, is exactly the same for both rich and poor, and is that which regulates the market price; and that in the case of the rich man, the series increases more rapidly, that is to say, the intensity of his demand increases more rapidly in proportion to the diminution of his consumption, than in the case of the poor man. I have chosen the example of provisions as being the most obvious and palpable, and as most frequently affording a practical instance of the principle which it illustrated; but the same observation is equally true, although not so strikingly, in every case in which a diminution of supply would occasion a diminution in any individual's consumption, without leading him to give up the use of the article altogether.

'RETALIATION, OR FREE TRADE?'

James A. Lawson

Source: James A. Lawson, *Five Lectures on Political Economy*: Delivered before the University of Dublin, Michaelmas Term, 1843, London: John W. Parker; Dublin: Andrew Milliken, 1844, pp. 133–47

SINCE the remark in the text was written, my attention has been directed to some views lately put forward by Colonel Torrens, on this subject. I have read the article in the 157th number of the *Edinburgh Review*, entitled, "Free Trade and Retaliation," and Colonel Torrens's Reply to that article. I have not seen the publication called the "Budget," in which those views were first put forward, at least so as to attract public attention; but as, in the remarks I have to make here, I do not mean to enter into the *minutiæ* of detail connected with the subject, and as I shall be careful not to assume any opinion as belonging to Colonel Torrens, unless it be adopted and advocated by him in his Reply, I trust that I shall be able to give a fair representation of his opinions, and a short but satisfactory refutation of them. I could not within the limits of this note, enter into a detail of all the points at issue between Colonel Torrens and Mr. Senior, the author of the article in the *Edinburgh Review*; nor would I be disposed to attempt to answer all the matters contained in Colonel Torrens's Reply, as I dare say they will be answered by Mr. Senior himself, with far greater ability than I could pretend to; I could not, however, let this little work go forth without noticing what I conceive to be a very plausible and dangerous error.

The opinion, then, the correctness of which I now dispute, is, "that the imposition of retaliatory duties, to countervail similar duties imposed by foreign countries, is expedient, and that such a course would raise prices in the country that imposed them; but that, on the contrary, a lowering of import duties upon the productions of countries retaining their hostile tariffs, would occasion an abstraction of the precious metals, and a decline in prices, in profits, in wages." I am sure Colonel Torrens will admit that these are substantially his opinions. Instead of examining the arguments used by him in support of this view, I now take the more direct course of demonstrating its fallacy, by the following argument:—

First—I shall point out the causes which regulate and determine the quantity of precious metals that circulate within any country;

Secondly—I shall examine whether the imposition of import duties exercises any influence on these causes; if not, the conclusion is inevitable, that the amount of the precious metals in the country will be unaffected by their imposition.

With regard to the first branch, I am sure that Colonel Torrens will not dissent from my propositions respecting it.

Colonel Torrens states his views in page 7 of his Reply—"that the precious metals have a constant tendency so to distribute themselves throughout the world, as to bring the currencies of different countries to par; or, in other words, to cause an ounce of gold, in London, to purchase (subject to a slight correction on account of carriage) a bill of exchange for an ounce of gold, payable in Paris, Amsterdam, Hamburgh." This is perfectly true, and when the currencies are thus at par, each country has its *natural* supply of the precious metals; but the absolute amount that circulates in each country is very different, and we now ask what determines that amount? Here again I agree with Colonel Torrens, who quotes and adopts Ricardo's view. It is regulated mainly by the productiveness of the labour employed in the raising of exportable commodities. In Mr. Ricardo's words, as quoted in page 9 of the Reply—"Of two countries, having precisely the same population, and the same quantity of land of equal fertility in cultivation, with the same knowledge too of agriculture; the prices of raw produce will be highest in that where the greater skill and the better machinery is used in the manufacture of exportable commodities." The same truth is stated with admirable clearness by Mr. Senior, in his "Lectures on the Cost of obtaining Money," which Colonel Torrens cites with approval. If an Englishman can in the same time produce double the quantity that an Irishman can, it is manifest that he will obtain, as the reward of his labour, double the quantity of gold that the Irishman will. The only other circumstances that determine what supply of the precious metals a country shall have, are these which affect the rapidity of the circulation and the number of exchanges, as pointed out by Mr. Senior, in page 27 of the *Edinburgh Review:* these latter circumstances obviously cannot be influenced by any change in import or export duties; they depend exclusively on the monetary regulations of the country, and on the civilization of the people; we may, therefore, safely put them out of view in the present inquiry, and then the only question we have to ask, is, *whether the imposition or removal of import duties has any effect upon the productiveness of the labour employed in making exportable commodities?* If their imposition increases that productiveness, it increases the supply of the precious metals, and Colonel Torrens's position is established; if it diminishes the productiveness, it diminishes the supply of the precious metals, and the very opposite of his theory is the truth; and if it exercises no influence upon the productiveness of labour, it produces no *permanent* effect, on the supply of the precious metals; and the same may be said, *mutatis mutandis*, of their removal;—I say *permanent*, because there may be a *temporary* variation in the supply, produced by the occurrence of anything unusual in the commercial world, such as the drain of gold caused by a deficient harvest. That it is *temporary* only, will be indicated by the exchanges, as Colonel Torrens states in page 7 of his Reply; and it is very different from any permanent change in the supply, which, as I have stated, can only be produced by a change in the productiveness of labour.

Let us examine, then, into the effect which a change in import duties can exercise upon the productiveness of labour. Suppose the trade between England and France to be *perfectly* free—a state of things which would meet the unqualified approval of Colonel Torrens: it is then evident, on the principles put forward by all supporters of free trade, that the industry of each country will be directed to those employments in which its labour is most productive. Now, let England impose an import duty on French articles, and, France continue to receive English articles duty free: Colonel Torrens would say that the consequence of this would be an increase of the supply of the precious metals in England, and a diminution of them in France. This cannot be, unless the productiveness of labour in France is diminished, and in England is increased by the change. Is it so, then? The first effect of the import duty would be to diminish the consumption of French articles in England. Those articles were procured by sending to France, in exchange for them, the produce of English labour, either in the form of English manufactures or in gold, or some other commodity procured by the export of English produce. The consumers of French articles in England, having discontinued or diminished their consumption of them, will, by some new mode of expending their income, give a different direction to this labour, which was formerly employed indirectly in procuring French articles for them—it is obvious, that the consumers of French articles suffer by the imposition of the duty, for this labour, which they are able to command, was most productive of enjoyment to them, when it was employed in procuring French articles for them, otherwise it would not have received from them this direction; the income they used to spend in the purchase of French articles must now be expended upon something which will produce less enjoyment; therefore, as far as English consumers of French articles are concerned, the productiveness of the labour at their command will be diminished; *is not, therefore, the productiveness of English labour diminished?* Labour is most productive when it furnishes us with the greatest abundance of all the articles we desire; and by the imposition of this duty, the number of desirable articles at the disposal of the English public is diminished, and their power to gratify their wishes impeded. This I call a diminution in the productiveness of English labour, and I know no other sense in which the words can be properly used. Take the article claret: suppose a man used, when there was no duty, to drink 100 bottles of claret a-year; and the duty is high enough to double the price: if he does not choose to spend more on claret than he did, he can only drink 50 bottles now: he pays for the 50 as much as he used to pay for the 100, and has only half the enjoyment, and the benefit is reaped by Government, at his expense, by the receipt of the duty. If he discontinues the use of claret altogether, the money which he used to spend on claret, he will spend in some other way less suited to his inclination. This may seem a trifling inconvenience, especially as some Political-Economists seem to regard the interests of consumers as of much less importance than those of producers; but if we read "corn" for "claret" in the illustration, the same will be true, and the results formidable in their character; for it is obvious that neither the corn nor the claret would be procured from abroad, if they, or articles to supply their place, could be raised at home as cheaply and as well. Now, would any injury be inflicted on France by the change? As the English demand for French goods would be diminished by the rise of price consequent upon the duty, those who had capital embarked in the business of supplying goods to the British market would suffer from a fall of profits until either a new market for those goods was discovered, or, if that could not be done, until some capital was withdrawn from this occupation. Nothing, however, has occurred to diminish the demand for British articles in France, and they can be obtained upon as favourable terms as before; they can no longer be all paid for by the direct exportation of French produce, and therefore some of the labour which is now not required to supply the British demand, will be employed in procuring something which England will take—for instance, in sending goods to Germany, and sending German goods into England; or in sending goods somewhere for gold, and sending gold into England. Now this change in the direction of industry is certainly *some* evil, but it is by no means of the same magnitude as that under which England suffers; the latter cannot be evaded, for the prohibited commodities cannot be introduced even indirectly from any other country, while France *can* evade the difficulty in the way of making her payments, by indirectly sending into England the produce of other countries which is not prohibited. Now, suppose France imposes a corresponding duty on English imports: how will this benefit her? It will bring upon France those evils which I have shown England experienced from the diminished productiveness of labour, for French consumers of British goods must now be satisfied with an article less suited to their wants and wishes. England would now suffer from the same evil which was confined to France before, namely, the diminished demand for British articles for the French market, but neither country would now have to resort to a round-about indirect mode of making their payments, as the direct exports and imports would probably balance each other, as they did in the time of free trade, which is the only advantage that can result, if advantage it be. But the final result of the imposition of duties by both countries is, that the productiveness of labour in each country is permanently diminished.

The same reasoning will prove that the lowering of import duties in England, in the face of foreign rivalry and hostile tariffs will not produce any permanent abstraction of the precious metals from England; because it will not diminish the productiveness of her labour, which is the regulator of the supply of the precious metals.

It appears to me, therefore, that unless Colonel Torrens can show, that the removal of import duties would diminish the productiveness of a country's labour, or the imposition of them increase it, it is impossible for him to sustain his present opinions. It is easy to *imagine* a case in which such a result would follow, for instance, if the effect of a large exportation of a country's produce were to compel her to export articles in which her labour was less productive; but in practice it is found that the greater the demand is, the greater is the productiveness of our labour. I have not embarrassed this argument by any considerations respecting the Exchanges; but I am sure Colonel Torrens will admit, that, if from any cause, a greater supply than usual of the precious metals is poured into a country, while the natural causes, which determine what that supply shall be, remain unaltered, the principle which he has pointed out in page 7 of his Reply will operate; the exchanges will become unfavourable to that country, and, by a well-known law, the gold will find its way out until the supply is reduced to its natural amount; and in the same way, if the supply of the precious metals is diminished, while the causes, which determine what the natural supply shall be, remain unaltered, gold will flow back, until the natural supply is restored. I will not enter here into the detail of the operation, by which the Exchanges bring about this result; every one at all acquainted with Economic Science is familiar with it, and it is stated with the utmost clearness in Mr. Senior's first Lecture "On the Transmission of the Precious Metals."

It is not my design, as I already stated, to reply to all Colonel Torrens's arguments, for the answer which I have given, if there be no error in the reasoning, is conclusive against them, and renders it unnecessary to entangle one's self in the perplexity of the imaginary cases he puts. I will, however, observe, that the reasoning which he has in some places employed, based as it is upon suppositions most remote from reality, illustrates the importance of the truths I directed attention to in the first of these Lectures.

I will, however, take his imaginary case of England and Cuba, and point out what very different results would take place from those which he predicts.

England and Cuba are supposed to be equal in territory, fertility, population, amount of capital, and general efficiency of labour, and that they have each a metallic currency amounting to £30,000,000; this supposition is strictly correct, for on the principles agreed on by both Colonel Torrens and myself, the supply of the precious metals in each would be equal. He also supposes that they trade only with one another, and that this supply of sixty millions of gold cannot be increased. England has superior productiveness in cloth and Cuba in sugar, and he supposes the exchanges between them, under a system of free trade, to be 1,500,000 cwt. of sugar, worth 30*s*. per cwt., and 1,500,000 bales of cloth, worth 30*s*. per bale. It is evident, then, that it requires the same amount of labour and capital to produce a bale of cloth in England as it requires to produce a hundred weight of sugar in Cuba. He then supposes Cuba to impose on cloth a duty of 100 per cent. and England not to retaliate. I will now trace the results according to the sound principles of the Science, as I understand them, and leave the reader to compare them with those arrived at by Colonel Torrens.

Cuba will now only consume 750,000 bales of cloth, and there will be a balance due by England to her after receiving 1,500,000 cwt. of sugar, which she must pay in gold, only the three articles, cloth, sugar; and gold, being supposed to exist—the amount will be £1,125,000.

> Cuba will now have . .   £31,125,000 of gold.
> England will have   .   .   £28,875,000 of gold.

This will alter the value of cloth and sugar in each country measured in gold, the supply of gold is altered, but the supply of cloth and sugar remains the same; and it is manifest that if, when there were £30,000,000 in Cuba, cloth was worth in Cuba 30*s*. per bale; when there are £31,125,000, it will fetch 31*s*. 1*d*. per bale, or thereabouts, and if when there were £30,000,000 in England, sugar was worth 30*s*. per cwt., when there are only £28,875,000 the English merchant will only give 28*s*. 9*d*. per cwt., or thereabouts, for it, exclusive of the duty; matters would therefore stand thus:—

> Cloth   will be worth in England   28*s* 9*d*.
> Cloth   ,,   ,,   ,,   in Cuba   31*s* 1*d*.
> Sugar   ,,   ,,   ,,   in England   28*s* 9*d*.
> Sugar   ,,   ,,   ,,   in Cuba   31*s* 1*d*.

It is manifest that the instant effect would be, to check exportation from Cuba to England, and to encourage exportation from England to Cuba.

But suppose, with Colonel Torrens, that England still imports 1,500,000 cwt. of sugar, and Cuba 750,000 bales of cloth,

> Sugar in England will only bring   28*s* 9*d*.
> Therefore England will pay—1,500,000 cwt. at 28*s* 9*d*.—£2,156,250
> Cloth in Cuba will bring . . . . .   31*s* 1*d*.
> Therefore Cuba will pay—750,000 bales   at   31*s* 1*d*.—£1,165,625
>
> _____
>
>   £990,625

The balance now to be remitted by England is £990,625 instead of £1,125,000 as on the last occasion, and if the exchanges go on, England will have to remit less on every occasion, till very soon she will get 1,500,000 cwt. of sugar for 750,000 bales of cloth.

The result therefore would be altogether favourable to England; she need only employ as much labour and capital as would make 750,000 bales of cloth, and the labour before required for the other 750,000 might be applied to some other purpose; or, if it was still employed in the same way, she would have the enjoyment at home of 750,000 bales of cloth, in addition to her usual supply of sugar, while the Cuba consumers would only have half their former supply of cloth, while they should devote the same amount of labour and capital to the making of sugar, and the only benefit derived by them would be an increased supply of gold, for which they are obliged to pay this penalty; and England, for the loss of the gold, would reap the advantages I have stated.

Let the reader compare these results with Colonel Torrens's deductions, bearing in mind, however, that the reasoning is about a purely imaginary state of things, for, except upon the supposition that the supply of gold in the world is incapable of increase and that there are no other trading countries, the supply of gold could not be permanently different in two countries, whose population, efficiency of labour, &c., are equal; and in this *imaginary world* it would not be attended with any evil to the country whose supply was lessened; in the *real world*, however, if such a permanent diminution were possible, it would be attended with great evil; but in the *real world* it never can happen; so that the circumstance of the existence of other trading countries, and of other supplies of gold, which would cause it to be an evil if it occurred, is the circumstance that effectually prevents its occurrence. For I take it to be clear to demonstration, that, if the productiveness of a country's labour is unaltered; if her goods will procure as much of the precious metals or other commodities in the market of the world as they ever did, and yet, if her supply of the precious metals be, from any cause, lessened, gold will flow into that country; for this simple reason, that gold is more valuable there than in any other part of the world, for in consequence of the diminution of its supply, it will procure in exchange more of the goods of that country than it did before, and those goods are of the same value in the market of the world as they were, for the productiveness of the country's labour is undiminished, and those goods will procure as much of every other thing as they did, except of *gold at home*; therefore, a clear profit is to be realized by bringing the gold there and getting those goods in exchange; and the same is to be said, *mutatis mutandis*, when the supply of the precious metals in any country is, from any cause increased, while the productiveness of its labour is the same. This is effected, as we all know, by the operation of the exchanges, which, by becoming favourable or unfavourable, lead to the import or export of the precious metals; the exchange can never be *at par* between two countries, unless the value of gold is equal in both, and it is not equal if it procure more of goods of the same value in one and less in another, that is to say, it can never be *at par* if the supply of the precious metals in any country is altered, while the productiveness of the country's labour remains the same. The immediate effect, therefore, of any change in the supply of the precious metals, is to produce a corresponding change in the exchanges; and when they return to par, it is manifest that the supply of the precious metals is the same as it formerly was, unless the productiveness of the country's labour has been changed. Colonel Torrens's mistake, therefore, consists in supposing, that the diminution of supply can be *permanent*, when the causes which regulate and determine that supply remain unaltered.

I would think it unnecessary to dwell so long upon a point which seems so clear to my own mind, but that the opinion which I have been combating would, if well founded, be fatal to the cause of Free Trade, and it has received the sanction of eminent Political-Economists: for instance, Dr. Longfield, one of my predecessors, whom I consider one of the ablest writers upon the Science, was led into this mistake, and puts it forward in page 108 of his 'Lectures on Commerce and Absenteeism.' I dare say Colonel Torrens will be glad to have such an ally.

Colonel Torrens is much displeased, because Mr. Senior identifies his view with the Mercantile System; but let the opinions be clothed in what language they may, their substantial import is, that it is advisable to compel a people to do without foreign goods, and to keep their gold, which, under a system of freedom, they would give for the goods—why is the gold given? because we prefer having the goods to keeping the gold; and this choice Colonel Torrens would prevent us from making. A large and sudden importation of foreign corn is complained of, because it produces a drain of gold; but if we had no gold to give, or were not allowed to give it, and if the foreigners would take nothing else, would we not be much worse off? we should then do without the corn, which is the alternative Colonel Torrens must recommend. If this be not the essence of the Mercantile System, I know not what is; and when Colonel Torrens defends himself by showing that he does not adopt *all* the opinions of the Mercantile School, while he admits the principle on which they are based, he only succeeds in proving his views to be *less* sound than theirs—they are *consistently*, he *inconsistently*, in error.

Great and unnecessary confusion has been introduced into the discussion of this subject, by mere verbal disputes, as to the principles which regulate *inter-national* exchange. Colonel Torrens, in his Reply, page 14, says, "I maintain that the terms of inter-national exchange are regulated, not by cost of production, but by demand and supply. You maintain that they are regulated, not by demand and supply, but by cost of production. My position is, that the relative value of foreign commodities is regulated by a different rule from that which regulates the relative value of domestic commodities;—your position is, that the relative value of foreign commodities, and the relative value of domestic commodities, are regulated by one and the same rule."

If there were any *real* difference of opinion between Political-Economists upon a matter so elementary as this, it would be a circumstance calculated to lower the public estimate of the Science, but in truth there is not, it is a *verbal* difference. Mr. Senior would admit, that "the value of foreign commodities is *not* regulated by *cost of production*," taken in the sense in which Colonel Torrens supposes him to have used the word; and, on the other hand, Colonel Torrens would, I trust, admit, "that the relative value of foreign commodities is regulated by the *same rule* as that which regulates the value of domestic commodities"—taking that proposition in the sense in which Mr. Senior employs it.

A simple statement of the principle which regulates the exchangeable value of *all things* will clear up the confusion.

It is a proposition always true, and of universal application, *that the exchangeable value of all articles depends upon their utility*, that is, upon their power to gratify the wants and wishes of man; in other words, upon the degree in which their possession is desired. This applies a like to domestic and foreign commodities, to manufactured articles and raw produce, to monopolized and unmonopolized articles—it is as true in a siege or a famine, as in the exchanges of every day occurrence.

Every other principle which has been assigned as the regulating cause of exchangeable value, is of partial and limited application, and subject to many restrictions and exceptions.

For instance, the "proportion between the demand and supply." It is very true that this influences the value of commodities, but it is only because it affects their *utility*, and only *when* it affects their utility. Thus, if A has a commodity called X, and B a commodity called Y, the proportion in which they will exchange for each other will be determined by the utility of X and Y—A will not part with X, or any portion of it, for any portion of Y, unless the portion of Y which he receives possesses more utility to *him*, that is, is more desired by him, than the portion of X which he gives. In like manner, B will not part with Y, or any portion of it, for any portion of X, unless the portion of X which he receives possesses more utility to *him*, that is, is more desired by him, than the portion of Y which he gives. Every child knows that this is the principle, and the only one, on which all exchanges are made. Demand and supply *generally* influence this utility; for instance, if A's supply of X be increased, this will generally diminish its utility to him, or the degree in which he desires its possession, for as our particular desires are capable of being satisfied, it is obvious that we may have more of one article than we wish to use, and therefore the retaining the possession of that surplus is less desirable to us: the exception to this is, when the article is not one which will spoil by keeping, and when we have a prospect of being able, by keeping it longer in our possession, to obtain more of what we want in exchange for it; hence it is that corn is very liable to fluctuations in value from changes in the supply, while some manufactures, which can be produced at pleasure, and which will not spoil by keeping, are comparatively uninfluenced by variations in their supply.

I think it was the existence of articles of this latter class, that led to the formation of the opinion now so general, that *cost of production* is the regulating cause of exchangeable value. This principle seems to account satisfactorily for the value of the latter class of articles, but was certainly inadequate to account for the former, and yet one class of Economists have vehemently contended that cost of production *only*, and the other, that demand and supply *only*, was the regulator of exchangeable value, although neither of them, by itself, will account for all the variations in exchangeable value.

Before we inquire into the influence of *cost of production* on exchangeable value, let us ascertain the meaning of the term, Mr Senior defines it to be "the sum of labour and abstinence necessary to production," and the general reader will readily understand it, as "the trouble and expense necessary to procure the article." Now it is obvious that the value of articles does not always conform to this: that class which I have mentioned as being peculiarly affected by changes in the demand and supply, does not obey this rule, and as a general rule, the cost of production is not the circumstance which influences a party in determining what he will pay for an article, it is, as I said, the utility of the article: the man who finds an article and offers it for sale, will get as much for it as another who has been for a long time labouring to produce a similar article; and if a workman takes three days to make an article, which another workman can make in one day, he cannot on that account get three times as much for it; so if a person is the sole producer of an article, he may charge any price he pleases for it. It is not true to say that the cost of production *regulates* value, though it is true that in many cases the value, which is determined by other considerations, happens to coincide with the cost of production. The reason why it so coincides, and the circumstances under which it does so, and the means by which the coincidence is brought about, are manifest. In a country where every man is free to choose his own occupation, it is evident, that, as a general rule, all labour is equally rewarded, as Adam Smith with great felicity shows; this establishes an average rate of wages and profits, and if the price received for any article is not such as to pay the average wages and profits to those engaged in it, it will be abandoned, and the supply of the article will be diminished, until the price rises to that amount; and, on the other hand, if the price be greater, the supply will be increased, until it falls to that level; so that value is only made to coincide with cost of production, *through the medium of a change in supply*, and when this cannot be brought about, there is no such coincidence and no tendency to it. Again, in measuring cost of production, we must suppose all labour of the same value; an article which required the day's labour of a skilful artificer to produce it, cannot be said to be equal in cost of production to one which required the day's labour of an unskilled workman to produce it. These two circumstances—the necessity of the existence of the power of changing from one employment to another, and the equality of the labour employed—explain at once the apparent difference between Mr. Senior and Colonel Torrens. The first proves that Colonel Torrens is right in saying that the value of foreign articles is not regulated by their cost of production, for an Englishman cannot become a foreigner at pleasure, they are therefore like those domestic commodities, the supply of which cannot be altered at pleasure, and whose value therefore is regulated by their utility, and does not coincide with the cost of their production: but Mr. Senior is equally correct in saying, that the value of foreign is regulated by the same rule as that of domestic commodities, and that is, by their power of gratifying the wishes of the world. Again, the quality of the labour is not necessarily equal, therefore the value does not coincide with the cost of production. Colonel Torrens says, "The question is, will the English yarn produced by a given quantity of labour, sell in the markets both of England and France, at the same price at which the French silks, produced by the same quantity of labour, sell in the markets both of France and of England? If this question can be answered in the affirmative, your case is proved; if it must be answered in the negative, my case is proved." Of course Mr. Senior would not answer this question in the affirmative, nay, even Colonel Torrens would not answer the corresponding question, with regard to domestic articles, in the affirmative. "Will an English watch produced by a given quantity of labour, sell at the same price in England as a piece of English straw matting, produced by the same quantity of labour?" "Certainly not," Colonel Torrens would reply, "for the labour of a watch manufacturer is skilled labour, but the labour of a person who weaves mats, is comparatively unskilled;" just as Mr. Senior would say in reply to the other question, "No, for English labour is more skilled than French."

Mr. Senior uses the term "cost of production," in the sense of *cost of production to the consumer*, and thus maintains, that the value of foreign articles coincides with the cost of production, because if we set about producing them ourselves we could not do it on better terms; but Colonel Torrens by "cost of production," means "cost of production to the producer," and in this sense he is right in saying, that the value of foreign articles does not coincide with their cost of production. However, I do not think that the value of foreign articles is at all regulated by their cost of production, even in Mr. Senior's sense of the word, it is never so high: who will say that the value of tea is regulated by what it would cost us to supply ourselves with tea grown at home? It appears to me, therefore, that the simple and obvious statement is, that the value of articles is governed by their utility, and if the labour of an Englishman for one day, can produce an article possessing double the utility in the market of the world, that an article produced by the day's labour of a Frenchman possesses, a day's labour in England will procure double the quantity of gold or of any other commodity, in the market of the world, that the day's labour of a Frenchman will, and will always continue to do so until the productiveness is diminished; and unless the imposition or removal of duties affects that productiveness, it can never permanently affect the supply of the precious metals. Of this we may be as well assured, as we are of any conclusion in Physical Science. That no such result as Colonel Torrens anticipates, has, *in fact* ever taken place, is shown in No. 22 of "The Economist," page 426.

19

AN INTRODUCTORY LECTURE ON POLITICAL ECONOMY

William Neilson Hancock

Source: William Neilson Hancock, *An Introductory Lecture on Political Economy*, Dublin: Hodges and Smith; London: James Ridgeway, 1849, pp. 5–20.

GENTLEMEN,

In pursuance of a plan which I announced in my first lecture last year, I propose in this course of lectures to apply the principles of Economic Science to the solution of our social difficulties, by endeavouring to point out some of the most important economic causes of the present state of Ireland. Before, however, entering on this subject, I shall in this introductory lecture give you a general view of the limits of Political Economy, of the philosophic method to be pursued in its investigations, and also a sketch of the elementary parts of the two theories of prices and of money, under which the principal laws of the science can be conveniently arranged. A general view of the subjects which fall within the limits of the science is of great use, in enabling us readily to distinguish those investigations which the economist is bound to undertake, from those which, however interesting in themselves, properly fall within the limits of some other branch of the social sciences. And this distinction must be marked with as much precision as the nature of the subject admits of, and must be observed throughout our investigations. We shall thus avoid the error of mixing up economic considerations with speculations on extraneous subjects, by which economists have frequently brought some of the best established principles of the science into disrepute.

The most correct view of the peculiar province of Political Economy can be obtained, by applying to the social sciences the principle of division by which the boundaries of the natural sciences are marked out. Each of the natural sciences is distinguished by the class of natural phenomena which is taken as the subject matter to be observed and explained. Thus, the movements and other phenomena of the stars and other heavenly bodies constitute the matter to be observed and explained by Astronomy. In the other

42

natural sciences, in like manner, such as Physiology, Botany, Mineralogy, and Geology, the phenomena to be observed and explained are those which are exhibited by the structure of the human frame, by plants, by minerals, and by the crust of the earth, respectively. Now the social phenomena which political economists propose to observe and explain, are that large and all-important class of human transactions known in common language by the terms "barter," "selling and buying," "letting and hiring," and all included under the scientific term, "exchanges." In all states of society, in all countries, and in all times, men have been found to possess the instinct which leads them to make exchanges with their fellow-men. This is such a distinguishing mark of humanity, that Archbishop Whately has proposed to define man as "the exchanging animal." Exchanges are not only of universal occurrence, but also of paramount interest, as the most important interests of mankind are involved in them. On exchanges each of us is dependent for the luxuries, the conveniences, and even the necessaries of life. On exchanges nations are dependent for their progress in wealth, happiness, and civilization. And hence it is that the definition of Political Economy which best indicates its limits is "the Science of Exchanges."

Having explained the limits of Political Economy, the next matter to be noticed is the philosophic method to be pursued in its investigations. This is the same as in the natural sciences, especially those which, like astronomy, do not afford facilities for experiments. First, the phenomena of exchanges are subjected to observations, so that the variations in them, both as to time and place, may be noted. Secondly, hypotheses are proposed to explain these variations, and lastly, further observations are made to test these hypotheses. Any hypothesis which, when tested, is found to be true, is enunciated as a law of the science. The laws thus discovered lead to the more accurate classification of the phenomena, which are again subjected to the same process of investigation. Thus more careful and systematic observations are made; new hypotheses are suggested to explain newly observed variations; these again are tested, and, if verified, lay the foundation of more complete laws.

Having explained the subject matter and philosophic method of the science, I have next to direct your attention to the most important circumstance in every exchange. This is the quantity of the one article which is received in exchange for a given quantity of the other article. This quantity is called the *value* of the article given in exchange estimated in the article received in exchange; and from the consideration of *value* thus entering into every exchange, it has been proposed by some economists to call Political Economy the Science of Value. The value of articles of wealth is observed to be subject to variations both as to time and place. Thus, some articles of wealth, although preserving the same average value for long periods, are subject to fluctuation for short periods, such as corn and labour. Other articles of wealth, such as the precious metals, are constant in value for short periods, but are subject to great changes at distant intervals of time. Again, some articles, such as the precious metals, preserve nearly the same value in all places at the same time, whilst other articles, such as labour and live stock, have very different values in distant places. The variations in value thus present to the economist an infinite variety of phenomena to be observed and explained.

But a difficulty presents itself in conducting investigations into value, and still more in explaining the results of such investigations to others, from the word *value* having more meanings than one. Thus, in common conversation you will find that this word is more generally used to denote utility, or what Adam Smith calls "value in use," than to denote the quantity of an article given or received in exchange, which he calls "exchangeable value." Thus, most persons would say that a thousand pounds' worth of wheat is more valuable than a thousand pounds' worth of children's toys. This ambiguity about value has been increased by some economists using the word as if it were synonymous with cost. Thus, when Adam Smith says, "equal quantities of labour at all times and places are of equal *value* to the labourer," and "that he must always lay down the same portion of his ease, liberty, and happiness;" and again when he says, "labour never varies in its own *value*," he used the word value in the sense of *cost* or sacrifice. This meaning has been perpetuated by Ricardo. Now there cannot be anything more injurious to the progress of science, than to have its truths enunciated in language which admits of the slightest ambiguity. For such ambiguities, besides exposing the propositions to be misunderstood by careless reasoners, and misrepresented by dishonest opponents, deceive even the most careful student. For as we all speak our native language before we learn science, the scientific signification attached to a word never entirely displaces in our minds its popular meaning. There is, however, a method of avoiding the use of the word value, without in the slightest degree diminishing the validity or even the convenience of the investigations.

The explanation of this method leads me to the next important circumstance with regard to exchanges, namely, that there is a particular class of commodities which are observed to be oftener exchanged for other articles of wealth, than all other articles taken together. The commodities included in this class have the characteristic of being the least changeable in value for short periods, and are comprized under the general name of *money*. From this circumstance they are best adapted for that most numerous class of exchanges, where the parties have not reciprocal wants, as where the shoemaker wants beef, but the butcher does not want shoes. The commodities used as money in this country are the precious metals, gold, silver, and copper. From the circumstance, then, that articles are oftener exchanged for money than for all other articles, in other words, that sales are much more numerous than cases of barter, it follows that the most important investigations with regard to value are those of the value of articles estimated in money; but this value is called their *price*. Now the word "price" is fortunately free from all ambiguity, and always means the exchangeable value of a commodity, estimated in the money of the country where the exchange takes place. Thus, every one would admit that a thousand pounds worth of wheat is of the same *price* as a thousand pounds worth of children's toys. And I find that the corresponding French word *prix* possesses the same advantage.[1] Now I propose to substitute observations into the variations in price, for observations into variations in value. Such observations, besides avoiding the ambiguity of the word value, are also more readily made in all civilized countries than other observations with respect to value. In fact, every market and every newspaper furnish statements with regard to the prices of commodities. If the variations in price can be explained, all other variations in value can be readily accounted for. Thus, if the value of wheat estimated in labour is found to vary, there must be a change in the prices of both wheat and labour, or else in the price of one of them. If we can explain these changes, we at the same time account for the variation in the value of wheat estimated in labour.

The first important result which has been ascertained by systematic observations of prices is, that there are two classes of variations in prices, perfectly distinct from each other. Thus, it is found that the price of a particular article often varies without any corresponding variations in the prices of other articles. At other times, the prices of all articles of wealth partake of a simultaneous change. Variations of the first kind are found to arise from causes acting on the particular article in the price of which they occur. They may, therefore, in reference to the article, be called intrinsic variations. Variations of the second class are found to be quite independent of the articles of wealth, but to arise from causes acting upon the value of money. They may, therefore, be called, with reference to articles of wealth, extrinsic variations in price. They arise from the same causes which produce intrinsic changes in the price of other articles, producing intrinsic changes in the value of money, and consequently extrinsic changes in prices in general. The explanation of the causes of variations in value, which forms by far the most important part of Political Economy, may therefore be divided into two parts, which, with reference to the classes of variations proposed to be explained, namely, intrinsic and extrinsic changes in prices, may conveniently be called—the former, the theory of prices, and the latter, the theory of money.

To proceed, then, with the theory of prices, it is found by observation, that no intrinsic variation takes place in the price of any commodity, except from one of two causes; either a change in the degree in which its possession is desired, or in its desirability; or a change in the force of the causes by which its supply is limited, or, in other words, by which it is made scarce. These causes operate separately. Thus, whenever a commodity is for any time, or altogether, incapable of increase, variations in its price depend entirely on changes in the degree of its desirability. On the other hand, whenever a commodity is capable of immediate increase, the variations in its price depend not on its desirability, but on the degree of its scarcity, or, in other words, on the force of the causes which limit its supply. The degree in which the possession of a commodity is desired, is measured by the number of persons able and willing to purchase at each amount of price. And it is observed that for commodities in general, their desirability increases very rapidly as their prices fall. The penny postage affords a familiar instance of this; the number of persons able and willing to pay a penny for the carriage of a letter, being an amazing increase on the number able and willing to pay the previous high rates of postage. All causes of variations in the desirability of a commodity, are to be measured by their effect on the number of persons able and willing to purchase at each amount of price. As very few commodities are capable of an instantaneous increase in supply, the intrinsic variations in prices for short periods depend almost entirely on the changes in the desirability of commodities. But as most commodities can be increased in supply, the permanent intrinsic variations in prices depend almost entirely on changes in the degree of their scarcity.

The chief investigations respecting prices relate to the causes of permanent changes therein, and hence the importance of explaining the causes by which the supply of articles of wealth is limited. This leads us to that branch of Political Economy which treats of the production of wealth. Commodities in general are produced from other commodities called raw materials, by human labour, and the assistance of natural agents, such as air, water, land, &c. employed for some time in the work of production. The very statement of this process implies a third instrument of production; for it is clear that some one must have had the raw produce at the commencement of the process, and the means of supporting the labourers, and must have been able to abstain from the use of these articles for his support or other purposes, during the time required for production. Such a person is called a capitalist, and the instrument he employs is termed "capital," and the act of employing it may be conveniently termed "savingness."[2] Commodities, then, are produced from other commodities by labour, savingness, and the assistance of natural agents.

If we trace the manner in which the laws of production act upon the prices of commodities, we shall find that raw produce is generally desirable and limited in supply, and therefore bears a price. In the same way, labour, savingness, and the assistance of natural agents are each desirable and limited in supply, and have, in like manner, each its price. The causes, then, which limit the supply of any commodity arise from the necessity of using raw materials, and the three instruments of production; and the force of these causes is estimated by the sums which have to be paid for their use, or, in other words, by the respective prices of the materials and of the use of the instruments of production. We arrive, then, at this very simple law of price, namely, that the price of any commodity, so far as the causes limiting its supply are concerned, depends on the amounts of labour, savingness, and assistance of natural agents necessary to be used in its production, and the prices of such labour, savingness, and assistance, together with the amount of raw produce and its price. From this general formula we may deduce several, with which you are no doubt familiar in the writings of distinguished economists. Thus, if we apply this formula to the price of the raw produce, and so successively to the price of each raw produce considered as a commodity, we must come ultimately to some elements, such as air, water, &c. which, being unlimited in supply, do not bear any price. The price of a commodity may therefore be said to be equal to the sum to be paid for all the labour, savingness, and assistance of natural agents necessary to produce itself, and all the elements from which it is composed; or, in other words, to the amount of labour multiplied by its price, added to the amount of savingness multiplied by its price, added to the amount of the assistance of natural agents multiplied by its price. But the price of labour is the same as the rate of wages, the price of savingness as the rate of profits, and the price of the assistance of natural agents as rent. We have, then, at once the formula of Adam Smith as to the component parts of the price of commodities. Thus, after speaking "of that part of price which resolves itself into labour, and that part which resolves itself into rent, and that part which resolves itself into profit," he adds, "In every society the price of every commodity finally resolves itself into some one, or other, or all of those three parts; and in every improved society all the three enter, more or less, as component parts, into the price of the far greater part of commodities."

We can also deduce from the formula I have given the conclusions of Mr. Senior, as to the extent to which the price of a commodity depends on its cost of production. He defines cost of production as "the sum of labour and abstinence necessary to production," and adds, "We have seen that under circumstances of equal competition, or, in other words, where all persons can become producers, and that with equal advantages, the cost of production on the part of the producer or seller, and the cost on the part of the con-sumer or purchaser, are the same; and that the commodity thus produced sells for its cost of production; or, in other words, at a price equal to the sum of the labour and abstinence which its production requires; or, to use a more familiar expression, at a price equal to the amount of wages and profits which must be paid to induce the producers to continue their exertions." Now, by "sum of the labour and abstinence," Mr. Senior obviously means what I have already explained as the sum of the amount of labour multiplied by its price, added to the amount of savingness multiplied by its price. He then gives what may be considered as his complete proposition as to cost of production:—"when we speak, therefore, of a class of commodities as pro-duced under circumstances of equal competition, or as the result of labour and abstinence unassisted by any other appropriated agent, and consider their price as equal to the sum of the wages and profits that must be paid for their production, we do not mean to state that any such commodities exist, but that if they did exist, such would be the laws by which they would be regulated; and that so far as labour, or abstinence, or both, are conducive to the production of any given commodity, it is to be considered as produced under circumstances of equal competition, and as worth the wages, or profits, or both, with which that labour, or abstinence, or both, must be remunerated." Now this is only another form of the statement, that the price of a commodity, so far as the causes limiting its supply are concerned, is equal to the sums to be paid for the labour, savingness, and assistance of natural agents required in its production.

The theory of prices, however, requires another set of investigations to render it complete. We have seen that the prices of commodities depend partly on the *amounts* of labour, savingness, and assistance of natural agents required in production, and partly on the *prices* of such labour, savingness, and assistance of natural agents. Now these *amounts* depend on the circumstances of production of each particular commodity, and any further investigation of them is beyond the limits of Political Economy. But how are we to ascertain the causes on which these *prices* depend? They enter into the prices of all other commodities, and seem to be the ultimate variables, by the changes in which most of the other changes in prices can be accounted for. The investigation of the causes of these variations, accordingly, is one of the most important parts of Political Economy, and at the same time one of the most difficult. It resolves itself into three parts, namely, the theory of wages, or, of the price of labour; the theory of profit, or, of the price of savingness; and the theory of rent, or, of the price of the assistance of natural agents. The method of commencing the investigation of these theories is the same in all; namely, by the application of the laws already stated with regard to other prices. The prices of labour, of savingness, and of the assistance of natural agents depend on the causes which make the use of labour, capital, and natural agents desirable, and limited in supply, or scarce. In my lectures last year, on the condition of the labourer, on the condition of the capitalist, and on the condition of the landlord, I noticed the theories of wages, of profit, and of rent, and I gave some illustrations of them. In some future lectures I propose to give a complete account of these theories, but for the present it will be sufficient to have called your attention to the important position which they occupy in the theory of prices, and to the most general manner of investigating them.

Notes

1 "L'usage veut que l'on appelle *prix* le quantité de monnaie que l'on donne pour le même objet."—*J. B. Say's Notes to Storch*, i. 72.
2 I propose to use the term, "savingness" as synonymous with Mr. Senior's term "abstinence," and Adam Smith's term "parsimony."

20

THE PRINCIPLES OF VALUE IN EXCHANGE

Lecture I

Arthur Houston

Source: Arthur Houston, *The Principles of Value in Exchange, Explained and Expressed in Simple and Comprehensive Formulae*, London: Longmans, Green & Co., Dublin: William McGee, 1864, pp. 5–50, 85–93.

GENTLEMEN,

In a former Lecture I endeavoured to explain the nature and origin of Value in Use, and to trace the connexion between Value in Use and Value in Exchange. Having disposed of these preliminary points, I purpose in this and the succeeding Lecture to consider the laws which govern Value in Exchange; in other words, the principles which regulate the proportion in which commodities exchange for each other. By "Value," therefore, in the further discussion of the subject, you will understand "Value in Exchange," unless the contrary be distinctly stated.

Value in Exchange, as has just been intimated, signifies the proportion in which a commodity exchanges either for a particular commodity, or for commodities in general, the latter being its more usual and proper signification. It is observed that this proportion varies at different times and places: that sometimes, for example, the value of an article rises; that this rise is but transient, the value after a while subsiding to its former level, or even sinking below it: or it may be, on the other hand, that this rise is permanently maintained, and even that the value is still further raised. The same phenomena, it is unnecessary to remark, are observed with regard to depressions of value. These fluctuations are generally revealed to us through the medium of prices; but if we lived under a system of pure barter, they would, though not perhaps so perceptible, equally exist, and would probably be more violent. Now Political Economy charges itself with the task of pointing out the source of such changes in value, whether they are temporary or permanent.

49

It is one of the characteristics of the science to combine the attractions which pure abstract speculations possess for the philosophic mind, with the immediate applicability to the concerns of every-day life, by which practical men measure the importance of a study. In no branch of Political Economy does this double recommendation present itself in a higher degree than in that which we are about to consider. While the laws that govern value are among the most curious and interesting of all those with which the science is conversant, a clear insight into them is of the utmost importance to the mercantile community. If the merchant and the manufacturer would make their calculations with that accuracy which is necessary to continued success in business, they must be able rightly to interpret the phenomena exhibited by the markets, and to refer changes in value to their true source. It is scarcely too much to say, that a commercial crisis seldom occurs which is not either due in its origin to, or aggravated in its intensity by, miscalculations arising from ignorance of these laws. The practical importance of the subject, therefore, no less than its speculative interest, will justify me in dwelling upon it at some length.

What then determines the proportions in which, at a given time and place, commodities are naturally exchanged for each other? or rather, what determines the proportions in which they would be exchanged, if those transactions which are now conducted through the instrumentality of money, were effected by the direct process of barter? Such is the problem for solution.

In order to simplify it as much as possible, we shall confine our attention to a single case of Exchange Value, namely, that of what are technically termed "freely-produced" commodities. By a *freely-produced* commodity you are to understand, one in procuring which no agent or material has been employed, that cannot be obtained by any person who is prepared to undergo the sacrifices which must, *in the course of nature*, be made in the acquisition of such agent or material. I say, *in the course of nature*, because there are many agents and many materials, the use of which we cannot obtain, without submitting to sacrifices which spring solely from the artificial constitution of society. Were all rivers as accessible to the angler as the open sea is to the fisherman, trout would be as much a freely-produced commodity as mackerel. But the State authorises private persons to exclude the angler from fishing a trout-stream, except on payment of a sum of money for the privilege. Thus, in addition to the natural obstacles lying in the way of procuring trout, the sacrifices which must naturally be made in order to obtain it, society raises an artificial obstacle, creates an extra sacrifice. Trout, therefore, is not a freely-produced commodity. Nor, indeed, can it be with safety asserted that any commodity is. The mackerel taken from the sea, for instance, cannot be obtained without the assistance of a variety of implements, which may have required in their fabrication the use of agents subject to that artificial limitation in supply, which I have illustrated by the case of a trout preserve. The timber in the smack, the metal in the looks, and the cord in the lines or net, may, one or all, have been obtained from sources affected by this influence, and if so, may, as we shall see, have had their values disturbed in a corresponding degree. A further pursuit of this same thread of inquiry would lead us to detect the influence of artificial obstacles in every stage of the manufacture of any article we chose to select. It would be impossible, therefore, to fix upon any commodity in the concrete as being in the strict sense of the term freely-produced. Many commodities, however, approach indefinitely near to such a standard; and we may, at all events, conceive of one that reached it, and reason upon the supposition without danger of falling into error, so long as we bear in mind the hypothetical nature of our premises.

Suppose, then, that two such commodities existed in the hands of two different persons, and that each of these persons had more of that commodity which he possessed than was sufficient for his necessities, and that each was therefore willing to exchange a part of his surplus for so much of the other commodity as he stood in need of; in what proportion would the articles be exchanged? To make our hypothesis complete, let it further be assumed that each party is equally competent to produce either commodity; is quite aware of, and ready to act in accordance with, his own interest; that the commodities are naturally of the same degree of utility[1]; and finally, that no pressing necessity exists why either party should not wait till he had time to produce the required article for himself.

Supposing all these conditions were fulfilled, in what proportion would the exchange of the two commodities take place? The answer is sufficiently obvious, namely, *in such proportion that the sacrifice on both sides shall be the same*. Where each party has the option of producing for himself the article which the other possesses, neither will, in the circumstances supposed, consent, for the sake of procuring that article, to surrender another, the effort to obtain which has cost him a greater sacrifice than what he would himself have had to undergo in the production of the article he receives in return.

This principle, that equality of sacrifice regulates the value of freely-produced commodities, simple as it may seem, is yet, when rightly understood, the very pivot upon which the entire theory of Exchange Value turns. Let us examine more closely what is signified by the proposition.[2]

When Ricardo and Smith were investigating the laws of Exchange Value, they reverted first to that rude state of society in which all natural agents[3] were equally accessible to all mankind. They concluded that in such a state, *labour* was the sole regulator of value. The deer and the fish which were respectively the average produce of one day's sport, naturally exchanged for each other: but if the labour was in one case more severe than in another, or was more disagreeable, or such as required more dexterity, then a smaller quantity of the produce of such labour would be sufficient to buy the produce of a whole day's simple labour.

In the primitive state of society to which Ricardo and Smith reverted, commodities are in the main freely-produced; so that we have here a state of things which coincides in the most important point with the conditions I have laid down. The conclusions at which they arrived are on the whole sufficiently in accordance with the principle of equality of sacrifice insisted upon in our fundamental formula, to pass for the present without qualification. But they require to be fully developed in order that their bearing on the theory of value should be properly estimated.

There are some employments naturally disagreeable, and some are rendered so by the disrepute in which they are held by society. Some again are in these respects indifferent; beyond the physical or mental exertion they necessitate, there are no associations, agreeable or the reverse, connected with them. Lastly, there are some which are positively delightful, or are held in such estimation by society as to confer corresponding pleasure on those engaged in them.

These facts are full of significance in relation to the subject of Exchange Value. In certain instances the enjoyment derived from the pursuit of an avocation is of itself quite sufficient compensation for any sacrifice of time or trouble it may involve. The thousands who study the fine arts without any view to pecuniary emolument, afford proof of this fact. Other employments, again, are such as to be *self-remunerative*, if I may so term it, in a certain degree, but not so altogether. Let us return to the hunters, the anglers, and, adopting the illustrations of Ricardo and Smith, the arrow-makers of primitive society. Of these three classes the first have perhaps the most exciting and pleasurable existence. The life of the second, if not so exciting, is at least safe, and pretty easy and agreeable. That of the last possesses little positive enjoyment, and of excitement presents none; it is sedentary, not disagreeable, not difficult. Of no one of the three occupations can it be said that it is actually disagreeable; while each has, perhaps, something to recommend it. Supposing then all three classes equally qualified to carry on any one of these three trades, in what proportion will arrows, fish, and game exchange for each other? The answer is:—*In proportion to the degree in which each of the employments is not self-remunerative.* The hunter is partly compensated for the dangers and toils of his occupation by the excitement of the chase, and the enjoyment of a life of freedom and activity: the angler is partly compensated for his time and trouble, and for occasional exposure to cold and wet, by days of pleasant wanderings by tree-shaded streams, and all the other quiet pleasures Isaae Walton so enthusiastically describes: the maker of arrows is partly rewarded for his patient toil by the satisfaction arising from the exercise of mechanical skill. But for whatever of toil, and trouble, and anxiety, and hardship there may be, beyond that for which such inseparable pleasures afford compensation, the hunter, angler, and arrow-maker must be further remunerated, by the portion of the produce of their labour they respectively retain for their own consumption, and by what they respectively receive in exchange for the remainder. It is not then the *absolute* sacrifices undergone in production that regulate the value of the product, but the *balance* of such sacrifices, after account has been taken of the pleasure derived from the mere exercise of the calling itself.

All this is clear while the argument is confined to that rude state of society in which no capital exists, and no land or other natural object is subject to appropriation. Adam Smith accordingly considered that it was only in such primitive state that labour *alone* regulated value. He held that when capital came into existence, *profits* also, as well as labour, operated to adjust the relative values of things made with the aid of capital. And further, that when land and other natural objects were appropriated, *rent* united with profits and with labour—or rather with *wages*, which he uses as an equivalent expression—in regulating the values of commodities produced with the assistance of appropriated natural agents as well as capital. I shall forbear to touch as yet upon the case of articles produced with the assistance of appropriated natural agents, and shall confine myself for a little longer to the consideration of commodities that are freely produced.

Such commodities, I have observed, are obtainable by every one who is willing to encounter the obstacles which *naturally* arise in the process of production. The difficulties of pursuit, capture, and destruction, in the case of wild animals, and the trouble of fabrication in the case of missile weapons, are of this nature. But there are other obstacles to be encountered in production not less important than mere *physical* exertion, such as alone is required in the chase of a wild animal or the construction of a material object. For instance, some articles before they arrive at perfection, must pass through a variety of processes; these processes require considerable time; the person, therefore, who undertakes to produce such an article, must await patiently the lapse of an interval more or less protracted, before he can hope to be rewarded for his trouble, and compensated for his outlay. Now, this clearly is an additional sacrifice, over and above whatever surrender of time and case the employment may otherwise necessitate; and for this additional sacrifice he will accordingly expect to be remunerated. Since the appearance of the article on Political Economy contributed by Mr. Senior to the *Encyclopædia Metropolitana*, this sacrifice has been known by the name of *Abstinence*.

The amount of abstinence required in the production of any commodity, and the proportion which it bears to the other sacrifices undergone in each particular case, depend on the nature of the processes through which the commodity passes in its progress towards completion. In order that a butt of grape-juice, or a young sapling, should attain the highest degree of perfection which they are severally capable of reaching, little is required except forbearance to drink the one, or to cut down the other. A watch or a coat, on the contrary, requires the application of manual labour at every stage of its progress. The value of the wine or the timber is due mainly to the extent to which *abstinence* must be practised: that of the watch or the coat, to the amount of labour and abstinence combined.

But labour and abstinence do not at all exhaust the catalogue of sacrifices undergone in production. The exertion of muscular power or of intellectual energy, when not excessive, is not disagreeable to the majority of people. It is seldom, however, that the mental or bodily faculties can be set to work for the purpose of production, without encountering other annoyances besides that of a mere surrender of case. Sometimes an occupation is in itself disagreeable, disgusting, unwholesome, or even dangerous; sometimes it is attended with public opprobrium or contempt. Now, it is clear that were all employments open to every one alike, and all persons equally qualified to engage in any one of them, every person would choose the more agreeable, or rather *less disagreeable* employments, if the remuneration were the same in all: it follows accordingly, that in order to induce persons to enter the less desirable species of employments, a rate of remuneration must be afforded by these employments, higher precisely in proportion as the net sacrifices they demand are greater than those demanded by other occupations.

This principle applies equally to the case of labourer and capitalist, though a different set of influences affect each class of producers. The ordinary workman is naturally more liable to be affected by what is disagreeable and disgusting to the senses, or dangerous to health or life: the professional man and the capitalist are more exposed to the influence of moral or social privations. The large gains of the "bill-discounter" are partly a compensation for the odium in which the practice of "usury" is still held by society. The high wages of the public executioner are partly compensation for the loss of human sympathy, and for all the other dreadful associations connected with his ghastly office. The miner who works in an atmosphere laden with mineral poison, must be paid more highly than the man who breaks stones above ground, because he is shut out from the light of day, and surrenders health and life to his employer. The physical exertion is perhaps the same, the concomitant sacrifices are very different.

The conclusions at which we have now arrived may be concisely stated thus:—

1. Freely-produced commodities tend to exchange for each other in proportion to the sacrifice undergone in their production.
2. The amount of such sacrifice depends upon the degree in which an employment is not *self-remunerative*, or, in other words, upon the degree in which the advantages inseparable from an employment are exceeded by the sacrifices it entails.
3. The sacrifices entailed by any employment may be classed under three heads, viz.:—

A—Those involved in mere labour, *i.e.*, in physical or mental exertion.

B—Those involved in mere abstinence, *i.e.*, in that forbearance to consume commodities which is a necessary condition of future production.

C—Physical or mental discomfort, other than that which is involved in ordinary physical or mental exertion, or in the practice of abstinence. That surrender of comfort, health, longevity, social position, or reputation, which disagreeable, unwholesome, or dangerous employments entail.

Combining the first and second of the above propositions we arrive at the following formula:—

"The value of freely-produced commodities is regulated by their Net Cost of Production." By Net Cost of Production is to be understood, the preponderance of the sacrifices incurred, over the advantages enjoyed, by the producer in the process of production.

Such of my hearers as are already conversant with the theory of value laid down by acknowledged authorities in Economic Science, will not fail to perceive that I have ventured to innovate slightly on the received doctrine. My object in so doing is to furnish you with a formula that will apply without modifications or explanations to all cases. In substance, indeed, the conclusions at which I have arrived do not differ from those you have already met in the works of Mr. John Stuart Mill, Mr. Nassau William Senior, and other modern economists of repute. But the theory, as I have presented it to you, when compared with that to be found in the treatises of these eminent writers, offers two points of contrast. The form in which it is presented by them is this:—Freely-produced commodities tend to exchange for each other in the ratio of their several costs of production; cost of production being defined to mean, "The sum of the labour and abstinence necessary to production." Thus the law of value, in the case of freely-produced commodities, when fully developed, is, according to these authorities, as follows:—Freely-produced commodities tend to exchange for each other in the ratio of the quantities of labour and abstinence they severally require for their production. Now, this proposition, you will see, requires afterwards to be qualified by making allowance for the collateral hardships undergone, and the collateral advantages enjoyed, by the labourer and the capitalist. But this supplemental clause in the law of value is incorporated into the body of the statute, if I may use a legal metaphor, by the arrangement I have ventured to adopt, namely, by analysing cost of production into three, instead of two elements, and employing the expression, Net Cost of Production, to denote that balance of sacrifice which constitutes the true regulator of value. It is in these two points that the law of value, as I have enunciated it for you, differs from that expressed in the formula usually laid down.[4]

The foregoing considerations enable us to perceive the abstract justice of the high value, which in a system of perfectly unrestricted competition, one commodity, or one service[5] may command, or the low value at which another may exchange, irrespective of their relative utility. But it is of importance to consider how this conformity between the actual value and that which corresponds to the net cost of production is brought about. It is not enough that there exist the most obvious reasons why in justice commodity A should bear a higher value than commodity B, or that the service rendered by C should be remunerated at a higher rate than that rendered by D. Unless there exist the means of compelling the public to consent to take these commodities, or hire these services, at this natural and proper rate, appeals to their sense of justice will be powerless to do so. To descend from abstract generalization to fact: it has been over and over again proved to demonstration, that the pay of a needlewoman is, in the majority of cases, insufficient to provide her with the commonest necessaries of life: and it is, if possible, more indisputable, that her work is of the most exhausting kind. Many and powerful appeals have been made by the philanthropist and the poet to the justice and the humanity of the public. The "tones" of the "Song of the Shirt" *have* reached "the rich." Efforts have been made to raise the scale of remuneration received by these hapless women. Yet, the source of the disease being misunderstood, the remedy has not reached beyond the symptoms; the cry of suffering is still heard from time to time through the periodical press: a spasmodic effort is made to afford relief: a blind attack is directed against the *employers* of needlewomen, the very people who do most to mitigate their distress; for without the employers they must starve, or worse.[6] The public having quieted its conscience by this inadequate assistance, and this misplaced censure, relapses once more into indifference, till awakened by the moans of some new victim.

If, then, the rule does not hold good in practice, if we find, as a matter of fact, that value, whether of services or commodities, is not obedient to the control of net cost of production, how, in the hypothetical case we have assumed, would it be *compelled* to submit to it?

To this question the answer is:—through the instrumentality of limitation of supply.

Net cost of production, it is hardly necessary to remind you, consists of the balance of the unavoidable sacrifices undergone, over the inseparable advantages enjoyed, by those engaged in production. The greater this balance in any employment, the greater will be the discouragement to engage in it, and the greater, therefore, must be the external inducements held out to producers. These external inducements consist of the articles which can be procured in exchange for the service or commodity, as the case may be. Now if the amount of such articles be less than what could be obtained in some other occupation, by the same net sacrifice as has been undergone by the producer of a given commodity, or the performer of a given service, that producer or that labourer will not continue in such employment, but will transfer his labour or his capital or both, to some other in which he will not be exposed to this disadvantage. The amount of commodities or of services,

in other words, their *supply*, being diminished by the withdrawal of the producer or the labourer in question, those persons who are in want of this
particular commodity or service, will, by their competition, raise its value. It
is thus, through the instrumentality of a check put on supply, that the value
of such articles or such services rises until a level is reached corresponding to
net cost of production. The fact of the value of some commodities, or some
services, being unnaturally low, involves, as a necessary consequence, that the
value of some others, if not all, shall be unnaturally high. If the undue
elevation of value be confined to one or a few, it is to these that the liberated
capital will be transferred: and the same change which diminished the supply,
and raised the value of those from which labour and capital were withdrawn,
will increase the supply and reduce the value of those to which they are
transferred.

But this assumes that the necessary transfer of labour and capital may be
effected without difficulty: that no obstacles, natural or artificial, obstruct
those movements of capital by which the re-adjustment of value to net cost is
effected. If this condition be not fulfilled, the transfer not being possible at
all, or not to the requisite extent, the supply will not be regulated in such a
manner as to allow the principle of equality of sacrifice to come into play,
and value, therefore, will deviate from its natural level in a corresponding
degree. Net cost of production is the *power* by which value is regulated:
limitation of supply is the *lever* by which that power is applied. If any force
interferes to prevent the free movement of the lever, to prevent its obeying
the impulse received from net cost of production, the power fails to produce
its proper effect, and value diverges from its natural course. Thus, on the one
hand, if producers, in carrying on their production, were actuated by any
motive different from self-interest, if they increased their supply without
regard to remuneration, no sacrifices they might undergo would affect the
value of the product. And on the other hand, whoever can set this lever,
limitation of supply, in motion, can control value, irrespective of the light-
ness of the sacrifices at which supply can be increased.

These two propositions bring me to the second branch of my subject. Let
us recall our hypothesis once more, take each condition separately, and
examine the effect of its absence on the conclusions we have reached.[7]

1. Each of the parties to the exchange was supposed to be fully aware of all
   the circumstances of the case, fully alive to his own interest.
2. They were supposed to be both disposed to act according to the dictates
   of that interest alone, without reference to any other motive, immediate
   or remote.
3. They were also supposed to be *able*, as well as *willing* to do so.
4. Both of the articles exchanged were supposed to stand in the same rank
   as regards utility.
5. And lastly, these articles were assumed to be freely-produced, *i.e.*,

obtainable without the assistance of any material or agent except those universally accessible.

The first and second of these conditions may be dismissed in a few words. It is obvious that if either of the parties concerned in a purchase or sale, or any other form of exchange, is ignorant or unmindful of his own interest, and if the other be ready to take advantage of this ignorance or indifference, the articles in which they trade will be exchanged in a proportion different from that which corresponds to the net sacrifices incurred in their production. In the trade between dealers and consumers, the latter being generally more or less in the dark as to the conditions under which commodities are brought to market, this deviation from natural value is the rule. But where parties have to live by the profits derived from purchasing and selling, that is to say, in transactions between manufacturer and dealer, or between dealers themselves, strict attention being paid to all the circumstances calculated to affect value, there is less likelihood of deviations from the natural level arising from this cause.

The same may be said with regard to the *desire* to act from a sense of interest. In retail dealings the purchaser often acts from feelings of pride or compassion. So far as be does so, he is likely to give in money more than an equivalent for the goods purchased. But wholesale dealers, whose profits depend quite as much on the rate at which they purchase, as on that at which they sell, cannot be supposed to act from any other motive than that of interest.

The third of the conditions in our hypothesis is to the effect, that not only are the parties *willing* to act according to the dictates of interest, but *able* to do so. It is quite obvious that the interference of moral or physical force to compel producers to surrender a portion of the advantages naturally within their reach, must disturb the proportions in which their products exchange, quite as much as a disinclination on their part to avail themselves of these advantages. It is true that the operation of such laws or customs as are supported in the last resort by physical force, will, when they conflict with the interest of individuals, be more or less evaded, especially when these laws want the sanction of public approval. Such was the case under the system of Purveyance or Preemption, by which our sovereigns were entitled to enforce the sale of articles for their own use, at an arbitrary price fixed by a government officer. No doubt this rule was frequently evaded by concealing or sending away commodities likely to be purchased at an under-value for royal consumption: but still, so far as the law was carried out at all, it necessarily did produce a disturbance in value to a corresponding extent. Such regulations, indeed, not unfrequently tend to produce effects the very opposite of those that were intended. They cause the supply to be so diminished by concealment or withdrawal, that the real price rises, not only much above the fixed maximum, but also above the natural rate that would have ruled if things had been left to adjust themselves. In any case, however, there will be a deviation from that level of value which corresponds to net cost of production, to which, in the long run, market value tends, in a state of freedom, to conform.

The next condition is one of very great importance. It has reference to the relative intensity of the demand for the commodities exchanged. Hitherto we have assumed them to be on a par in this respect. Had we not done so the result would have been very different. No better illustration of this point could be adduced than that of Esau and his birthright. The hunter was famishing; his death was imminent unless timely succour was afforded. The intensity of the demand for food was the highest conceivable, and, consequently he surrendered all he held dearest in life for a "mess of pottage." Here we have a striking instance how much perturbations in the value of articles are affected by the imperiousness of the desire they are calculated to satisfy. The same thing is observable on a smaller scale in the case of a besieged city. Everything that can support life attains a value augmenting in a constantly increasing ratio, as the scarcity of provisions becomes more intense. The same phenomenon occurs in the time of famine: and whenever a scarcity of the staple article of national consumption actually exists, or is imminent, a result similar in kind, though less in degree, is produced. Thus it is said that a deficiency in the average yield of corn, in any year, amounting to .1, will produce a rise in price of .3, and a deficiency of .5, a rise of 4.5. If we compare these figures with the rise in the price of cotton goods, produced by the recent stoppage of supplies of the raw material from America, we shall readily perceive how much the greater imperiousness of the desire for food affects its value.[8] To sum up, when commodities, the subject of exchange, require some time before a new supply can be procured, scarcity, actual or apprehended, will give rise to a deviation from natural value, greater or less in proportion to their utility, or, in other words, in proportion to the imperiousness of the desire they are adapted to satisfy.

Lastly, we come to the consideration of by far the most important of all the conditions of our hypothesis, namely, freedom of production. Freely-produced commodities we defined to be such as were obtained without the assistance of any agent, or any material, not universally accessible. It has been already remarked, that to fix upon any commodity produced under such circumstances would be next to impossible. The great instrument at work in production is human agency. Man's labour is ever present in production, from the primitive contrivances of the savage, to the loftiest triumphs of mechanical ingenuity to be found in the most perfect form of civilisation yet attained. But the powers of all men are neither similar in kind, nor equal in degree. It is obvious, therefore, that leaving out of consideration such things as are produced by the agency merely of those faculties which are common to all human beings, nothing is in strictness "freely-produced."

In the case of all commodities not included in this exception, a deviation from natural value will take place—so far as not counteracted by other causes—proportionate to the rarity of the faculties which the production of the particular commodity requires. Nothing can be more delightful than the exercise of the faculty of poetical composition. Those who possess it exercise it constantly without any view to reward, beyond the pleasure inherent in the act itself. It is in the highest sense self-remunerative. If then the faculty were universal, the product of the poet's brain and pen would bear no value. But such not being the case, the rarity of the talent causes the supply of good poetry to be limited, and confers on the literary product a value corresponding to its excellence. Again, if all the world were trustworthy, it would not be necessary to remunerate confidential agents so highly as at present. This high remuneration is the result, partly of the rarity of the quality, and partly of the necessity, where its existence cannot be certainly known, of making fidelity worth the while of the trusted agent, of making honesty his best policy.

Thus it appears that this diversity of talents among mankind produces a corresponding effect on values, making them, in most cases, deviate from their natural level, namely, that which corresponds to net cost of production. But it is not his own powers only that man can employ for his own advantage: the powers of Nature also are generally susceptible of appropriation. Wherever this is the case the appropriator may, without any additional sacrifices being entailed on himself, obtain an increased portion of the world's produce. Suppose that in an island in which there is but one waterfall, a man set up a handmill for grinding corn: he will have to work hard to convert his neighbours' grain into flour, and must, perhaps, employ others to assist him. Imagine then, that by some circumstance he is enabled to avail himself of the water-power of the island for this purpose; henceforth he will be able, most probably, to dispense with the greater part of the manual labour hitherto necessary in the process. He may be the sole gainer by the change: his sacrifices will henceforth be all the less: but it does not follow that his customers will reap any benefit from this circumstance. If he act altogether from a narrow sense of his own interest, he will demand the same remuneration for grinding their corn as before, and as in the case supposed he need fear no rivals, they will have to submit.

This is but one instance of the effect of natural agents becoming the subject of appropriation. If they existed in such quantities as to be accessible to all, no addition to the value of the commodities made with their assistance would be made on account of that assistance. Fish caught in the open sea, on the one hand, and those caught in a preserved stream, on the other, illustrate the two opposite cases. Agricultural produce, minerals, everything obtained by the aid of natural agents limited in quantity, bear in their value traces of the influence of this limitation. Nor is the case different where the discovery of some chemical or mechanical process can be kept secret, or its exclusive use otherwise secured by the inventor, or to any other individual, or body of individuals. These parties are in exactly the same position as the miller who took advantage of the stream, instead of employing manual labour or horse-power. The sacrifices which must now be undergone in producing a commodity by the new process, are less in amount than those undergone when the old alone was in use. A smaller number of workmen, a smaller quantity of material, or implements, less labour, less abstinence, less hardships of any kind, may be necessary. The net cost of production is diminished: but if the method by which this saving is effected be the subject of monopoly, the value of the product will not of necessity be influenced by the alteration. Just in the same way, if the right to use the magnetic wire-gauze respirator, worn by needle-makers, had been confined to one establishment, the sacrifice of health previously undergone by the hands employed there would have been avoided; but the value of needles would not necessarily have fallen. The same principle holds good with reference to the invention of the Davy-lamp for the protection of miners from the effects of fire-damp, and to others of the same class.

What then determines the value of commodities not freely-produced? Is it in any degree influenced by the forces which regulate that of freely-produced commodities? We shall find that in two very important particulars it is. In the first place, the *immediate* regulator of value in this case is exactly the same as in that of freely-produced commodities. Limitation of supply is here too the lever by which their value is raised or lowered; but the *power* that works this lever is different. In freely-produced commodities we have seen that net cost of production is the influence which it obeys: in things not freely-produced the function of net cost of production is confined to setting limits to the permanent elevations or depressions of value. The will of the owner of the monopolised source of production, acting of course in subservience to his interest, is the force which in this case supply obeys; but where the article produced by the monopolised agent can also be produced by any other agent, of less productive power, but capable of producing the article in sufficient quantity, the owner of the former cannot, by limiting his production, raise the value to a height beyond that which corresponds to its net cost when produced with the assistance of the inferior agent. Suppose the case of a patented process by which an article can be manufactured at a net cost of production only one-half of that involved in processes available to all the world: the patentee may here so restrict his production as to keep up the price to any height not greater than that which corresponds to the net cost of producing the article by unpatented processes. Should he attempt to do more, he will at once render it profitable for others to resort to these processes, and the increase of supply thence resulting will bring value down to its former level. Further, it is only if the patentee can, and will, supply the whole market, that the value will be at all affected permanently by the discovery. The first effect of a discovery is to increase the supply for sale: this reduces value, and renders every producer but the patentee a loser by the business. Probably, therefore, some of them will withdraw from the business, and most will contract the scale of their operations. This process will continue till either, first, the patentee has, by successive augmentations of the supply, constantly kept the value below that which corresponds to the net cost of producing the article by means of unpatented processes, and thus forced the original producers to relinquish their trade, and attracted the entire custom to himself: or secondly, till he ceases to extend his production, and therefore leaves a certain number of the original manufacturers still engaged at the business. In the latter case the value of the article will remain at its pristine level, and even in the former, if he adjusts the supply so as to coincide exactly with that formerly produced by the superseded process, the value will remain unaltered. If, however, he pushes his production further, he will lower the price against himself. It must not be supposed, however, that such will necessarily prove a losing speculation for him, as it is possible—nay, probable—that his gains on the larger quantity at the lower value, would be greater that those on the smaller quantity, at the higher.[9]

It may happen, however, that from some circumstance the possessor of the superior facilities cannot supply the whole market. It may be that there are several degrees of productiveness in the various processes or agencies employed in production. Capitalist A may possess a material or a machine superior to that possessed by B, who, in turn, possesses one superior to that employed by C, while A and B cannot, by the utmost exertion, produce enough of the commodity which they are all engaged in manufacturing, to supply the entire market. It remains to inquire, then, what, under such circumstances, will be the value of the commodity produced by these various processes?

Of course its value cannot fall permanently below the cost value to C, otherwise he would withdraw from the business. But can it rise above that level? That will depend on the state of the demand: for should there be a demand for so much of the commodity at the value which corresponds to C's net cost of production, that the united efforts of A, B, and C, cannot satisfy it, the value of the commodity will necessarily settle above the level which corresponds to the cost to C. At what point, then, will the rise in value be arrested? If there be no other resources available from which to obtain an increased supply, the value will rise till an elevation is reached at which the demand is brought within the limits of the quantity that A, B, and C can jointly produce. If there *be* other resources available, then the value may not reach so high a point; for the rise in value may render it remunerative to call into play some of the other resources, though they are inferior in productive power to those employed by any of the three original producers. But in all cases the value will settle at a level at or above that which corresponds to the net cost of production to that producer who brings the commodity to market under the least favourable conditions.

What the worst kind of agency employed shall be, depends on the state of the demand. Suppose, for example, that there are ten agents, or processes, of as many different degrees of productive power, available for the manufacture of a particular commodity. In a certain state of the demand, the best of these alone might be employed; but if the demand increases till it can no longer be supplied by the sole assistance of such agency, then the second in order of efficiency will be brought into play; and so on until all ten processes or agents are in operation. If the demand continues still in excess of what can be provided, even with the assistance of the least effective of the ten, value will rise above the point corresponding to the net cost of producing the commodity by such means.

From these considerations, we see that the laws of value, applicable to things produced by means of agents or processes not universally accessible, to commodities *not* freely-produced, in other words, are these:—First, the immediate regulator of their value is demand and supply; and so far they are exactly on the same footing as freely-produced commodities. Second, though their value does not tend to conform to net cost of production, yet net cost of production is not altogether without influence on it. For, as their value never can fall permanently below that point which corresponds with the net cost of production to the producer who has had the most advantageous process, or the most efficient agent, at his command, so it never *does* fall permanently below that which corresponds to the net cost of production to that producer who is obliged to employ the least advantageous process, or least efficient agent. And lastly, the value of such commodities can never rise above that point which corresponds to the net cost of production to the community in general, in case the commodity is one that can be obtained with the assistance of inferior agents or processes which are universally accessible.[10]

As I have already observed, there is scarcely a commodity in existence that has not been produced with the assistance of agencies which are beyond the reach of producers in general. The personal qualities of one workman, or of one professional man, or of one merchant, or of one manufacturer, differ in kind and in degree from those of other members of the same industrial class: the productive resources of one tract of soil, of one mine, fishery, or water-course, differ materially from those of other natural agents of the same species: and these means of production are, besides, generally the exclusive property of a body of owners forming but a small minority of the community at large. But scarcely any commodity can be brought to market without the assistance of some one or more of these agencies, and therefore scarcely any commodity can in strictness be said to be freely-produced. The relative values of commodities are, however, less affected by this circumstance than might at first sight be supposed, since in practice the exceptional powers required for the production of some commodities, are counter-balanced by exceptional powers, of a different kind perhaps, brought into requisition in the production of others; so that relative value, as between such commodities, remains pretty much as it would have been in the absence of all such disturbing causes. Thus, for example, to write an entertaining work of fiction, to paint a beautiful picture, and to execute a statue of unusual excellence, all demand exceptional abilities, and these articles there-fore bear a high value when compared with things in general. But probably the rarity of the endowments required in each of these cases is very much the same; accordingly their values *inter se* are almost unaffected, and pretty nearly correspond to the net cost of their production severally.

APPENDIX.

Appendix A.

Referred to on page **12.**

ADAM SMITH seems on one occasion to have touched for an instant on this principle, that natural value is regulated by the sacrifices undergone in pro-duction. Speaking of labour as being the true measure of value, he observes—"The real price of everything, what every thing really costs to the man who wants to acquire it, is the *toil and trouble of acquiring it.*"—Wealth of Nations, Bk I., Ch. V. Further on, speaking of the labourer, he observes—"In his ordinary state of health, strength, and spirits, in the ordinary degree of his skill and dexterity, he must always lay down the same portion of *his ease, his liberty, and his happiness.*" Had Smith recognised the existence of Abstinence, and been a little more careful to employ in a uniform sense each term that he had occasion to use, there would have been little to find fault with in his theory of value, or at least much of the confusion in which it is involved would have been avoided. Even the word 'value' itself does not escape the influence of this tendency to ambiguity. He speaks of "equal quantities of labour" being "of equal value to the labourer," because they cost him the same portion of ease, liberty, and happiness; a sense of the term value quite inconsistent with his definition of either 'value in use,' or 'value in exchange:' unless, indeed, we consider the labourer as *metaphorically* bar-tering his labour with *Nature* for the treasures of her storehouse. The same ambiguity affects the meaning of the word 'price' in the chapter of the Wealth of Nations already quoted.

APPENDIX B.

Referred to on page 24.

There seem to me to be very cogent reasons for not including such sacrifices under the term Labour, as is done impliedly by those who would reduce Cost of Production to that single element, or even to that element combined with Abstinence. In the first place, the term 'Labour' had already, before the birth of Political Economy, acquired a certain meaning which it would be highly injudicious to seek to disturb. Labour is universally understood to signify the *active* exercise of some faculty, mental or physical, and not the mere *passive* endurance of any privation. To extend its signification so as to make it embrace the latter, would be an innovation calculated to mislead not only the reader, but also the writer himself. Furthermore, it is to be observed, that such sacrifices make up by far the most important portion of the cost of producing many articles, and are the most potent causes of the value of many services: hence to assert that labour regulates their value is often only to put the investigator of economic truths on an entirely wrong track. Moreover, these sacrifices are very frequently found in connection, not with labour, but with abstinence, to which indeed they approximate much more nearly in their nature, being, like that great element in cost of production, of a moral description. Lastly, such an analysis of cost of production as I have ventured to suggest has this advantage, that so long as it is kept in view, it is impossible to overlook any of the circumstances affecting natural value. When natural value is said to depend on the sum of the labour and abstinence necessary to production, there is always the strongest probability that in investigating any particular case of value, these two elements alone will be taken into consideration. But when a third direction is clearly pointed out in which further influences may reasonably be expected to be found at work, such incomplete researches are not likely to occur.

The impossibility of finding a measure or standard of value, by comparison with which the value of any article at any time and any place could be ascertained, is now universally recognised. It has been well observed by Mr. Mill with reference to this subject, that Smith and the earlier economists, while apparently in quest of a measure of value, were in reality upon the track of a measure of cost of production.[11] Now if they had discovered such a measure, and had devised a proper method of applying it, they would have gone thus far towards finding the object of their search, that they would have enabled us to determine the relative values of such freely-produced commodities as were obtained under conditions that did not vary with time or place, and under circumstances that did not confer any special advantage on the producers. If it had been true, for example, that *labour* was the sole element of cost of production, and that the same thing always and everywhere required the same expenditure of labour in its production, then freely-produced commodities, the act of producing of which did not directly or indirectly confer any special pleasure, would exchange for labour, and for each other, in inverse proportion to quantities of labour they respectively required in their production. Labour under such circumstances would so far have furnished not only a measure of cost of production, but a standard of value. Since, however, cost of production consists of so many other elements besides labour, labour is far from being a measure of cost of production; and since most occupations possess some special attraction, and since there is nothing the conditions of whose production are constant, labour is still farther from being a standard of value.

But though it be impossible to find a standard of value, it does not seem impossible to find, or at least conceive of, a measure of net cost of production, which should be of as much service towards ascertaining the values of commodities, as labour would have been in the circumstances above supposed, that is to say, which should enable us to determine the relative values of freely-produced commodities so, far, and so long, as the conditions of their production did not vary.

The real essence of cost of production is *sacrifice*, pain or discomfort or privation of some kind; and this could be employed as a measure of cost of production, and within certain limits as a measure of value, in the following way. First let a unit of sacrifice be fixed upon, such, for example, as the amount involved in one hour's ordinary labour to the average workman. It would then be necessary to determine the relative values of different species of sacrifices *inter se*; for example, what amount of the kind of sacrifice involved in mere physical labour, would be equal to a given amount of that kind which is entailed by abstinence, physical discomfort, or mental suffering. Further, it would be necessary that we should determine the relative values of the different kinds of pleasure accompanying different pursuits: for example, what amount of that kind of pleasure which flows from social eminence would be equal to a given amount of that kind which accompanies intellectual exertion. Lastly, it would be requisite to determine the amount of sacrifice to which a given amount of satisfaction would be equivalent. In order to ascertain the relative values of two commodities fulfilling the conditions before specified, it would then only be necessary to measure the net cost of producing each, and compare the results. For example, let the unit of sacrifice be represented by the symbol s, and let commodity A require in its production a quantity of labour involving an amount of sacrifice represented by $m\,s$, and a quantity of abstinence involving an amount of sacrifice represented by $n\,s$. Let these be the sole elements in its cost of production, and let the occupation of producing it occasion an amount of pleasure which would be compensation for an amount of sacrifice represented by $p\,s$. The net cost of producing such a commodity would be $m\,s + n\,s - p\,s$ or $(m + n - p)\,s$. Let there be another commodity, A′, in which the corresponding sacrifices are represented by $m's$, $n's$, and $p's$. The net cost of producing this latter

66

commodity will be represented by $(m' + n' - p')\ s$, and the value of A will stand to that of A′ in the ratio of $(m' + n' - p')\ s$ to $(m + n - p),\ s$, or as, $m' + n' - p' : m + n - p$.

APPENDIX C.

Referred to on page **44.**

It is perhaps worth while to inquire what this depends on. It depends, *ceteris paribus*, on the rate at which value falls with increase of supply, in other words, on the extensibility of the demand. It will always be for the advantage of the patentee to endeavour ultimately to drive all the old producers from the market, as he will thus gain the full benefit of his invention on the largest possible quantity of goods, the value, as we have seen in the text, being the same whether he supplies the entire market, or only a portion of it. But it may be a question whether he ought to push production beyond this point. The remunerativeness of such a speculation will depend on the following considerations:—1. The profits that might have been made on the additional capital invested, had it been otherwise employed. 2. The loss on the price of the smaller supply. 3. The gain on the increase of supply. Thus, for instance, if an article had been originally made at an outlay of £1,000,000, and profits averaged 10 percent., and by an improvement the cost of production were diminished one-half, the calculation would stand thus. Original price of the article, £1,000,000 *plus* 10 per cent. that is, in all £1,100,000. The capital required by the new process would be £500,000, and if only this amount were employed, as the article would sell for £1,100,000, a gain of £600,000 would be realized. Suppose the supply doubled. This would require the investment of a second sum of £500,000, and would reduce the price, say, one-fourth. The supply now produced would sell for £1,650,000, which is double £1,100,000, less one-fourth, shewing a gain of £650,000. If from this be deducted £550,000,—the half million additional invested, *plus* the profit on it at 10 per cent, there will remain £100,000, instead of £600,000, the sum which was realized by an investment of but one half million. Thus, in the circumstances supposed, there would be an enormous disadvantage in doubling the quantity of produce. But if the fall in price had been not one-fourth, but one-fortieth, the gain on the larger supply would have been within £5000 of that on the smaller; and had the fall been but one-fiftieth, the gain on the larger would have been £5000 above it.

APPENDIX D.

Referred to on page 48.

It may not be out of place to remind the reader that, between agricultural produce and products obtained from agents of irregularly varying degrees of fertility, there exists an important distinction too often overlooked, namely, that while the market value of agricultural produce is regulated by the net cost of producing that portion of it which is raised at the greatest expense, such is not at all the case with respect to mineral and other produce obtained from agents of a different order. The late Mr. M'Culloch more than once fell into error through inattention to this fact. Thus, in his note to a passage in which Adam Smith lays down that the price of coals at any given coal mine is regulated by the best mine in the neighbourhood, he says, "This is an error. The price of the coal extracted from the least fertile mine which it is necessary to work, in order to supply the demand, will determine the price of the coal extracted from all the other mines."—*Wealth of Nations, note* 1, *page* 76, 4*th Edition*.

Mr. J. S. Mill has clearly pointed out the distinction of which we are speaking, in his chapter on Value as dependent on Cost of Production. Yet, singular to say, in another place he seems to have forgotten it. In the ninth chapter of his Third Book, which treats of the Value of Money as dependent on Cost of Production, he says, "Of the three classes into which commodities are divided—those absolutely limited in supply, those which may be had in unlimited quantity at a given cost of production, and those which may be had in unlimited quantity, but at an increasing cost of production—*the precious metals, being the produce of mines, belong to the third class. Their natural value is, therefore, in the long run, proportional to their cost of production in the most unfavourable existing circumstances, that is at the worst mine which it is necessary to work in order to obtain the required supply.* . . . The average value of gold is made to conform to its natural value in the same manner as the values of other things are made to conform to their natural value. Suppose that it were selling above its natural value . . . a part of the mass of floating capital which is on the look out for investment, would take the direction of mining enterprise: the supply would thus be increased and the value would fall." Now is it not clear that the diversion of floating capital to mining enterprise in the circumstances supposed would be conditioned on the existence of a mine as yet unwrought, which, at the existing value of bullion, it would pay to work? Suppose the next best mine to that already in operation were 20 per cent, inferior to it, and that the market value of bullion was but 1 per cent. above natural value, would any floating capital be directed to its working? It is true that floating capital might be directed towards mining explorations, but unless these explorations *happened* to lead to the discovery of a mine of exactly such a degree of fertility that the market value of bullion coincided with its cost value at that mine, the future value of the precious metals would not be thereby rendered coincident with the cost of their production at the worst mine. The new mine brought to light might happen to be of any degree of fertility above or below this standard, and might therefore pay its own expenses and leave a rent, or not pay its own expenses, and therefore cease to be worked at all, so soon as the true character of its resources was ascertained. Far different would be the case with a rise in the value of agricultural produce. Capital can always find an investment in agriculture which will exactly return the ordinary rate of profits, and no more and no less. But this arises from the fact that land exists of every conceivable degree of fertility below that of the best in cultivation. From this peculiarity of that great natural agent results this peculiar fact in reference to the value of agricultural produce, that in the main its market value coincides with its cost value on the worst land actually cultivated. It is different, however, with the produce of other natural agents, whose productiveness varies in a scale descending by wide and irregular intervals.

Notes

1 By this is meant, that the strength of the desire, the imperiousness of the necessity, they are respectively calculated to satisfy, is the same in both cases. Thus the utility of food may be considered as about on a level with that of drink, and above that of shelter. These distinctions will appear more clearly hereafter. See p. 34.

2 See Appendix A.

3 By a Natural Agent is to be understood, adopting the language of the late Mr. Nassau W. Senior, "Every productive agent, so far as it does not derive its powers from the act of man."

4 See Appendix B.

5 I employ these terms here in the sense attached to them by Mr. Senior, who defines "service" as "the act of occasioning an alteration in the existing particles of matter," and "commodity," "the thing as altered."

6 Of course, I am not to be understood as seeking to palliate, much less defend, the inhumanity with which some employers, taking advantage of the utterly helpless condition of their workwomen, treat them. I am merely drawing attention to the fact, that every employer of female labour is, as such, a benefactor to female labourers generally, raising the remuneration of the class by the amount he expends in wages.

7 See above, p. 11.

8 The full table of alterations in price resulting from variations in the supply of corn, as given by Mr. Gregory King, is as follows:—

Where the deficiency is	.1, the advance of price is	.3,
.2,	,, ,,	.8,
.3,	,, ,,	1.6,
.4,	,, ,,	2.8,
.5,	,, ,,	4.5.

These statistics lead me to doubt whether what was stigmatised as "*Engrossing*," might not be so practised as to ensure to the benefit of the engrosser, without conferring any corresponding advantage on the consumer. When the area from which supplies could be procured was so small as it was before commerce was facilitated by good roads, might not a dealer, by making speculative purchases, so raise the price of corn, that for a portion of his stock he would get a price equal to, if not greater than, that at which he bought the entire?

9 See Appendix C.
10 See Appendix D.
11 Principles of Political Economy, Book iii., chap. 15, § 2.

21

'OF HUMAN WANTS' AND 'OF EXCHANGE'

William Edward Hearn

Source: William Edward Hearn, *Plutology: Or The Theory of the Efforts to Satisfy Human Wants*, London: Macmillan; Melbourne: George Robertson, 1864, pp. 12–23, 235–53.

CHAPTER I.

Of human wants.

§ 1. Life in every form with which we are acquainted, is subject to waste and repair. The living structure in no case continues unchanged, but is maintained by a series of reparative acts. If any of these acts be discontinued, life ceases, and the organism quickly disappears. In the case of animal life, provision is made by the agency of pleasure and pain for securing the proper supply of reparative material. Every animal is possessed of sensibility; and the acquisition of those materials which are necessary to keep in activity its vital powers is attended with pleasure; while the privation of them involves an equally distinct pain. Food, drink, air, and warmth, are the most urgent of these necessities. If these or any of them are withheld beyond a certain small degree or a certain brief time, the animal must die. These necessities man shares with all other animals. He must have a constant supply of pure air; he must have a sufficiency of such food and drink as his organs can assimilate. In colder climates at least, since nature has not furnished him with the protection that the lower animals enjoy, he must have more ample means than they require of retaining the vital heat. If any of these essential conditions be unfulfilled, the human animal like any other animal must die. If they be but partially fulfilled, his powers whether muscular or nervous are proportionately feeble. If he have complied with all these conditions of his existence, these powers are in a proper state for their due exercise. The satisfaction, therefore, of his primary appetites is imperative upon man. Of all his wants, they are the first in the degree of their intensity; and in the order of time they are the first which he attempts to gratify.

§ 2. But while the superior organism thus possesses all the desires that belong to the inferior, it has also by virtue of that superiority many more. Man has not only the mere animal faculties and their corresponding wants: he has also beyond all other creatures other faculties, which, beside their own requirements, seriously affect the gratification of the primary appetites. For man is able not merely to satisfy his primary wants, but to devise means for their better and more complete gratification. The food of the dog or of the horse of our time is, except where it has been modified by man, the same as that of the dog or the horse a thousand years ago. The bee constructs its cell, the spider spins its web, the beaver builds its dam, with neither greater nor less skill than that with which bees and spiders and beavers in all known times have worked. In the quality of their work, in the kind of material they employ, in the modes in which they deal with those materials, there is no improvement and there is no decline. Man alone, of all known animals, exhibits any such improvement. He alone has cooked his food. He alone has infused his drink. He alone has discovered new kinds of food or drink. He alone has improved the construction of his dwelling, and has provided for its ventilation. He alone clothes his body, and varies that clothing according to the changes of the temperature, or his own ideas of decoration. He alone is not content with the mere satisfaction, in whatever manner, of his physical wants, but exercises a selection as to the mode of their satisfaction. So strong in him is this tendency to the adaptation of his means, that, in favourable circumstances, he regards the preparation of the objects which are intended for his gratification as of hardly less importance than the gratification itself. Thus the comparative range of human wants is rapidly increased. When the question of degree is admitted in the satisfaction of the primary appetites, and when the greater or less adaptability of various objects to satisfy these appetites is recognized, the extent of human desires is bounded only by the extent of human skill.

§ 3. As the attempt to satisfy the primary appetites thus gives rise to new desires, so the actual increase of these desires tends of itself to a still further development. The enjoyment that a man has once received he generally desires to renew. The mere repetition soon becomes a reason for its further repetition. By the powerful influence of habit the desire becomes a taste; and the taste quickly passes into an absolute want. Nor is this all. The mere exercise of the faculties strengthens them; and gives rise to a comparison of results and a desire for further improvement. The man whose senses are educated to a certain point, who has had to a certain extent experience of different modes of satisfying his desires, and has formed a judgment upon the comparative efficiency of these modes, will seldom in favourable circumstances stop at that point. Not merely would a return to what pleased his untaught faculties be intolerable to him; but the actual enjoyment which he derives from his discovery stimulates him to further advances, and suggests the modes of obtaining them. Thus while man is not guided and limited by a blind instinct but each individual is left free to rise or fall according to the exercise of his powers, provision is made even in the primary wants of our nature both to prevent the retrogression of the species, and to secure its advancement. The number of wants that belong to this class is therefore limited, as I have said, by our knowledge of the properties of matter or of material objects fitted to satisfy our wants, and by our skill in their adaptation. This knowledge and this skill continually increases; and as the limit they present recedes, the range of our tastes and of our artificial wants increases with them.

§ 4. These principles may be readily verified. It needs no elaborate proof to show that men constantly desire an increase of physical comforts; that when they have acquired such comforts they are pained at their loss, but that their acquisition does not prevent them from continuing to desire a further increase. The universal experience of mankind is conclusive on these points. We feed and clothe and lodge our felons in a way that, to an Australian blackfellow, would seem an unspeakable luxury. The mechanic that daily complains of his hard lot would be shocked if he were reduced to use no better light, or no more convenient measure of time, than that by which Alfred wrote and by which he distributed his labours. Two pounds of tea were presented to Charles II. as a present worthy of a king. A century afterwards, the steady perseverance of the Americans in abstaining from their unjustly taxed tea was rightly regarded as the most remarkable case of national self-denial that history records. Tobacco was unknown to our ancestors, and even now is unused by not a few; yet its deprivation was in the eyes of the Irish pauper the most cruel aggravation of work-house constraint.

"It is a phenomenon, says Bastiat,[1] well worthy of remark, how quickly, by continuous satisfaction, what was at first only a vague desire, quickly becomes a taste, and what was only a taste is transformed into a want, and even a want of the most imperious kind. Look at that rude artizan: accustomed to poor fare, plain clothing, indifferent lodging, he imagines he would be the happiest of men and would have no farther desires, if he could but reach the step of the ladder immediately above him. He is astonished that those who have already reached it should still torment themselves as they do. At length comes the modest fortune he has dreamt of, and then he is happy—very happy—for a few days. For soon he becomes familiar with his new situation, and by degrees he ceases to feel his fancied happiness. With indifference he puts on the fine clothing after which he sighed. He has got into a new circle, he associates with other companions, he drinks of another cup, he aspires to another step, and if he ever turns his reflections upon himself, he feels that if his fortune has changed, his soul remains the same, and is still an inexhaustible spring of new desires."

§ 5. There are other important respects in which human wants differ from those of the inferior animals. In addition to those primary appetites which he shares with the humblest living creature, and which relate exclusively to things, man has also in a peculiar degree affections which relate to persons; and various desires which are only conceivable with reference to abstractions, and result not from any physical antecedent, but from operations of the mind. By the aid of memory, which recalls the past; and of imagination, which represents the distant, the absent, and the future; and of reason, which exercises a judgment upon the utility present or prospective of an object, and upon the means of obtaining it, man forms desires concerning his personal safety, his family, and his property. These desires like those already described become by the force of habit, daily more persistent and intense. To this class of desires no limit can be assigned other than the mental powers of each individual.

These wants, except those relating to the family, might arise in a man isolated from all other beings of the same kind. But man is by the constitution of his nature a social being. Beginning with the family he soon forms relations with other men; and lives, and moves, and has his being, in society. Hence arise new desires; each of which, like every other desire, is intensified and confirmed by habit. Man is imitative; and so seeks to have what his neighbor enjoys: he is vain; and so desires to display himself and his possessions with advantage before his fellows: he loves superiority; and so seeks to show something that others have not: he dreads inferiority; and so seeks to possess what others also possess. Hence it is that, as daily experience teaches us, no man ever attains the state in which he has no wish ungratified. The greater the development of the mental and moral faculties, the greater will be the number of desires; the more continuous the gratification of these desires, the more confirmed will be the habit.

§ 6. Human desires are indefinite not only as to their extent, but as to their objects. The capacity of desire is strengthened, and extended by exercise; but the desire is not necessarily felt for the same things. There are some objects to the use of which strict physical limits are set. There are others of which the pleasure depends, in a great degree, upon their scarcity. But in hardly any case does the increase of the object bring with it a proportionate increase of enjoyment. The sameness soon palls upon the taste; and if, as is usually the case, an extraordinary quantity of one object involve a corresponding diminution in the supply of others, one faculty or class of faculties is gratified to the full extent that its nature will bear; while the other faculties are left unsupplied.

Not merely is the amount of human desire indefinite, but the modes in which desire in many different individuals is manifested, are equally without any practical limit. Even in the primary appetites, there is room for great diversity, according to differences of climate, age, sex, and other considerations, in the choice of food, and the construction of houses, and the fashion of clothes. In the desires which are peculiar to man, we seldom find agreement. The diversity of individual tastes is proverbial. Two persons will often regard with very different feelings the same object. The same man will at different times and in different circumstances experience great changes in his desires and his aversions. There is, however, a remarkable distinction in the facility with which desires can be appeased. It is in those cases in which the commodity is essential to our existence or our comfort that the limit to our gratification is soonest reached. Our most irrepressible appetites are the most quickly satisfied. Our most insatiable desires are the most easily repressed. Were it otherwise, with the present predominance of the self-regarding affections, the accumulation of the wealthy might interfere with the existence of the poor. Desire too is never transformed into a want, strictly so called, that is into painful desire, until it has been made such by habit; in other words, until the means of satisfying the desire have been found and placed irrevocably within our reach.[2]

§ 7. It is not difficult to perceive the cause of this diversity of desire; or to trace the circumstances on which the development of our wants depends. That cause is found, where at first it might not be expected but where its presence is consistent with a deeper investigation of our nature, in the state of our intellectual development. Beyond the mere primary appetites, no other want can make itself known, except through some mental operation. Our actions depend upon our will; and our will depends upon our judgment. If we seek to obtain any object, it is because we desire it; if we desire it, it is because we have formed some notion of its nature, and some judgment upon its suitability to our purposes. According, then, to the degree with which we are acquainted with external objects, and to the power that we possess of judging of their relations to ourselves, and to other things, our capacity of desire will be extended. Our desires, too, are subject to our will; and admit of being repressed or encouraged without assignable limits. It therefore depends upon the education, in the widest sense of that term, of each individual, and upon his character as mainly resulting from that education, how many and what kind of objects, and with what degree of persistency he desires. The more complete the intellectual development, the wider will be the field of desire; and, by the usual reaction in our mental nature, the wider the field of desire, the stronger will be the inducements to intellectual effort for the continuance of means to gratify these desires. On the contrary, the narrower our field of thought, the more contracted and the more humble will be our desires; and the less consequently will be the inducement to incur that continuous exertion of mind or body that industry implies. Where intelligence therefore prevails, the number of desires and the power of satisfying them will be alike great; where intelligence is small, the number of desires and the power of satisfying them will also be small. If this principle be true of individuals taken separately, it will not cease to be true of them when they are regarded as forming the aggregate that we term a nation.

§ 8. It requires but little observation to perceive the confirmation which these reasonings obtain from actual experience. We know that the desires of educated men are more varied and more extended than those of persons without education. We know that the wages of educated men are higher, and consequently their means of gratifying their desires greater, than those of the uneducated. If an educated man be reduced by misfortune, we sympathize with the disproportion between his desires and his means of satisfying them. If an uneducated man become suddenly rich, we see that, from the limited extent of his former wants, and the undeveloped condition of his desires, he literally does not know what to do with his money, and rushes into the most extravagant and ludicrous follies. We see that if a man be content, like a dog, to eat his dinner and to sleep, his nature will gradually sink to that of the brute. The higher faculties will waste from disuse; the lower in the absence of restraint, and from habitual exercise, will acquire a complete predominance. On the other hand, those nations, and those classes of a nation who stand highest in the scale of civilization, are those whose wants, as experience shows us, are the most numerous; and whose efforts to satisfy those wants are the most unceasing.

§ 9. Nothing, therefore, can be farther from the truth than the ascetic doctrine of the paucity and the brevity of human wants. So far from man wanting little here below, his wants are indefinite; and never cease to be so during his whole existence. Nor is there anything immoral in such a view. The supposed inconsistency arises from a confusion of apathy with content. The former term implies that the development of desire is repressed; the latter that it is regulated. Content is a judgment that, upon the whole, we cannot with our existing means improve our position, along with an unmurmuring submission to the hardships, if any, of that position. Its aim is, not to satisfy desires; but to appease complaint. It is consequently not inconsistent with the most active efforts to alter that combination of circumstances upon which the judgment was formed. "The desire of amelioration, it has been[3] truly said, is not less a moral principle than patience under afflictions; and the use of content is not to destroy, but to regulate and direct it."

§ 10. So far from our wants being unworthy of our higher nature, we can readily trace their moral function and appreciate its importance. They not only prevent our retrogression, but secure our advancement. Our real state of nature consists not in the repression, but in the full development and satisfaction, of all those faculties of which our nature consists. Such a state is found, not in the poverty of the naked savage; but in the wealth of the civilized man. It is the constant and powerful impulse of our varied and insatiable desires, that urges us to avoid the one state, and to tend towards the other. "Wants and enjoyments," says Bentham,[4] "these universal agents in

76

society, after having raised the first ears of corn, will by degrees erect the granaries of abundance, always increasing, and always full. Desires extend themselves with the means of gratification; the horizon is enlarged in proportion as we advance, and each new want, equally accompanied by its pleasure and its pain, becomes a new principle of action. Opulence, which is only a comparative term, does not arrest this movement when once it is begun; on the contrary, the greater the means, the greater the field of operations, the greater the reward, and consequently the greater the force of the motive which actuates the mind. But in what does the wealth of society consist, if not in the total of the wealth of the individuals composing it? And what more is required than the force of those natural motives, for carrying the increase of wealth to the highest possible degree?"

But these wants do not stimulate our acquisitive and inventive powers only. They also serve to discipline our moral nature. Many of man's proceedings are slow in their nature; and so he must practise patience. In like manner, he must expend some of his acquisitions with the view of acquiring more; and thus in addition to patience he must exercise hope. One great means of increasing his power is co-operation with his fellow-men: he must therefore, to some extent, subordinate or at least assimilate his will to theirs; and so he must learn forbearance. Thus the efforts that we make for the satisfaction of our wants supply the means for developing both our intellectual and our moral faculties.

§ 11. The subject of this inquiry is the efforts made by man to secure enjoyment. The particular character of any enjoyable object is, therefore, for the present purpose indifferent. The question is not whether a given object be conducive to our general well-being; but simply whether it be enjoyable. If it be enjoyable, it is foreign to the purpose to consider whether the enjoyment to which it contributes be unmeaning or even immoral; or whether it be embodied in a tangible shape; or be merely a fleeting gratification of the sense; or be a permanent benefit to the body or the mind. We pass no judgment upon the character of the want, or upon the manner in which it should be regulated. For our purposes, wants are simply motives of varying power which universally exist, and the laws of which we propose to investigate. We have to deal with them merely as forces, without any other estimate of their characters than the intensity with which they are felt by the persons who experience them. Nor are we any more concerned to appreciate the character of the means of enjoyment, than we are to appreciate the character of the want. It is enough that the want is felt, and that it can be satisfied.

CHAPTER XIV.

Of exchange.

§ 1. I now approach the consideration of that great agent which with an excusable exaggeration some writers have regarded as the sole subject of economic science. Although a less exalted rank has been assigned in these pages to the theory of exchange, this lower view of its position does not proceed from any insensibility to its influence. Coming into at least full operation at a late period of industrial development, exchange quickens into new life as well the primary elements of production as its own fellow industrial auxiliaries. It suggests to the labourer new wants. It at the same time provides the easiest means of satisfying these wants. It enables the ignorant and the weak innocently to profit by the learning of the wise, and the vigour of the strong. It extends to the inhabitants of different regions a share in those natural advantages of which nature seems to have granted to each region the exclusive possession. It affords larger means for the accumulation of capital, and an ampler field for its profitable occupation. To its demands for increased facilities both of production and of intercourse some of our most important inventions are due. Above all, it is the complement and the crown of co-operation, carrying out the full effects of that great auxiliary to an extent that would otherwise he impracticable, and establishing not only between unacquainted individuals but remote and jealous nations an unpremeditated and almost unconscious, yet not the less complete or effectual, system of association. Nor must we omit, although they hardly come within the range of the present inquiry, the indirect benefits of exchange. It enlarges the sphere of men's observation and so of their knowledge. It substitutes for the ferocious antipathies of an earlier age the friendly relations which spring from a sense of reciprocal advantage. It renders both parties dependent on each other for a multitude of their daily enjoyments, and thus binds them in a sort of unacknowledged yet powerful frankpledge. Disputes consequently whether private or national tend to become more odious in conception and less facile in execution. Thus by a method that the most obtuse cannot overlook, and the most wilful cannot misunderstand, it teaches the great moral lesson that the benefit of each is the benefit of all; and that a wrong done to one class is sure to extend its influence over the whole community.

Exchange may be described as the voluntary transfer by one person to another of one instrument of enjoyment in consideration of the reciprocal transfer of a different one. There must therefore be two parties to every exchange; and there must also be a consideration. It is this latter circumstance which distinguishes exchange from other forms of giving and receiving. A free gift is something different from an exchange: so is a robbery: so too is a tribute. All these transactions fail in the essential condition of reciprocity. There is no *quid pro quo*. But as in an exchange there is something received, so also there is something given. There are two parties, each of whom is influenced by the desire of enjoyment and the dislike of effort; and to each of whom the transaction presents itself in a different light. Each has an inducement and a sacrifice; but the inducement and the sacrifice are reciprocally inverted. Each obtains at a smaller cost than he otherwise could the means of satisfying a desire or of accomplishing a purpose: and each therefore finds, or expects that he will find, the exchange beneficial. From these considerations the conditions of exchange may be deduced. In every such transaction there must be enjoyment; and in like manner there must be cost. There must also be a proportion between that enjoyment and that cost; and that proportion must be more or less in favour of the enjoyment. Further, as there are two parties to every exchange, the principles now stated must apply equally to each of the two, and therefore the transaction must be, at least in their opinion at that time, beneficial to each.

§ 2. Some attempt however imperfect may be made to illustrate by a numerical expression the extent to which exchange reduces cost. "We annually import into this country," says Mr. Senior,[5] in a work written nearly thirty years ago, "about thirty million pounds of tea. The whole expense of purchasing and importing this quantity does not exceed £2,250,000, or about 1s. 6d. a pound, a sum equal to the value of the labour of only 45,000 men, supposing their annual wages to amount to £50 a year. With our agricultural skill and our coal mines, and at the expense of above 40s. a pound instead of 1s. 6d., that is at the cost of the labour of about one million two hundred thousand men instead of forty-five thousand, we might produce our own tea and enjoy the pride of being independent of China. But one million two hundred thousand is about the number of all the men engaged in agricultural labour throughout England. A single trade, and that not an extensive one, supplies as much tea, and probably of a better sort, as could be obtained if it were possible to devote every farm and every garden to its domestic production."

A curious calculation has been made[6] to show the loss formerly entailed upon the agricultural classes in France by the prohibitory duty then imposed on English iron. The lands then cultivated in France amounted to about fifty-seven millions of acres. From the quantity of land that a team of oxen could plough, the number of ploughs required for the cultivation of such an extent of land was taken to be a million and a half. The annual use and waste of iron on each plough has been estimated to be from forty to fifty kilogrammes. The whole consumption therefore at ninety francs per kilogramme amounts to two millions seven hundred thousand pounds. Although this estimate is said to be too high for an average calculation, the iron could undoubtedly have been imported at half the price; and the annual loss to agriculture alone must be taken at above one million sterling. The indirect loss arising from the use of wooden ploughs or iron ploughs of an inferior description cannot perhaps be computed; but it probably represents a far greater sum.

§ 3. It is not difficult to understand the nature of the assistance which exchange affords, and the mode of its operation. Exchange is an interchange of superfluities. Men give objects which they desire less, in return for objects which they desire more. The parties to an exchange have their superfluities and their deficiencies inverted, because their natural powers are different; because their acquired powers are not less varied; because the natural agents within their reach from differences of time place or circumstance are also different; and because the opportunities of these parties and their appliances for dealing with these natural agents present still greater degrees of diversity. Without the aid of exchange the satisfaction sought could in many cases either never be obtained or be obtained only at the cost of a greatly increased effort. No possible effort on his part would enable a landman to perform on himself an important surgical operation; or to ascertain and establish his rights in a complicated suit in equity. No physical training on the other hand would enable a weak and puny clerk to carry the load of a porter or a coalheaver. No artificial contrivance could raise tin in Durham or coal in Cornwall. Spices or pineapples may be grown in the British Islands; but only under such conditions of cost as would place them beyond the reach of ordinary consumers. In tropical countries these articles grow in abundance; and the inhabitants part with them for so small a consideration that even after a long sea carriage they can be sold in England at a very moderate price.

Exchange not merely acts as an economical form of production, but without it a large part of our ordinary production would never have taken place. It implies the existence in the purchaser of wants previously ungratified or unknown, and the power of rendering his labour or his properly available for their satisfaction. It thus utilizes, or at least increases the utility of, labour or of property that otherwise would have been useless, or at the most have afforded an incomplete enjoyment. When a savage discovers that the stones, or the skins, which are to him so common as to claim no special attention, can obtain for him beads or nails or other objects of his desire, be learns to prize and collect those commodities. When a labourer who wastes over his work the time for which he received no appreciable reward, finds full employment at piece-work, every minute acquires in his estimation a very different importance. When we hear that trade is brisk or markets lively, we know that capital is well remunerated. In all these cases the new value attached to the stones or the peltry, the increased reward for labour, the rapidity with which the capital is turned over, indicate a new demand. This demand may be caused either by an absolute increase of the population, or by an increase in the number of the buyers arising from increased facilities for exchange. This new demand gives to the vendors an increased power of satisfying their wants; and incites them to new or to increased industrial efforts. It supplies them with a motive, or more accurately it places them under industrial conditions, that did not previously exist. It is this effect that both many economists and the ordinary forms of speech indicate by such phrases as the finding a new market, an outlet for the surplus produce of the country, and similar expressions. They do not mean to deny that the benefit of an exchange to a purchaser consists in the incoming, not in the outgoing, in that which he acquires, not in that with which he parts. The expression is the same loose form used in the ordinary demand for employment, that is for labour not indeed for its own sake, but for the sake of the reward that accompanies it. These terms merely imply that the labour which was previously idle or comparatively inefficient, now becomes remunerative, or more largely remunerative than before. Exchange then has a double function. It both aids labour, and it stimulates it. It not only reduces to a minimum the effort required to satisfy any want; but it excites certain efforts which otherwise would never have been made.

§ 4. Since exchange is a method of procuring upon advantageous terms some means of satisfying a want, the object which a man seeks to acquire by exchange must be, or must appear to him to be, in some manner desirable. It is immaterial whether the object be really capable of gratifying the desire or of accomplishing the purpose; or whether the desire or the purpose be one which a good or a prudent man should entertain. It is sufficient if the object be one which the purchaser, whether rightly or wrongly, desires to possess. But as exchange professes only to reduce, not to abolish trouble, as it necessarily implies a consideration, it follows that the desirable object must also be one which is difficult of attainment. The cause from which this difficulty proceeds, is as little material to the exchange as is the nature of the desire. It is enough that the difficulty does in fact exist. It was at one time said by many economists that value depended on limitation of supply. But scarcity is only one out of several causes of difficulty. An object may be difficult of attainment, not only from its absolute rarity, but from the time or trouble that its appropriation requires, or from the general inability or reluctance from whatever cause to render the particular service. In a Canadian forest for example a man may obtain any quantity of timber by merely cutting it down, or any quantity of wild strawberries by merely picking them up; yet the trouble and the inconvenience of wood-cutting or of strawberry-picking are so great, that men are always willing to pay a price for having the work performed for them by others.

Again, as the peculiar method used in exchange of reducing trouble is transfer, it follows that those desirable objects which are difficult of attainment if they be subjects of exchange must also be transferable. To say that an exchangeable object must be transferable seems almost equivalent to the proposition that an exchangeable object must be exchangeable. Where the transferability is natural, the idea of exchange never arises. The heat and light of the sun, personal health and beauty, mental endowments, although both desirable and by any human exertion unattainable, are never in the market. We can purchase their use or their results; but the things themselves cannot be transferred. It is the artificial obstacles to transfer that direct our attention to this condition. Of these obstacles I shall elsewhere have occasion to treat. At present it is enough to indicate the great quantities of land which under family settlements are for many years together inalienable. There are also many unmarketable titles to real property. The holder of such property may be sufficiently secure from dispossession; but his title is open to dispute, and purchasers will not buy a lawsuit. He can thus comply with two conditions of exchange, but not with the third; and consequently his property is for the time not an exchangeable object. The value of the land thus rendered inalienable under the old system of real property law in England and Ireland was enormous. Some estimate of its extent may be formed from the fact that the Commissioners of Incumbered Estates in Ireland sold land which would otherwise have been inalienable to the amount of upwards of twenty-three millions of money.

There is yet another condition of exchangeability. The transfer of one such desirable object as that already described for another such object implies that the two objects are dissimilar. There is no motive for the interchange of objects that are precisely alike. A man parts with his property, or exerts his labour, to obtain something which he could not on equally advantageous terms otherwise obtain. If he receive in return something substantially the same as that which he gave, he has had all the trouble of the transaction without any of the expected advantage. At best the exchange, if it be not an actual burden, has ceased to be of any use. Accordingly we find that it is between men in different occupations, and not between men whose occupations are the same, that the great bulk of exchanges takes place. A carpenter seldom deals with a carpenter, or a mason with a mason; but they both deal with the butcher and the baker. No miner seeks to change his gold for other gold; and no farmer buys wheat with similar wheat. Diversity is essential to exchange. Like the condition of transferability, this condition is so involved in all our ideas of exchange that any illustration or enforcement of it seems absurd; and even its formal statement sounds like a truism. But although it is so obvious in its simple form, it brings with it consequences that are not equally apparent.

In every such transaction both parties must be free agents. Each man judges for himself of the comparative merits of the proposed inducement and the proposed cost. The idea of compulsion at once suggests a disturbing element. Every true exchange is voluntary. This limitation of exchange would not have required any special notice, were it not that an eminent writer[7] has denied its accuracy. It has been urged that if this view were correct the expressions "voluntary exchange" or "forced exchange" would be improper.

But the impropriety consists rather in the undue extension than in the undue limitation of the term. It is only by a kind of metaphor that we can speak of a forced exchange. That expression denotes something that has the appearance of an exchange but yet is different from it. Presents made on the tacit understanding that an equivalent will be returned are not really gifts. So a transaction without such a consideration as the party interested is willing to accept may perhaps be a theft, but is not really an exchange. Taxation has been cited as an instance of involuntary exchange. But a tax is the equivalent for the service of protection rendered. In a free State, either an endowment in the form of an hereditary revenue is provided by the original constitution of the country, or the people by their representatives consent to and determine the amount of their payments. In less favoured countries, the Government it is true both determines the remuneration and judges of the quality of the service. I am not however concerned to justify the practice of such governments, or to defend them from any charge that their opponents may bring against them. It is no objection to the true meaning of the term either that it is sometimes coupled with superfluous or incongruous epithets: or that it like many other terms bears its silent but emphatic testimony against the injustice of some rulers of mankind.

§ 5. In every exchange there are two points to which a purchaser must look. He must consider the strength of his desire, and the cost at which he either by his own net, or by the agency of others can gratify that desire. As either party in an exchange is in turn vendor and purchaser according to the point of view from which we regard him, the same considerations influence each. The amount of any other exchangeable object which any object can command in exchange is said to be the value of that object. When this value is expressed in money, it is called price, a term which as it is free from the ambiguities inseparable from value I shall habitually use. Although in every exchange the conditions both of desirability and of difficulty must co-exist, yet that of difficulty is generally the more active. The strength of the desire can only be tested by the difficulty which it will overcome. Without such a test, its force remains unknown even to the person who feels it. If the difficulty exceed the purchaser's desire, no exchange can take place. The motive for the exchange, the saving of sacrifice, will have ceased to operate. The point then at which the sacrifice is felt to be fully equal to the enjoyment, is the extreme limit which price can reach. The price may fall short of this point by any degree, but can in no case exceed it. It is however in rare and exceptional cases that price even approaches this limit. For although the excess of difficulty over desirability is fatal to exchange, the opposite condition of an excess of desirability is most conducive to it. In such circumstances the motive to exchange is in full operation; and the only subject of doubt is the precise amount of the difficulty. This question is determined by the mutual consent after free discussion of both parties. The purchaser considers the convenience to him of the subject of the transaction, and the difficulty he would have in otherwise procuring it. The vendor considers the convenience to him of the price offered, and the difficulty he would have in otherwise procuring that price. Neither of the two has any concern with the convenience of the other. Each seeks merely the smallest possible amount of sacrifice for himself. But exchange is ordinarily effected by the intervention of money. The simple barter thus becomes a complex transaction. There are two exchanges in place of one. There is a sale and a purchase, and then a purchase and a sale. The first vendor employs the purchase-money he has received from his purchaser in the purchase from a third party of the object he desires to use. Our attention is thus directed at each time to one part only of the transaction. We accordingly consider the sale and purchase of a single article and the circumstances affecting the price of that article, assuming for the time that money is an accurate standard of value. In this manner, without the complication of the second set of considerations, the circumstances may be traced which affect the price of any exchangeable object. A man purchases an object because be wants it, and because its attainment involves an effort. His want is personal. His effort admits of delegation, and so of exchange. He pays therefore not for the satisfaction of his want but for the effort which he has been spared. He does not consider the sacrifice incurred by the vendor. What he regards is not the labour that another has undergone, but the labour that he himself can avoid. Accordingly, price varies with the difficulty of attainment. If that difficulty increase, price will rise; if that difficulty be diminished, price will fall. The range of these variations is between the excess of desirability over difficulty, and the entire absence of the latter. If the element of difficulty be in excess, there can be no exchange; because one of its essential conditions has ceased to exist. If that element disappear, the same result and from the same cause, the absence namely of an essential condition, will ensue. The superior limit then, of price is the point at which the difficulty equals the desirability; its inferior limit is the point at which difficulty disappears.

There are however two parties to every exchange, to both of whom the exchange must be beneficial. It is possible that an exchange may take place which is far from being really beneficial to one of the parties, but which is effected because a partial loss is better than a total loss. A man may from error or from misfortune have misapplied his labour; and he prefers to escape with a reduction in price than to incur an absolute loss. But on whatever terms an isolated exchange at any particular time or place may be effected, a series of exchanges cannot take place, or in other words a trade cannot be established or retained, if the exchange should prove constantly disadvantageous to either of the two parties. One man will not continue to render a service to another, if he thereby entail upon himself a sacrifice greater than the consideration that he receives. The element of difficulty will in his estimation of the transaction exceed the element of desirability; and consequently no exchange can be effected. The price therefore in any given instance is determined by the trouble that the purchaser avoids; but that saving of trouble must on an average of cases coincide with the expenditure of trouble that the vendor incurs. Price therefore constantly tends towards the cost of production.

§ 6. The difficulty of attainment is composed of two elements. One is the actual cost of reproducing the object itself. The other is the number of persons who are prepared to purchase the existing quantity. Where there are more than the two parties, the desirability of the object to the other purchasers presents a difficulty in the attainment of that object to each individual competitor. Difficulty then may he said to depend partly upon the smallness of the supply, and partly upon the largeness of the demand. When both these elements of difficulty concur, the difficultly reaches its greatest height. When they are inverted, the difficulty is at its minimum. When both the supply and the demand are large or are small, the degree of difficulty is intermediate; and may be greater or less according to the circumstances of each case. The element of supply may be controlled by the presence or the removal of some natural obstacle, or of some artificial restriction, or by any of the circumstances which influence production. The demand may be affected by an influx of population, by a caprice of fashion, by any circumstance which induces an unusual number of people to pursue at the same time the same conduct or by any similar cause. But the rise in price consequent upon any such altered demand is not produced by any change either in the properties of the object, or in the purchaser's estimation of its use. Price in such circumstances rises, because each individual finds it more difficult than before to procure the article. In like manner when the supply is reduced, the rise in price is occasioned, not by any change in the intensity or the extension of the demand, but by the increased difficulty of attainment.

The cost of re-production may vary in every degree from a slight obstacle up to absolute impossibility. Those degrees however admit of some classification. The quantity of the object desired either is or is not susceptible of increase. In the latter case, the price will only be checked by the desirability of the object to the purchaser. This is the case of monopoly. Obvious instances are paintings by the old masters, rare coins, first editions, the vocal talents of a prima donna, all which command what is usually called a fancy price, that is a price the limit of which is merely subjective. The opposite case is the ordinary one where the quantity of the object may be indefinitely increased at the same or even a less amount of labour. In this case the limit of price will be objective. The effort requisite for procuring the article will exchange for an equivalent effort in producing it. The difficulty of attainment will be equal to the cost of production.

There may however be more than one cost of production. It may happen that an increase of production is required, but can only be obtained at a greater proportionate cost than the former amount. It may happen that while the quantity required remains unchanged the cost of part, but not of the whole, of that quantity is reduced. In both cases, and for the same reason, there will not be the two prices of the two differing costs, but one price. The purchaser pays for the difficulty of attainment. He has nothing to do with the vendor's labour. That labour may be greater or may be less in any given instance, although its average amount tends towards the difficulty of attainment. Consequently, the increase of the cost increases the difficulty of the attainment not to one person only but to all. The price therefore rises; and the producers at the original cost gain the whole difference between the old, and the new or increased, cost. But on the same principle that a partial increase of cost produces a general rise of price, a partial decrease of cost will leave prices unchanged. In such a case, the difficulty of attainment will remain as before; and the producer at the new cost will gain the entire difference between the new or diminished, and the old, cost. This advantage is generally regarded as extra profit, if the producers personally enjoy it; if they transfer their right to others, the consideration which they receive is termed rent. In a subsequent chapter it will appear how in the one case a desire to share in the advantage gradually brings into general notice the means of the partial cheapness of production, and ultimately tends to reduce the price to the lower or improved cost; and again how the increase of price urges men to seek for improved processes which enable them to neutralize the increased cost which sometimes follows an increased demand.

Prices then within the limit of desirability vary with the difficulty of attainment. In cases of strict monopoly, the price is guided solely by the desire of the purchaser, and has no tendency towards any other limit. In cases of the absence of monopoly, where there is one cost and one price, the price whatever may be its occasional perturbation, steadily tends towards that amount of sacrifice which is involved in rendering the service, and which is called the cost of production. In cases of partial monopoly, where there is a diversity of cost and a uniformity of price, the price in like manner tends to the cost of production of the most costly part. Its residual phenomenon, the difference in amount between the two costs, either augments profit, or appears as rent.

But the cost of reproduction is in some cases modified in a remarkable manner by the character of the demand. As there are degrees in difficulty, so there are degrees in desirability. Men either can or cannot forego the objects of their desire. Some things are absolutely essential to our position in life or to our very existence. With other things, however desirable, we can dispense. These two classes are differently affected by an increase of cost. In the case of superfluities there are always some purchasers for whom the price is at its maximum. In their estimation, the desirability of the object and the difficulty of its attainment are nearly equal. Even a slight increase of cost therefore destroys as far as they are concerned the conditions necessary for exchange. They will cease to satisfy that particular desire. The difficulty will ascend the scale, but not to its full extent. Price will rise, but not to the height that might at first have been expected. There is a counteracting influence at work. The demand of the excluded class was an element of difficulty to other purchasers, and this demand is now withdrawn. The difficulty therefore, although increased at one side, is reduced though not to the same amount on the other. The price will rise to the amount of difficulty caused by the increased cost, less by the amount of difficulty which the suppressed demand represents. In like manner any reduction in cost will bring under the conditions of exchange persons who were previously excluded. Their demand will consequently form a new element of difficulty; and the fall of price will to that extent be checked. The price therefore of superfluities is modified by the diminution or the increase of purchasers. The rise consequent upon the increase of cost is checked by privation. The fall consequent upon a decrease of cost is retarded by enlarged enjoyment.

But the case is otherwise with things that are indispensable. In their case price has no such modifying influence. All men must have food; and no man can use more than a very limited quantity. Hence an increase in the cost of food will not be checked, to the same extent at least as in other cases, by privation. People prefer to sacrifice other sources of enjoyment than to reduce considerably their consumption of food. Accordingly a deficient harvest, brings with it a very disproportionate rise in price.[8] A deficiency of one-third of the crop, even when relieved by foreign supplies, has been sufficient in England to treble the ordinary price. Such a state of things brings with it a general reduction of expenditure in every direction. A famine at once prostrates all industrial exertion with the one sad exception of the trade in food. But the extension of the demand, whatever its intensity may be, is not great. There is no very marked difference in times of abundance and of dearth between the consumption of people in tolerable circumstances. Consequently a plentiful harvest will not bring with it a proportionate increase of consumption. Since people do not require more than a certain quantity of food, the desirability is brought below the difficulty. There is no increase of difficulty arising from increased demand. The expenditure saved is directed towards other sources of enjoyment. Accordingly after a good harvest, trade in its other branches is always brisk, and the price of food falls very low. As the check that controls the rise of price in necessaries is absent, so also is the check that moderates its fall.

§ 7. Both desirability and difficulty are obviously relative terms. They vary accordingly to the circumstances of the person to whom they are applied. Apart from the primary appetites common to the species, both the number and the intensity of human desires are indefinite. The same desires, or the same degrees of desires, are not found in two persons of different nations, or of different generations, or of different years, or of different occupations, or of different sexes. They are not found even in the same person in different circumstances. In like manner the obstacle which to one man is insuperable is scarcely regarded by another. A porter will carry a weight which a man of ordinary muscular power will hardly move. So, one man will easily satisfy a given desire at a cost which to another man would be ruinous. What may be a reasonable indulgence in one person may be a criminal extravagance in another. What is an absolute necessity in some cases may in others be an idle luxury. But our intense desires are few, and our moderate desires are many; and a large amount of purchasing power, like a large amount of muscular power, is comparatively rare. Hence each increase of difficulty excludes a constantly increasing amount of desire, while every dimination of effort brings larger and larger classes within the necessary conditions of exchange. Every permanent increase therefore of cost rapidly increases the amount of human privation. Every permanent decrease of cost extends in ever widening circles the amount of human enjoyment.

It is but of late years that this principle, obvious as it appears, has been fully recognized. Experience however has now fully confirmed its truth. In those branches of manufacturing industry in which the use of machinery has been most extensive, the demand for labour has so rapidly increased that wages, so far from falling before the competition of invention, have largely risen. In the cotton manufacture for example, where beyond all other cases machinery has been most influential, wages were increased between the years 1830 and 1859 on an average from ten to twenty-five per cent. The reason of this unexpected result is universally admitted to have been the immense increase in the consumption of these goods, which sprung from the reduction in their price. Again, books and newspapers, which if sold at the current prices of thirty years ago would not pay their expenses, now afford when their prices bring them within the reach of numerous readers a liberal return to all who are connected with them. It is now an axiom in finance that the higher the rate of duty upon articles in general use, the less will be the produce. "In no instance is an increase of duty followed by an equal increase of revenue, but on the contrary the produce will be less and less according as the duty advancees until there is no increase of the revenue but a falling off."[9] In like manner it is stated as the result of all past experience in railway affairs that "there is hardly an exception to the rule that a high fare produces a low amount of traffic, and stints its growth, while a low or moderate fare collects a large amount of traffic and fosters increase."[10]

Notes

1 *Harmonies of Political Economy*, p. 52, (English Translation).
2 Bastiat *Harmonies*, p. 58.
3 Dr. W. C. Taylor's *Natural History of Society*, vol. i. p. 145.
4 *Works*, vol. i. p. 304.
5 *Political Economy*, p. 76.
6 Porter's *Progress of the Nation*, p. 289.

7 Archbishop Whately's *Lectures on Political Economy*, p. 10.
8 Porter's *Progress of the Nation*, p. 429.
9 Levi *on Taxation*, p. 63.
10 *Journal of Statistical Society*, vol. xxii. p. 295.

22

'NORMAL VALUE'

John E. Cairnes

Source: John E. Cairnes *Some Leading Principles of Political Economy: Newly Expounded*, London: Macmillan, 1874, pp. 43–96.

§ 1. THE attribute of normal or usual value implies systematic and continuous production. We can not predicate normal value of a commodity of which the supply is limited and can not be increased—for example, of a picture of Turner's; because, although it would be possible from a number of sales of such pictures to strike an average, this average would merely represent the mean of fluctuations uncontrolled by any presiding principle, and so, as having no tendency to keep themselves within any certain bounds, incapable of being made the ground of expectation as to the course of future prices. But when a commodity is systematically and continuously produced, the existence of a normal value soon reveals itself. It is perceived that, however greatly the price may vary from time to time, the variations do not occur at random, but obey a hidden principle, and tend to conform to a certain rule. The price of wheat may be unusually high one year, but this at once calls into action forces which control the advance, and ultimately bring back the price to its usual level; or the price may be exceptionally low, and then the same forces are ranged on the opposite side, and the price rises. In this way the fluctuations of the market are kept within certain, not perhaps precisely determinable, but still real, limits, with a constant tendency to approach a central point—the point of "normal value" of which we are in quest.

I have remarked that an average of the actual sales effected of a commodity, that is to say, of its market prices, does not necessarily represent its normal price or value, because the commodity may exist under conditions which do not supply any controlling principle to its fluctuations, and consequently do not develop any tendency in these to revolve round a central point. But it is still true that, where the conditions for evolving a normal value do exist, that is to say, where a commodity is systematically and continuously produced, the normal value will generally be coincident with the average of actual sales, if only the number of instances taken be sufficient to eliminate the effects of what we may call disturbing causes—causes, that is to say, which interfere with the adaptation of supply to demand.[1] The number of instances necessary to effect such elimination will vary greatly with the nature of the commodity. It will in general be least in articles of ordinary manufacture, much greater in those of raw produce, and greatest of all in products of the animal kingdom. These, however, are points which will be more conveniently elucidated in connection with the subject of market values.

One word more of explanation. Normal values, though, in contrast with market values, they may not improperly be described as average or permanent values, must not be supposed to represent any thing absolutely fixed or constant in the exchange relation of commodities. There is no such fixedness or constancy to be found in that relation. All that we can properly understand by the permanency predicated of such values is that they remain the same so long as the conditions of production remain the same. In point of fact, the conditions of production of all commodities undergo change, and those of most commodities frequent and extensive change. In general, however, these changes, where they are of much importance, occur at intervals of some duration, and in the intervening periods the normal price remains constant. The centre about which market prices oscillate is thus not a fixed, but a movable centre; moving, however (as will be fully set forth in a subsequent chapter[2]), for the most part in constant directions, determined by the character of the commodity and the circumstances under which it is produced. Thus in most manufactured goods the course of normal prices in this country has for some centuries been steadily downward; while on the other hand, the normal prices of raw produce, and more particularly of produce of the animal kingdom, have pretty constantly risen.

So far as to the character of the phenomenon which now claims our attention. It remains to consider the conditions which determine it.

§ 2. The current theories of value connect normal value (called by Adam Smith and Ricardo "natural value," and by Mr. Mill "necessary value," but best expressed, it seems to me, by the term which I have used[3]) with one set of conditions only, those, namely, comprised under the phrase "cost of production;" and some writers would, under this notion, distinguish such values as "cost values." But this, it seems to me, is to take a much too limited view of the range of this phenomenon. The essence lies in the tendency of the exchanges of the market to gravitate toward a central point; wherever that tendency is observable, we can predicate of the commodities which exhibit it the possession of a central, usual, or normal value. Now, to go no farther at present, such a tendency exists in the relative values of the commodities exchanged by different nations, or, as they are called, "international values." In other words, trading countries exchange their productions in certain proportions, which, in any given state of industry, manifest the condition of normality. Deviations may, and do occur, but forces are in existence which tend constantly to bring back the proportions to the normal line. International values, however, are admittedly—or at all events are demonstrably—not governed by cost of production, and we have thus normal values which are not connected with cost, but come under the influence of some other principle. And I shall afterward have occasion to show that, even in domestic exchanges, cost of production is by no means coextensive with the range of this phenomenon.

Cost of production, however, is undoubtedly the principal and most important of the conditions on which normal value depends. Not only, as will be shown, does it absolutely determine that relation over a very wide field of exchange transactions, but over perhaps a still wider it exercises, not a decisive, but a powerful influence, and within certain limits controls the results. It is therefore necessary, at the outset of our discussion, to ascertain the true nature of Cost of Production, a clear perception of which, I may observe, quite irrespective of the theory of value, is indispensable for the solution of most of the problems of production and distribution.

The following is the analysis of Cost of Production given by Mr. Mill, and which, so far as I know, has been acquiesced in, either expressly or implicitly, by economists alike in this and in other countries:

> "The component elements of Cost of Production have been set forth in the first part of this inquiry. The principle of them, and so much the principle as to be nearly the sole, we found to be Labor. What the production of a thing costs to its producer, or its series of producers, is the labor expended in producing it. If we consider as the producer the capitalist who makes the advances, the word 'labor' may be replaced by the word 'wages:' what the produce costs to him, is the wages which he has had to pay. At the first glance, indeed, this seems to be only a part of his outlay, since he has not only paid wages to laborers, but has likewise provided them with tools, materials, and perhaps buildings. These tools, materials, and buildings, however, were produced by labor and capital; and their value, like that of the article to the production of which they are subservient, depends on cost of production, which again is resolvable into labor. The cost of production of broadcloth does not wholly consist in the wages of weavers; which alone are directly paid by the cloth manufacturer. It consists also of the wages of spinners and wool-combers, and, it may be added, of shepherds, all of which the clothier has paid for in the price of yarn. It consists, too, of the wages of builders and brick-makers, which he has reimbursed in the contract price of erecting his factory. It partly consists of the wages of machine-makers, iron-founders, and miners. And to these must be added the wages of the carriers who transported any of the means

and appliances of the production to the place where they were to be used, and the product itself to the place where it is to be sold." . . . "Thus far of labor, or wages, as an element in cost of production. But in our analysis, in the First Book, of the requisites of production we found that there is another necessary element in it besides labor. There is also capital; and this being the result of abstinence, the produce, or its value, must be sufficient to remunerate, not only all the labor required, but the abstinence of all the persons by whom the remuneration of the different classes of laborers was advanced. The return for abstinence is Profit. And profit, we have also seen, is not exclusively the surplus remaining to the capitalist after he has been compensated for his outlay, but forms, in most cases, no unimportant part of the outlay itself. The flax-spinner, part of whose expenses consists of the purchase of flax and of machinery, had had to pay, in their price, not only the wages of the labor by which the flax was grown and the machinery made, but the profits of the grower, the flax-dresser, the miner, the iron-founder, and the machine-maker. All these profits, together with those of the spinner himself, were again advanced by the weaver, in the price of his material—linen yarn; and along with them the profits of a fresh set of machine-makers, and of the miners and iron-workers who supplied them with their metallic material. All these advances from part of the cost of production of linen. Profits, therefore, as well as wages, enter into the cost of production which determines the value of the produce." . . .

"Profits, however, may enter more largely into the conditions of production of one commodity than of another, even though there be no difference in the *rate* of profit between the two employments. The one commodity may be called upon to yield profit during a longer period of time than the other. The example by which this case is usually illustrated is that of wine. Suppose a quantity of wine and a quantity of cloth made by equal amounts of labor, and that labor paid at the same rate. The cloth does not improve by keeping; the wine does. Suppose that, to attain the desired quality, the wine requires to be kept five years. The producer or dealer will not keep it, unless at the end of five years he can sell it for as much more than the cloth as amounts to five years' profit accumulated at compound interest. The wine and the cloth were made by the same original outlay. Here, then, is a case in which the natural values, relatively to one another, of two commodities, do not conform to their cost of production alone, but to their cost of production *plus* something else. Unless, indeed, for the sake of generality in the expression, we include the profit which the wind-merchant foregoes during the five years in the cost of production of the wine: looking upon it as a kind of additional outlay, over and above his other advances, for which outlay he must be indemnified at last."[4]

And finally he thus sums up:

"Cost of Production consists of several elements, some of which are constant and universal, others occasional. The universal elements of cost of production are the wages of the labor and the profits of the capital. The occasional elements are taxes, and any extra cost occasioned by a scarcity value of some of the requisites."[5]

§ 3. Such is the view of Cost of Production which must be considered as now generally accepted by economists. But in spite of the great authority properly attaching to any doctrine propounded by Mr. Mill, and enhanced as this is in the present instance by the general concurrence of economists, I am compelled to dissent from it. It seems to me that the conception of cost which it suggests is radically unsound, confounding things in their own nature distinct and even antithetical, and setting in an essentially false light the incidents of production and exchange; further, I think it will appear that it leads to practical errors of a serious kind, not merely with regard to value, but also with regard to some other important doctrines of the science.

Of all ideas within the range of economic speculation, the two most profoundly opposed to each other are cost and the reward of cost—the sacrifice incurred by man in productive industry, and the return made by nature to man upon that sacrifice. All industrial progress consists in altering the proportion between these two things; in increasing the remuneration in relation to the cost, or in diminishing the cost in relation to the remuneration. Cost and remuneration are thus economic antitheses of each other; so completely so, that a small cost and a large remuneration are exactly equivalent expressions. Now, in the analysis of cost of production which I have quoted, these two opposites are identified; and cost, which is sacrifice, cost, which is what man pays to nature for her industrial rewards, is said to consist of wages and profits, that is to say, of what nature yields to man in return for his industrial sacrifices. The theory thus in its simple statement confounds opposite facts and ideas, and further examination will show that it involves conclusions no less perplexed, and in conflict with doctrines the most received.

For, first, if the analysis in question be accepted, and wages and profits be taken as the constituents of cost of production, this conclusion follows: that the cost of producing commodities, taking industry as a whole, is a constant condition, incapable, however great of universal the progress of industrial improvement, of undergoing change. Suppose, for example, the general productiveness of industry were increased; this would mean that the aggregate results of industry in return for a given exertion of labor and abstinence were increased: in other words, that the fund from which wages and profits were paid had increased in relation to the labor and abstinenece expended. Wages and profits, therefore, as an aggregate would rise exactly in proportion as industry had become more productive; and the cost of producing a given commodity, measured in wages and profits, would thus remain precisely as before. There would be less labor and abstinence exerted, but this smaller exertion being more highly remunerated, the cost, measured in the remuneration, would suffer no change. I may mention that this is no fanciful deduction of mine, but has in effect been applied by at least two writers to the solution of a practical question. In a paper read some years ago before the Dublin Statistical Society, it was argued by Dr. Hancock that the cost of producing gold had not been reduced by the gold discoveries; and what was Dr. Hancock's proof of this assertion? Simply this, that the wages and profits of the producers of gold had increased as much as the labor and abstinence required for the production of a given quantity of gold had diminished, leaving thus, he said, the cost of production unchanged. The facts were undoubtedly as the argument assumed, and the inference was strictly in accordance with the accepted view of cost of production. But the inevitable conclusion (which Dr. Hancock did *not* draw) would be that the depreciation of gold is impossible.[6]

Take another example of the consequences involved in this doctrine. If it be true that the wages and profits received by the producers of a commodity are the measure of its cost of production, then it follows that all commodities whatever, it matters not under what circumstances produced, whether of competition or of monopoly, exchange, and can not but exchange, in proportion to their costs of production. This results at once from the consideration that the value of a commodity, where it is continuously produced, constitutes for the producers the fund from which wages and profits are paid. Accordingly, such as the value is, such will be the wages and profits of the producers; but such as are the wages and profits of producers, such, according to the theory, is the cost of production. When, therefore, two commodities exchange for each other, or, varying the expression, when their values or prices are the same, their costs of production, according to the view we are considering, will necessarily be the same. It is evident that this argument applies to every case of value and price, and is wholly irrespective of the circumstances, whether of freedom or monopoly, under which commodities are produced. In truth, the principle that "cost of production determines value" becomes, when thus understood, little more than the assertion of an identical proposition, since it merely amounts to saying that values are in proportion to the aggregate of the elements of which they are made up.

That a doctrine open to objections so fundamental should have obtained the currency and prestige which this has acquired may seem scarcely credible; and I am in some dread lest I should be suspected of misrepresenting the view I am combating. But that I have not done so will be admitted on consideration of the following sentences occurring in the passage quoted above, in which Mr. Mill discloses with perfect clearness the line of thought by which the view in question has been reached: "What the production of a thing costs to its producer, or its series of producers, is the labor expended in producing it. *If we consider as the producer the capitalist who makes the advances, the word labor may be replaced by wages; what the produce costs to him* is the wages which he has had to pay." In other words, the point of view is shifted from the ground of human interests to the partial and limited stand-point of the capitalist employer; and the cost of producing an article, which really consists in the sacrifices required of human beings for its production, is only considered so far forth as it is "cost to him," that much more important portion of the cost which is cost to the laborer being put altogether out of sight. This point of view being once taken, the rest follows simply and naturally. What is cost to the capitalist, that is to say, his advances, consisting of the profits of previous producers as well as of the wages of laborers, profits as well as wages, must evidently be included in cost; and not only the profits of previous producers, but, in order to meet the case of different periods of advancing capital, the profits of the producer of the particular commodity whose cost is considered—an extension of the theory which involves this curious consequence, that among the elements of the cost of producing a commodity is counted the profit obtained on that commodity by the producer, a profit which I need scarcely say is not realized till *after* the commodity is produced. Such is the line of thought by which the view in question has been reached; and it is not difficult to see why, once adopted, it should find easy and general acceptance. The vocabulary of commerce is, for obvious reasons, framed almost wholly from the capitalist's stand-point; and Political Economy is for the most part compelled to draw its nomenclature from the vocabulary of commerce. A doctrine, therefore, of cost of production which resolved all cost into capitalist's cost would easily fall in at once with the general phraseology of economic science, and with the preconceptions and prepossessions generated by commercial modes of thought.

That the laborer's share in the industrial sacrifice is by the current doctrine excluded from the conception of cost of production does not appear to have been seen, or, if seen, to have been adequately appreciated by its adherents. Mr. Mill's language seems to imply that the wages advanced by the capitalist—though he admits they only represent "the cost of producing *to him*," may yet in some way be taken to represent the cost to the laborer also, for, having dealt with this portion of the case, he leads on to the next with the words: "Thus far of labor *or wages*, as an element of cost of production. . . . There is also capital," etc. But I must absolutely deny that wages can in any sense be taken to represent the labor element in cost of production. Wages, as Mr. Mill observed in the passage already quoted, may be regarded as cost to the capitalist who advances them; though perhaps it would be more correct to say that, so far as they go, they *measure* his cost, which really *consists* in the deprivation of immediate enjoyment implied in the fact of the advance. But to the laborer wages are reward, not cost; nor can it be said that they stand in any constant relation to that which really constitutes cost to him. If they did, wages in all occupations, in all countries, and in all times, would be in proportion to the severity of the toil which they recompensed; whereas the proportion fails, not only in different occupations and in different countries, but whenever a general advance or decline takes place in the conditions of productive industry in the same occupations and in the same countries. That it fails in different occupations in the same country Mr. Mill himself allows; rather, let me say, he has been the first economist strongly to insist upon the importance of this fact; that it fails on a comparison of the condition of labor in different countries is too obvious to need proof; and that it fails in the same country and in the same occupations on the occurrence of important changes in the conditions of productive industry we may satisfy ourselves by simply observing the events now passing before our eyes. The remuneration of labor has for some years been pretty steadily advancing in the majority of occupations in this country—advancing not merely in its money amount, but in the real reward it procures for the laborer. And wherever this has happened without a corresponding increase in the severity of the toil undergone (and in general it has been accompanied rather by a reduction than an extension of working time), the proportion between sacrifice and reward has been altered. I repeat, therefore, that not only do wages not constitute the laborer's share in the cost of production, but they can not be taken in any sense to represent that cost. Where they are advanced by the capitalist they measure, so far as they go, the capitalist's sacrifice, and the capitalist's alone; and an analysis of cost of production, therefore, which takes no account of any sacrifices but those represented by wages, simply omits altogether the most important element of the case.

§ 4. The point for which I am contending will possibly appear to some persons to involve a purely theoretical issue. A theoretical issue no doubt is at stake, but I believe a better example could not easily be found of the intimate connection between theory and practice, and of the way in which an unsound theory can invert for people the true relation of phenomena and mislead in the practical business of life, than is furnished by this doctrine. The truth of this statement will only fully appear in the later chapters of this work; but even here I may give an example or two. What, for instance, is now the grand argument with the people of the United States for the maintenance of protection? Why, the high cost of production in that country. And what is the evidence of this high cost of production? Simply the high rates of wages which prevail. How, they ask, can we, with our high-priced labor, compete with the pauper labor of Europe? I must frankly own that, accepting the point of view of the current theory of cost, I can find no satisfactory reply to this question, and I am quite sure that Mr. Wells, who implicitly adopts this point of view, has wholly failed to furnish one. But to pursue the argument further here would be to anticipate what will come more naturally under review at a later stage of our investigation.

Nor are our commercial writers here entitled to plume themselves on the superiority of their economic notions to those of American protectionists, at least as regards this question of cost of production. In dealing with the labor question, the arguments of our capitalists do not differ in principle from that which I have just criticised. Consider, for example, the significance of such passages as this which I find in the work of so well-informed and thoughtful a writer as Mr. Brassey, and which fairly represents the economic doctrine that pervades it:

> "It is the opinion of Mr. Lothian Bell, one of our highest author-ities, that, after all the efforts of our iron-masters to contend with the difficulty of high-priced labor by the improvement of machinery, labor costs fifteen per cent more in England than on the Continent, and this disadvantage, in his opinion, entirely neutralizes the advan-tages we derive from our great facilities in the proximity of our iron-mines to our coal-beds. Our workmen are not sufficiently alive to the necessity for the exercise of the utmost efforts of ingenuity, in order to enable capital invested in England to holds its own in the industrial campaign."[7]

Now, I ask, what inverstion of the true relations of things can be more complete than to represent high-priced labor as an obstacle to production in the same sense in which the proximity of our coal-beds to our iron-mines constitutes a facility? Dear labor neutralizing the advantages of our coal-beds and iron-mines! As well speak of the large fees reaped by a successful barrister as neutralizing the advantage of his skill; for not more certainly are the large fees the consequence of the barrister's legal skill, than the high wages of our artisans are the consequence of the industrial advantages under which they work. Now what is the explanation of this singular confusion of thought and perversion of facts? Obviously this—the whole problem of industry is looked at exclusively from the capitalist's point of view. "The advantages *we* derive" from our coalbeds and iron-mines are the advantages which capitalists derive from them. "British trade" means capitalists' profits; and, as the only cost taken account of in production is the capitalists' cost, so naturally the capitalists' remuneration is the only remuneration thought worth attending to. Hence high wages are represented as "neutralizing" industrial advantages, as if nothing were gain which did not come to the capitalist's maw; and the liberal remuneration of the working-people is deplored as a national calamity because it sets limits to the capitalist's share in the produce of their joint exertions. "Dear labor," says Mr. Brassey (p. 142), summing up the argument of a chapter, "is now the great obstacle to the extension of British trade."[8] It does not occur to him that high profits are an obstacle in precisely the same sense. If British laborers and capitalists will only consent to accept a lower scale of remuneration for their services they may have the satisfaction of indefinitely extending British trade and achieving the great goal of commercial ambition by underselling all the nations of the earth. Each, however, halts, and would prefer that the other should take the initiative in the patriotic sacrifice, desiring, like the French soldiers at the battle of Fontenoy, to give to his opponent the honor of firing first.

§ 5. It seems to me that a sufficient case has now been made out to justify an attempt at a fresh exposition of the doctrine of Cost of Production. I therefore proceed to submit to the reader that view of it which such reflection as I have been able to give to the subject has led me to form.

And here I must, in the first place, insist that cost means sacrifice, and can not, without risk of hopelessly confusing ideas, be identified with any thing that is not sacrifice. It represents what man parts with in the barter between him and nature, which must be kept eternally distinct from the return made by nature on that payment. This is the essential nature of cost; and the problem of cost of production as bearing on the theory of value is to ascertain how far and in what way the payment thus made by man to nature in productive industry determines or otherwise influences the exchange value of the products which result. To find an answer to this question we need not go beyond that fundamental principle of conduct which leads men to seek their ends by the easiest and shortest means. The end of engaging in industry is the acquisition of wealth; and the means, self-denial, toil, forethought, vigilance. The problem of industry is, therefore, to attain wealth at the least expenditure of those bodily and mental exertions—or, as we may say, at the least sacrifice or cost. And the law of cost of production, as governing value, is merely the practical consequence and outcome of the pursuit of wealth under this condition.

In order to perceive this, it is only necessary to keep steadily in view the two following facts: First, that under the influence of the motive just indicated, men, in selecting their occupations, whether as laborers or as capitalists, will, *so far as they have the power of choice*, select those which, in return for a given sacrifice, yield, or promise to yield, the largest rewards; and secondly, the fact that, under a system of separation of employments, industrial rewards consist for each producer, or, more properly, for each group of producers, employed on a given work, in the value of the commodities which result from their exertions. I say in the *value* of the commodities, not in the commodities themselves; for it is not always that the man who is engaged in industry needs the particular commodity on which his own exertions are bestowed, and it is seldom that he needs more than at most an insignificant quantity of what he produces; consequently his remuneration must come, not from the direct but from the indirect results of his labors—from those things, whatever they are, which the commodity he produces enables him by sale and purchase to command—in other words, from its value. Given the productiveness of a man's industry, this alone will not enable us to determine the amount of his remuneration. In order to this, we must further know the proportions in which what he produces will exchange for what he wants— that is to say, for the articles of his consumption. The value of the product resulting from industry forms thus the source from which, under the actual state of things, industry is remunerated. Nor is this conclusion invalidated by the fact that, under the industrial organization prevailing in this and other civilized countries, the laborer commonly receives his reward in the form of wages advanced by the capitalist before the product is completed; since what he receives is subsequently recouped to the capitalist, the sum being drawn from the value of the product; so that it is still *the value of the product* from which the remuneration of all concerned in the creation of that product ultimately comes. Wages and profits in each branch of industry are thus derived from the value of the commodities proceeding from that branch of industry, and, as (with the exception of the case where rent is also an element in the value of commodities—a case which, those acquainted with the economic theory of rent will perceive, does not affect the general argument) wages and profits also absorb the whole of that value, it follows that, other things being the same, the aggregate of wages and profits received by any given group of producers will always vary with the value of the aggregate of commodities which they produce. Where wages and profits, therefore, in different occupations are in proportion to the sacrifices undergone, the value of the commodities proceeding from those occupations will also be in proportion to the same sacrifices, that is to say, the commodities will exchange in proportion to their costs of production. Now wages and profits will be in proportion to the sacrifices undergone wherever, and only so far as, competition prevails among producers—wherever, and so far only as, laborers and capitalists have an effective choice in selecting among the various occupations presented to them in the industrial field. Give them this effective choice, and the correspondence of remuneration to sacrifice, not indeed in every act of production, but as a permanent and continuing state of things, is secured by the most active and constant of human motives. Each competitor, aiming at the largest reward in return for his sacrifices, will be drawn toward the occupations which happen at the time to be the best remunerated; while he will equally be repelled from those in which the remuneration is below the average level. The supply of products proceeding from the better paid employments will thus be increased, and that from the less remunerative reduced, until supply, acting on price, corrects the inequality, and brings remuneration into proportion with the sacrifices undergone. Competition, therefore, is at once the security for the correspondence of industrial remuneration with sacrifice, and also, and because it is so, the security for the correspondence of the values of commodities with the costs of their production.

The indispensable condition to the action of cost of production as the regulator of normal values is thus the existence of an effective competition among those engaged in industrial pursuits; and the point to which we have now to turn our attention is the extent to which such effective competition is actually realized in industrial communities. Confining our attention for the present to England, we find competition here active and widely prevalent. In trade, as distinguished from industry, I mean in the buying and selling of commodities as distinguished from their production, it may be said to be universal and unlimited. Every one is at liberty, and not only at liberty, but in general has the practical power, to sell his commodity,[9] whatever it may be, in any market in the country. Again, every one, speaking broadly, is free, so far as the law is concerned, to engage in any industrial pursuit he pleases, from hedging and ditching up to the learned professions. But for the present purpose something more than this is necessary. Not only must there be for dealers the right and power of selling the commodity where they please, and for workmen the legal right of admission to whatever occupation each prefers, but there must be, for laborers and capitalists respectively, the practical power of employing their labor and capital in whatever direction each may please—in a word, an effective choice in deciding on the destination of the instrument of which they have each to dispose. It matters not what the obstacle may be to the effectiveness of the choice, whether law, ignorance, or poverty—if there be an obstacle, if the producer can not pass freely from the less to the more lucrative occupation, competition is defeated, so far as regards the requirements of the law of cost, since there can be no security under such circumstances that remuneration shall be brought into correspondence with sacrifice. This is the sort of competition through which cost of production, as a regulator of value, works; and the question is, How far does competition in this sense prevail in this and other industrial communities?

There is a school of reasoners who will not hesitate to answer this question by flatly denying the existence of competition at all in the sense defined. I shall be told that the assumption so readily made by economists, that capital and labor may be shifted about from one occupation to another in search of the highest remuneration, is a mere figment of the economical brain, without foundation in fact. Once embodied in a form suited to actual work, capital, it will be urged, is for the most part incapable of being turned to other uses. The buildings, plant, and material required for one kind of manufacture can rarely be adapted to any other, and, even where the conversion is possible, the process will only be accomplished at great expense and loss. The difficulty of transferring labor, it will be contended, is even greater, since we are here in contact with mental as well as physical obstacles. Industrial skill is not a thing to be acquired in a moment, and that which a man possesses is the result, in general, of considerable time and outlay devoted to its acquisition. Is it likely that, having spent his time and money in acquiring this skill and fitting himself for a particular occupation, a workman will desert the line of life he has chosen on the first sign of an advance in remuneration elsewhere? We are reminded how long the hand-loom weavers persisted in their unprofitable labors after power-looms were in general use; and we can imagine how extreme the case would be which would cause a carpenter to become a smith, or a smith a carpenter, still more, which would cause either to take to hair-dressing or tailoring. On such grounds, it has been contended that competition, such as I have defined it as necessary to the action of the principle of cost, has no real existence, and that consequently all theories assuming its existence fall to the ground. Alike with regard to capital and labor, it is held that either, once embarked in a particular employment, is practically committed to that employment, and may therefore be regarded as taken out of the field of competition with agents of the same kind engaged in other branches of industry. I am anxious to do the fullest justice to the quantum of truth contained in this argument, and I admit at once that the facts alleged are substantially true. But I think it will not be difficult to show that they by no means sustain the practical conclusion they are adduced to support, and that, taking account of other conditions of the case which the argument overlooks, they are perfectly compatible with the existence of an effective industrial competition.

In the first place, it may be remarked that, in order to secure an effective industrial competition—such a competition as shall bring rewards into correspondence with sacrifices—it is not necessary that every portion of capital, or that every laborer, should be at all times capable of being turned to any selected occupation. It is enough that a certain quantity of each agent— varying according to circumstances—should be thus disposable. Suppose some branch of industry to be specially flourishing and to be realizing exceptional gains, there is no need that the whole industry of the country should be disturbed to correct the inequality. A small diversion of capital and labor—small, I mean, in comparison with the aggregate embarked in any important industry—will in general suffice for the purpose. Even on extraordinary occasions, when unlooked-for events in the political or commercial world disturb ordinary calculations and give an enormous advantage to particular industries—such occasions, for example, as occurred in the early years of railway enterprise, or again in the linen trade on the breaking out of the American civil war—even on such occasions, the equilibrium of remuneration and cost can always be restored, not indeed in a moment, but after no long delay, through the action of labor and capital still uncommitted to actual industrial employment, and without any sensible encroachment on the stock already actively employed. All that is necessary, therefore, with a view to an effective industrial competition, is the presence in a community of a certain quantity of those instruments of production existing in disposable form, ready to be turned toward the more lucrative pursuits, and sufficiently large to correct inequalities as they arise. Now, it will not be difficult to show that this condition is fulfilled in many industrial communities, completely in the case of capital, and less perfectly, but still within certain limits really and effectually, in the case of labor also.

The existence of a large amount of capital in commercial countries in disposable form—or, to speak less equivocally, in the form of money or other purchasing power, capable of being turned to any purpose required—is a patent and undeniable fact. Nor is it less certain that this capital is constantly seeking the best investments, and rapidly moves toward any branch of industry that happens at the moment to offer special attractions.[10] It is plain, too, that the capital thus disposable is sufficient for the purpose we have here in view, namely, to render competition effective among the various industries; since we find a portion of it constantly moving abroad for foreign investment—a destination it would scarcely receive while there was a prospect of reaping exceptionally high returns from investment within the country. We have, therefore, in the existence of this fund all that is required for a practically effective competition, so far as *one* instrument of production is concerned, and this without necessitating any serious encroachment on the capital actually engaged in productive operations. But is the corresponding condition satisfied in the case of labor? A little consideration will show that, within certain limits and subject to certain qualifications, it is fulfilled in this as well.

For here also we have a disposable fund, capable of being turned, as remuneration may tempt, in various directions. Granted that labor, once engaged in a particular occupation, is practically committed to that species of occupation; all labor is not thus engaged and committed. A young generation is constantly coming forward, whose capabilities may be regarded as still in disposable form, fulfilling the same function in relation to the general labor force of the country which capital, while yet existing as purchasing power, discharges in relation to its general capital. The young persons composing this body, or others interested in their welfare, are eagerly watching the prospects of industry in its several branches, and will not be slow to turn toward the pursuits that promise the largest rewards. Individual tastes, no doubt, will go for something in the decision, but varieties of tastes, taken over a large area, may be assumed pretty well to balance each other; and there will remain a steady gravitation of disposable labor toward the more remunerative callings. On the other hand, while fresh labor is coming on the scene, worn-out labor is passing off; and the departments of industry, in which remuneration has from any causes fallen below the average level, ceasing to be recruited, the numbers of those employed in them will quickly decline, until supply is brought within the limits of demand, and remuneration is restored to its just proportions. In this way, then, in the case of labor as in that of capital, the conditions for an effective competition exist, notwithstanding the practical difficulties in the way of transferring labor, once trained to a particular occupation, to new pursuits. But, as I have already intimated, the conditions are in this case realized only in an imperfect manner, and this involves, as a consequence, certain limitations on the action of competition in the labor market, and certain corresponding effects on the values of commodities. What the nature of those limitations are I shall now proceed to point out.

I remarked just now that the youthful labor constantly coming forward to recruit the labor market might be compared to the capital still existing in the form of purchasing power, and ready to be applied to any occupation, according as the prospect of profit might determine. In one important respect, however, the analogy fails. Of the capital existing in this disposable form any portion may be applied to any industrial purpose. But of the disposable labor each element—that is to say, each individual laborer—can only choose his employment within certain tolerably well-defined limits. These limits are the limits set by the qualifications required for each branch of trade and the amount of preparation necessary for their acquisition. Take an individual workman whose occupation is still undetermined, he will, according to circumstances, have a narrower or wider field of choice; but in no case will this be co-extensive with the entire range of domestic industry. If he belongs to the class of agricultural laborers, all forms of mere unskilled labor are open to him, but beyond this he is practically shut out from competition. The barrier is his social position and circumstances, which render his education defective, while his means are too narrow to allow of his repairing the defect, or of deferring the return upon his industry till he has qualified himself for a skilled occupation. Mounting a step higher in the industrial scale—to the artisan class, including with them the class of small dealers whose pecuniary position is much upon a par with artisans, here also within certain limits there is complete freedom of choice, but beyond a certain range practical exclusion. The man who is brought up to be an ordinary carpenter, mason, or smith, may go to any of these callings, or a hundred more, according as his taste prompts, or the prospect of remuneration attracts him; but practically he has no power to compete in those higher departments of skilled labor for which a more elaborate education and larger training are necessary, for example, mechanical engineering. Ascend a step higher still, and we find ourselves again in presence of similar limitations: we encounter persons competent to take part in any of the higher skilled industries, but practically excluded from the professions. It is true, indeed, that in none of these cases is the exclusion absolute. The limits imposed are not such as may not be overcome by extraordinary energy, self-denial, and enterprise; and by virtue of these qualities individuals in all classes are escaping every day from the bounds of their original position, and forcing their way into the ranks of those who stand above them. All this, no doubt, is true. But such exceptional phenomena do not affect the substantial truth of our position. What we find, in effect, is, not a whole population competing indiscriminately for all occupations, but a series of industrial layers, superposed on one another, within each of which the various candidates for employment possess a real and effective power of selection, while those occupying the several strata are, for all purposes of effective competition, practically isolated from each other. We may perhaps venture to arrange them in some such order as this: first, at the bottom of the scale there would be the large group of unskilled or nearly unskilled laborers, comprising agricultural laborers, laborers engaged in miscellaneous occupations in towns, or acting in attendance on skilled labor. Secondly, there would be the artisan group, comprising skilled laborers of the secondary order—carpenters, joiners, smiths, masons, shoe-makers, tailors, hatters, etc., etc., with whom might be included the very large class of small retail dealers, whose means and position place them within the reach of the same industrial opportunities as the class of artisans. The third layer would contain producers and dealers of a higher order, whose work would demand qualifications only obtainable by persons of substantial means and fair educational opportunities—for example, civil and mechanical engineers, chemists, opticians, watch-makers, and others of the same industrial grade, in which might also find a place the superior class of retail tradesmen; while above these there would be a fourth, comprising persons still more favorably circumstanced, whose ampler means would give them a still wider choice. This last group would contain members of the learned professions, as well as persons engaged in the various careers of science and art, and in the higher branches of mercantile business. The reader will not understand me as offering here an exhaustive classification of the industrial population. I attempt nothing of the kind; but merely seek to exhibit in rough outline the form which industrial organization, under the actual conditions of modern life, tends to assume; my object being, by putting the fact in a concrete shape, to furnish help toward a more distinct apprehension of the limitations imposed by social circumstances on the free competition of labor than would be obtained from more general statements. As I have already said, I am far from contending for the existence of any hard lines of demarkation between any categories of persons in this country. No doubt the various ranks and classes fade into each other by imperceptible gradations, and individuals from all classes are constantly passing up or dropping down; but while this is so, it is nevertheless true that the average workman, from whatever rank he be taken, finds his power of competition limited for practical purposes to a certain range of occupations, so that, however high the rates of remuneration in those which lie beyond may rise, he is excluded from sharing them. We are thus compelled to recognize the existence of non-competing industrial groups as a feature of our social economy; and this is the fact which I desire here to insist upon. It remains to be considered how this organization of industry is calculated to modify the action of the principle of cost of production.

The reader will remember that there are two distinct sacrifices undergone in the business of production—the sacrifice of the capitalist, and the sacrifice of the laborer. As regards the former, the competition of capital being, as we have seen, effective over the entire industry of each commercial country, it follows that so much of the value of commodities as goes to remunerate the capitalist's sacrifice, and which may be regarded as the "profit fund," will correspond throughout the range of domestic industry with that portion of the cost which falls to the capitalist. The defalcation from the principle of cost occurs not here, but in that other and larger element in the value of commodities which goes to remunerate the laborer. The nature of the failure may be thus described: The exchange of all commodities produced by laborers belonging to the same industrial group, or competing circle, will be governed by the principle of cost—this results necessarily from the fact that competition *is* effective within such groups or circles; but the exchange of commodities produced by laborers belonging to different groups or competing circles will, for the opposite reason, not be governed by this principle. Thus all the products of unskilled labor will exchange for each other in proportion to their costs; as will also all the products of ordinary artisan labor *as among themselves*. But the latter products will not exchange against the former in proportion to their costs, nor will the products of artisan labor, or of unskilled labor, exchange in proportion to their costs against those of the higher industrial groups. The price of a deal table and the price of a common lock will be found to correspond to the sacrifices actually undergone by their producers; or again, the price of a barometer and the price of a watch will be found to correspond to the same conditions; but if we compare the price of either of the latter commodities with that of either of the former, we shall find that the correspondence fails; the prices of the barometer and of the watch will bear a far larger proportion to their respective costs than those of the deal table, or of the common lock, to theirs. If any one questions the fact, the evidence is to be found in the relative remuneration of the producers of the several articles. That remuneration, as I have shown, comes from the price of the commodity in each case; but, while it is in proportion to the relative sacrifices of production in the case of the workmen who are in competition with each other, it is not in proportion to those sacrifices where the workmen are excluded from mutual competition. The result, then, is that the principle of cost of production controls exchange value in the transactions taking place within certain limited industrial areas; while, in the reciprocal dealings of those several areas with one another, its operation fails.

This is the principal modification suffered by cost of production in consequence of the circumstance we are considering. In reality, however, the effects of that state of things are a good deal more complex than would appear from the statement just made; for in that statement account was not taken of the fact that the same commodity is very frequently the product of labor belonging to different industrial circles. For example, a house is mainly produced by masons, brick-layers, carpenters, plasterers, and others, who would all rank in the class of artisans; but a considerable quantity of purely unskilled labor is also employed in attendance upon these, as labor of a higher degree of skill than that of the ordinary artisan is employed in the finishing and decoration of the house. Now suppose a commodity of this kind, the joint production of workmen of different orders, to be exchanged against one produced by workmen belonging to some one industrial group, or to several groups, but in proportions different from those obtaining in the other case, what principle would here govern exchange value, or—to express the conception in a more familiar form—the relative prices of the commodities? Manifestly more than one principle will be engaged in determining the result. So far as the two commodities are the products of workmen in competition with each other, their values will be governed by cost of production, but so far as they proceed from workmen not in mutual competition, they will be governed by that other principle, yet to be ascertained, which governs normal value in the absence of competition. Supposing the commodity with which a house is compared were produced exclusively by the artisan class, the cost principle would be mainly operative in determining the exchange relation; but it would not be entirely so, since a portion, though a small portion, of the house has been produced by workmen not in competition with the producers of the other article. On the other hand, if the comparison were made between a house and a commodity produced either wholly by unskilled labor, or wholly by labor of a degree of skill superior to that of ordinary artisan labor, the relative values would follow, but in a slight degree, the rule of cost of production, being mainly controlled by the principle prevailing in the absence of the conditions which secure the action of cost. This example will serve to show the great complication that arises in the relative values of commodities under the actual conditions of their production. And if we bear in mind that all manufactured commodities are produced from raw materials which are very frequently the product of workmen not in competition with those who per form the manufacturing process, we shall see how widely the range of this sort of complication extends. Still we must not exaggerate its importance. What mainly happens is, that the bulk of the value of each commodity follows one law—say the law of cost, or what we shall afterward find to be the law of reciprocal demand, while a small remaining element is governed by a different principle. Thus, reverting for a moment to a previous illustration, a barometer and a watch are in very large proportion the products of workmen of a high order of skill, and in industrial competition with each other; in a very insignificant degree, of workmen of an inferior order; as, on the other hand, a deal table and a common lock are mainly the products of ordinary artisan labor, though, it may be in some small degree, also of labor not in competition with the labor of artisans. In so far, however, as any portion of the labor employed on the barometer is out of competition with some portion of that employed on the watch, and in so far as the same is true of the labor employed on the other compared articles, to that extent we were not justified in asserting that the commodities in question exchanged, either pair of them, in proportion to their costs of production. Nevertheless, it is certain that our statement was substantially true, since the chief portion, and so much the chief portion as to be nearly the whole, of the labor employed on each pair fulfilled the required condition; and this would govern a corresponding proportion of their values. A similar qualification would be needed in the case of most assertions of a like nature. In strictness, we can seldom say that the values of two commodities are in their whole extent governed by their costs of production: we can only say that they are so mainly, and in their chief elements. In effect the point in question is of little more than theoretic importance. As a point of theory it is proper to notice it, but the circumstance it deals with has little sensible effect upon the facts of exchange.

The mode in which the cost of producing commodities operates in regulating their values has now, I trust, been made tolerably clear. It will probably have been observed, that as I have departed from the current doctrine in my view of the elements of cost, so also have I departed from it in my manner of representing the operation of the law. That law is ordinarily regarded as a principle governing value *universally* wherever it affects value at all— governing, that is to say, the value of certain classes of commodities *in all exchanges*; so that, the conditions of their production being known, the law of their value is supposed to be known, whatever may be the nature or the conditions of production of the commodities against which they are exchanged. For example, the price of calico would commonly be said to be governed by its cost of production, and this would be laid down without any limitation as to the article which might form the other member in the exchange. If, however, the exposition contained in the foregoing pages be sound, this conception of the law can not be correct. For what has there appeared is a tendency in commodities to exchange in proportion to their costs of production *only so far as there exists free competition among their producers*. The exchange, therefore, in proportion to cost would only take place within the limits of the field of free competition; and a commodity produced within this field, but exchanged against one produced by workmen from beyond it, would not in such case exchange in proportion to its cost of production. Supposing, for example, A, B, C, D, E, F, to be commodities, the producers of which are all in free competition with each other, such commodities would exchange among themselves in proportion to their costs. Again, supposing X, Y, Z, to be commodities produced by workmen also in free competition with each other, but excluded from competing with those who had produced A, B, C, D, etc.; here again the values of X, Y, Z, in the exchanges of these commodities against each other would be governed by the principle of cost. But now suppose the exchange to be made of a commodity belonging to the former category against one belonging to the latter—value would in this case be no longer governed by cost of production, inasmuch as there was no longer free competition among those who had produced the commodities exchanged. Now if the reader will recall the description that has been given of the various non-competing groups of which our industrial system is made up, he will perceive that the case last supposed represents no inconsiderable proportion of all the exchanges which take place within such a country as this; and that, therefore, the action of cost of production in regulating value is by no means as extensively prevalent, even within the limits of the same country, as the current theory would lead us to suppose. The same commodity follows the law of cost of production in some exchanges and does not follow it in others; nor is it true that the value of any commodity conforms to the principle of cost in all exchanges. In order that this should happen, effective competition should be established among producers over the entire field of industry—a condition which, I need hardly say, is very far yet from being anywhere fulfilled. The true conception of the law of cost is thus, not of a law governing universally the values of any class of commodities, but that of one governing the values of certain commodities in certain exchanges.

§ 6. In what has gone before, cost of production has been discussed without more than a passing reference to the nature of the elements which compose it. There was no need to discriminate those elements with particularity while we were occupied in establishing the general principle, but the evidence for that principle having now been set forth, it will be desirable to attempt some analysis and characterization of the constituents of cost.

There can not be much difficulty in determining the principal elements of cost of production, once we have firmly seized the fact that, as cost means sacrifice and not reward, so cost of production means the sacrifice involved in production—in the act or acts of rendering certain objects supplied by nature fitted for human purposes, not the beneficial result or return upon such acts. This sacrifice, so soon as industry has passed its most primitive stage, assumes two distinct forms—first, that involved in the physical or mental exertion incident to taking part personally in the work of production, which we may call briefly the sacrifice of "labor;" and, secondly, that involved in supplying the prerequisites of productive operations, or capital— a form of sacrifice which is conveniently expressed by the term "abstinence." These are the principal kinds of sacrifices involved in productive industry; but there is also a third, the liability, namely, of producers to certain evils over and above the usual and calculable sacrifices incident to their work, which we may call "risk." There is no reason in the nature of things that these several sacrifices should not be undergone by the same person, that is to say, that the same person should not be at once laborer and capitalist, and also incur all the risk of the industrial operation; and in point of fact this arrangement has place more or less in every country, and in some countries, especially those in which peasant proprietorship prevails, to a great extent. In

England, however, and in all the non-agricultural industry of most civilized countries, the sacrifices of labor and abstinence are, for the most part, undergone by distinct classes, who are named, accordingly, laborers and capitalists. The sacrifice of risk, on the other hand, falls on both classes of producers alike, though the nature of the risk differs according as it affects one or the other. Affecting the capitalist, it is risk to his property; affecting the laborer, it is risk to his bodily and mental faculties or life, but in either case it is an element of cost; being a real sacrifice incurred by a producer, and demanding consequently a corresponding compensation in the value of the product.[11]

Our analysis, then, of cost of production resolves it into three principal elements, which, I may remark, are also *ultimate* elements[12]—Labor, Abstinence, and Risk; the first, under the prevailing industrial arrangements of this and other civilized countries, borne by the laborer, in that enlarged sense of the term in which "laborer" includes all who take a personal part in the business of production; the second by the capitalist; the third falling upon laborer and capitalist alike. A few remarks on each of these elements will suffice for my present purpose.

Considering labor as an element of cost of production, the principal remark that seems called for is that, in estimating it in this character, three circumstances, and three circumstances only, must be taken account of— namely, the duration of the exertion, the degree of its severity or irksomeness, and the risk or liability to injury of any kind attending it. As commodities differ greatly more in the duration of the exertion, or the quantity of the labor required for their production, than in the severity of this labor or the risk attending it, the former is obviously the most important circumstance in the case, and it was to it alone that Ricardo, in his analysis of cost, had regard; but manifestly his exposition was in this respect defective. The labor employed in producing different commodities differs in severity and in liability to accident as well as in mere quantity, and, in proportion as it is more severe or more liable to accident, implies, other things being the same, a greater sacrifice, and therefore a larger cost. This greater sacrifice will require corresponding compensation, which, as in other cases, can only be furnished from the value of the product. Commodities, accordingly, will exchange—if we confine our attention to the labor element of cost—not simply in proportion to the quantity of labor employed in their production, but in proportion to this multiplied by the severity of the labor or the risk attending it. When, however, we have taken account of quantity, irksomeness, and risk, we have taken account of every incident in virtue of which labor is an element of cost of production, and affects through this principle the value of commodities.

It will be observed that in the brief analysis just given I have not taken any account of skill as an incident of labor entering into the cost of production. In making this omission, I have no doubt I shall be considered by many to have omitted a principal element of the case. Nevertheless, I must maintain that skill, as skill, is no part of the cost of production, and I add, that no article is dearer than another simply in virtue of the skill bestowed upon it. Let me explain. Skill, I say, is no element of cost, but it may be, and generally is, an indication of that which is an element of cost—namely, the sacrifice, whether in the form of labor or abstinence, undergone in acquiring the skill. Now, so far as skill is the product of such sacrifice, it undoubtedly represents an element of the cost of production; but the point to be attended to is, that the addition thus made to the cost of production is in proportion, not to the skill, but to the sacrifice necessary to the acquisition of the skill. As a matter of fact, the products of most kinds of skilled labor exchange against those of unskilled in a proportion much more favorable to the former than cost of production, as I have defined the doctrine, would prescribe. But this does not prove that skill is an element of cost; because it will be found that, where the products of skilled labor command these high terms of exchange, the conditions of production are not those in which cost of production would govern value; in other words, the result in question only occurs where skilled labor represents a monopoly. If we desire evidence of the powerlessness of skill, as such, to affect the value of commodities, we have only to consider the very low prices which many works of the highest literary and scientific excellence fetch, as compared with products of a far lower degree of skill. The eminent skill embodied in such works does not prevent their selling at a price far below their cost of production, as measured by the prices of commodities representing skill of a different order; and if in other instances the products of skill command prices far above what the law of cost would prescribe, no more is this elevated value due to the skill which such products represent, but to the circumstances which limit the possession of this skill to a small number of persons as compared with the demand for their services.[13]

The true relation between skill and value may be expressed in the following propositions:

First, skill, as skill, produces no effect upon value; in other words, commodities do not under any circumstances exchange for each other in proportion to the degree of skill bestowed upon them. Secondly, skill, though in itself inoperative on value, nevertheless affects it indirectly in two distinct ways: first, where competition is effective among producers, through the cost which must be undergone in acquiring the skill—in such cases the value of skilled products will, *cæteris paribus*, exceed that of unskilled by the amount of the normal returns upon this cost; and, secondly, in the absence of effective competition, through the principle of monopoly, by limiting the number of competitors in skilled occupations, and so acting on the supply of skilled products. In either of these ways skill may raise value; but, as skill, that is to say, in virtue of its own excellence, whether measured by the standard of utility or of artistic merit, it is powerless for this result.

There is, indeed, a mode of speaking sanctioned by the language of some economists, and much in favor with those who seek to justify in all things existing industrial arrangements, which implies that skill, as such, is a source

111

of value, and that high or low wages and prices are to be explained by reference simply to the results of the skill which services or commodities embody. For example, we constantly hear it said, in reply to complaints of wages being unduly low in certain industries, that this must be so, inasmuch as the services remunerated by these low wages are of little worth, while the higher wages obtained in others are explained by reference to the high worth of the services rendered by the workmen employed. Employers, we are told, can not afford to pay any class of workmen more than their services are worth. Now, what is the standard of "worth" here adopted? There would seem to be but two standards possible; first that furnished by the exchange itself: in other words, the "worth" of a service may be measured by the money it commands. According to this conception of "worth," the statement that wages are low because the services they remunerate are of little worth, and high because the worth of the services is high, merely means that wages are high or low because they are high or low, which does not much elucidate the problem; while, in the assertion that employers can not pay their workmen more than their services are worth, the point at issue is formally begged, since—the standard of worth being the actual terms of the exchange—it amounts to saying that employers can not afford to pay their workmen more than they actually do pay them, which is just what the complainants deny. In truth, however, though this is the standard of worth upon which those who use the argument I am considering would, if pushed, probably rely, their language really suggests something more than this—the idea, namely, that industrial "worth" is something varying with the utility embodied in the services, or, what comes nearly to the same thing, with the skill which is productive of this utility. Some such sense as this must be assigned to their words if they are not to be taken as expressing barren truisms; but in any such sense, the statements in question are wholly unfounded. No such connection between wages (it will be understood that I speak now of *comparative* wages) and the utility or skillfulness of the services rendered exists as the language assumes, any more than a similar connection can be made out between these qualities and the prices of commodities. The true connection is not with either utility or skill, but, where competition is effective, with cost of production, and in the absence of effective competition, with monopoly, more or less qualified, and acting through supply and demand. To return from this partial digression, we find labor, as an element of cost of production, measurable by reference to three of its incidents, and to three of its incidents only—1st, the duration of the exertion, or the quantity of labor; 2d, its severity or irksomeness; and 3d, the risk attending it. In whatever other qualities various sorts of labor may differ, unless so far as these are indications of onerous effort expended, they are no portion of the labor element of cost, and must be regarded as irrelevant to the question now in hand.

The term "abstinence" is the name given to the sacrifice involved in the advance of capital. As to the nature of this sacrifice, it is mainly of a negative kind; consisting chiefly in the deprivation or postponement of enjoyment, implied in the fact of parting with our wealth so far at least as concerns our present power of commanding it. The term, indeed, would imply that the sacrifice is wholly negative; but I am inclined to include in it a certain small positive element, namely, that low degree of risk which is never absent from the advance of capital. That some degree of risk always accompanies the act in question is evident from the nature of the case, since it implies either the trusting of one's wealth to other persons, or, where it is employed by the owner himself in productive industry, the putting of it, with a view to future results, into forms not capable of being directly converted to his uses. It will be more convenient, I think, to consider this slight and inevitable risk, which is always present where abstinence is exercised for economic ends, as an incident of that sacrifice, than as a substantive element of cost to be associated with "risk" as I have defined it in that character. I shall, therefore, so understand it, and shall accordingly define "abstinence" as the act of abstaining from the personal use of wealth with a view to employing it in productive industry, combined with that low degree of risk inevitably attaching to every such act.

This being the nature of abstinence, the question will suggest itself how far it may be properly considered as an industrial sacrifice needing a stimulus to its exercise in the form of specific reward, and to be co-ordinated with labor in an analysis of the sacrifices of production. It must be admitted that its connection with production is not so intimate as that of labor, since capital, however it may augment the efficiency of industry, is not absolutely indispensable to it. What we have to deal with, however, is not industry, as it may exist among savages or in very primitive communities, but industry as it exists in civilized countries; and to industry in this sense, to industry as it must be carried on if the populations now inhabiting civilized countries are to continue to exist, capital is absolutely indispensable. But, if so, then abstinence, the act by which capital comes into existence, must be regarded as a necessary condition toward the efficacious prosecution of industrial pursuits.

But is it properly a sacrifice? a sacrifice which needs, in order that it be undergone, the prospect of a specific reward? To put the question in another form, are profits to be placed on the same line with wages in an analysis of the economy of production? As to the economic foundation of wages, the case is very clear. Wages are necessary, first, to support the laborer, and secondly, in a free community, to induce him to work. Capital has no need to be fed and clothed, but, in order to its existence, there must be an adequate motive offered to the owners of wealth to induce them to employ it in this way. At present this inducement is found in profit; and the question to be considered is, whether, consistently with the maintenance of capital, this inducement can be dispensed with. There are those who think it may, who hold that capital may be maintained without any deduction in favor of the capitalist from the value of the product which results from its use, and which they would assign in its entirety to those who take a personal, not to say a manual, part in the business of production.[14] Assuming that those who take this view understand the process by which capital exists and grows, we must suppose them to regard the act of abstaining from present enjoyment as in itself agreeable, and, coupled with the risk which always attends abstinence when practiced for industrial purposes, as constituting in some inscrutable way, irrespective of the gains which flow from it, its own reward; so that, the present inducement being removed, the accumulation and increase of capital would go on with unabated force. It is scarcely necessary to remark on the perfect gratuitousness, not to say preposterousness, of such a notion. It is true, indeed, that abstinence may be for the rich, with whom its exercise rarely implies any sensible encroachment on customary comforts and luxuries, and still less on necessaries, but a trifling sacrifice; but even in their case, when practiced with a view to industrial investment, it means, as we know, risk also; which is certainly a sacrifice great enough not to be undergone without the clear prospect of adequate compensation. And even if we grant that a reservation of a portion of their wealth from immediate consumption would still be practiced by prudent and well-to-do people, even though the specific reward which now attends it were taken away (since there would still be the desire to provide for the future), it does not follow that what was thus reserved would necessarily go to assist productive industry; nay, it is pretty certain that this would not be its destination, since it might with much less risk be converted into gold or silver, and hoarded. Even for those, therefore, with whom the sacrifice of abstinence would be slightest, a specific reward would be needed to secure its exercise. But with those who are not included among the rich, with that great class of dealers and producers, from the ranks of unskilled labor upward, whose aggregate savings form the main support of the capital of civilized states, abstinence, far from being a slight, is always a serious, and often a very severe sacrifice. The mere act of resisting the temptation to present enjoyment, and of repressing the urgent requirements of the moment, often constitutes in itself a severe discipline, and demands for its accomplishment no little strength of character; and to this has to be added the inevitable risk incident to industrial investment. Even as matters stand at present, the inducement is found for many to be all too weak; but take away this inducement, exclude the prospect of future gain as the compensation for present trials, and what reason have we to suppose that such trials will be undergone?

I seem to be laboring to prove a truism; and, indeed, I am inclined to attribute the opinion I am combating rather to blank ignorance, or, at the least, profound mystification, on the part of those who hold it, respecting the nature and source of capital, than to deliberate acceptance of the premises on which alone it can logically rest. That the conversion of wealth to the purposes of productive industry, in other words, the creation of capital,[15] involves self-denial, is what probably has never crossed their imaginations: much more likely, if they have speculated on its origin at all, it would be connected in their minds with the issue of paper money and other operations of banking. But, however unsettled for them be the question as to the origin of capital, on one point they have no hesitation or doubt. Governments, it is a fixed article in their economic creed, have an unlimited command over capital, and may possess themselves of it at all times, in any quantity required. Where such notions respecting capital prevail, it is natural enough that profits and interest should appear superfluous institutions. Unfortunately for the speculations in question, capital is not the creation of Banks, nor has Government any means of obtaining it, except through the crude expedient of taking it from those to whom it belongs. Unfortunately, again, the process by which capital is brought into existence, maintained, and increased, is, for the great mass of those who take part in the work, a really painful one. Under such circumstances compensation and reward for those who perform this function is plainly an indispensable condition to the effectual prosecution of industry—a consideration which justifies us in co-ordinating abstinence with labor among the elements of cost of production, as we co-ordinate profits with wages in relation to the value of the product.

Perhaps it may be well here to guard against a possible misapprehension of the doctrine just laid down. It has been assumed in the argument that capital is indispensable to the prosecution of systematic industry; and the act, creative of capital, saving, parsimony, or abstinence, has been characterized as a sacrifice distinct from labor. It must not be supposed from this that there is any economic necessity, or any economic reason whatever, at least derivable from the arguments just used, that capitalists should form a distinct class from laborers. The distinctness of the sacrifices constitutes no ground for assigning them to different sets of persons. The same person may both labor and abstain, and, performing the double sacrifice, become entitled to the double reward. So far, indeed, am I from thinking that there is any thing in this combination of the parts of capitalist and laborer in one person which militates against the true economy of productive industry, that it is precisely in this direction that, for my part, I am disposed to look for an escape from the growing embarrassments and difficulties that now beset the relations of capital and labor. But this is a point the consideration of which will more properly fall within another part of this work.

Another possible ambiguity it may be well here to clear up. As was intimated just now, the sacrifice involved in a given act of abstinence is very different in the case of different persons. A rich man abstains from the consumption of his superfluous wealth, and is scarcely conscious, perhaps quite unconscious, of having suffered any deprivation whatever: his surplus income goes to his capital account, which continues to grow, while his expenditure remains precisely as before. On the other hand, the same or a much smaller amount of wealth reserved from personal consumption by an artisan or a small tradesman will frequently demand the most rigorous self-denial. The same individual, too, feels very differently the pains of abstinence at different stages of his career—in the struggling outset and at the successful close. And it is similar with labor. The laborious effort fitted to produce a given result does not represent the same sacrifice for different people: it is one thing for the strong, another for the weak; one for the trained workman, another for the raw beginner. This being so, the question arises—How are such differences to be dealt with in computing the cost of production? Are we to take account of what is personal and peculiar to the actual producers, and regard the cost of the commodity as higher or lower according as it has been produced by a weak or a strong workman, or by capital the result of painful or of painless saving? The answer must be in the negative. The sacrifices to be taken account of, and which govern exchange value, are, not those undergone by A, B, or C, but the average sacrifices undergone by the class of laborers or capitalists to which the producers of the commodity belong. A few remarks will enable us to make this clear.

What at bottom maintains the connection between value and cost of production is, it must always be remembered, the power of choice residing in laborers and capitalists to decide between different occupations. Now what is it determines the choice? No doubt the prospects of the pursuit, the remuneration being compared with the sacrifice. But what sacrifice? Plainly the sacrifice about to be undergone by the particular workman or capitalist who has to make the choice. Each takes account of the incidents of the course proposed as it bears upon himself, and considers how it stands in the comparison with others equally open to him. The conclusion he arrives at on this point determines his decision. Through a process of this kind every laborer and capitalist, either personally himself, or vicariously through a parent or other adviser, passes. Carried on over any given field of industrial competition, it is evident the result of this proceeding must be not to bring the remuneration of each of the individuals comprised within it into conformity with the sacrifice which each undergoes, but to establish this conformity among the aggregates of those engaged in the several competing occupations; so that the total remuneration falling to each branch of industry shall bear the same proportion to the total sacrifices undergone in that branch as the total remuneration falling to any other within the same field bears to the sacrifices undergone in that other. The total remuneration falling to any branch of industry, however, consists of the total value of the commodities proceeding from it. This value, therefore, will bear the same proportion to the sacrifices undergone in producing it, as the value proceeding from any other industry within the same field of competition bears to the sacrifices of which it is the result. It follows that the relation which competition establishes between cost and value is one, not between the value of particular commodities and the sacrifices of the individual or individuals who have produced each such commodity, but one between commodities taken as sorts and their cost of production. We can not, for example, assert that a particular pair of shoes will exchange against a particular coat in proportion to the sacrifices undergone respectively by the shoe-maker and the tailor in the actual ease; but we may assert that, within a given field of competition, shoes, as one sort of commodity, will exchange against coats as another in this proportion. The costs, therefore, to which the values of particular commodities correspond are not the particular sacrifices undergone in producing each commodity, but the average sacrifice undergone in producing each sort of commodity. We may, therefore, state broadly, that differences in the sacrifices incident to production, whether of labor or of abstinence, which are due to peculiarities either in the physical, mental, or social circumstances of individuals, are to be excluded from consideration in estimating cost of production. What we have to do with is, not individual sacrifice, but the average sacrifice of each industrial class.

This point being cleared up, we can have no difficulty in seeing how cost in its principal elements is to be computed. In the case of labor, the cost of producing a given commodity will be represented by the number of average laborers employed in its production—regard at the same time being had to the severity of the work and the degree of risk it involves—multiplied by the duration of their labors. In that of abstinence, the principle is analogous: the sacrifice will be measured by the quantity of wealth abstained from, taken in connection with the risk incurred, and multiplied by the duration of the abstinence.

§ 7. We have now treated the subject of normal value, so far as it is regulated by the principle of cost of production. But, as I stated in the opening of this chapter, the phenomenon in question is by no means confined to cases in which the conditions necessary to the action of cost of production exist. The essence of normal value, as I then remarked, is a tendency in the exchanging proportions of commodities to gravitate toward a central point, and this tendency is observable in departments of exchange where effective competition among exchanging producers has no place. The most important example of this kind is furnished by international trade. As between the producers in different nations, whether laborers or capitalists, there is no effective competition, nothing, therefore, to secure that industrial rewards in different countries shall be brought into correspondence with industrial sacrifices; nor, consequently, that international values shall correspond with cost of production. Nevertheless international values, or, let us say, the relative prices of the products of different nations, do not vary at random irrespective of rule or measure, but exhibit precisely the same tendency to gravitate toward a central point as is manifested in those exchanges which are governed by cost of production. A less striking and hitherto, so far as I know, unnoticed, example of the same kind meets us in domestic trade. As I have pointed out, cost of production does not control value universally even within the limits of a single country: in respect to a considerable class of exchanges—all those, namely, which take place between what I have called non-competing industrial groups—its action fails. Yet not the less we observe here, as in international trade, the phenomenon of normal value. The exchanges between the non-competing groups—or, let us say, the relative prices of the products of such non-competing groups—though unamenable to the law of cost, are not without a controlling force which restrains their fluctuations and guides them toward a normal result. This is the phenomenon with which we have now to deal; and the question to be considered is the nature of the force or forces which, in such cases, come into play.

Fortunately the problem has already, in principle at least, been solved for us by Mr. Mill. Mr. Mill has not, indeed, carried his solution beyond the case of international values; but his doctrine is manifestly applicable to all cases in which groups of producers, excluded from reciprocal industrial competition, exchange their products. Such cases, as I have shown, occur in domestic trade in the exchanges between those non-competing industrial groups of which I have spoken. The principle, therefore, which operates in international trade must operate here; and little more needs to be done, to complete the theory of this part of our subject, than to point the application of Mr. Mill's doctrine to this strictly parallel case.

That doctrine may be thus briefly stated: International values are governed by the reciprocal demand of commercial countries for each other's productions, or, more precisely, by the demand of each country for the productions of all other countries as against the demand of all other countries for what it produces; the result of this play of forces being that, on the whole, the exports of each country discharge its liabilities (of which the principal are on account of its imports) toward all other countries.[16] Whatever be the exchanging proportions—or, let us say, whatever be the state of relative prices—in different countries which is requisite to secure this result, those exchanging proportions, that state of relative prices, will become normal— will furnish the central point toward which the fluctuations of international prices will gravitate, the rule to which in the long run they will conform. Such is the law governing international values, called by Mr. Mill "the Equation of International Demand." What we have now to consider is the mode in which this principle operates in the case of the non-competing groups of domestic trade.

And first, in what sense are we to understand "reciprocal demand" as applied to non-competing industrial groups? Manifestly, in conformity with the analogy of the international case, as the demand of each group for the products of all other groups compared with the demand of all other groups for what this group produces. How, again, are we to measure such demand? Again I say, in conformity with the same analogy, by the quantity of the products of each group available for the purchase of the products of other groups; while the products of other groups available for the purchase of the products of any given group will measure their demand for the products of that group. Lastly, how are we to understand the "Equation of Demand," as applied to non-competing groups? Still following the international analogy, I reply, as such a state of exchanging proportions among the products of the various groups—or, let us say, as such a state of relative prices among such products as shall enable that portion of the products of each group which is applied to the purchase of the products of all other groups to discharge its liabilities toward those other groups. The two cases thus run strictly on all-fours, and the play of the forces in action is in all respects the same. As in international trade an increased demand for the products of other countries will, other things being equal, affect international values—or, let us say, affect the relative prices of the products of different countries—unfavorably for the country whose demand is increased; and as, again, the converse of this condition, an increased demand by other countries for the products of a given country, will operate in the contrary direction; so it will be in the exchanges which take place between non-competing domestic groups. What-ever increases the demand of a given group for the products of outside, that is to say non-competing, industries, or (what comes to the same thing) what-ever increases the supply of its products available for the purchase of the products of such industries, will, other things being the same, depress the prices of its products in relation to the prices of the products of the indus-tries against which they are exchanged, and *vicè versa*; while whatever increases the demand of the outside industries for the products of a given group will have the contrary effect, and will raise the level of its prices in relation to those of the non-competing groups with which it trades, and *vicè versa*. The relative position, commercially considered, of each group may thus be affected either by an increase or diminution of its own products not consumed within the group, or by an increase or diminution of the products of other groups, so far as those products are disposable for the purchase of the products of the group in question. Such is the nature of "reciprocal demand," and of its mode of action as between the non-competing groups of domestic industry. As the reader will observe, it is simply "supply and demand" taken twice over, first in the sale and then in the purchase, or, rather, we may describe it as Supply and Demand contemplated at once from both sides of a completed exchange.

But it may not be at once apparent how a principle of this character is fitted to accomplish the result ascribed to it—that of determining *normal*, as distinguished from temporary or market, value. As I have remarked, Reciprocal Demand is merely duplicate Supply and Demand regarded in its full significance; but Supply and Demand, as we are most familiar with their action, are, in their relation to prices, merely proximate agencies, governing indeed the fluctuations of the market, but themselves controlled by forces lying deeper in the economy of production. How then does it happen that, in the cases under consideration, those agencies are capable of doing more than this—capable of determining, not simply the fluctuations of the market, but the rule to which, in the long run, the fluctuations of the market conform?

The answer to this question is to be found in the circumstances which give stability to Reciprocal Demand in the class of exchanges we are now considering. Reciprocal Demand, or, if the reader prefers it, Supply and Demand, in relation to a particular commodity, or even to a considerable number of commodities, may, as we know, vary in almost any conceivable degree, and with great rapidity. But when we consider them as affecting aggregates of transactions carried on between limited bodies of producers—for example, between independent nations, or between non-competing industrial groups—the case is very different; and the limits within which variation is possible are in fact pretty strictly determined; for in this case the measure of the aggregate demand of each trading body will be the total of its productions, and the measure of its demand for the productions of the bodies with which it trades will be the proportion of its total production which it desires to apply to the purchase of the productions of those bodies. Now, in the absence of any great changes in the conditions of productive industry, and of legislation specially contrived for this purpose, neither the aggregate production of a community nor the proportion of its means employed in interchanges with other communities can easily undergo on a sudden serious variation. The total production will depend on the nature and extent of its resources; and the proportion employed in external trading on the comparative character of those resources as they stand related to those of the communities with which it trades. These, indeed, are not circumstances which can be regarded as absolutely fixed. On the contrary, the conditions of productive industry over the best portion of the industrial world are and have for long been pretty steadily progressive. But the progress, though steady, has in general been slow. Sudden changes, at least on a scale large enough to effect great aggregates of transactions, but rarely occur; and further, what is pertinent to our purpose, where important improvements in productive industry do happen, they are seldom confined to a single community, but, after an interval more or less brief, are in general shared by other communities, so that the relative positions of the various trading bodies are in the end but slightly affected. It follows that the demand of such bodies, however it may vary in respect to particular commodities, can not easily as an aggregate undergo any great or sudden change; while their reciprocal demand for each other's productions, which expresses their relative industrial condition, will be still less liable to serious or abrupt disturbance. Here, then, we find the conditions fitted to produce that stability of exchanging relations which is implied in the term "normal value." While the prices of particular commodities may fluctuate indefinitely in international as in other trade, the same possibility does not exist for the prices of aggregates of commodities exchanged by definite groups of producers, such as independent nations, or the non-competing sections in domestic industry. The limits to such fluctuations are set in the limited purchasing power, incident to the limited productive power, at any given time possessed by such trading groups. It is in this way that a normal relation arises in the terms of the transactions carried on, and that a central point is furnished toward which the fluctuations of the market gravitate, performing in such trade the same function discharged under a *régime* of competition by the principle of cost.

Cost of Production and Reciprocal Demand in the sense explained, it thus appears, perform in certain circumstances similar economic offices. It remains now to point out an important difference in their modes of action and in the character of the results which flow from them. They each, as I have said, furnish a centre about which market values gravitate; but there is this difference between the two cases: The centre furnished by Cost of Production stands related to the fluctuations of the individual commodity; that supplied by Reciprocal Demand to the average fluctuations of considerable aggregates of commodities. A reduction in the cost of producing a hat will lower its price, but will have no tendency to affect the price of any other thing. But an alteration in the reciprocal demand of two trading nations will act upon the price, not of any commodity in particular, but of every commodity which enters into the trade. What such an alteration necessitates is a change in the *average* terms on which the trade is carried on; but it decides nothing as to the details by which the required average shall be attained and maintained. This is determined, not by international demand, but by those circumstances in the internal industries of each country which regulate in each the relative prices of its products. And similarly in the interchanges of non-competing domestic groups, what the reciprocal demand of the groups determines is the average relative level of prices within each group; the distribution of price among the individual products being regulated by the cause which governs value within it, namely cost of production.

The net result would seem to be this: Reciprocal International Demand determines the average level of prices throughout the entire trade of each commercial country in relation to that prevailing in other countries in commercial connection with it. Reciprocal Domestic Demand determines certain minor relative averages extending over classes of articles, the products of non-competing industrial groups; while Cost of Production acts upon particular commodities, and, in each case, within the range of industrial competition, determines their relative prices. The actual price, therefore, of any given commodity will, it is evident, be the composite result of the combined action of these several agencies.

Another distinction needs to be noticed between Reciprocal Demand and Cost of Production in their operation upon normal value. The former is, on the whole, far more steady and equable in its action than the latter. The reason is plain. Changes in cost of production depend mainly on the progress of the industrial arts, and this has for some time been and, we may perhaps assume, is likely for a long time to continue to be, remarkably rapid.

Thus we find in the course of the present century an immense reduction in the costs of producing a large number of articles of general consumption, accompanied by a corresponding reduction in their value. On the other hand, changes in reciprocal demand are chiefly due to moral, social, and political causes, operating on a scale large enough to affect the relative positions of considerable bodies of men. Such changes are necessarily of slow accomplishment; and consequently the variations in value which result from them are rarely of a striking character, and in general proceed so slowly that they can seldom be perceived unless the comparison be made between prices taken at periods separated by considerable intervals of time. Still such changes do occur, and international values, as well as the corresponding class of values in domestic trade, respond to them. For example, I think we may assume that the adoption of free trade by England has improved her international position in the trade of the world. I do not refer to the extension of her trade, which, as all the world knows, has been enormous, but to the terms on which it is carried on. A given exertion of English industry will now command in the exchange with foreign countries the product of a larger exertion of foreign industry than formerly. In the domestic sphere, probably the most potent agency affecting reciprocal demand is the progress of popular education. Supposing, for example, that the system of primary education now being established in this country proves as successful as the friends of education desire; and supposing again, and more particularly, that effective provision is made in it for facilitating the ascent of promising boys from the lower to the higher educational levels, I think we may with some confidence predict that the movement will issue in a considerable change in the relative prices of certain classes of commodities in this country; nor can we have much difficulty in perceiving what will be the general direction of the change. Plainly the effect will be to augment the number of skilled workmen in relation to the unskilled, and of highly skilled workmen in relation to workmen possessing skill of the more common sorts. The social wall of partition which now divides the non-competing groups will to a large extent be broken down, and many of those occupying the lower levels will take advantage of the breach to press into those above them. The result will be a change in the reciprocal demand of the several groups. The demand of the groups representing the higher sorts of industrial skill will increase relatively to that of the groups representing the lower; or, to put the same point in a different form, the supply of the products of the former groups will increase relatively to that of the products of the latter. The inevitable consequence must be a change in relative prices unfavorable to the higher, and in a corresponding degree favorable to the lower sorts, of skilled industry. In a word, the qualified monopolies resting upon social conditions which now exist will be still further qualified: the range of competition will be enlarged; and, just in proportion as these results are attained, relative prices, and with them relative wages, will be made to approximate, more closely than at present, to the rule of cost. We may illustrate the case by the state of things in new colonies. There, owing to causes precisely similar to those which the educational movement is tending to develop here—owing, that is to say, to the great equality of conditions prevailing among the industrial population—the coarser kinds of labor and the lower sorts of skill are not merely positively, but comparatively, in relation to the finer and higher sorts, far more highly remunerated than they are at present with us. The explanation is that which has just been given: competition has there a wider range; and wherever this is so, prices and remuneration will represent more truly the actual sacrifices undergone by producers.

Notes

1 For the precise sense in which these words are used the reader is referred to *ante* pp. 40, 41.

2 See chap. v. of this Part.

3 I have adopted the term from M. Cherbuliez's excellent work, "Précis de la Science Économique."

4 "Principles of Political Economy," book iii., chap. iv., § 1, 4, 5.

5 Ibid., book iii., chap. vi., § 1.

6 The same argument, in principle, will be found in the sixth volume of Tooke and Newmarch's "History of Prices," part vii., § 14.

7 See "Work and Wages," p. 19.

8 I cannot resist quoting the sentence which follows: "But we see how cheap labor at the command of our competitors [continental capitalist employers] seems to exercise the same enervating influence as the delights of Capua on the soldiers of Hannibal" (p. 142). To which this, from the *Times's* money article, may serve as a pendant: "It must be borne in mind that no discovery of fresh supplies [of coal], either in Europe or America, would cause any decisive benefit, because the present difficulty in those parts of the world is not from want of coal, but from want of labor. . . . The East is the only quarter *where labor is untrammeled*; and it would be interesting to the English public to learn, as far as the coal question is concerned, why, in a British settlement, where labor and material are both in abundance, nothing can be accomplished to mitigate an evil which promises to become one of the most serious ever inflicted upon the industry of civilized nations." It is not clear whether the evil deprecated is the scarcity of coal or the high price of British labor; but, from the point of view both of the *Times* and of Mr. Brassey, these would both be evils of the same order.

9 I say his "commodity," not his "service." The grounds for not including labor and commodities in the same category, in an exposition of the theory of value, will be found stated further on (part ii., chap. i.).

10 "Political economists say that capital sets toward the most profitable trades, and that it rapidly leaves the less profitable and non-paying trades. But in ordinary countries this is a slow process, and some persons, who want to have ocular demonstration of abstract truths, have been inclined to doubt it because they could not see it. In England, however, the process would be visible enough if you could only see the books of the bill-brokers and the bankers. Their bill-cases, as a rule, are full of the bills drawn in the most profitable trades, and *cæteris paribus* and in comparison empty of those drawn in the less profitable. If the iron trade ceases to be as profitable as usual, less iron is sold; the fewer the sales the fewer the bills; and in

consequence the number of iron bills in Lombard Street is diminished. On the other hand, if in consequence of a bad harvest the corn trade becomes on a sudden profitable, immediately 'corn bills' are created in great numbers, and if good, are discounted in Lombard Street. Thus English capital runs as surely and instantly where it is most wanted, and where there is most to be made of it, as water runs to find its level."—"Lombard Street," p. 13, by WALTER BAGEHOT.

11 In the usual exposition of the doctrine of cost of production the only risk taken account of is that incurred by the capitalist; but this is merely a consequence of that habit of contemplating the work of production exclusively from the capitalist's stand-point, of which I have already spoken.

12 As I understand the word, "an ultimate element" in the subject-matter of any science is either an element which in the actual state of knowledge does not admit of being farther resolved, or one the resolution of which belongs to some other department of knowledge. In this sense labor, abstinence, and risk are ultimate elements in Political Economy, since, though they all admit of being traced to prior conditions and so "explained," the task of performing this process falls within the province of other sciences. In what sense profits and wages can, in any case, be considered *ultimate* elements of cost I am at a loss to understand."

13 The reader will observe that the doctrine here laid down as to the relation of skill to the value of commodities and, as depending on this, to the relative remuneration of services, relates to skill of different kinds as existing in the different departments of industry. *Within the limits of the same trade or profession* differences of skill will, in general, under free competition, be accompanied with corresponding differences of remuneration. What the capitalist employing labor looks to is not the labor, but the result; and, consequently, where two inferior workmen only produce the same result as one of superior skill, it will be worth his while to pay the latter double what he could afford to pay either of the former. Relative wages, therefore, *within the same occupation*, will, where competition prevails, be, in general, pretty accurately adjusted to the different degrees of skill: *in different occupations*—and it is only with these, as furnishing the occasion of exchange, that a theory of value has to do—they will be affected by skill only in the manner pointed out in the text.

14 The language of some of the manifestoes of the International justifies this representation; but I argue the question throughout as if it was only proposed to deprive the capitalist of his profit.

15 "Parsimony, and not industry, is the immediate cause of the increase of capital. Industry, indeed, provides the subject which parsimony accumulates. But whatever industry might acquire, if parsimony did not save and store up, the capital would never be the greater."—*Wealth of Nations*, McCULLOCH's edition, p. 149.

16 As the doctrine is ordinarily stated, the exports of each country are said to balance its imports, but, as I shall hereafter show, this mode of stating it is not accurate. See *post*, part iii., chap. iii.

Part 2

DISTRIBUTION THEORY

23

Extracts from

AN INQUIRY INTO THE PRINCIPLES OF THE DISTRIBUTION OF WEALTH

William Thompson

Source: William Thompson, *An Inquiry into the Principles of the Distribution of Wealth Most Conducive to Human Happiness; Applied to the Newly Proposed System or Voluntary Equality of Wealth*, London: Longman, Hurst, Rees, Orme, Brown, Green, and Wheatley and Adlard, 1824, pp. 6–20, 24–28, 144–51, 173–8

SECTION 1

Wealth is produced by labor: no other ingredient but labor makes any object of desire an object of wealth. Labor is the sole universal measure, as well as the characteristic distinction, of wealth.

A few illustrations will perhaps be sufficient to demonstrate this proposition, whether as applying to articles the unaided production of nature, or to those in which the agency of man is alone conspicuous. But first let us state what is conceived to be a just definition of wealth; in the support of which all our illustrations will terminate.

The word, *wealth*, signifies "that portion of the physical materials or means of enjoyment which is afforded by the labor and knowledge of man turning to use the animate or in-animate materials or productions of nature."

Perhaps it may be useful to bear in mind in more compendious, if not as accurate terms, that wealth is "any object of desire produced by labor."

Value in exchange is not necessary, though it almost always attaches, to the idea of wealth: for small communities have been rich and happy by labor in common, without any exchanges. Would not woollen cloth be wealth though every man made his own coat? Without value in exchange, an article, ever so much an object of desire to him that owns it, and produced by ever so much of his labor, can have no marketable value: it will not in a market be exposed for sale to those who have no desire for it: but that does not make it the less

127

an object of wealth to him who desired it because it was useful, and who wisely employed himself in its fabrication for his own use.

Without labor there is no wealth. Labor is its distinguishing attribute. The agency of nature constitutes nothing an object of wealth: its energies are exerted altogether equally and in common, in the production of all the means of enjoyment or desire, whether objects of wealth or not objects of wealth. Labor is the *sole* parent of wealth.

National wealth is nothing more than the aggregate of the individual masses of the matter of wealth.

Land, air, heat, light, the electric fluid, men, horses, water, *as such*, are equally unentitled to the appellation of wealth. They may be objects of desire, of happiness; but, till touched by the transforming hand of labor, they are not wealth. Of these, air, heat, light, the electric fluid, and frequently water, though objects of desire and utility, even of necessity, not only to health, but to the continuance of life, are not objects of wealth. Why so? Because it requires no *labor* to produce them, to gather them together for use, to enjoy them. They exist in such quantities, and are used and enjoyed with so little exertion, some of them requiring—as air, light, and heat—a positive exertion for the exclusion of their operation upon us, that no sort of labor is necessary to gratify our desires for them. Droves of horses or horned cattle abounding in regions thinly peopled, are not objects of wealth any more than the air or light. There are more of them than are wanting for use: no human exertion has produced them: whoever will employ the labor necessary to appropriate any of them, becomes their owner: and the mere labor of acquisition makes that an object of *wealth* which before was merely an object of possible desire. The *value* of the animal depends entirely on the average quantity of the labor of men of ordinary strength and skill, necessary to convert it to use, whether as a beast of burden, or for the use of the flesh, or of its skin merely. What renders a fine horse an article of wealth in civilised society? What nature has done for him? No such thing. Nature has done as much for the wild horses of South America; and they are not articles of wealth. Has nature done more for the trained horse? No; but man has done it: and the horse, exulting in his strength, stands, pawing the earth, the representative of the labor employed in producing the things he has consumed, and for which *his* labor has not yet compensated, from the time he was born till his exhibition for sale. His trifling value at birth is but a mere equivalent for the consumption of food during the time lost from labor by his mother, when nourishing him before and after birth, and for the expenses incurred on the father in fitting him for his idle Turkish occupation of pleasing 100 concubines. Thus, as articles commonly esteemed objects of wealth, lose that quality under circumstances in which no labor is requisite for their production; so do other articles, not esteemed objects of wealth, gain that quality when under circumstances making labor necessary for their enjoyment. By day, when light profusely flows every where over the illumined half of our planet, that species of light, the light of the sun, the most useful and grateful of all light, is not an object of wealth. But let the earth continue its revolution and avert from the sun its lately illumined portion, and let light be still desirable for human convenience, and it will become immediately an article of wealth under the name of the substances from which it is in scanty portions extracted. The value of candles, oil, gas, &c., is only the value of the light extracted from them; and as science improves and the modes of extracting are increased and facilitated, the value of light diminishes with the smaller quantities of labor necessary for its extraction. Till directed by labor under the guidance of knowledge, the powers of nature, in point of useful production of articles denominated wealth, are beneath estimation. Where nature would give the means of mere existence to a few individuals, of shelter, clothing, or comfort to none, labor does, out of the same materials, produce all the means of happiness to thousands. Let the labor of any community cease but for one year, and how many of that community would be preserved in life, by the *materials or energies of nature*, to tell the perilous experiment to the succeeding year? Not only the comforts but the very *existence* of all nations depend on the eternal operation of labor. While the mouth consumes, the industrious arm is reproducing.

Wealth is limited to the *physical* means or materials of enjoyment. Labor or muscular exertion can be occupied on physical things alone: they only are capable of accumulation. There are numerous means of enjoyment besides those of a physical nature, besides those which are tangible, visible, or which tend, through any other of the senses, to the production of happiness. All of these numerous means of enjoyment, though founded on and resolvable into exterior and interior sensation or feeling, may clearly and usefully be considered apart: physical enjoyment, meaning those pleasures only which *directly* affect the senses. There are moral and intellectual, as well as physical, pleasures; and what the two former want in intensity is more than compensated by their facility of acquisition or cheapness, their permanence, and facility of reproduction. With these moral and intellectual sources of happiness we are not now concerned, as they are not directly comprehended in the meaning attached to the word, wealth. There are also numerous *physical* means of happiness which come not under the definition of wealth. Light, by its varieties of colors, gives pleasure to the eye, water to the taste, the sexes to each other; yet are neither of these means of happiness denoted by the term wealth, because they are the gift of nature alone, without any addition made thereto by the labor or skill of man.

The mere utility of a thing carried to any extent and superadded to its mere existence, or what we call its production by the hand of nature, constitutes nothing an object of wealth till labor in some shape becomes identified with it: then it is separated from all other objects of desire, all other means of happiness, and becomes *wealth*.

What is wealth also in one country is not wealth in another, because the very same article which in one region, whether from the constitution of our nature or from mere caprice, is an object of desire requiring labor for its production, in another region causes pain, and of course no labor is expended in its acquisition or preparation.

Thus ice in equatorial civilized regions is an article of wealth and luxury; while approaching the poles, it becomes the bane of existence. In parched sandy countries, a well of water is a source of wealth; while the land is the property of no one, not being worth the trouble of appropriation. Labor was not necessary to make the well, nature, we shall suppose, having produced it; nor is the labor of drawing out the water to be alone estimated. But the existence of the well in that spot *saves the labor* that would be otherwise necessary to bring water there from its nearest supply; and the value of the well is to be measured by the quantity of labor thus saved.

Men and women, at different times and places, have been converted into mere objects of wealth; compelled by brute force, without any equivalent, to administer to the pleasures of their owners; and still this disgrace to humanity continues, upheld by the two nations, at either side of the Atlantic, who boast most of their love of liberty and their regard to human happiness. The two circumstances necessary to constitute wealth being, "objects of desire" and "procured by labor," or effort, apply to human beings, like any other substances, such as iron or sheep, when tyrannically converted into objects of wealth. Not only is an expense of labor, of force or effort, necessary, in the first instance, to make human beings slaves, and thus objects of wealth, but also to retain them in slavery. And this expense of effort is of the most irksome kind, and attended with constant risk; differing for the worse, in these particulars, from ordinary labor. False calculations of partial interest give birth to the desire of possessing slaves. Whether human beings ought (*i. e.* whether it promotes the happiness of them and their masters, collectively and individually taken) under any circumstances, to be so converted, is quite another question. Other principles will show the wickedness, because the overbalance of misery, produced by such appropriations.

It will not be objected, that, by including effort and force under the head of labor, every act of violence and robbery would constitute any thing desired by the ferocious, an object of *equal praise* with that acquired by peaceful industry. It will prove indeed that such objects of desire as are by force sought after, must in all probability be objects of wealth; but not that those objects of wealth ought to be enjoyed by any one who can seize them. Scarcely would risk and effort be superadded to ordinary labor in the acquisition, if the articles were not esteemed articles of wealth. The simple question now discussed is, not to whom these articles of wealth ought to belong—which we shall presently discuss—but what circumstances they are which constitute any objects of desire articles of wealth; the possession, the distribution of them, so as to produce the greatest quantity of happiness, being the main subject of this inquiry.

As to violence exerted to constrain, say the person of a woman to submit involuntarily to man's inclinations; wherever this violence is permitted, women become property, to people harems, as men do to cultivate the soil or to work in domestic thraldom.

It would be little better than impertinence, in an inquiry addressed to a civilized community, formally to except human beings from becoming objects of desire and of appropriation to each other: nor would it be necessary; for, wherever these most pernicious desires have existed, so as to lead to appropriation, property has followed, and they have been constituted matters of wealth, like any other materials animate or inanimate. Wherever the *power* of appropriation has accompanied the fatal *desire*, the appropriation, and the sometimes illegal, but always unjust, conversion into property or wealth, has followed of course.

Numerous are the objections that may be made, from partial views of particular objects, to this simple explanation of what constitutes an object of wealth. To explain them all would be an endless task. It may suffice to notice a few of the most conspicuous and apparently of the most difficult explanation. Of all the physical objects of desire to man, few are more attractive than the possession of a rich and well-cultivated piece of land, yielding every year teeming harvests of grain and fruits, or sending forth from its bosom useful minerals, such as iron, tin, silver, rock-salt or coal. Is this land, or are all its products objects of wealth? First, are this land and all its products *objects of desire?* Circumstances evidently may exist under which neither the land nor any of its products, internal or external, may be objects of desire in the way of appropriation; as where rude hunters occupy it, as half a century ago was the case with all the fruitful lands and immense *materials*, or things capable of being converted into wealth, in the territories of the United States, west of the Alleghany mountains. Vast tracts of these lands, now cultivated by men flourishing and happy in as far as free, and erected into states, were not then objects of desire to any human beings. Want of knowledge as well as of inclination arising from acquired habits, concealed from their savage occupants the uses to which they might be applied. Remoteness, want of security, necessarily prevented civilized strangers from thinking at that time of settling on them. Though abounding in all the physical materials of happiness, they were not therefore objects of wealth, because not objects of desire. But when the scene changed, and civilized men turned their eyes and footsteps towards them, desiring to convert them to the means of happiness; were they then converted into objects of wealth? They were simply in the way of becoming so: but they were not yet so converted. Labor was wanting to be superadded to mere desire, and in proportion as labor was bestowed upon them, they were transformed from mere objects of desire into objects of wealth. The first settler cleared the timber and erected a shed, and affixed the value of his labor to that part of the soil on which it had been expended, and to those contiguous spots rendered by it more convenient for use. A second settler, paying for the labor under the name of the land, still added to its value by expending more labor upon it, in clearing a larger space, cultivating useful crops, and improving the sheds, and perhaps rearing and domesticating some animals. A third settler pays an increased value for all these products of labor under the name of the soil to which they are attached, introduces stock and machines, all produced by labor, and leaving the former erections for subordinate or temporary purposes, erects houses and makes fences suited for permanence and convenience. Thus is a piece of rich land which was a few years ago an object of no value, now converted into an object of wealth. What has nature done towards this conversion? Nothing. What has man, what has man's labor done? Every thing. All that we call the work of nature, the mere existence of the land and its capabilities, were in as palpable existence before the land was converted into wealth as after it. Nay, by repeated culture the capabilities of the best land are frequently impaired or exhausted. But, all this time, the minerals lying on the surface of the land, or arranged in its interior, though capable of the most extended use, have not been regarded, have not been esteemed articles of wealth. Whence comes this new phenomenon? In general, because none of these articles have been all this time objects of desire, and therefore no labor has been expended upon them. Some of them, such as coal, have not been objects of desire, because other articles procured with *less labor*, such as wood, necessarily cleared away to fit the ground for cultivation, have been used instead of them. Others, such as iron, from want of the skill and machinery necessary to convert them to useful purposes on so limited a scale, have been disregarded, in as much as *less labor* applied to the soil would procure articles sufficient to get them, or rather things fabricated from them, *in exchange*. But let an increase be made in population, let the number of those requiring such articles be such as to afford constant employment to the machinery and skill of a few, let the timber be cut down and exhausted; then will the neglected iron-stone and the coal become objects of desire; then will labor be bestowed upon them and they will become objects of wealth. A new value will be given to the land; not because nature has done any thing to increase the capabilities of useful application of the objects of which the land consisted, but because circumstances have led to the formation of desires for their appropriation, and in consequence of such desires, labor has been bestowed upon them.

If it be objected that these lands are bought, before any labor has been expended upon them, of the United States government; it may be observed, that the moderate price paid is but a very small remuneration for three benefits which the comparatively weak individual occupant derives from the powerful community from whom he purchases; by which he is saved a hundred fold in risk and labor in the cultivation, in the enjoyment of his land.

1st, Immediate peaceable possession; 2d, Guarantee by the national force from savage attack or fellow citizens' annoyance, permitting the whole of the cultivator's exertions to be directed to improvement, none of it being abstracted for defence; 3d, *Security of title* in future enjoyment or transfers, the original appropriation becoming a public act registered and authenticated; thus saving litigation resolvable into loss of wealth or useless expenditure of labor, with its accompanying vexation and consequential evils to an interminable extent.

Nor does the fertility or barrenness of the soil require any modification to be made in the definition given. If the land be so barren as not to afford an adequate return in the means of comfort for the labor that might be bestowed upon it, that labor will be withheld; and this desire will depend on the facilities of getting from other sources by means of less labor, the objects contemplated by the application of labor to the land in question. No matter whether the land be rich or poor, let the desire of making it, or any thing attached to it, tributary to enjoyment, be once produced, and let labor be in consequence applied, the value of the land will necessarily depend on the quantity of labor guided by ordinary skill and judgment bestowed upon it. If land more fertile be discovered, after lands less fertile have been cultivated, and so near and convenient in point of situation as to come in competition with them, the new land may be cultivated in preference; and that part of the labor bestowed on the old which had not been returned by means of the crops but expended in more durable changes, called permanent improvements, would be lost. That particular parcel of land first cultivated, ceasing, from whatever cause, to be an object of desire, the labor expended upon it would no longer preserve it an article of wealth, as the labor of drawing stones, not objects of desire, from the sea, would not convert them into articles of wealth. Let any thing be once an object of desire, labor is the only ingredient necessary to erect it into an article of wealth. The desire removed, no labor will, except by compulsion, be employed upon it. The desire excited and the object not to be obtained without exertion, labor is bestowed upon it, and it is converted into an article of wealth.

Suppose a trading colony settled on a confined barren spot, as the British on the island of Malta, for the mere purposes of commerce: What will determine the value of the few barren spots of ground in their neighbourhood? The quantity of labor that has been expended upon them. What determined that quantity of labor? The quantity that it has been necessary, or that it would be necessary, to expend upon them in order to afford for sale whatever articles the climate and convenience permitted, on the same terms that articles equally good could be imported from the cheapest accessible market. If more money were demanded for a vineyard, an orange-grove, or a corn-field, than this mass of labor, with the necessary profits of capital as they are called and superintendence, would amount to, it could not be given without loss; because the productions of the spot would not repay the interest of the capital deposited with the yearly expenses of culture necessary to meet the rival foreign article. The value again of the articles brought from abroad would depend on the quantity of labor there necessary to produce them.

Suppose that instead of being barren, the spots of the island had been very rich; their value would be equally determined in the same way, either by the quantity of labor expended upon them, or (whether to the whole amount expended or not) by the quantity of labor, or the worth of labor, they would save the proprietor, the amount which without them he would have to pay in freight, first cost, and attendant expenses, for a quantity of produce equal to that which his home culture could produce.

In such way would the value of a piece of land be determined for agricultural purposes on such an island. In what way would it be determined for building or for pleasure-ground? The value of building ground depends on the quantity of labor in carriage and otherwise which the situation would save, and in the probability of quicker sale or letting it would afford; all which are resolvable into the saving of labor. The price of pleasure grounds depends on the competition of the desires of the rich. To these, when wealth is viciously divided, and when great ignorance is joined to great wealth, it is hard to assign a limit. The loss of other enjoyments, which the acquisition of a spot, so over-valued by caprice beyond its agricultural or building value, would entail on its acquirer, is almost the only check to this competition. If labor somewhat beyond what could create agricultural sites, could create new sites equally suited to caprice for pleasure-grounds; the amount of this labor would stamp the value. But these favorite pleasure-grounds are in general limited in quantity, and such as cannot be imitated by labor. They have therefore a surplus value of their own, arising from the competition of desires, more or less reasonable, on a supply necessarily limited. But this surplus, over and above their agricultural or building value, or value for health or any other useful purpose that can be estimated by labor, could scarcely have place, or but to a very small extent, as we shall see, under the natural, unconstrained, and most useful distribution of wealth. This surplus is a mere artificial value, not appreciable or worthy of being appreciated in the scale of the wealth and happiness of any community. Still however, in all cases, the two ingredients of desire and labor are necessary to constitute an article of wealth. If nature have limited the supply of the article so that labor cannot furnish the demands of desire, the artificial value of caprice commences: but whereas, in ordinary cases, the value of an article of wealth extends to the smallest quantity of labor that could produce it, here the value of caprice cannot extend even as far. Scarcely any amount of labor, not such as any individual fortune could purchase, could create a new river for instance and form sites upon it, or continue exploring the earth till new diamonds or similar baubles, equal in size to the largest known, were discovered. Even this surplus artificial value therefore comes within our rule: for not only can it never *exceed* the amount of labor necessary to produce similar articles, but it seldom reaches that amount. The amount of labor expended or saved on objects of desire, is therefore in all cases the utmost limit of their value, and what constitutes them articles of wealth.

Though the proposition heading this section, asserts that labor is the *sole* measure of the value of an article of wealth, it does not assert that this sole measure is in all cases an *accurate* measure. As an article must be an object of desire to be an article of wealth, and as these desires and preferences are apt to vary with circumstances both physical and moral, particularly with the quantum of knowledge, (of science and art) of the means of converting to use the materials and energies of nature; it is evidently impossible that the absolute quantity of labor can be any accurate index to these. Superfluous trinkets without use are sought after by the savage and the courtier. Under representative self-government, they would be equally disregarded as things conferring merit, and reduced to their commercial value, to the value of real use. Uninformed nations may disregard the sea-weed and the siliceous sand on their shores; by the union of which, by means of heat, into one substance, light and warmth might be enjoyed in their dwellings; and should other substances supply the place of these, in cheaper substitutes, they would, if not wanted for other purposes, be equally disregarded by civilized nations. What is asserted, is, that in any given state of society, with any given desires, at any particular time, labor, employed with ordinary judgment on objects of desire, is the sole measure of their values; and under such circumstances, an accurate measure. While the quantity of land and the supply of the materials of many articles remains stationary, population and knowledge at the same time increasing; while desires or tastes vary as the moral and intellectual condition of mankind improves, no accurate measure of value, as applied to wealth, can be given. To seek it, is to hunt after a shadow. Nothing but labor or effort bears any relation to the converting of objects of desire into objects of wealth: they may by possibility all change their characters, and be at one time objects of wealth, while at another they are mere objects of desire; or may cease to be even objects of desire.

Greater skill it is evident is exerted in one species of labor, and by one laborer at the same work, than in another. But these are resolvable into the ordinary labor of the community. If by extraordinary skill at a particular employment, or by ordinary skill at an employment requiring a considerable expenditure of previous labor to learn, an individual accomplishes that in two days which ordinary skill or untaught skill could not accomplish in less than four, this labor is double the value of ordinary labor. The estimate of the value of a day's labor is that produced by ordinary skill and diligence in the ordinary occupations of the laborious part of the community. There are also other circumstances, such as danger, noxious smells, noxious airs, moisture, cold, extra-exertion, which increase the value of particular species of labor. The products of these species of labor being objects of desire, the repulsiveness of the work requiring greater effort must be met by increased remuneration, if it cannot be obviated by indirect means requiring more labor or time. Thus, though labor is not an accurate measure of the relative value of articles of wealth under the varying circumstances of human society, it is the best approximation to such a standard; and is the only standard by which we can judge whether an article of desire is or is not an article of wealth.

There is no one article of desire, usually esteemed an article of wealth, which has not been, and which is not, in many places, denied that title. There are tribes, by whom neither corn, nor cottons, nor woollens, nor gold, nor rice, nor silver, would be esteemed articles of value, or wealth: but there are no tribes, there are no human beings, with whom human labor is not esteemed an article of value. Ignorant or enlightened, poor or rich, depraved or beneficent, labor is every where, to all men, an article of value: it is every where the price paid for the continuance of existence as well as for the means of enjoyment. It is the only universal commodity. No where without human labor or effort can objects of desire be obtained in such quantity or state of preparation as to support life.

Enough, it is hoped, has been said to prove, that "wealth is produced by labor; that labor is the sole ingredient by which an article of desire is converted into an article of wealth; and that labor is the sole universal, though still not an accurate, measure, of the value of wealth."

From what has been said follows also the truth of these propositions,

First, The mere desirableness of, or desire for, any physical, or other, object, does not constitute it an object of wealth.

Second, Nor does its rarity, nor its beauty, nor the pleasure, ever so pure, intense or permanent, that may be afforded by it, nor even its necessity for existence, constitute it an object of wealth.

Third, Nor, of course, does its *utility*, or its subserviency to any or all of the above, or to any other, uses, constitute it an object of wealth.

Fourth, Labor alone, added to the desire for physical things, constitutes them objects of wealth.

There are also two circumstances to be noticed, which when combined exclude physical things, though objects of desire, from having labor bestowed upon them so as to be constituted articles of wealth, viz.

First, The exhaustless supply of some physical objects of desire.
Second, Their existence in a state fit for use.

Such are the light of the sun, the air, sometimes water, atmospheric heat, &c.

Having a clear idea of what wealth is, we shall be able to understand each other when we speak of its distribution. Let us proceed then to our next section.

SECTION 2.

The object to be aimed at in the distribution of wealth, as in its production by labor, is to confer thereby the greatest possible quantity of happiness (i. e. of PLEASURES, whether of the senses, or of a moral or intellectual nature) on the society producing it.

OUR organization has made us *sentient* beings, that is to say, capable of experiencing pleasure and pain from various sources. Happiness denotes that continued state of well-being which is compounded of the different items of pleasurable feeling, experienced during a considerable space of time. Pleasures are the component parts, of which happiness is the aggregate, or the result. There is no space here for making an estimate of the different species of pleasures which compose happiness. The only rational motive to exertion of any sort, whether to acquire wealth or for any other purpose, is to increase the means of happiness, or to remove or lessen causes of annoyance, immediate or in prospect. To add to happiness therefore, wealth is produced. If nature produced spontaneously an abundance of food and all other comforts for the use of man, as she does of air for his respiration, no effort would be made to produce or appropriate them, no *distribution* would be thought of: every one would take and consume as his wants demanded. With the sole view of adding to happiness, wealth, which nature does not give, is produced by labor: and the greater the happiness produced, the more satisfactory must be the effort. If we are delighted with one portion of happiness as arising from our wealth—be it enjoyed by whom it may—we must be more delighted with two portions, and with three still more than with two; and so on with any increase, to any extent of the number of portions. And as wealth can only be produced with a view to being made the means of comfort or enjoyment by its use or consumption, and as it must be distributed in order to be consumed, that distribution must be the best which gives the greatest number of portions of enjoyment, which gives the greatest possible quantity of happiness to those, the society or community, that produce it. The community producing the wealth will not send the fruits of their labor to add to the happiness of a neighbouring community, because that community possesses equal facilities for the production, because there is no reason to suppose a greater capacity for happiness amongst other communities, and because such gratuitous supply would annihilate the motives to production in the idle community receiving, as well as in the giving, unrequited, community.

The organization of man is so constituted as to enable him to enjoy an extent of happiness indefinitely greater than that of such an animal as an oyster or any number of oysters, or perhaps even of any number of horses: therefore is his comfort to be preferred indefinitely to the comfort of such inferior animals, whenever their happiness is incompatible with his. Between the capability of happiness of man and those animals that are unprovided with one or more of the five senses, as the oyster, the distance is immeasurable. Between man and the most perfect of other animals, as the ape, the distance is perhaps as great as between the ape and the oyster, or perhaps greater. This is to be attributed to the superior organization of man's extremities, his organs of voice, and particularly his brain, the organ of thought or feeling. From the development of this latter, comes *foresight*; by which he guides his future conduct by inferences from the past, and is liable to the pleasures of memory and anticipation. In this, and from this, in his immense capacity for knowledge and all species of intellectual and moral pleasures, those of association included, stands the pre-eminence of man; the anticipations or other intellectual capacities, and thence the capacities for happiness, of even the most intellectual of other animals being extremely faint, hardly equalling that of a child of a year old. If now any one human being could demonstrate that his organization so excelled that of his fellow men as to enable him to experience indefinitely greater happiness than the rest of his species, his claim, like that of man above the oyster, ought to be allowed, and wealth and all other means of happiness ought to be applied to him, as by such application they would be the most productive. Even such a state of things would not violate our present rule. The greatest quantity of happiness, wherever it may be found to alight, must be pursued.

If, on looking round into society, we find the actual distribution very different from what we could expect from the principle of so distributing as to produce the greatest possible sum of happiness, it is quite another question to inquire how, under such circumstances, the happiest distribution could be brought about. We are now investigating first principles, unshackled by any fortuitous combination in any community.

Time was when this proposition, which some may *now* perhaps deem too trivial to be used as a basis of moral reasoning, too plain and too universally admitted to need illustration, would not have been endured. In days of ignorance the principle, both acted on and avowed, was, "We are possessed of the means of gratifying our appetites and passions, and will keep what we have: we have the power of adding indefinitely to these means, and will use that power to make the happiness of others subservient to ours. We know of no greatest happiness but the greatest happiness to ourselves." To this selfishness, this short-sighted selfishness, the reply was obvious,—"If your happiness be all to you, the happiness of every other individual is all to him, and so of any number of individuals: but to a third person, say a calm reasoner or legislator, it would be unimportant whether A. or B. enjoyed the happiness; his object would be to produce the greatest quantity by whomsoever enjoyed." The only reason that can be given for the *production* of wealth at all, is, that it adds to the means of happiness: the only reason that it should be *distributed* in one way more than another, is, that it tends more to produce, to add to the stock of happiness, the object of its production, by one mode of distribution than by another. The object being happiness, the greater quantity of happiness held in view and attainable, the more completely is that object accomplished, and the greater, of course, the efforts to produce it. What possible reason can be given that a smaller quantity of happiness, enjoyed by whom it may, should be preferred to a larger quantity of happiness? The state of things here supposed, is previous to distribution, whether of things supplied by nature or by labor, before any one has expended any labor, or acquired any property. What reason under such circumstances could any one give, that his avowedly smaller happiness should be preferred in the distribution to larger portions of happiness of one or more of those around him? If it could be proved that more happiness on the whole would accrue to society by centering the whole sum of wealth in many or a few individuals, such should be the distribution of wealth, in full accordance with this first principle. It assumes nothing as to the sort or numbers of persons to whom the distribution is to be made; but merely puts those to the proof, who assert that the greatest sum of happiness would be produced to society by distributing its enjoyment to them rather than to others. Consistently with this principle, if the slavery of nine out of ten and the superlative happiness of the tenth increased the sum total of happiness, *that* distribution, of slavery, should be pursued. All that is asked by this first principle, is, that the greatest quantity of agreeable sensations, both in intensity and duration, should be the object aimed at in the distribution of wealth. To deny it, would be to affirm that pain is to be preferred to pleasure, that no sensations are preferable to agreeable ones, that not feeling, which is tantamount to non-existence, is to be preferred to feeling or existence. Unfortunately, in older times there were few calm observers; all were influenced by the state of things and prejudices in which they had been brought up; and from the immediate necessities of life, every one pursued his own immediate apparent interest, without thinking, or being able to think, of first principles. Happiness in the abstract, and the greatest possible quantity of it, being then our first object, let us proceed to ascertain what mode of distribution will ensure the most of it. Our next proposition is,

SECTION 4.

The happiness of the greater number is to be preferred to the happiness of the lesser number; otherwise the object in view, the production of the greatest possible quantity of happiness, would be sacrificed.

THIS proposition necessarily follows the preceding; for if all sane persons are, by similar treatment, capable of equal portions of enjoyment; to say, that the happiness of two of these equals is to be preferred to one, is no more than saying that two or any other number are more than one. Happiness being the object, the sum total would be lessened by the abstraction of any portion of it. Why then the necessity of stating a self-evident proposition? Because, though sometimes admitted in theory as to smaller associations, it has been most flagrantly and lamentably neglected *in practice*, not only as applied to society at large, but even in its application to these minor associations. To enumerate the practices that prevail in violation of this principle, would be to enumerate almost every case of privilege and exemption. It must be observed again, that though this, like the other propositions, is expressed in general terms as applicable to every species of happiness, to happiness derived from all other sources as well as from wealth, because they are thought to be universally true; yet is our general argument concerned with no more than this, that *that* portion of the happiness of the greater number, which *is derived from wealth*, is to be preferred to that portion of the happiness of the smaller number which is derived from the same source. The *direct* operation of wealth is chiefly to afford the means of more extensive pleasures of the senses: it is only indirectly that it operates to increase our moral and intellectual pleasures; and when unequally distributed, and in very large masses, it tends, as will be proved, to eradicate almost entirely these higher moral and intellectual pleasures.

There can be therefore no possible reason why the happiness of a smaller number of individuals should be preferred to that of a greater number. How are we to find out who this favoured smaller number shall be? the *already rich?* This circumstance might be a very good argument in leading us to direct our attention to those not yet provided with the objects of wealth or happiness; but it is surely the worst of all possible reasons why we should do again what was already done, (supply the rich with the means of more happiness or more wealth,) and neglect that which is undone, supplying those who are unsupplied, and who want those means. Of all the perversities of human selfishness distorting human reason, there is perhaps no where to be found more lamentable absurdity than is too often exhibited under this head; confounding the pursuit of security of wealth obtained by labor or voluntary transfer, with an interminable effort to add to the heap by usurpations on the right of the poor to free labor and free exchange of the products of labor. If this smaller favored number are not to be the *already rich*, who are they to be? The individuals, virtuous or vicious, happy or miserable, actually in possession of the collective *power* of the society? If we do not name them, will they, having the power, convert it to any other distribution of wealth amongst any other favored number of individuals, the literati, the moral, or the religious? The very thought, the very statement of the question, seems absurd. If they are not convinced to use their power, as far as it can or ought to influence the distribution of wealth in preferring the happiness of the greater to the smaller number, if any exception be allowed to this rule, they will naturally make the exception in their own favor; for we are all the best, the most worthy of happiness, in our own eyes. The alternative is therefore evident and pressing. Either the general principle of impartial justice set forth in our proposition, must be adopted, or philosophy must sanction the law of brute force, the empire of the strongest: for to what number of individuals less than the majority shall we leave the decision as to those to be elected into the favored few, for whose particular enjoyment the distribution of wealth is to be fashioned? If we leave it to the majority, they will naturally determine in favor of their own happiness, and thus establish our principle. But we shall find as we proceed, that whatever really useful advantages the favorers of any smaller number may expect from their system of direct favoritism, these advantages will be attained in a more easy and effectual manner by adhering to our rule of universal justice, without producing any of the ill consequences, selfishness, jealousies, murmurs, arising from their arbitrary preferences. We shall find that in every thing the unrestrained tendencies of things, aided by knowledge, will produce more of happiness, than any artificial arrangements.

But should not the happiness of the intelligent and the moral, some will still perhaps weakly ask, be preferred, in the distribution of wealth, to the happiness of the ignorant and vicious? First, it was dissimilarity of treatment alone that made the one enlightened and the other ignorant, the one moral and the other vicious. None so ready to proclaim this truth as the intelligent and the moral. Ask them from what sources their happiness is derived: ask them how much of it proceeds directly from mere wealth, and you will be astonished at the scantiness of the proportion of their enjoyments arising from that source, beyond the supply of the average comforts of life. Will *they* wish, will they demand that the physical enjoyments of others should be deliberately sacrificed to theirs? that the distribution of wealth should be directed out of its natural channel of free labor and voluntary exchanges, to favor them? Will *they* desire by any artificial regulations, to obtain the fruit of other men's labor without their consent, and for which there is no equivalent given?

Far from the intelligent, far from the moral, would be such a wish: if they want to obtain additional wealth, an additional supply of those means of happiness which wealth bestows, they will desire no more than that free competition, which the rest of the community do, or ought to, possess. If they want wealth and have no moral or intellectual equivalent to offer, they will devote themselves to industry, instead of wishing by fraud or rapine, open or disguised, to appropriate the products of other men's labor without their consent. The happiness of the wise and good could not be promoted by such means; they require the forced sacrifice of no man's happiness, of the happiness of no portion of their fellow-creatures, to promote theirs. Such injustice would but mar their happiness instead of increasing it. To the slave-driver they would resign the sweets extorted from the unrequited labor of the slave. The more abundant their sources of happiness independent of wealth, the more unjust would they feel it to be to wring from those who have no other sources of enjoyment, a portion of that scanty source which is left to them. They respect the happiness of all other men equally with their own. But suppose the case were the reverse; suppose that the wise and moral did, in this unwise and immoral way, require the sacrifice of the happiness of others, of the greater number, to theirs, how should we find out who were the moral and the wise? By the forming of such wishes? Who would not then put in his claim for morality and wisdom? Every individual would assert his exclusive claim. To avoid this confusion, we give—to whom?—the power of deciding who are to be the favored virtuous and wise. If to those in power, whose legislative measures regulate the distribution of wealth, will they prefer the interest of the wise and good to their own exclusive interest? Or will they not find out at once that they are the wise and good; that to themselves and their friends, as the wisest and the best, the preference should be given; if the happiness of a smaller is to be preferred to the happiness of a larger number?

Let us turn to which side we may, it will be impossible to find any rational ground for preferring the happiness of the smaller number as derived from wealth, or indeed from any other source, to the happiness of the larger number. If we took any side on this question of preference and exclusion, it would be that directly opposed to those notions which have been generally entertained and acted upon. Were there ten persons, wise, rich, powerful, and nine unenlightened, poor, and unprotected, making nineteen in the whole; and were the question asked in whose favor should the distribution of wealth be turned, in order to produce the greatest quantity of happiness on the whole?—should the tendency of wealth and its enjoyments be rather directed to the greater or the smaller number, to the ten or the nine? we should—were we forced to be unjust to one of the parties—prefer the injustice to the most destitute, though the fewest in number, and would rather direct wealth by artificial means to those whose wants were the most pressing, and who were debarred from other sources of enjoyment. If any argument for preferring the happiness of the smaller to the larger number could be listened to, it would be evidently in favor of those who are *in the most need*; therefore even of the minority—if in the most need. This is however an impossible case: the minority of society are never in the most need: the most destitute are also the majority. They have therefore the double title, in all communities, of being the most in number, and the most in need, the most destitute of those means of happiness which wealth affords. The happiness of the greatest number must therefore be always kept in view by the moralist and legislator, without any regard to morals, manners, intellectual or other qualities. In fact, our argument does not incumber itself with the supposition of the actual existence of any inequalities of character or circumstances. We take mankind as actually constituted by nature, and as capable by similar treatment of being fashioned by circumstances; and under these data, we ask what is best to be done in the way of the distribution of wealth? A future stage in the inquiry will lead us to an investigation of the best mode of introducing our natural arrangement into a society laboring under the evils of forced and artificial arrangements for distributing wealth.

The happiness of the greater number is therefore to be preferred to the happiness of the lesser number, in whatever arrangements may be made respecting the distribution of wealth.

*   *   *

SECTION 13.

That inequality in the distribution of wealth, and that alone, which arises from securing to every man the free use of his labor, and its products, and the voluntary exchanges thence ensuing, should be upheld; because, without that extent of inequality, there would be no SECURITY, without security no production, without production no wealth to distribute.

WERE food and all other objects of wealth supplied to man, like light, air, and in most places water, in such quantities as to be abundant for all, without the necessity of any human effort for their production; and were it proposed, *in order to make them produce more happiness*, to limit their consumption by the greater number of individuals of the community, that the remainder might have more than they could consume; who is there that would not exclaim against the absurdity of such a proposal? Or, were they only in such quantity, but still unconnected with human exertion, as to afford but a limited supply to all, enough for mere necessary use but not for superfluity; would not the person, in this case also, be deemed irrational who should propose to increase the sum total of the happiness of the community, by any inequality of distribution, taking from some what was merely necessary, in order to load others with satiety? The absurdity and the mischief in the latter case would be the greatest: for those who had at best but merely necessaries, would suffer more pain in being deprived of them to add to the superfluities of others, than those who previously possessed abundance. Suppose a third case, that a given supply, any how obtained, but without the intervention of human exertion, that would give but a treat to all, were every year, every month, or every day, acquired by a community; the enjoyment of any individual using at the same time 500, 1000, or any other number of those portions, would scarcely, from the laws of our organization, double the enjoyment of any one of those from whom one of the single shares was taken or withheld. This, it is hoped, has been already made evident in sections 8 and 9, and will be further proved when we inquire into the effects of *excessive* inequality of wealth on the happiness of a community.

In all cases then, whether of a large or small supply, where human effort has not been concerned in the production, equality of distribution is the rule of justice. Let the reader pause, reflect, and speculate, and assign if he can any other justification amongst beings similarly constituted, capable of equal degrees of happiness, of a departure from the law of equality in distribution, than the necessity of human exertion for the production. There can be no other justification of a departure from equality of distribution. Its blessings are so transcendently great, so productive of immensely increased agreeable sensations, peace, and benevolence, that never but when justified by the necessity of continued production should they be departed from. To this superior *necessity*, and to this alone, must they yield; and to this necessity must they be strictly limited.

What is the circumstance which distinguishes the objects of wealth as means of enjoyment, from other means of enjoyment which come not under the name of wealth? The necessity of *labor* for their production. In nothing but in being the creatures of human labor, do they differ from other sources of enjoyment. Without labor they could not exist. Without security—which means the exclusive possession by every man of all the advantages of his labor—labor would not be called forth. Therefore in the distribution of such articles where labor is employed, called articles of wealth, and in these alone, equality must be limited by security, because in no other case are equality and production incompatible with each other. What is the reason of this? that equality is not, wherever attainable, to be desired? is it that equality itself is not founded in justice and productive of happiness? Far from it. But because its paramount blessings cannot be obtained, when applied to one particular class of objects of desire, those which are produced by labor, called objects of wealth, without destroying the source, the supply of such objects. Were it possible to ensure a reproduction by labor of the articles equally consumed, all the advantages of equality would be as fully derivable from the equal distribution of objects of wealth, as of any other objects of desire or materials of happiness whatever. A celebrated practical as well as philosophical inquirer, conceives that he has demonstrated *experimentally* that reproduction and equality are *not* incompatible even when applied to objects of wealth, produced, as they all are, by labor. He conceives that he has proved that other motives, besides *individual* necessity and the love of the factitious pleasures of superiority of wealth, can be found, and made to operate with sufficient energy, to ensure a constant reproduction of abundant wealth, for the equal use of the whole community. As *almost* all falsehood and violence, and as *all* stealing proceeds from inequality of distribution of wealth; *he* would certainly be no mean benefactor to his species, who could demonstrate the practicability of thoroughly eradicating, by removing the causes of, these the most numerous by far of human miseries and vices. The mischiefs arising from the mis-regulation of our appetites, passions, and desires, and from the want of knowledge and loss of the pleasures of intellectual culture, would be the only ones to which the attention of society would be then anxiously directed: and the whole attention being concentrated on these, the prospects of indefinite improvement would be captivating indeed. In a separate chapter will be investigated Mr. Owen's views, which are by no means regarded as visionary speculations, but as some of the most important problems of social science that were ever submitted to the consideration of mankind.

In the course of our argument in this inquiry, we have, however, all along reasoned on the supposition of labor by *individual competition*, and taken it for granted, in opposition to Mr. Owen, that the re-production of wealth and security were incompatible with equality of wealth. By no scheme or combination affecting a whole community, have these discordant principles been ever yet in human practice reconciled. But to assert that they could not, as moral wisdom improved, be found reconcileable, would be as presumptuous reasoning from ignorance, in morals, as to assert, in physics, (and not many years ago the writer heard the assertion made by an experienced naval officer, who now owns a steam-vessel and practises what he pronounced impracticable,) that it would be impossible to apply steam navigation to the ocean or to strong river currents. No part of our argument is built even on the practicability of reconciling these two hitherto rival principles of security and equality; or rather of reproduction and equality; for although equality might leave every one secure in the possession of his equal share by taking away the motives to plunder, it would remain still, under such circumstances, to *supply motives to production*. This is the real difficulty; which Mr. Owen conceives he has solved. Conceding therefore so much on the one hand, we must strictly guard, on the other, against the abuses and false inferences that may be drawn from this concession. Wherever inequality is not called for by the clear necessity of security, not of that false security which is partially applied to soothe the imaginary alarms of the rich, protecting mere possession however acquired, while it overlooks violence applied to the very means of existence of the poor; but of that equal and just security which is alike to all; *equality* is to be pursued as the means of the greatest happiness derivable from distribution. Quite opposite to this has been the current philosophy, in order to uphold the enormous practices every where in operation, and outraging equally the principles of security and equality. There is scarcely a violation of the principle of security, for which the maintenance of that principle has not served as a pretext. The word, security, once laid hold of by the lovers of exclusive privileges and possessions, and but partially understood or wilfully misrepresented, has been reserved for the protection of the rich and powerful alone, to guard their possessions, however acquired, though at the expense not only of equality, but of the security of the rest of the community, and has been by the rich used as a cover for every oppression, may as a justification of the most atrocious cruelty, the worst species of vice. To justify that transcendent enormity, the slave-trade, including in itself all the complicated evils combined arising from the violation of the principle of security, the name of that same principle of security has been as unblushingly as absurdly profaned. Allowing for a moment that our demonstration of the sole original right to *property*, as founded on free labor and voluntary exchanges, is erroneous; allowing that it would tend to the happiness of a community that property should be acquired by its members by force or fraud, and that such acquisitions should be eternally by force or fraud maintained; still the simple question of *security* comes to this. There are *two* human beings, the slave and the owner, equally concerned in the maintenance of this principle of security. If the slave were a house or an ox, or any such species of property, and *not a sentient being like the owner*, the principle of security would then apply to the owner alone; but wherever man and labor are concerned, the principle of security will apply. To the owner the principle of security says, "Your property, that is to say, the free use and direction of your labor and all your faculties (not interfering with similar rights in others), and the right of voluntary exchanges for the products of that labor; and also, as an item of this your property, your expectation of so much happiness from *the use* of the living machine (provided it was acquired by free labor or voluntary exchange) shall be awarded to you." But to the slave the same principle of security says, "*Your* property, that is to say, the free use and direction of your labor and all your faculties (not interfering with similar rights in others), and the right of voluntary exchanges for the products of that labor, shall be awarded to *you*." How can justice in this case reconcile security with security? the security of the master with the security of the slave? It is impossible. But in such and a thousand similar cases, where two moral duties interfere with each other, and it is impossible to perform them both, what is the conduct which necessity, in compliance with the principle of the greatest good, requires? *That the lesser duty should be sacrificed to the greater*: making always such compensation, where practicable, to the party suffering as will not be attended with other preponderant mischief. In cases like the present, where the injustice has been sanctioned and upheld by the public regulations and public force, the compensation should be paid by the public. Compensation or not, the smaller evil, the smaller breach of duty, must be preferred to the greater. The greater security of the sentient and rational being, the slave, must be preferred to the smaller security of the sentient and rational being, the owner. In the security of the slave are comprehended *all his rights*, all *his means of happiness*, not only those arising from wealth, but from all other sources; all compromised and annihilated by slavery. In the security of the master is comprehended that additional *balance* of enjoyment which the forced labor of the slave could give him over and above the paid voluntary labor of any hired laborer. This *balance*, taking the large interest on the original cost into the account, is demonstrably, in most cases, no balance at all in favor of, but is against, the slave-owner. Whether in *any case*, under circumstances ever so favorable, the balance of *profit* to the agriculturist or manufacturer, is in favor of slave over free labor, at an equal cost, seems not to be fully ascertained. The amount of the *gross produce*, of the mass for consumption and happiness, is always diminished by forced labor or slavery:

the only question is as to the share of the employer, whether *that*, putting down the interest or enjoyment of the forced laborers, the slaves, as nothing, is not always diminished by substituting slave for voluntary labor. The loss, to the owner, of the malignant gratification of domination and cruelty, we pass by, as more than counterbalanced by the disquietudes, precautions, and efforts necessary to uphold forced labor. The security of the master consists in the preservation to him of a *very doubtful* balance of enjoyment in *one item* of all the numerous sources of happiness incident to human beings. The security of the slave consists in the preservation to him of *every item of all possible sources of happiness*, of which slavery robs him, and lodges in the caprice of another person. Thus then, on the principle of security alone, so ignorantly and so grossly profaned by the owners of slaves and the forcible retainers every where of their fellow creatures' rights, do their practices stand condemned.[1] The principle of "security" is the mortal foe of slavery, and of all injustice. *The security of acquired property, the produce of labor, is only a branch of the security of labor: and the security of labor is only a branch of general security, guarantying equal rights to all sentient and rational beings, founded on their similar organization and the equal utility of these rights to all.* Where two masses of security are incompatible with each other, the sacrifice of the smaller mass is to be preferred.

Having thus shown, in so flagrant a case, the mischiefs practised and justified under the pretext of doing homage to the principle of security, it will be easy to detect its abuse in all other cases. Equality of enjoyment, arising from equality of distribution, is never to be sacrificed, but when a real, not an imaginary, security demands it; when a real balance of security demands the sacrifice as necessary to reproduction. For what purpose should any, the smallest, portion of inequality not necessary for production be maintained? To maintain the happiness of those who profit by the inequality? But you thereby destroy a much greater portion of happiness of those at whose expense the inequality is acquired. There is no other reason than the necessity of supplying motives to production for any portion of inequality of distribution. Were there no fear of deficient reproduction, were not voluntary labor the necessary ingredient in that reproduction, why reward one person more than another, and at the expense of that other, with what is equally necessary, or would give equal enjoyment, to all? Were the human race like the race of many other animals, as that of the cats, in which the lion or the tiger requires ten times the food of the common cat, it might then be right to assign to the Liliputians of the human species, of two feet high, food, clothing, and habitations proportionate, and of course unequal to those of their larger brethren of six feet in height and corresponding wants. In such case, *wants* being unequal, equality of supply would produce the same mischief that inequality now causes; repletion to some, with scarcely any addition of enjoyment; scarcity to others, with the pains, moral and physical, of privation. Men being, as they are, of equal capacities of enjoyment from the sources of wealth, equality must be the object desired, where not destructive of, or tending to weaken, the motives to production.

An unanswerable reason—were any further reason wanting—why inequality of distribution is not desirable beyond this its natural limit, is, that this limit alone would always have upheld, though the additions made to it by force and fraud had been entirely suppressed, great absolute inequality of wealth; though, contrasted with what now actually takes place, it would be a comparative approach to equality. How far this approach to the blessings of equality may be carried, when all obstacles of force and fraud to the entire development of free labor and voluntary exchanges shall have been removed, and when knowledge shall be equally afforded to all members of a community, it would be hazardous to predict. That it would approach however very nearly to Mr. Owen's system of mutual co-operation by common labor, there can be no doubt. And as every approach to this state consistent with the greatest production, is always to be kept in view, hence arises the peculiar duty of those who seek the greatest happiness of the community in which they live, to oppose every institution, regulation, and effort, tending to add to those unavoidable evils of inequality which security requires. If equality and security, or production, can be reconciled by the difusion of knowledge; or, in other words, if motives equally or more efficient than those arising from personal gain, can be put into operation to ensure an equally large production, no doubt social motives ought to be preferred to selfish. This phenomenon however remains to be exhibited in practice, as well as proved by theory: and as all its operations must be eminently and essentially *voluntary*; as all force and fraud must be equally excluded from its establishment and continuance; the system here advocated, of free labor and voluntary exchanges, will quietly lead to the adoption of every thing useful in it.

It may be said that we are conceding the very basis of our argument, when we admit, for a moment, the *possibility* of reconciling security or production with equality of distribution. True, as far as concerns the system of labor by *individual competition*, the ordinary system of human labor, and the only one yet spoken of, security is not reconcileable with equality of distribution. We have been hitherto contrasting the system of free labor by individual competition with the employment of force, compulsion, or restraint of any kind. Of production by mutual co-operation resting on individual security, or *voluntary* equality in the distribution and enjoyment of the products of united labor, a succeeding chapter will treat at length. If production can be hereafter obtained without the pressure of those hitherto necessarily attendant evils of inequality, surely so much the happier for mankind. Our object is to show how vast a mass of happiness is in the power of every civilized community, *in spite* of these and all other obstacles, whether real or the work of nature, or artificially fabricated by man: it being the duty, as it is the interest, of society to remove all obstacles but those which are unavoidable, or the removal of which would bring in their train preponderant evil.

On the whole then it is evident, that that portion of inequality in the distribution of wealth, whatever it may be, which unavoidably arises from the maintenance of *equal* security, must be submitted to, in order to procure the greatest happiness derivable from wealth.

SECTION 15.

General inferences from the foregoing premises. Statement of the "Natural Laws of Distribution," or general rules or principles, the observance of which is necessary in order to attain the greatest happiness derivable from wealth.

IF we have entered with great earnestness and minute detail into the proof of the propositions at the head of the several sections of this chapter, it has been with the view of establishing a few simple, intelligible and most important rules, to serve as first principles in the distribution of wealth. As we have hitherto proved directly their truth, that is to say, their accordance with the organization and circumstances of man and their tendency to promote the greatest happiness to be derived from wealth; so shall we frankly and unhesitatingly follow in subsequent chapters wherever truth may further lead us, in the development of all the other consequences interesting to mankind, that appear to flow from an undeviating adherence to these simple rules. These are what may be called the *natural laws of distribution*. The observance of these rules or laws will lead, without effort, to the enjoyment of the greatest portion of the benefits of equality that can be had without preponderant evil, *i.e.* without violating security, and with security curtailing, and ultimately annihilating, production itself. Every person exercising them is of course bound to respect the same rights in every other member of the community. The grand secret demonstrated is, that it is the *interest* of all communities to substitute reason and voluntariness, for force, in the distribution of wealth, as well as in all their other concerns; that in the distribution of wealth, as in every other department of morals, the duty and the interest of individuals coincide, mingle with, and form the aggregate of national happiness.

In the preceding sections what have we proved? First, it is evident that if we wish to extract from wealth the greatest happiness it is capable of affording those who produce it, we shall be of opinion that "all labor ought to be free and voluntary as to its direction and continuance."

All labor should be "free" from external compulsion as to its direction and continuance. On all unappropriated articles labor ought to be free, because, no appropriation having been made, no rival claim can be set up; no consent is to be asked. On appropriated articles labor is to be free from all external compulsion, the consent of the appropriator having been obtained. Why render this consent necessary? Because without it *force* must be employed;

and the employment of force annihilates, as far as it goes, the motives to reproduction, and consequently production itself. Without it the producer could not enjoy the products of his labor. Without it the laborer himself would establish a precedent which would lead to the abstraction from himself of the product of whatever his labor might appropriate by giving it a value or adding to its previously acquired value.

All labor should be "voluntary" as to its direction and continuance; that is to say, not only should no external compulsion restrain its action on any unappropriated or conceded appropriated article; but even to direct it to any of these, no motives but those capable of moving the *will* through the reason, the affections, or both, should be employed. Man can only be induced to act through the will or by force: there is no alternative. Delusion is still voluntariness, and knowledge is its appropriate cure. While knowledge, not force, is employed to remove the delusion, no force should be used directly or indirectly to support it: if the laborer do not choose to labor at all or in any given direction, if he refuse to obey his interest and to listen to persuasion, let no force be employed to compel him; leave him to the punishment of nature: such is the dictate of even-handed justice, of utility seeking the greatest happiness.

Perhaps the word *voluntary*, used in its widest signification, embracing the different meanings above used, might be sufficient for our purpose, and supersede the use of the additional word "free." If the meaning be more clear by the employment of an additional word, its use will not be regretted. For the lengthened proof of this first rule or law of distribution, the reader is referred to the five first sections.

What is the second rule that the preceding facts and inferences have proved? "All the products of labor," it has been shown, "ought to be secured to the producers of them."

The object being to promote happiness, and of course the greatest quantity of happiness; and this quantity depending, other things being equal, on the quantity of articles of wealth produced to promote that happiness; that quantum of use of the products of labor ought to be enjoyed by the laborer which will call forth this greatest happiness and greatest production. True, that the additions by use of wealth, to the happiness of the producers, will decrease continually in their pleasure-producing qualities: but exactly in proportion to the decrease of the enjoyment from the production, will be also the decrease of motives to continue that production. Decreased energy of motive requires increased excitement: but as the produce of the last hours of labor always affords less and less enjoyment than the preceding, there is *more* necessity, instead of less, for the use of those products to continue the stimulation of these continually decreasing tendencies to exertion. There is doubtless a portion of exertion, that necessary to existence by means of food, which absolute want will command: there is also a degree of exertion so oppressive to the over-wrought faculties, that no pleasures of enjoyment will keep them long engaged to that extent. But within these two extremes are placed all the degrees of industrious exertion: and as *habit* will not supply motive, but merely keep up the tendency to be at all operated upon by appropriate motives, and as these motives are apt to flag towards the termination of exertions, hence arises the more commanding necessity for the use of the last products of labor than for any of the intermediate products, every preceding portion of which furnishes a stronger incitement to an increased tendency.

No doubt, in the present artificial and fortuitous combinations of society, from the monopoly of knowledge and the numberless and ever-varying expedients in which force and fraud are the agents of insecurity, the laborer is *compelled*, by the necessity of living, to exert his productive powers beyond that first produce, which if left to himself would be abundantly sufficient for his support: nor is it probable that, if left to himself to consume the whole products of his labor, he would persevere in that unremitting though under the new circumstances richly-requited) toil, which is now exacted from him under the pain of destitution and death. Under the present system of things, the producer is, as to *happiness*, at the very lowest point of the scale at which he can be kept consistently with the continuance of his efforts. As to *production*, the expedients of insecurity restrict the acquisition of skill and the use of capital (the materials of production) to so few, and render such numbers utterly useless to production, that with one half the labor which is now extracted from the misery of a few, four times or perhaps ten times the quantity of production on the whole would be obtained from the active energies of an equally-informed and skilful community, all enjoying the whole of the products of their individual exertions. The accumulation of the general capital of the community—for a few accidental exceptions, to a small amount, would cause no perceptible derangement—in any other hands than those of the real operative laborers, necessarily arrests the progress of all industry but that which will leave the usual remuneration of capital which the time and circumstances afford, to the holders of the capital. Though millions might be made happy by employment on the existing capital,—land, food, houses, machines,—of any community, if rendered skillful and permitted to use them at a profit, say one fourth, or any proportion, less than that which a very few skilful laborers of the same community could be *made*, by limiting, by direct and indirect means, their enjoyments to nothing, to yield to the holders of the capital; yet as long as that force-supported organization of things continues, by which one set of men possess the productive powers alone, and another possess the physical means of putting those productive powers into operation, so long will the latter, the capitalists, use the means in their power to render the labor and the happiness of all laborers subservient to their greatest interests; so long will the happiness of the whole human race be sacrificed, if necessary in the estimation of capitalists, to produce an additional quarter per cent. profit. The laborers in their place would do the same, being all equally the creatures of the circumstances surrounding them. As long as two hostile masses of interest are suffered to exist in society, the owners of labor on one side and the owners of the *means* of laboring on the other, as long as this unnatural distribution is forcibly maintained—for without force wielded by ignorance it could not be maintained—so long will perhaps as much as nine-tenths of attainable human productions never be brought into existence, and so long will ninety-nine hundred parts of attainable human happiness be sacrificed. To obviate these evils, by excluding force altogether from the distribution of wealth, it is necessary to observe our second rule, "All the products of labor should be secured to the producers, of them." By means of it alone will all pernicious inequality be prevented from arising where it does not already exist; and where it does exist, it will be gradually exterminated, simply by renouncing the future employment of force in all operations respecting wealth.

It will not be supposed that by the word "secured," in the above rule, is meant to be conveyed any notion of coercion. To secure to the producer the products of his labor, no display of force is necessary. To abstain from the use of force, is all that is wanting. To protect the laborer in the repelling of force that would abstract the product of his toils, is the only meaning to be applied to the word "secured." For the lengthened illustration and proof of this second rule of equal security in respect to property or wealth, see sections 6, 8, 9, and 10.

There is still another rule to be deduced from the preceding sections, making with the two former what we call the "natural laws of distribution," or principles of security respecting property or wealth. "All exchanges of the products of wealth ought to be free and voluntary." In sections 7, 11, and following, this proposition is proved. Though the faculty of freely exchanging may be said to be implied in the entire use of the products of labor, it was deemed necessary to treat it apart, in order to afford room for those further developments which the important subject of exchanges demanded. Considerable space was therefore taken to show the utility of unshackled exchanges and the pernicious consequences of any forcible interference with them, of any other interference than that arising from persuasion and the diffusion of knowledge.

As in the first rule, principle, or law respecting the direction and continuance of labor, so in this respecting exchanges of the products of labor, the word "free," as well as "voluntary," is made use of. Exchanges must be free as referring to external constraint, and must be voluntary as respects the intelligent agent. Were the word "free," not made use of, it might perhaps be said, "All the exchanges that are permitted, ought to be voluntary; but there are many exchanges which it would be unwise to permit." To obviate therefore the possibility of misunderstanding the meaning, the second word is introduced; though the first alone in its fair signification might be sufficient to convey the whole intended meaning. In section 12, this rule of exchanges has been developed.

Our lengthened discussions, it will be seen, have had for their sole object to remove all regulations and interferences with labor and its products depending on force; and to substitute knowledge and persuasion for them in all matters relating to wealth, by means of intelligible and simple first principles or rules of action, the observance of which, constituting what is called *security* as to property, would lead of itself, without effort, to the utmost possible, nearly approaching to a perfect, equality of distribution of wealth, and thus to the greatest happiness derivable from it.

These rules of action, or natural laws of distribution—so called because they require no artificial or factitious arrangements for their support—as illustrated and proved in the foregoing sections, are the three above stated.

First. All labor ought to be free and *voluntary*, as to its direction and continuance.

Second. All the products of labor ought to be secured to the producers of them.

Third. All exchanges of these products ought to be free and *voluntary*.

The literal and impartial execution of these laws of distribution, will produce, without further effort, the greatest happiness to a community, to be derived from that portion of wealth, whatever it may be, of which it may happen to be possessed, or which it may be in the yearly habit of producing and consuming, and will ensure the greatest reproduction of wealth. The penalty attached by nature to the breach of these her laws of distribution, or, to speak without metaphor, the penalty ensuing from the constitution of men and of things surrounding them, is, the loss of the objects of wealth and of the happiness to be derived from them, in proportion to the magnitude of the offence, to the extent of departure from these laws.

Note

1 It is pleasing to observe that one of the first acts of the Congress of the representatives of Columbia, under the presidency of General Bolivar, has been, the gradual emancipation of all the slaves of the nation, nearly on this basis,—Freedom to the slave: compensation, by the nation upholding the wrong and participating in the wickedness, to the owner.

24

LECTURES ON POLITICAL ECONOMY

Lectures IX and X

Mountifort Longfield

Source: Mountifort Longfield, *Lectures on Political Economy*, Dublin: William Curry, Jun., London: Longman, 1834, pp. 180–221.

Lecture IX

GENTLEMEN,—The theory of rent which I endeavoured to explain in a preceding lecture, has been made the foundation of a most ingenious theory of profits. It supposes, and correctly, that as population advances, there arises a necessity of resorting to inferior soils for the requisite supply of provisions, or of forcing the soils already in cultivation to yield a more abundant produce. In either case, labour and capital become less productive. The same amount of labour and capital is employed to raise a less quantity of corn. That this must be the case, when inferior soils are resorted to, is evident, the inferiority of the soils consisting in this, that to the same expense of cultivation they yield a less return, or at least that their produce does not bear so high a proportion to the expense of cultivation as in the case of better land. The same consequence follows when the additional supply, or any part of it, is forced from the land already cultivated; it being a property of all lands to yield each additional supply required from it, at a more than proportionally increased expense. Agricultural improvements have a contrary tendency; they diminish the cost of production, and thereby render the labour and capital employed in farming, more productive. This effect of improvements is sometimes less than, sometimes equal to, and sometimes greater than, the opposite effect produced by the increase of population, and accordingly the productive powers of agricultural labour sometimes diminish, sometimes remain stationary, and sometimes increase, as the society advances in population. On the whole, however, it is generally supposed that the march of population is more certain and constant than that of improvement, and

154

must outstrip it in the long run, and therefore that there must be a constant tendency to decrease in the productive powers of agricultural labour. Whether this tendency is counteracted wholly or partially, it leaves undisturbed the theory of rent, which rests upon this principle, that if a less abundant supply of corn were required, it could be produced at a less proportional expense than the actual present supply; or that if a larger quantity were acquired, that addition could only be produced at a greater proportional expense. From these principles, it evidently follows that some corn is raised with a less cost of production, exclusive of the rent, than other portions are; but all corn of the same quality will have the same natural and average price, viz. such a price as may be sufficient to remunerate the grower of that quantity which, in order to satisfy the wants of the society, must be raised under the most naturally disadvantageous circumstances. But the corn which is raised with less expense, under more favourable circumstances, being sold at the same price, will leave an excess of profit to the grower of it. This excess, originating not in the superior skill of the farmer, but in the superior advantages of his farm, will necessarily be required and paid as rent. Thus rent equalizes the profits upon all farms, since whatever advantage one farm, from its fertility or situation, may have over another, is demanded by the landlord as rent.

But it is alleged, and I think without sufficient reason, that rent exercises a considerable influence over profits, and some of the most distinguished writers have adopted the theory, first, I believe, proposed and explained by the late Sir Edward West, which considers profits to be almost entirely regulated by the fertility of the last and worst soil that is brought under cultivation. Mr. M'Culloch, in his "Principles of Political-Economy," page 486, lays down the doctrine in the following words, which he prints in italics:—"*The decreasing fertility of the soil is therefore, at bottom, the great and only necessary cause of a fall of profits.*" The theory is an ingenious one, and I should feel much pleasure in assenting to it, and it is with corresponding regret that I have come to the very contrary conclusion, namely, that the decreasing fertility of the soil has scarcely any direct effect upon the rate of profits, and that it exercises only a remote influence, if any, by its effect in retarding the increase of population.

The proof usually given of the theory to which I have alluded, may be thus briefly stated. When inferior lands are taken into cultivation to satisfy the increasing wants of the society, the same amount of labour and fixed capital produces a less return than before; but this diminution will not, and cannot, entirely fall upon the wages of labour, since the labourer could not support himself and family if it took place; some part of it must therefore fall upon the profits of agricultural capital, and since the profits of capital employed in different trades will preserve their usual level, this permanent depression of the profits of agriculture must be accompanied by a corresponding permanent reduction of profits in all other trades; and thus as society advances in population, and is compelled to resort for subsistence to corn raised at an increased expense of capital and labour, the profits of every trade must, at the same time, decline.

The supporters of this system universally, I believe, maintain, that the increase of capital in any country, unaccompanied by an increase of population, has not even any tendency to reduce the profits of capital, since they say that the last capital employed in any manufacture will necessarily be as productive as the first, and probably more so; and they exemplify it by saying, that if a thousand hats were required, the last would not be made at a greater cost of production than the first, and so on for any greater number.

Before I proceed to give what I consider a more accurate system of profits, and of the causes which determine their amount, and produce their rise or fall, I shall briefly point out the fallacies in the two arguments of which I have just given you a sketch. In the argument used to prove that the decreasing fertility of the soil is the great and necessary cause of a decline of profits, it is, I conceive, unwarrantably assumed, that the effect cannot be entirely borne by the labourer, and that therefore of necessity some part of it must fall upon capital. This necessity I cannot perceive. As population was advancing, the wages of labour must have been more than what would be necessary to the subsistence of the labourers, with such families as would keep up an unvarying population; they may sustain some reduction, and why not the entire amount of the reduction that has taken place in the returns made to labour and capital? It should be remembered that these diminutions in the returns to capital and labour proceed by imperceptibly small differences, and not by sudden steps, and that as long as population increases, the labourer may sustain some reduction in his wages. And even if the labourer cannot bear the entire reduction, and continue to support himself and his family as usual out of the diminished wages, what is it that determines how large a portion of the reduction shall be borne by *him*, and how much, from *his* inability to bear the whole, will be thrown upon the capitalist? To say merely that part must be borne by the labourer, and the rest by the capitalist, is a very loose way of regulating a matter which must be settled by contract. Even on the principle against which I am contending, I see no way of determining how much of the diminution the labourer can bear, except by leaving him such wages only as shall be sufficient for his subsistence, and that of such a family, on an average, as shall sustain a merely stationary population. This cause, therefore, of a reduction of profits, can only operate at the period when population ceases to increase. But I do not say that it is expedient that the wages of his labour should be thus reduced, but merely that while population is increasing, he cannot occasion a fall in profits by his inability to bear a reduction of wages. The matter is left open to contract, where the only circumstance which increases or causes the rate of wages is the competition of the employers, and this will not be increased by an increase in the number of labourers, unaccompanied by an increase of capital.

In the argument used to prove that the increase of capital has no tendency to diminish the rate of profits, the fallacy, I conceive, lies in the assumption, that without an increase of population an increased supply of any article can find purchasers without a reduction of price, and that therefore the additional capital can be employed in the same manner, and with the same rate of profits, as the old capital was before such addition took place. This I think is not true, but it is enough to say that it has never been attempted to be proved.

But I shall content myself with those allusions to the fallacies contained in those arguments, since the most satisfactory refutation of any error is the proof of the opposing truths; and for my purpose, it is enough if you will grant me your attention for a few moments, without rejecting any proposition merely because it is inconsistent with the theory to which I have just alluded. I think that were it not for the progress of improvements and discoveries in the arts, and the increase of population, the rate of profits would continually decline, as the quantity of capital accumulated in the country increased.

Capital is useful, by advancing to the workman the value of his labour, before the produce of his labour is sold to the consumer. It also assists the labourer materially, by supplying him with instruments, tools, and machinery. These, which I may call by one general name, machines, are of various degrees of efficiency. By their help the labourer can execute more work than he could possibly do without their assistance. Some make his labour twice, some four times, and some ten times as efficient. It is however evident that the owner of a machine which gives assistance in this manner to the labourer, will be paid for the use of it in proportion to its value, and the injury it receives from use, and the time during which it is lent, and not in proportion to its effect in increasing the efficiency of labour. This is an immediate consequence of the principle of competition, which produces an equality between all the advantages and disadvantages of the different modes of employing capital. If the owner of one machine could obtain more for its use than the owner of another of equal value and durability, people would purchase, and artificers would then make the former rather than the latter, until the profits of each were reduced to their level. This level must be determined by the less efficient machine, since the sum paid for its use can never exceed the value of the assistance it gives the labourer. Thus, if with the aid of any instrument a labourer could execute exactly twice the quantity of work which he could perform without its assistance, then its use cannot be worth more than half the value of the work which the labourer performs with its assistance, that is, equal to the wages of the labourer during the same time. If more were demanded, the labourer would find it more advantageous of forego its assistance, and the employer would have the same quantity of work performed more cheaply by two labourers unassisted, than by one with the machine. Thus the sum which can be paid for the use of any machine has its greatest limit determined by its efficiency in assisting the operations of the labourer, while its lesser limit is determined by the efficiency of that capital which without imprudence is employed in the least efficient manner; and these principles are not altered, whether the use of the machine is paid for in the first instance by the labourer, or his employer, or whether they make or purchase the machine, and reimburse themselves by its profits for the labour or expense it costs them. The profits of capital employed in every industrial undertaking must find their level, and the height of that level must be determined by the profits of that capital which is naturally the least efficiently employed.

In order to consider more accurately the manner in which different portions of capital are employed, with different degrees of efficiency, in assisting labour, and rendering it more productive, I shall make the supposition of a society, which for simplicity I shall suppose perfectly destitute of capital at the commencement, but possessed of all the skill and information which exist among the inhabitants of these countries at the present day. Capital operates in rendering labour more productive, principally by these means—1st. By assisting the labourer with suitable machinery, including under this term all instruments, from the rudest and simplest tool, to the most exquisite and complicated machine. 2ndly. By advancing to the labourer the means of his subsistence, or the value of his labour during the progress of his work, and thus enabling him to remain steadily at his work, disengaged from the necessity of producing his own subsistence. Without capital applied in this manner, and belonging either to the labourer or his employer, little progress could be made: every man would be constantly occupied in producing the means of his own subsistence, and it is evident that little, if any, machinery could be produced, as the labourer is not supposed to have provisions to maintain himself while making such instruments. This application of capital to the support of the labourer, until his work has arrived at maturity and is fit for consumption, is therefore prior to the former, which consists in the introduction of machinery. They both agree in this, that by means of capital properly employed, labour, at the end of a certain period, will have produced goods of more value and utility than it could have done if it had been set directly to the production of such goods, without deriving any assistance from capital.

It is not easy to conceive by what slow steps the first accumulations of capital must have been made. Capital appears entirely the product of labour and previous capital. All, even the simplest kind of machinery, is itself produced by labour and machinery; that labour itself requiring to be supported by provisions already accumulated; that is, in other words, by capital. The matter appears to go in a circle, capital being alike the offspring and the parent of capital. Imagine a number of intelligent and industrious men, placed in a fertile country, in full possession of all the gifts of nature, but utterly destitute of capital. With what difficulty would they eke out a miserable subsistence, possessing no tools except what they could fashion with their hands, and teeth, and nails. It is probable that they would quickly relapse into barbarism. But if undaunted perserverance and industry should rescue them from such a fate, they would have immense difficulties to encounter, and their first progress in wealth would indeed be slow. If, however, any succeeded in procuring something beyond the means of his present support, and that some should do so is necessary, on the supposition of any progress in wealth taking place, he would then be able to command a certain quantity of the labour of other people, by offering them in exchange for it as much of the means of subsistence as they could have procured by employing it for themselves. This capitalist must then make it his business to endeavour to make that quantity of labour which he can command as efficacious as possible. This will probably be effected by employing part of his capital in paying labourers for making tools, and part of it in paying labourers who use those tools when made. Those tools must of course be such as, in proportion to the cost of production, or labour expended in their fabrication, will be most efficacious in increasing the productive powers of labour. Suppose those tools to be spades, or any other instruments of agricultural or manufacturing labour. As soon as one is made, he may put this first machine into the hands of the ablest labourer be can find, paying him as wages, so much as, without the aid of such an instrument, he could earn for himself. The profits which the capitalist or owner of this instrument will reap, will be the difference between the quantity of work which the labourer can do with and without its assistance. But as the number of such instruments increases in the hands of the same or different capitalists, other and inferior labourers must be employed to use them, and according to the principle which I have already laid down, the rate of profits must be determined by those cases in which the efficiency of capital is the least; that is, on the supposition I have just made, the profits of a single tool will be equal to the difference of the quantities of work which the feeblest labourer could execute with and without its use. It cannot be more, for then the labourer could earn more by declining its assistance; and it ought not to be less, for as there are not supposed to be instruments enough for all, the competition of labourers will compel the inferior labourers to accept such wages as will leave this profit to the capitalist, as the latter will have the choice among several labourers equally good, some of whom must necessarily work without any capital. But as the quantity of capital increases within the country, other causes will come into operation to diminish the profits of this kind of instrument: as soon as a sufficient number of those instruments is in existence to satisfy the wants of the society with the goods produced by their means, more cannot be employed with equal effect, since their products in such cases could not continue to be sold at the usual prices: and the owners of capital now becoming more plentiful, must sustain a reduction of profits, either by employing more in the usual manner, and selling their goods at reduced prices, or by furnishing their labourers with tools, which, though more effective than those hitherto used, are expensive in a still greater proportion, or by giving it altogether a different direction, and making other instruments to assist labour of some other

159

kind. But in every case the profits of capital will be regulated by that portion of it which is obliged to be employed with the least efficiency in assisting labour, since none will be diverted to this employment as long as the owner thereof can derive a greater profit by giving it any other direction.

This extends to the profits of capital that principle of an equality between the supply and the effectual demand which in all cases regulates value. The price is always equal to that sum which is compatible with the entire supply being disposed of. Much more than this it never can be, since on this supposition a part of the supply would remain unsold, the proprietors of which, to avoid the loss consequent upon having a useless stock of articles left on their hands, will reduce their prices, and by competition, diminish the price of the article elsewhere. Neither can it be much less, since the possessors of goods will not readily sell them for a less price than they can get. But from the very meaning of the terms, it is manifest that all can get that price which produces an equality between the supply and the effectual demand. In the case of capital and profits, this equality between the supply and the effective demand is produced by such a rate of profit as is equal to the assistance which is given to labour by that portion of capital which is employed with the least efficiency, which I shall call the last portion of capital brought into operation: and for the reasons already mentioned, the rate of profits cannot be much higher or lower than this. This subject may perhaps be made clearer, if we pursue a little farther the analogy between the price of goods and the profits of capital. In each alike we may remark, that there generally exists among some an intensity of demand, which however exercises no influence upon price or profits. The intensity of the demand is the sacrifice one would make to obtain any commodity, if the alternative were to be compelled to remain without it. The high price to which provisions rise in times of scarcity, is a proof of the intensity of the demand for them at all times. It proves the price which persons are willing and able to pay for them, when the alternative is to starve. And yet, although the desire of food is equally imperious among the rich in times of plenty, it does not lead them to pay this high price for provisions, because when food is abundant, it could not all be disposed of at such prices; it must fall to such a sum as will bring the effectual demand to an equality with the supply, and then, however intense any man's desire may be, it will not lead him to pay a high price for that which he can as well procure on cheaper terms.

In the same manner, if a spade makes a man's labour twenty times as efficacious as it would be if unassisted by any instrument, $\frac{1}{20}$ only of his work is performed by himself, and the remaining $\frac{19}{20}$ must be attributed to the capital. And this is the measure of the intensity of the demand for such an instrument. A labourer working for himself would find it for his interest to give $\frac{19}{20}$ of the produce of his labour to the person who would lend him one, if the alternative was that he should turn up the earth with his naked hands; or if he worked for another, his employer might pay a similar sum for the purpose of supplying him with an instrument. But this profit is not paid, because on account of the abundance of capital in the country, much must be employed in cases where, in proportion to its quantity, it is not so capable of multiplying the efficiency of the labourer; and the profits on this portion must regulate the profits of the rest.

You may remember that the effect of demand and supply, in regulating the price of commodities, is frequently slightly influenced by the cost of production, which determines the average prices, and prevents buyers and sellers, especially in the case of the more durable manufactured commodities, from departing very far from those prices to which they know the value of the article will soon conform itself. But of capital there is not, properly speaking, any cost of production, except that sacrifice of the present to the future which is made by the possessor of wealth, who employs it as capital instead of consuming it for his immediate gratification. The amount of this sacrifice varies very much in different ages and countries, and even in different persons of the same age and country. In many instances it is very slight, since we find that many persons save without any prospect of profit, but merely from the love of accumulation, or the preference of the future to the present. On the other hand, many spend, in their present gratification, what they know they might profitably employ as capital. This prospect, however, of deriving a profit from their accumulations, is a strong additional motive to save, although its influence will vary considerably, according to the manners, habits, disposition, circumstances, and general situation of the country. It will not generally be strongest where the rate of profits is highest, although, *cæteris paribus*, it would necessarily be so. But without departing from my present purpose, I cannot now enter upon the enquiry of the circumstances, which combined with the rate of profits, will have most influence in strengthening the principle of accumulation in any country.

From what I have said, it may sufficiently appear that some portion of capital must be employed to less advantage, principally on account of the following causes:—Ist. Inferior labourers must be employed to use the instruments provided by the capitalist. This, although a real, is yet a slender source of the diminished rate of profits. 2ndly. In order to find employment for all the increased capital, machinery must be resorted to, of greater value in proportion to its efficiency, when labourers are not numerous enough to create a demand for all the instruments of the more efficacious kind that can be procured for them. 3rdly. Articles which are produced partly by means of capital, will overstock the market for them, and must be sold cheaper; and more articles will be made by various descriptions of machinery, which with a higher rate of profits could not exist, as such profits could be procured only by means of such prices as purchasers would be unwilling to pay. These causes of low profits, the effects of capital accumulated in the country, generally come into operation all at the same time, although it is convenient to consider them separately. Each capitalist will endeavour to get as much profit as he can, and his interest, and the necessity of the case, will be his guide in determining him to employ more labourers, or to give higher wages, in order to prevent other capitalists from withdrawing them from him, or to sell his article cheaper, in order to prevent the goods, now produced in greater quantities than heretofore, from remaining on his hands unsold.

It may be thought that this analysis of profits is imperfect, as applying only to the profits of that portion of capital which is employed in machinery, or in assisting labour; but that I appear to have left altogether out of consideration the profits of that portion of capital which is employed in paying the wages of the labourer, or in advancing to him the means of his subsistence while the product of his labour is incomplete or unsold. This is usually called circulating capital, and it is evident that the profits of this must be regulated by the profits of fixed capital. Both must keep their level, or bear their natural proportion to one another; and I have confined my investigations to fixed capital, because I conceived that its profits admitted more readily of a comparison with labour, being regulated by that portion which the necessity of employing all the capital within the country compels to be least efficiently employed.

The additional capital is so mixed up with the former quantity, that no separation can be made, except in imagination. A machine may render labour 1,000 times more productive, and yet may partly consist of that capital which is least efficiently employed, since perhaps a similar machine, made in a less expensive manner, might be nearly as efficient in increasing the productiveness of labour. In such a case, I consider the difference in expense between the two machines as the last application of capital in this respect, and the difference of their efficiency is the measure of the efficiency of such last application. On a future occasion, I shall attempt to point out the secondary causes which influence the rate of profits, and the effects which low profits, produced by increased capital, exercise upon the prosperity of the country. In my next lecture I shall call your attention to the primary causes which regulate the wages of labour.

Lecture X

GENTLEMEN,—Our next subject of enquiry is naturally relating to the wages of a labourer, and what it is that determines their amount. In their whole science of Political-Economy, there is no subject more important than this. The class whose livelihood depends upon the wages they receive as a remuneration for their labour, is a very numerous one. In Ireland it is, I believe, more than equal to all the other classes. In England not quite so much. There is no question, therefore, that we should feel so desirous of resolving with accuracy as this, how far, and by what means, legislation can promote the prosperity of this numerous class of our fellow countrymen— whether by directly regulating their wages by law, or by making such wise rules for the promotion of trade and industry as will enable the labourer, by fair contract, to procure from his employer an adequate remuneration for his toil. What adds a peculiar importance to such enquiries as those we are now entering upon is that the opinions held respecting them may exercise an immense influence over the peace and happiness of the country, independent of the effect they may have upon legislation. This it is that makes it so important that all should be aware of the truth. As far as legislation is concerned, false opinions held by a few might be disregarded; but obedience, peace, and order, are more likely to prevail where every person sees that he cannot attribute his misfortunes and difficulties to the state of the laws. Those who live upon the wages of their labour, form not only the most numerous, but also the poorest, and the most ignorant class of society. It comprises those who, when they suffer, are the least able to assist themselves, or to investigate the causes of their calamity. Sudden vicissitudes in their small incomes generally arise from causes which they cannot be aware of, and over which, even if they knew them, they could exercise very little control. The rich man whose income is diminished, may retrench a little from his superfluities; but to the poor labourer, a diminution of income means a deprivation of some of the necessaries of life. I shall not at present enter upon those enquiries which relate solely to the vicissitudes of trade, and those periods of unusual prosperity or adversity which occasionally throw a momentary light or shade upon the condition of every order of society. I shall for the present confine myself to those causes which determine the permanent, natural, or average rate of wages.

There is one cause commonly assigned for the relative wages of labour in different countries, to which I cannot agree, and which is generally supported by a confused species of reasoning, confusing primary and secondary causes, and mixing metaphor and analogy with apparent demonstrative reasoning. The doctrine I allude to is this, that the value of labour, like every thing else, depends upon the cost of production, and that the cost of production of a labourer is that sum which according to his natural or artificial wants, is sufficient to support the labourer, together with, on the average, such a family as is necessary in order to keep up the population of the country, and to enable it to increase or remain stationary, according as the wants of the nation require an increasing or a stationary population. We know how the cost of production of any article has the power of regulating its average price, since the being able to procure such a price is the only and the necessary condition on which any persons will continue to produce the article. But the attempt to prove this truth by analogy, and to find out what is the cost of production of common labourers, appears to be a trifling with a serious subject. No such calculations are made previous to the production of a common labourer. He is not produced for the sake of what he can afterwards earn. The expression therefore, "cost of production," is merely metaphorical when applied to such a case; and no argument can be drawn from it, since the

analogy is deficient in the very circumstance through which the cost of production affects the price of articles of commerce. But it is said that if the
country requires stationary population, the labourer must earn so much as,
according to the scale of living which habit or necessity has introduced
among his order, will be sufficient to support himself, and on an average,
such a family as will keep up a stationary population: and if an increasing
population is required, he must earn more in order to maintain a larger
family, in proportion to the rapidity with which the population is required to
increase: for that otherwise the stationary in the one case, or the increasing
population in the other, would fail to be kept up.

In this I have given, I trust, a fair statement of the arguments generally
used to prove that the wages of the labourer depends upon the expense of his
maintenance and usual style of his living, instead of his expenses and his
mode of living depending pretty much upon his wages, as most people, and I
confess myself among the number, would most readily imagine to be the
case. The argument, if logically stated, would assume the form of a hypo-
thetic syllogism, in which the premises, viz. the major, which contains the
substance of the argument, and the minor, which is usually suppressed, as if
it were self-evident, are both false. But laying aside the rules of logic, as a
reference to them is not often a very intelligible or popular mode of explaining the subject, you may observe that the argument consists of two propositions, connected by the alternative phrase "otherwise." Thus—the labourer
must earn certain wages according to his real or imaginary wants, otherwise
the population required by the country would not be kept up. The validity of
this argument requires that the second proposition should be impossible, and
should follow from the denial of the first. Now, is this the case? Does a
population fall short or decrease, or does it ever cease to increase, in consequence of the wages of labour proving insufficient to support the necessary
family? If such an event ever takes place, which no one attempts to prove
impossible, it is an instance of that alternative case, on the impossibility of
the existence of which, the argument depends; unless, indeed, such an interpretation is given to the phrase "population required by the country," as will
deprive both the argument, and the proposition proved by it, of all meaning.
Indeed the argument and proposition are generally stated without this latter
phrase, and I think the omission has the advantage of rendering them more
intelligible. But even granting that population will always march on at its
proper pre-determined pace, and that the wages of labour will always be
sufficient to sustain it on its march, does it never happen that this increase of
population has the effect of depriving the labourer of some of the comforts
which he had heretofore enjoyed; may not the labourers, by descending a
little in the scale of comfort, be enabled to support that average family which
is necessary to increase the population? Indeed those who hold the opinion
which I am combating, generally maintain, although not very consistently,
that the increase of population frequently deteriorates the condition of the

labourer, and diminishes his comforts; that in fact it is the most usual and natural cause of such a change in his situation. Is not this an admission that the circumstance of the labourer's being used to a certain degree of comfort, is not sufficient to procure it for him permanently, by keeping down the population to such a quantity as is consistent with his obtaining his usual rate of wages, since, notwithstanding such habits, the population does increase, so as to compel the labourer frequently to surrender many of his accustomed enjoyments. I do not deny that it is for many reasons desirable that the labourer should be accustomed to think a certain degree of comfort indispensable. Such habits, such wishes on his part, if not the cause of his receiving suitable wages, are at least the effect of his prosperity, and therefore imply that his situation is such as we should all desire it to be. Such wishes and habits may even lead to a continuance of his prosperity, by inducing him to make extraordinary exertions, rather than forego those comforts and decencies which he has been used to consider indispensable to his happiness; and it may prevent him from forming those reckless matrimonial engagements which are supposed to produce a redundancy of population, inconsistent with the comfortable subsistence of the labourer. All I am contending for is, that the wages of the labourer depend upon the value of his labour, and not upon his wants, whether natural or acquired, and that if his wants and necessities exercise, as they do, some influence upon the wages of his labour, it is indirect and secondary, produced by their effect upon the growth of the population, and that this effect is not analogous to the effect which the cost of production has upon the price of commodities. My present enquiry is not what has brought this or any other country to its present state, but what it is that in the present state of population, science, and civilization, has the power of determining the amount of wages which the labourer receives.

I have already remarked that we ought, in Political-Economy, carefully to distinguish between the primary or immediate causes of any phenomenon, and those whose influence is remote or secondary, and which either act through their effect upon the primary causes, or perhaps in some instances modify the effect of those primary causes themselves. The neglect of this distinction has had the effect, if I mistake not, of producing among political-economists many disputes about words, or which might almost be disregarded and considered as merely verbal, were it not that we often see deductions of serious consequences drawn from propositions originally founded on verbal subtleties or misapplications of language. I think that the doctrine which makes the price dependent upon the cost of production, and be regulated by it exclusively, has its origin in this source. The cost of production does indirectly or mediately affect the supply in most cases, and in some it influences even both the supply and demand, or at least the effect which the existing state of supply and demand has upon prices. But all this influence upon prices is indirect and mediate. The importance of the question, whether rent ought to be considered a part of the cost of production, is caused by the same confusion, to which we naturally become more liable as we approach more complicated questions.

There are many matters which have the most powerful effects upon the fate of the labourer, and in common conversation it might be allowable to attribute his prosperity or misery to causes which affect him very remotely; and this follows from the nature of the language used to communicate our ideas to each other. Most effects are produced by a variety of causes, all concurring to the same effect, and all essential to its production; so that if any one of those causes had been absent, the effect would not have been produced. Some of those causes are generally certain laws of nature, others are mere facts, and properly speaking they altogether combine to form one cause. But in ordinary conversation, if we were asked the cause of any event, we should not answer by stating all the causes which concurred to produce it. We should attend more to the object which the interrogator had in view, and merely inform him of that cause which we supposed him previously ignorant of; and we should not hesitate to say that that was the cause, whether it was a fact or a law of nature, and whether its connection with the event enquired about, was immediate or remote. Hence the word cause is used in a very extended sense. But this does not make it the less important to distinguish the immediate and primary, from the mediate and secondary causes, and to examine and lay down accurately the rules by which they are connected. We shall then be able to form clear ideas, and what is scarcely less important, to use correct and consistent language respecting the operation of those causes, and we shall not be involved either in a confusion of ideas or a verbal controversy, if we find, as we frequently shall find, the primary causes producing a certain effect, and that effect reacting upon the secondary causes, in such a manner as through them to influence the primary causes, and thus to prevent the first effect from being permanent. Examples of this species of rotation are very numerous, and I shall mention some of them at another time: to do so at present would be a disorderly digression. I may however remark that such instances shew very strongly the necessity of studying the subject methodically, as very little progress can be made by detached arguments. By merely selecting what part of the circle he begins with, any man may by tolerably specious reasoning, draw any consequence he pleases. But before I engage further in any argument to shew that the wages of labour do not depend upon the wants of the labourer, it may not be out of order to shew upon what I think they do and must depend.

It is evident that the wages of labour, like the exchangeable value of every thing else, must depend upon the relation between the supply and the demand. It is also plain enough, that the supply consists of the present existing race of labourers. But on what does the demand depend? Undoubtedly, in the case of the great body of labourers, the demand is caused by the utility or value of the work which they are capable of performing. Menial servants, and those labourers usually termed unproductive, must be maintained by funds derived from other sources: but the wages of the great mass of labourers must be paid out of the produce, or the price of the produce of their labour. This, then, supplies us with a measure which we can apply to the wages of certain labourers, and by proportion to which, on the principles mentioned in a former lecture, the wages of every class of labourers can be ascertained. This gives us the measure of each labourer's wages in the articles which he contributes to produce, and by proportion we ascertain the quantity of any other article which he can procure in exchange for them. The average value of any article depends upon the quantity and value of the labour which called it into existence, considering as one of the causes of the superior value of labour, in forming part of the cost of production, the greater length of time which must elapse before the article on which it is expended can come into the consumer's hands. It is true that this addition to the value of the labour, does not appear in the form of increased wages to the labourer, because the latter requires his wages for his immediate subsistence, and the ultimate value of his labour is, as it were, discounted for him by his employer, who keeps the work, and when disposing of it, charges the full value of the labour if he sells it to the consumer. But if he gives it to any intermediate merchant or manufacturer, he in return has, as it were, to pay discount for the interval between the time at which he parts with it and the time at which it is ultimately sold to the consumer. In other language, he receives profits only proportioned to the length of time which has elapsed between his payment of the labourer's wages and his receiving the price of the article in the state in which he disposes of it. But each person thus receiving a profit on the advances which he was compelled to make, while the commodity was in his possession, it comes to the consumer or ultimate purchaser charged with a profit proportional to the time elapsed between the payment of each labourer's wages and the ultimate sale of the finished article. In this manner the relative values of any two things are found, by comparing the quantity and the kind of labour employed in the production of each; taking care in the comparison, to make an addition to the value of each day's labour, proportioned to the rate of profit in the country, and the interval that must generally elapse between the execution of that labour and the completion and sale of the entire work. The share of the article which each labourer will receive, is found by computing how much of the entire value consists of labour, and how much of profit, and then dividing the former share among the labourers, in proportion to the quantity and value of each man's labour. Thus, if the rate of profits is ten per cent. per annum, and a commodity is fabricated by the labour of ten men, each contributing equal quantities and values of labour, and each being paid his wages, on an average, a year before the sale of the article. Then the wages of each labourer must be $\frac{1}{11}$ of what it sells for, the remaining $\frac{1}{11}$ going as profit to the capitalist; and this must equally happen whether the article is one of luxury or necessity. A similar result would take place, if instead of ten, the work was executed by nine labourers, one of whom was entitled to double wages, on account of the difficulty, hardship, or disagreeableness of the employment, the skill required to execute it, or any of those circumstances which make one man's labour more valuable than another's. He will receive $\frac{2}{11}$ of the price of the work, the rest of the labourers and the capitalist will receive $\frac{1}{11}$ each. Hence the real wages of the labourer, that is, his command of the necessaries and comforts of life, will depend entirely on the rate of profits, and on the efficiency of labour in producing those articles on which the wages of labour are usually expended. To make this clearer, suppose that a single labourer employed for a year in the cultivation of that inferior soil which yields no rent, or more accurately speaking, employed in the production of that corn in the price of which rent does not enter as an ingredient, can raise 44 quarters of corn, then profits being at 10 per cent., his wages must amount to 40 quarters: and if a cotton weaver's labour is, on the ground of superior hardship, or skill, or any of those principles to which I have already alluded, equal to once and a half that of an agricultural labourer, then the wages of such a manufacturer for one year must be 60 quarters of corn; and if 20 quarters are sufficient for the consumption of himself and his family, then the one will have the price of 20, and the other that of 40 quarters, to expend in the purchase of other necessaries, comforts, or luxuries. Now suppose that the labour of 20 men for a year can produce calico enough to clothe 330 families, then the rate of profit remaining as before, each weaver must receive as wages the price of as much calico as would clothe 15 families, and of course this would be the same as the price of 60 quarters of corn. Hence the agricultural labourer could procure sufficient calico to clothe his family for the price of 4 quarters of corn. But if manufacturing industry was one half less productive, then 20 labourers would earn only the clothing for 150 families, and the price of the clothing of a labourer's family would be equal to the price of 8 quarters of corn; that is, to $\frac{1}{5}$ instead of $\frac{1}{10}$ of the agricultural labourer's wages.

In the same manner may be calculated how much of any commodity can be procured by any labourer in exchange for his wages, viz. by first calculating what portion will be received by the labourer employed in its fabrication, and then, on the principles which determine the relative wages of labour, determining the proportion that must exist between the wages of this latter labourer and those of the one whose wages we desire to ascertain. A labourer will not receive for his wages either more or less than the amount of what he produces, minus the profits received by the capitalist. The proportion of the price of the article which will go to profit, will depend upon the rate of profit in the country, and on the length of time for which the advance is made. If the rate of profits was 10 per cent., and every man's labour was of equal value, and employed at the average interval of a year from the production of each commodity: then of the price of every article, $\frac{1}{11}$ should go to the capitalist, and the remaining $\frac{10}{11}$ should be divided among the labourers in proportion to the quantity of labour which each devoted to its fabrication, and the prices of articles should be proportional to the quantity of labour employed in its production; and the wages of the labourers would depend upon the productiveness of labour: the more they produced, the more they would receive.

Now how does the supposition I have made, differ from the real state of facts? Ist. One man's labour is not equal in value to that of another. 2nd. There is an immense difference between the various lengths of time that elapse between the employment of a labourer, and the sale of the commodity in producing which he has been employed. Of those circumstances, the first has evidently only the effect of introducing a new consideration into the calculation, which distributes to each labourer his share of the price of the finished commodity. The rate of profits being the same, the sum to be divided among the labourers will be also the same, namely, $\frac{10}{11}$ of the value of the entire article, and each man's share will be proportional to the quantity and relative value of his labour jointly. The principles on which the relative values of different kinds of labour are to be computed, I mentioned in a former lecture. They are the natural effects of free competition, and of circumstances which tend to diminish the competition among labourers in certain employments, by rendering many persons unwilling to engage, or unable to succeed in them. The fact, therefore, that labour of different kinds is of different degrees of value, does not in the least interfere with the truth of this proposition. *The wages of labour depend upon the rate of profit and the productiveness of labour employed in the fabrication of those commodities in which the wages of labour are paid*, and therefore the comforts of the labourer will depend upon the rate of profits, the relative value of his labour, and the productiveness of that labour which is employed in fabricating those commodities on which he wishes to expend his wages. Now, is the truth of this proposition affected by the second circumstance which I mentioned, namely, that different lengths of time must frequently elapse between the employment of the labourer and the ultimate sale of his work? I think not in the least. It renders the calculation more complex, and therefore more difficult to be described, though not more difficult to be conceived; but it leaves unaltered the principle on which the calculation is to be made. The proportion of the wages of the different labourers employed in making any article is to be estimated on the same principle as before, namely, by a reference to the value of each man's labour, and to the quantity which he gave; but there is a little more complexity in the computation of the proportion of the entire work which is to be divided among the labourers. Compute it thus: to each man's wages is be added a profit proportional to the interval that must elapse between their being advanced and the sale of the article. This will give the proportion of the total value of the article to the share distributed in wages among the labourers. Observe that this last calculation does not suppose that

I know the absolute amount of wages paid to any labourer; it only supposes that I know the proportion of their wages one to another, and I have already attempted to explain the circumstances upon which this proportion depends. Let an ordinary day's labour of some particular description be taken as the unit or standard, by relation to which every other kind of labour is to be measured. It is not necessary that this unit should be of an average value between the extremes. By relation to this, the value of the labour which any man bestows upon an article may be expressed by a number, and another number will express the profit on the advances made to him. The wages of the other labourers and the corresponding profits may be similarly expressed, and the sum of those numbers will represent the entire value of the article. In the same way, the value of any other article may be calculated, and therefore the quantity of any commodity or commodities which a man may receive in exchange for the labour of a day, a week, or a year. It is true that in many cases no man could make those calculations; but the principle of competition leads to the same result with as much certainty as if such calculations were made and acted upon in every instance; and it is useful to bear in mind the principle of this calculation, because it shows the circumstances upon which the wages of the labourer depend, and to which we should direct our attention when we wish to ameliorate his condition. We must diminish the rate of profits, or increase the productiveness of labour. It is demonstrably true, that nothing else can procure him any increase of wages.

He cannot gain much by a reduction of the rate of profits. If a labourer earns 8d. a day, advanced to him at an average interval of a year before the produce of his work is sold, a reduction of profits from 10 to 5 per cent. would not add $\frac{1}{2}$d. a day to his wages, and the total surrender of profits could not raise his wages to 9d. a day; besides, it is utterly impossible for any direct act of legislation to diminish profits in such a manner as to improve the condition of the labourer. This can only be effected by the gradual increase of capital, and by the spread of peace, and order, and justice, and freedom, and security; in short, by every law, and custom, and circumstance which would enable capital to accumulate, or invite it to come, or induce it to stay. From the wages of the labourer must be necessarily abstracted a certain sum proportional to the rate of profit, and an additional sum for an insurance against fraud and outrage. Every destruction of property by fraud or violence increases the amount of this insurance, and thus the irresistible nature of things imposes a tax upon the labourer sufficient to indemnify his employer for every injury occasioned by his misconduct. Another necessary consequence from what I have proved to you to-day is, that taxes, unless so far as their sudden imposition disturbs the channel in which industry has been accustomed to flow, cannot affect the condition of the labourer, except when they are imposed upon the commodities on which he would desire to expend his wages. The payment of a tax may be considered as part of the cost of production of the commodity on which it is imposed, and in all cases it falls upon the unproductive consumer; that is, upon the person who consumes it in such a manner as that the mere consumption does not transfer its value to any thing else.

At first, this consequence might seem to follow from what I have stated respecting the proportion in which the price of any commodity is divided between the labourers and the capitalist, viz. that the introduction of machinery might sometimes diminish wages, for that taking, as we must, the expense of making the machine as a portion of the cost of production of the article, some of the labour must have been expended at a greater length of time before the sale of the commodity, and therefore a greater proportion of its price will consist of profits, and this will have the same effect in depressing wages, as if an increase was made to the rate of profits. The answer to this is, that a machine is never resorted to, except for the purpose of producing commodities more cheaply, that is, more cheaply independent of any reduction in the wages of labour or the rate of profits. Such reduction would produce a corresponding reduction of price, independent of the machinery. Therefore from the cost of production there must be more labour subtracted than there has been profit added, and each man's labour will purchase more of the article than it did before.

I trust, Gentlemen, that you will attend to the difference between a proof founded on an abstraction, and one founded upon a supposition. The former cannot but lead to truth, although its application may be a matter of some difficulty; the latter may lead to truth or falsehood, according as the supposition upon which it is founded is or is not conformable to the reality of things. The doctrines respecting rent, to which I called your attention this Term, are founded on a supposition which I attempted to shew was verified by experience. The theory of profits which I attempted to prove on Tuesday, is founded partly upon facts lying within the knowledge of all, and partly upon abstract reasoning. The theory of wages which I explained to-day, is founded upon mere abstract reasoning, and cannot be false in any time or country. Other circumstances may powerfully affect the rate of wages, or profits, or rent, but they must do so in some manner not inconsistent with the propositions which I attempted to explain to you. In my next lecture, which will conclude the business of this Term, I shall show some of the consequences that result from those propositions, and the manner in which rent, wages, and profits, vary in relation to each other with the progress of society.

25

RENT, PROFITS, AND LABOUR
A lecture

Isaac Butt

Source: Isaac Butt, *Rent, Profits, and Labour: A Lecture*, Dublin: William Curry, Jun., London: Samuel Holdsworth, 1838, pp. 7–32.

IN the Course of Lectures which were delivered last year, I endeavoured to bring before those who heard them a few of the leading of those truths that have been called Political Economy. I endeavoured also to point out the importance of the science to the welfare of mankind, and its deep interest to the Christian philosopher; and to meet those objections which had been made to its investigation, whether proceeding from narrowness of intellect, or weakness of faith, or grounded upon the errors, and worse than errors, which some of its professors have dignified with the name of Political Economy.

The regulations under which this Professorship is placed make it impossible for the person holding it to attempt any thing like a regular course of instruction in Political Economy. Perhaps, the science is not yet far enough advanced to make such a course altogether desirable in a University education. Much, unquestionably, has been done by the institution of this Professorship, in directing the attention of the students of the University towards subjects upon which, without such direction, their notions would be very vague and erroneous. Public attention, too, has been, in some measure, awakened to the subject by the lectures which have been delivered from this chair. The published lectures of my predecessor have not only attracted attention in this country to the science, but also made most important additions to its discoveries. In all this, much good has been accomplished. If the lectures delivered in this place have the effect of introducing among those receiving their education here, a habit of reasoning on questions connected with Political Economy, the Lecturer has not spent his time altogether in vain. It is not easy to calculate the good that may result, if out of the numbers that each year pass from this University with the credentials of her degree, even a small proportion bear with them into after life the habit of submitting to patient and scientific investigation, matters upon which, unfortunately, most persons form opinions without thinking. A very few years, indeed, will make manifest the influence which may thus insensibly, but powerfully, be exercised upon the tone of public opinion. Questions of economical legislation will be gradually redeemed from the province of passion and declamation, and brought within that of argument and reason. As there mingles with the mass of society a number of persons who have once learned to make such matters subjects of the calm inquiries of science, public opinion will gradually become a tribunal where, in the decision of those questions, prejudice will have less power and reason more.

That this may be, in some degree, effected by the lectures delivered from this chair, it is not altogether vain to hope. Much, I am persuaded, will be done by the recent institution of the annual examination, and the offer of the stimulus of honorary distinction. Without some such stimulus, it was hardly to be expected that young men would devote their time to the study of Political Economy; while for proficiency in other sciences there were held out so many brilliant rewards.

If we can direct the attention of even a few among the students to the science—if we can succeed in accustoming some, at least, to apply the strictness of scientific investigation to subjects upon which every man considers himself entitled to have opinions, and scarcely any one believes it necessary for him to think,—we will have done much service to the country. It will be much to have scattered through the professions, and the avocations of life, a number of men forming their opinions on these matters from thought, and supporting them by reason. It will be much to have so diffused through society a class of men capable of appreciating the tendency and the effects of any measure professing to interfere with the production or distribution of wealth, and therefore alive to the magnitude and importance of the interests it may involve. How much this is wanted in Ireland, we need no more striking illustration than the fact, that at this moment legislators are preparing to apply to Ireland a measure professing to be for the relief of her destitute population; which, whether wise or unwise, is an experiment of the most fearful magnitude and perilous character—an experiment which not only involves the interests of hundreds of thousands of our fellow-countrymen, but actually and literally affects the landed property of every individual to its entire amount: and yet public opinion appears as perfectly indifferent to its introduction, as if it were only a turnpike bill that were passing through parliament.[1]

I express no opinion upon the provisions of the new poor law bill: I merely employ it as an illustration. The indifference respecting it through Ireland certainly appears to me the strongest proof of the necessity that exists for employing every means of directing public attention to the science of Political Economy. We are not accustomed, as a nation, to be over-careless as to the retaining our own properties; certainly not to be indifferent to the condition of others. When a measure like the new poor law bill excites not interest in public feeling, we may presume that it is because we do not perceive the vital interests it involves. The truth is, that the great mass of the educated public—for it is of these that I speak—have never been accustomed to investigate such matters—to trace out the results of economical causes producing their economical effects by fixed and ascertainable laws. They see nothing in the bill but a measure for building a certain number of brick houses, and feeding a certain number of poor people.

It is in correcting this habit of carelessness in the public mind—in accustoming a portion, at least, of educated society to reason on the tendency of economical measures, that, I believe, the institution of this Professorship may produce important results. Perhaps, you will imagine that I am providing an excuse for myself, when I say, that its immediate object is not so much directly to extend the boundaries of the science, by new discoveries, as to interest and engage the minds of the students in its established investigations. But I am persuaded that this humble task is the proper duty—the other only the incidental office, of a public teacher. It were to he wished, indeed, that no educated person should remain in entire ignorance of the common principles that regulate the distribution and production of wealth. Under the present regulation of the Professorship, we can only make advances towards this. More than forty years have elapsed since it was first proposed, by one whose name is still an ornament to this University, to make the elementary truths of Political Economy a part of the course of university education.[2] It was reserved for the munificence of the distinguished founder of this Professorship to make the first step towards giving the science its proper importance in an institution designed, as was this University, to elevate the intellectual and moral character of a people. Much has been done, even in the immediate consequences of this step: more will yet result from it, if those who may be elected to this chair will faithfully and honestly follow out the intentions of its founder, (and not to do so, gentlemen, were worse than a fraud,) by endeavouring to make it efficient in encouraging the study of Political Economy, until we may, perhaps, hope that eventually it may lead to the establishment of some regular system of general academic instruction in the principles of the science.

In the mean time, however, we must do what we can to diffuse a knowledge of the principles, and create a taste for the investigations of the science: and this can best be done by endeavouring to exhibit the laws which we can ascertain to regulate the economic process, in their simplicity, unencumbered with the disquisitions and theories of those, too many of whom have but "darkened counsel by words without knowledge."

It had been my intention to have proceeded to apply the principles of the science to some of the questions of practical interest, upon which no person of ordinary intelligence can avoid feeling curious. The currency—free trade—the national debt—the economic effects of the extension of the railroad system—these, and many other questions of the same character, present subjects of inquiry popular enough to be generally attractive, and yet affording abundant opportunity for elucidating and applying the strictest reasonings of science. There are, however, some elementary abstract propositions with which it is of such importance that the mind should be familiar, that, on consideration, I have determined to occupy your attention by a brief review of them. From the fluctuating nature of this class, it is, of course, more than probable that I now address many who were not present at the lectures of last year; even to those who were it may be advantageous to exhibit the same truths in a new form.

We see that man, by the arrangements of his all-wise Creator, has been placed in such a relation to the external world, that many things possess the power of gratifying his wishes, and ministering to his wants. This power, which is a relation of things to our nature, we call utility.

We, furthermore, perceive that it is in the power of man so to modify things as to make them subservient to his uses: that is, to create utility that did not exist before. This creation of utility we call production. Wherever throughout this lecture I use the expression 'the product,' you will understand me to speak of the utility created by the operation of any agent.

We see, also, that in the process of production instruments are employed, which may, in the first instance, be classed under the heads of natural agents, and labour: but along with these there must, generally, be united a disposition, on the part of man, to prefer remote to immediate results. When articles possessing utility, which we call wealth, are devoted, not to present enjoyment, but to assist the process of further production, we call them capital.

Upon the nature of production, and its instruments, I do not now consider it necessary to dwell. Last year, we discussed the subject at length. The slightest reflection will teach you, that all the wealth which is in the world is produced by the agency of these instruments. The powers of nature—the industry of man—and the powers of accumulated wealth or capital, these are the agents by which is created all that ministers to the gratification or supplies the wants of man. With a very few remarks, I will now dismiss the subject of production.

That labour is a great instrument of production, it will need no words to prove. You will find the truth written in the great record of man's destiny. To till the ground was the occupation of his innocence. "In the sweat of thy brow, thou shalt eat bread," was the sentence of his fall. Exertion is the law of our being,—toil the penalty of our guilt. Were labour to cease, the human race would, in a short time, be swept by famine from the globe. The universal law of all God's gifts admits of no change or deviation: they are abundant and beneficent to the industrious, but stinted to those who will not work for them. The earth is sterile to the idle—yielding, perhaps, the miserable sustenance of the wild berry to his indolence, while all the while the rich storehouse of plenty lies but a few feet beneath the unproductive surface upon which he starves; and when the hardy husbandman drives the ploughshare down through the clod, and unlocks the treasuries of teeming vegetation that were stored beneath, then the soil is no longer barren, and man finds that nature was richly generous in her gifts; and the waving field of golden plenty proclaims that the gracious blessings of nature's God were but waiting to be drawn forth by the co-operation of man.

Labour, then, is the great instrument of production—the source of all human wealth; a lesson, which, if you have learned from Political Economy, you may carry with advantage to every transaction in which you are engaged. But man's unassisted labour would avail but little: it is the spade or the ploughshare that breaks the stubborn sterility of the clod. Wealth must be directed, not to enjoyment, but to assist in the process of a fresh production, or man's advance in civilization would be staid at its very starting.

Wealth, so applied, we call capital; and the power of capital ranks with natural agents and labour as an instrument of production.

Natural agents we may divide into two classes. There are some which bear a part in the process of production which human labour never could supply, such as the vegetative powers of the soil; others, like the powers employed in a water-mill, which merely supersede a certain quantity of human labour.

In the same way, the assistance of capital is two-fold. The subsistence yielded to workmen in large establishments, or tedious works, by which the division of labour is carried into effect, is capital; and the tools, implements, and appliances by which the labourer performs his work, are also capital.

You will find it convenient to bear this distinction in mind. Under the latter species of capital, we include the materials necessary for any business, the buildings and machinery of a manufactory, the store of goods in a retailer's shop; in a word, every application of wealth to the purposes of production which is not in the shape of subsistence to workmen.

I ought, perhaps, to observe, that last year, when I entered more fully into the subject of production, I explained that the retailer was a producer. He creates the utility of bringing goods nearer to the consumers; and his store of goods occupies just the same position in the production which he carries on, as the leather in the production carried on by a bootmaker.

You will find much that is interesting in the investigation of the means by which wealth is produced. In this brief review, I can only rapidly glance at the topics upon which we have already dilated more fully. I must now claim your attention for a few minutes to the subject of exchange.

That men will give a large quantity of one article of wealth for a small quantity of another, is a proposition scarcely worth announcing. Upon what, then, does this difference depend?—in other words, what is it that regulates value?

This is a question to which, I think, the commonest experience of buying and selling will enable you to give a reply. Go and stand in any of the markets of this city, and you will gain, certainly in a few days, most probably in a few hours, all the experience that is necessary for you to decide. You will find that articles of all kinds are dear as they are scarce, and cheap as they are plenty; and that their value appears to be regulated by nothing else than their utility and scarcity.

If before breakfast hour to-morrow morning some unfortunate accident should sweep all the loaves of bread in Dublin into the Liffey, except one dozen, the fortunate holder of that dozen would procure a most exorbitant price: but if, at the same time, the population were reduced to twelve families, he would get no more than the present price. It is but the double competition between sellers and between buyers that regulates price. Each buyer is anxious to get what he wants, and will, of course, endeavour to outbid the rest to procure it, according to his means and the strength of his desire for the article. But the sellers are engaged in a similar competition. Each of these is anxious to get rid of his entire stock, and, of course, will endeavour to undersell the others. By this double competition the price is fixed, evidently rising in proportion to the utility and the scarcity of the article.

In all this, I should hope you find nothing very difficult to understand, or nothing to which you can refuse your assent. You may satisfy yourselves of the truth of what I state by the observation of the dealings of any market. This is all the experience that is necessary to gain a knowledge of the motives that influence human beings in the act of exchange; and yet if you fully comprehend this process of adjustment of price by the competition of buyers and sellers, you will have but little difficulty in tracing out from this simple principle the general leading propositions of Political Economy.

Let us suppose that there are two articles in the market, both produced by labour alone without any assistance, upon which an equal quantity of labour has been expended; let us suppose that by the operation of the principles already explained, one of these articles is of greater value, owing to its being scarcer than the other,—the result evidently is, that the labourer who works at this article is better paid than the labourer who works at the other. Now, as every one who works desires to procure as much as possible in exchange for his labour, the consequence will be that more persons will set themselves to produce the high-priced article, and fewer will work at the lower. The effect of this will, eventually, be to reduce the value of the one, and raise that of the other, until the labourer at each is equally remunerated. This is, of course, supposing that the labour is of the same kind. Indeed, when we include in our supposition that the articles were produced by labour alone, we necessarily presume that the labour was not skilled, but such as every workman is capable of performing.

You will, I think, have little difficulty in making the inference, that such articles will generally exchange for each other; and that, generally, articles produced by labour alone will exchange in the inverse proportion of the labour expended on their production.

You will remember that in this you must make allowance for different kinds of labour. Our proposition is, that articles produced by an equal quantity of the same kind of labour will exchange for one another. But there are many circumstances which make a difference in the value of different kinds of labour; but you may take the unskilled labour of an ordinary workman as the standard, and with this you may compare all the different species of labour. I believe there is but little to be added to what has been said by Adam Smith on the subject of the different remuneration of different kinds of labour.

The great principle to bear in mind is, that, in a free state of society, no labour will be long permitted to receive a remuneration more than other labour receives, taking the advantages and disadvantages of each kind into account. And we may generally lay it down as a principle, that, making the same allowance, the value of things produced by labour is just in proportion to the labour expended on them.

Now, the same thing is true of capital, making a similar allowance for the greater risk and uncertainty of some trades than others: but, making this allowance, we may lay down the proposition—that things produced by an equal expenditure of the powers of capital will exchange for each other.

Indeed, we might state the propositions without qualification, and be accurate after all; for the high wages of some workmen is not a greater remuneration for their labour, but a payment for some other circumstances—such as uncertainty of employment, necessity of an expensive education, disagreeable nature of the employment. The values of equal quantities of labour in the abstract are equal; and so the high profits of hazardous occupations of capital will not be more than what would cover the increased insurance. Generally, therefore, the propositions are clear: that things produced by equal quantities of unassisted labor exchange for each other; and that things produced by an equal expenditure of the unassisted powers of capital would also exchange for each other.

But this does not settle the question—What is it that will regulate the exchange between things both produced by the joint operation of labour and capital? or, between things produced by labour and those produced by capital? The question, however, may be as easily solved upon the same principles.

Of course, the production of any thing by the unassisted powers of capital is a mere hypothesis. The powers of capital are assistant to labor, and united with it in the task of production; and this gives us an opportunity of comparing the value of any quantity of labour with any quantity of capital.

Capital is, of course, first expended in that manner in which the greatest assistance is given to labour; and if all the capital in the country could be expended in this way, the exchange between the powers of capital and labour would be regulated by the amount of this assistance. Thus, if all the capital in the country could be expended, as some of it unquestionably is, in multiplying the productiveness of labour to twenty times what it would be if unassisted, then, no doubt, the powers of that quantity of capital which would assist one labourer could exchange for the labour of nineteen.

But if the capital in the country were more than could be expended in such assistance, a competition would arise among its possessors, which would reduce the value of its powers; and this would go on with the increasing accumulation of capital, until it found employment in some new mode— suppose, for instance, in multiplying the powers of labour fifteen times—in which case the fall of its value would stop at the point at which it would exchange for the labour of fourteen men; until it had increased beyond the amount that could find employment at this reduced rate of assistance,—the process would then go on again; the competition of capitalists would again reduce its value, until the fall was again checked by its employment in a new, but still less efficient, mode of assistance.

This, then, gives us an opportunity of comparing the value of capital and labour, and determining in what proportions they exchange for each other. The least efficient assistance which the powers of capital actually render to labour, is at once the check and the measure of the fall which the competition of capitalists has caused.

Let us suppose, for instance, that a machine which cost £10,000 would make 100 men do the work of 120, and that it were possible, by expending an additional £10,000 in improving it, to make them do the work of 130 men: now, it is quite evident that the owner of the machine will not expend the money until the relative value of the power of labour and capital has reached the point at which £10,000 worth of capital will be equal to the value of the labour of ten men.

I stated this last year in a somewhat different form. It seems obvious and simple enough, but until the appearance of Dr. Longfield's lectures it was not thought of. With the exception of the discovery of the theory of rent— and, perhaps, even the propriety of this exception is questionable—no such important service has been rendered to the science since the days of Adam Smith.

It is of such importance that you should clearly understand the principles by which the relative value of the powers of capital and labour are ascertained, that I may, perhaps, repeat the substance of what I have said. By the assistance of capital, the powers of labor are multiplied, in different degrees, in a descending scale, descending as capital multiplies. The relative value of labor and capital will be determined by that point in the scale at which all the capital in the country can be employed.

You can easily understand that a spade, which cost two or three shillings, multiplies the productiveness of a man's labour infinitely more than two or three shillings expended in some refined improvement on machinery. A man with a spade could do, at the very least, fifty times as much as one without its assistance—an expenditure of capital to the amount of three shillings gives him this assistance, which is equivalent to saving the labour of forty-nine men. Go into one of our large factories and ask one of the enterprising men who are carrying the manufactures of Britain to an extent that seems almost like miracle—how much capital he would be willing to expend on a machine that would make one man do the work of fifty. He may perhaps answer your question by shewing some refined improvement of machinery on which he has expended several thousand pounds, with a result not much more greater in multiplying the productiveness of labour than is produced by the expend-iture of three shillings on the spade. This will place strongly before you the principle that capital in different modes of employment offers to labour an assistance very different in degree.

Now if you reflect a little you will see that between the spade which costs three shillings, and the newest improvement on machinery which will cost perhaps three thousand pounds with no greater result, there are multitudes of occupations of capital offering to labour an assistance varying in almost all possible degrees of intensity; so that you will have no difficulty in forming the conclusion that the assistance of capital to labour may be regarded as regulated by a descending scale of graduation from the highest assistance which it affords, to a limit infinitely small.

Now, supposing this graduated scale, you will see at once that it is the increase of capital that forces it downwards. If all the capital of the country could be expended, at the highest point in the scale, it never would descend to the lower and successively so through all the gradations of descent. If all the capital were not more than is required for spades, none of it would be employed in a less efficient mode of assistance, and the owner of a spade could evidently get for the use of his spade from a workman the difference between what a man could do with or without its assistance; but when the accumulation of capital exceeded what could find employment in the making of spades, each man would offer his spade for less than the full measure of its assistance, and some would in the end be forced to turn their capital into other and less efficient employments, but evidently not until competition had reduced the price paid for the higher assistance of capital to that which would be given for the lower.

In this lower rate of assistance, however, a new employment would be found for the overflowing capital, and until it had outgrown the additional vent thus provided for its abundance, no further alteration in the relative value of the powers of capital and labour would take place; but by degrees the multiplication of capital would force it into employments in which the assistance given by it would be constantly less.

I trust enough has been said to place the principle clearly before your mind, and that you fully understand what it is that regulates the relation in exchange between the powers of capital and labour.

You will observe that what we ascertain by this is the relation in exchange between the product of the powers of capital and the product of unassisted labour; and this, of course, gives us the proportion in which their joint product is divided between the capitalist and the labourer.

And just, by a parity of reasoning, we can calculate the relation in exchange between the product, whether of human labour, or of the powers of capital, and the product of a natural agent. Both the former we have already, so to speak, reduced to one denomination, and shewn how the value of labor can be expressed in that of the powers of capital, or the value of the powers of capital in that of labour. It now remains that we should shew how the value of a natural agent can be expressed in the terms of either.

Natural agents we have divided into two classes: those which merely supersede human labour, and those which perform a part in the process of production which no labour can supply. Now, it is evident, that, competition apart, the product of an agent of the first class would exactly exchange for the product of the labour it supersedes. But if this natural agent be so wide as to be incapable of appropriation—if, like the bleaching properties of the air and sun, it be open to every person without let or hindrance, to employ—or if, like the power of steam, it can be put in requisition by every one who can spend the capital that is necessary to employ it; then the very fruitfulness of nature's gift deprives it of all value in exchange; and no man would give the product of any, the smallest, quantity of labour in exchange for the product of what was wrought by the gratuitous and unappropriated agencies of nature. It is possible, however, speaking generally of the entire class, just as the principle of competition comes into play—a principle which, in its full operation, thus reduces the value of the agent to nothing—it is possible, I say, for the product of a natural agent that thus performs the works of men to vary in its power of exchange, up to the quantity of labor which it supersedes—a limit which it is obviously impossible for it to exceed.

But of the natural agents which do that which no human labour can perform, how are we to compare their services with that labour to which they seem to have so little affinity? Let us take the most important—the vegetative powers of the soil.

Now, if these powers could be infinitely drawn on—if land were boundless in extent, and exhaustless in fertility—if men had but to go to the utmost furrow of last year's cultivation, and find new plains and valleys baring the bosom of the soil to the ploughshare—or, if the tiller had but to continue his labor on the field to ensure an indefinitely increasing return; then would the value in exchange of these powers be nothing: and no man would give the product of labor in exchange for the product of these powers, which were teeming in exhaustless activity around him, and which he had but to strike his spade into the ground to call out into an energy to which no limits could be assigned.

But this is not so. The powers of the soil are capricious and varying; and very different, indeed, is the return which is made to the same expenditure of capital and labour. It is by means of this difference that we ascertain the value of the powers of vegetation in terms of the powers of capital or labour.

I will not now trouble you by going over again the subjects connected with the theory of rent, to which, last year, we devoted three lectures: a short explanation, however, may not be out of place.

That the soil of the country is possessed of different and unequal powers, I need scarcely stop to remind you. That men will first employ these powers which will yield them the greatest return to their expenditure, requires no proof. As long, however, as any of the first class powers remain unemployed, the value of the produce of the soil is merely that of the capital and labour expended in raising it; for the competition of producers will prevent it rising higher. But when all the highest class powers of the soil are insufficient to supply the demand for its produce, immediately the competition of buyers raises the value of the produce, and it will exchange for more than the product of capital and labour equal to that expended in raising it. The difference is the value of the vegetative powers of the soil.

Now, it is evident, that, if producers were limited to these first class powers, the rise in the value of the produce might go on to an indefinite extent: but a recourse to second class powers keeps it down. The product of these powers will exchange for the product of capital and labour equal to that expended in raising it; and until all these powers are employed, the value of produce will cease to rise—when they are occupied, precisely the same process will be repeated, and by a recourse to third class powers the rise will again be checked.

Supposing the same amount of capital and labor applied to any two soils—one of which has the lowest powers of vegetation then in employment—the produce of the last will exchange for exactly the product of the capital and labour expended on it: the excess of the produce of the first over this is the value of the higher class natural agent.

Thus any given quantity of agricultural produce will always exchange for the product of capital and labour equal to the amount of both which would be necessary to raise it, by the least efficient vegetative powers which the demand for such produce has called into action.

The product of capital will exchange for the product of labour equal to that which the assistance of the given capital might be equal to, in the least efficient mode of assistance to which the competition of capitalists obliges capital to have recourse.

You will thus easily perceive the simple principle by which we measure the value both of the powers of the soil and of the powers of capital in labour. We can regard both, in fact, as equivalent to the labour which they save. We can measure the labour which is saved by any power of the soil, by computing the difference between the labour which will raise a certain quantity of produce from it, and from the lowest power which the demand for produce has called into employment. We can measure the labour which is saved by the employment of capital, by the assistance which is rendered in the least efficient mode by a recourse to which the entire capital of the country can be employed.

These propositions have, generally, been stated as the theory of rents, and the theory of profits. I have thought it better to place them before you in the simple form of propositions, asserting the relation in exchange between the products of the three great instruments of production. The product of so much labour will exchange for the product of so much of the powers of capital; and the product of such vegetative powers of the soil will exchange for the product of so much of either labour or the powers of capital. This is, in reality, all that is asserted either in the theory of rent or profits. But the introduction of these terms has led to much discussion, and to many mistakes, which might have been avoided by presenting the propositions in their naked form. Men would then have known exactly what was asserted, and would neither have taken up their time in changing the terms of propositions into others, and then announcing the change as a discovery; nor yet drawn conclusions, which are nothing better than ingenious puzzles, and which appear paradoxical, because in the ordinary acceptation of language they are false.

It is, perhaps, time that this lecture should be brought to a close. I fear that you have found it dry and uninteresting. I have endeavoured, however, to compress into its compass a view of the leading propositions of Political Economy. In my next lecture, I will proceed to an inquiry which may, perhaps, demonstrate that these abstract inquiries are not without their practical value.

Next lecture, I propose to inquire into the circumstances which determine the condition of the labouring classes.

In the mean time, I will trouble you to bear in mind the principles which determine the relation in exchange between labour, capital, and natural agents.

The product of any given quantity of labour will exchange for the product of so much of the powers of capital as render to production an assistance equivalent to that labour, at the lowest rate of assistance to which capital is forced by its abundance to have recourse.

It will exchange for as much of the produce of the soil as could be raised by that labor, or the equivalent powers of capital, at the least productive expenditure to which the demand for produce has compelled the community to resort.

Notes

1 This was written early in last December. The indifference alluded to in these observations no longer exists. Public opinion in Ireland began to be excited about the measure when it had made considerable progress in the second session of Parliament, in which it had been discussed.
2 This was proposed by Dr. Burrowes, the present Dean of Cork, then a Fellow of the College, in a pamphlet published by him, in 1795.

26

'ON THE ENGLISH AND IRISH ANALYSES OF WAGES AND PROFITS'

Robert Vance

Source: *Transactions of the Dublin Statistical Society*, 1 (1847–49): 3–10. [1848]

By the Irish analysis of wages and profits, I mean that written by one[1] of the Vice-Presidents of this society, in his lectures upon the distribution of wealth. I call it the Irish analysis, because it is written by an Irishman, and because in its order, and in some important conclusions to which it leads, it is wholly at variance with the English analysis. And I take this opportunity of noticing the peculiarities of both, feeling convinced that the merits of this Irish analysis have not as yet been appreciated generally, either in this country or in England, as they deserve.

To show how little this work is known by English writers upon the subject of Political Economy, I shall mention an incident that occurred in my own endeavours to acquire an accurate knowledge of this science. A few years ago, having a considerable portion of my time occupied by the business of my profession, and wishing to economise as much as possible the remainder of my time, and to employ it in acquiring a knowledge of this science, I anxiously inquired for some brief history of the science, with the object of obtaining, as it were, in the first instance, a cursory glance at the leading outlines, and afterwards filling up the intervals as time might be allowed me. And I was delighted to find a work which exactly professed to answer my purpose. It was entitled, "The Literature of Political Economy," by J. R. M'Culloch, Esq., and professed to give a classified catalogue of the different works of merit upon the subject, together with a brief summary of their contents. It was published more than ten years after the Irish analysis of the distribution of wealth; and in that Irish analysis many of the principles which had been laid down in Mr. M'Culloch's previous works were canvassed and confuted; and yet, in "The Literature of Political Economy," I observed that the Irish Analysis was not noticed—even the name of its author was not mentioned. I suppose Mr. M'Culloch never thought of looking into *Irish* works upon the subject, under influence of the sentiment conveyed by the question, "Can anything good come out of Ireland?"

English writers upon the distribution of wealth treat of wages *before* profits, and found their analysis of profits upon that of wages. The Irish analysis does the very reverse: it treats of profits before wages, and founds the analysis of wages upon that of profits. Again, the English authors, in their treatises, write about wages as commodity wages—that is, commodities purchaseable by money wages: the Irish analysis treats of wages, primarily, as money wages. It is from these two sources that the chief distinctions between the two analyses are derived.

That money wages and commodity wages, at the same time and place, represent the same value, there can be no doubt. Further, that commodity wages form a better test than money wages do of the labourer's condition, there can also be no question. But though commodity wages are the best test of the labourer's condition, I maintain that commodity wages cannot form a basis upon which there can be erected a useful analysis of wages and profits; and that it is because the English analysis of profits is founded upon wages, and wages are used in this sense, that their whole analysis is in its reasoning confused, and in its result comparatively useless, as amounting to nothing more than a mere identical proposition.

When any man founds his reasoning in moral or political science upon a definition; for example, when a man writing upon Political Economy defines a word in a sense at variance with its popular signification, and founds his reasoning upon that definition; he can, as a general rule, arrive only at an identical or a trifling conclusion. And hence, when the present Professor of Political Economy in Oxford (than whom no abler, and, in some important particulars, no more useful writer upon the subject has appeared), when he defines wages to be commodity wages, and upon that definition founds his analysis of wages and profits, he arrives at the conclusion, "that the difference between the values of the advances and returns depends on the amount of labour which, at a previous period, was devoted to the production of wages, compared with the amount of labour which those wages when produced could command;" a conclusion which, when we estimate the advances and returns by the common measure of labour, and translate the expression, simply signifies, "that the difference between the values of the advances and returns depends on the difference between the values of the advances and returns"—a purely identical proposition.

One will now naturally ask himself, how is it that a writer of such eminence did not perceive his conclusion to be merely an identical proposition? I propose to explain this in the following way. One of Mr. Senior's chief objects, in his analysis of wages and profits, appears to have been to overthrow the system of Ricardo. Ricardo had adopted the definition of commodity wages, and reasoned upon it. This was one error of his system which Senior did not observe, and he himself fell into it. But Ricardo committed another error which Senior did observe and attack, namely, the using the fraction whose numerator was the labourer's share of the produce, and whose denominator was the entire produce,—the using this fraction sometimes simply as the labourer's share, and sometimes as the proportion of that share to the produce.

Now, it so happens that, by a curious compensation of errors, the result elicited from the reasoning in which these two errors are combined is true, and conformable to the *popular* signification of the word wages. Hence Senior, not observing any mere identical proposition as the result of Ricardo's reasoning, and knowing that he himself had founded his reasoning upon the same signification of wages as Ricardo had done, would not be likely to spend a thought upon any such result of his own reasoning, and in that way the defect might naturally enough remain unnoticed by him. But Senior did not observe the compensation of errors, whereby Ricardo, setting out upon a definition of wages *at variance* with the popular meaning of the word, arrives at a conclusion *conformable* to the popular meaning of the word. This compensation of errors was thus effected. He set out with the definition of commodity wages; then, agreeably to such definition, the rate of wages is the proportion of the amount of wages to the entire produce; and the rate of profit, consistently with this, is the proportion of the amount of profit to the entire produce. Now, this expression for the rate of profit is *one* error. Then he supposes these two proportions or fractions to be simply shares or amounts, and not proportions, which is the *second* error. Then, in order to arrive at the proportion of these two fractions considered as shares; that is, the proportion of the capitalist's share of the produce to the labourer's share of the same; he divides one of these fractions by the other, in which process the common denomination, "entire produce," vanishes, leaving as the result the fraction, whose numerator is the capitalist's share of the entire produce, and whose denominator is the labourer's share of the said produce; which fraction is the same as that whose numerator is the capitalist's share of the value of the produce, and denominator the labourer's share of the said value—which latter fraction is the popular meaning of the expression, "rate of profit," on the suppositions—first, that the time of advance is constant, and next, that the capital is all advanced in the form of wages.

It was partly by this compensation of errors that Ricardo's system was enabled to obtain the currency and popularity which it enjoyed. Ricardo's "principle" regarding wages and profits was, that wages rose as profits fell, and fell as profits rose. He meant by the word wages commodity wages, and he supposed the entire produce constant. And on that supposition, and for that meaning of the word wages, his "principle" was right; because, if the whole produce is constant, and is divided between the capitalist and labourer, the more the one receives the less the other shall receive. But, if the produce is supposed variable, then, even on the supposition of commodity wages, the principle is erroneous, as Mr. Senior at once observed; for both the labourer's share and the capitalist's share may increase together. But the "principle," that "profits rise as wages fall," is true, in reference to *money* wages, when we use the term profit in one particular sense—namely, when we consider profit as the price of capital employed in *paying* labour; for profit is then merely the discount which the labourer allows to be subtracted from his wages, in consideration of being paid at the time the work is done, in place of at the time the work is sold. And it was the truth of this "principle," in this sense of the word profit, and in reference to money wages, that greatly aided its reception and general currency.

Mr. Senior, restricting his consideration to commodity wages, did not view Ricardo's principle in this light, and therefore did not see how it could obtain currency with the public. He expresses his great astonishment that such a principle had received the sanction both of theoretical and practical men, alluding especially to Ricardo and to some practical men who had been examined by the Commons' Committee of Manufactures; and he wondered how such men could, in their evidence before such committee, declare "that prices are but little affected by variations in the amount of wages," "while profits are very much affected thereby." Now, the fact is, that both these propositions are true, and have been proved by eminent writers to be so, if we understand wages in the popular sense of money wages. Thus, Adam Smith shows that while increased capital is employed in paying labour—that is, in wages—and while the price of the article is thus *increased*, there is also, as a general rule, increased capital employed in assisting labour; and thus, in increasing the quantity of the article; and thus, in *diminishing* its price; and that compensating effects being in this way produced upon the price, it may happen that it will, in the result, be very little affected by a variation in the wages. And the author of the Irish Analysis has shown that a very slight variation in the wages may produce a very considerable effect upon the profits; for he has shown that, if the rate of profit were 10 per cent, and that a labourer received, as wages, eight-pence a day, at an interval of a year before the sale of his work, the increase of his wages one penny a day would completely annihilate the entire profit.

That Senior did not admit these truths, and was amazed at their reception, arose from the founding his investigation upon commodity wages. Adam Smith had long before expressly distinguished the two meanings of the word "wages," its popular sense as money wages, and its philosophic sense as commodity wages. Ricardo adopted the philosophic sense, and his system is greatly indebted for its reception to a compensation of errors, and to the fact that his fundamental principle was understood according to the popular signification of the words. Senior adopts the philosophic sense; and, in his attack upon the confusion caused by Ricardo's language, he falls himself into the very confusion which he reprehends. In the very paragraph where he is successfully showing the confusion of Ricardo in using "the rate of wages" sometimes as a share, and sometimes as a proportion, he is himself causing a similar confusion by using "the rate of profit" in two totally distinct senses. And it could not have been otherwise. Any man who founds his analysis of profits upon that of wages, and adopts the philosophic sense of wages, *must*, if his reasoning is consistent, fall into confusion in his use of the expression, "rate of profit." Thus, adopting the sense of commodity wages, then the meaning of "rate of wages" is the proportion of the labourer's share of the produce to the entire produce; and, consistently with this, the meaning of the "rate of profit" is the proportion of the capitalist's share of the produce to the *entire produce*. Now, according to popular language, the expression, rate of profit, is never used in this sense. In the popular signification, rate of profit means the proportion of the capitalist's share of the produce, or of the value of the produce, not to the entire produce, but to the *capital advanced*— not to the returns, but to the advances. Hence it is that Mr. Senior, in showing the absurdity of one of Mr. Ricardo's conclusions, expresses himself thus:—"The usual supposition is, that the capitalist turns his capital once a year, and receives *one-tenth of the value of the produce*; but I think," he says, "the average rate of profit in England is rather greater, and the average period of advance rather less; for, on making inquiries upon the subject at Manchester, I found the general opinion to be, that the manufacturing capitalist turns his capital twice in the year, and receives on each operation *a profit of 5 per cent.*" Thus he compares one-tenth of the value of the produce in the whole year, with a profit of 5 per cent. in each half of the year; that is, he compares one-tenth of the value of the produce with a profit of something more than 10 per cent.; as if one-tenth of the value of the produce, and a profit of 10 per cent. meant the same thing. But one-tenth of the value of the produce, and a profit of 10 per cent. mean quite different things; they are not comparable quantities; they are altogether distinct fractions; their numerators are the same, but their denominators are different. And, in the analysis of profit, every man must fall into a similar confusion who adopts the English mode of analysis, and reasons consistently. And, hence, Stuart Mill falls exactly into the same confusion. Ricardo is no exception, for he does not reason consistently, and he avoids *this* confusion, as I have already observed, by a remarkable compensation of errors.

How, then, does the Irish analysis avoid this confusion? It inverts the order of analysis. It first analyzes profits, and then founds the analysis of wages *upon* that of profits. And although, in the resulting conclusions, wages are sometimes used in the philosophic, and sometimes in the popular signification of the word, yet the particular sense is easily seen from the context, and no consequent error arises from the use of the word in its philosophic sense, because no analysis of profit is founded upon it.

Thus, the expression, "rate of profit," is taken in its common popular signification, as the proportion of the amount of profit to the capital employed for a given time. Then, two suppositions are made—namely, the time or interval between the payment of the wages and the sale of the work is supposed constant, and the capital employed is supposed to be all employed in the payment of wages. And all the cases are reducible to this form, when we consider *labour* as the common measure of value; just as when we consider *money* to be the common measure of value, we express the amount of a man's property (though consisting of several kinds of property) by so much money. On these two suppositions, the *rate of profit* is expressed by the proportion of the capitalist's share of the value of the product, to the labourer's share of said value.

Then, in order to determine the *amount of profit*, it becomes necessary to distinguish the different meanings of the word. Thus, profit is the price of the use of capital; now, capital is money capital or mental capital. And money capital has two uses, viz.:—to *pay* labour and to *assist* labour; so that profit, being the price of the use of capital, must, of course, have two meanings corresponding to these two uses. As to the profit of mental capital, though it is of the highest importance, and must always be considered in the results, yet it cannot be made the subject of analysis like the profit of money capital.

Considering, then, money capital as employed in *paying* labour, the amount of profit is merely the discount which the labourer allows to be deducted from his wages in consideration of prompt payment; and, in this sense, profit has a direct effect upon wages—the less the sum subtracted, the greater the sum received by the labourer; the less the discount or profit, the greater the wages. But, still, as this discount, at the common rate of discount, bears but a small proportion to the amount discounted, so does profit (considered in the sense we are now using it, namely, as the price of capital employed in paying wages) bear but a very small proportion to the amount of wages. Profit, considered as the price of capital employed in *assisting* labour, has not, necessarily, any effect upon money wages. Neither has profit, considered as the price of mental capital, any necessary effect upon money wages. And, therefore, the rate of profit of the capitalist, such profit being considered as composed of the profit of his capital employed in paying labour, and of the profit of his capital employed in assisting labour, and of the profit of his mental capital, necessarily affects the rate of the labourer's money wages only through the medium of the rate of discount. And this is the reason why a considerable variation in the rate of profit produces but a slight change in the money wages—so slight that, as I mentioned before, the reduction of the rate of profit by 10 per cent. did not raise the labourer's wages a penny a day.

Considering profit as the price of capital employed in *assisting* labour, the amount of profit is necessarily confined within certain limits. Thus, it cannot be less than the interest of the capital so employed; for the capitalist will not undertake the trouble of superintending the employment of his capital in assisting labour, if he can obtain the same return without any trouble at all, by putting his money out at interest. Again, the amount of profit, in this sense, cannot be greater than the value of the assistance given to the labourer by the least efficient machine in use for the purpose to be accomplished; otherwise, competition would reduce it to this value.

Having thus ascertained what it is that regulates the amount of *profit*, the Irish Analysis proceeds to investigate what it is that determines the amount of *wages*—using wages in the popular sense of money wages, or the price of labour. And setting out upon the principle that wages, or the price of labour, must be determined, as the price of any other article, by the demand for it, and the supply of it; and then, for simplicity sake, excluding the consideration of a variation in the supply, and thus getting rid of the question of emigration; and excluding also, the consideration of an increased demand arising from the use of increased capital, and thus getting rid of the consideration of extended markets, and of the question of free-trade as consequent thereon; the analysis shows that the demand for labour, and, therefore, the amount of money wages, must depend on the quantity and quality of the work done, coupled with a consideration of the length of interval between the production and sale of the work, and a consideration of the rate of profit during that interval. The analysis then shows that very little effect will be produced upon money wages by a variation in the rate of profit, or by a variation in the interval between the production and sale of the work; and, therefore, it concludes that the only sure and permanent ground upon which the labourer can rely for an increase in his wages is his own exertion—an exertion evidenced by an increase in the quantity, and an improvement in the quality of his work. The two other sources whence an increase might be expected to be given to the labourer's wages, and which were excluded from the analysis for the sake of simplicity, depend not on the labourer himself, namely, the sources of free-trade and emigration. But, apart from these considerations, the Irish Analysis has demonstrated that the labourer has not, and cannot have anything to rely upon for any important accession to his money wages, save his own individual exertion and good conduct.

However, if we use wages in the philosophic sense of the word, as meaning the commodities upon which the labourer expends his money wages, then, it is manifest, that whatever increases the quantity of the produce, and thus diminishes its price, must increase the wages of the labourer. Wages, in this sense of commodity wages, have reference to the labourer as a consumer; wages, in the common popular sense of money wages, have reference to the labourer as a producer. If we wish to have accurate notions upon the subject, we must keep these two meanings distinct. If we confound them, the whole subject of wages and profits becomes one mass of confusion. For example, if I use wages in its popular sense, it is true to say that "profits have little or no effect upon wages." This I have already shown. But, again, if I use wages in its philosophic sense, it is equally true to say, that "profits have a very considerable and important effect upon wages." Thus, using wages in its philosophic sense of commodity wages, every one of the three kinds of profit of which we have spoken, separately contributes to the increase of wages. As to the first kind of profit—namely, the profit of capital employed in paying labour, if the labourer were not paid until the work was sold, in place of having his wages advanced to him when the work is done, the price of the article produced would be greater than it is, since the loss to the labourer by the delay of payment (which loss would have to be made up to him) would be greater than the amount which he permits to be deducted for discount or profit; so that this kind of profit contributes to diminish the price of the product, and thus to increase commodity wages.

Again, as to the second kind of profit, namely, the profit of capital employed in assisting labour, the quantity of produce is increased by the assistance given to labour, and, therefore, the price of the produce is diminished, and, therefore, commodity wages increased. And, again, as to the third kind of profit, namely, the profit of mental capital, the quantity of produce is increased by the application of mental capital, and, consequently, the price of the produce is diminished, and commodity wages increased.

So that, while a diminution in the rate of profit may produce but a very small increase in the money wages, as operating through the medium of the discount, it may produce a very considerable increase in the commodity wages, as operating through the medium of the price. And though this difference would not be of any consequence to a particular labourer at a particular time and place, yet it is of such consequence in our reasonings upon the subject, that if we neglect it, we may give up all hope either of accuracy in our reasoning or of usefulness in our results. But if a person would keep in view the two distinct significations of wages, and the three senses of profit according to the meaning and employment of capital, I am sure he would get rid of many apparent contradictions, and I think he would thereby obtain more readily a scientific knowledge of the subject.

Note

1 Mountifort Longfield, Esq., Q.C., LL.D.

27

'ON COTTIER RENTS'

William Edward Hearn

Source: *Transactions of the Dublin Statistical Society*, 2 (1849–51): 3–8. [1851]

WHEN the principle of the appropriation of natural agents has once been established, the payment of rent follows as a necessary consequence. The assistance given to production by the monopolised natural agent, whether as compared with any other means of production, or with an inferior agent of the same kind, places the proprietor in a better condition than his less fortunate industrial competitors. If, however, the proprietor does not wish himself to use this advantage, he will readily find many others who are willing to take it from him; and the question is on what terms shall he part with his monopoly. Now, all profits have a general tendency towards equality; for if profits are unusually high or unusually low in any particular occupation, so many competitors will soon be attracted to or deterred from it as to reduce them to the ordinary level. If, then, the monopolised agent is put up to public competition, its price will be the exact difference between its productiveness and the productiveness of the ordinary application of capital. It will not be less; because if it were, the purchaser or lessee would still obtain higher profits than his neighbour. It will not be more; because, if it were, his profits would be lower than those obtained by the ordinary branches of industry. No one will, therefore, give more than the difference, and no one will give less; for, if one refuses to give the full amount, another will give it. It is evident that, in such a case, it is not the competition that causes the rent, but that which is the cause of the competition itself—namely, the demand for the use of the monopolised agent. The word *competition* merely expresses the intensity of the effectual demand. Men compete for an object because they desire it, but they do not desire it because they compete for it. There are thus three points connected with the payment of rent which we must observe:—First, that the rent is caused by the demand for the monopolised agent; second, that this demand is carried into effect and so the rent is procured, by competition; third, that this rent so caused and so procured, is limited, as a general principle, and as nearly as may be, by the difference between the produce of the monopolised agent and the produce of unassisted industry.

Applying, then, these general principles to the particular case to which the term rent is generally restricted, we shall find that the rent of land is caused by the demand for its produce, is procured by competition, and is limited by the difference between the returns of capital when employed on soils of varying advantages, or when employed in agriculture, and when employed in other industrial occupations. Mr. Mill observes that the difference of which we have spoken "is not, nor was it ever intended to be the limit of metayer or of cottier rents, but it is of farmers' rents." "The competition which economists speak of," says Dr. Hancock' "is a competition of capitalists; a competition of people who pay, not of paupers who promise." As the latter class, unfortunately, form at present a rather important portion of the community, and as the subject has not, perhaps, obtained as full an investigation as it deserves, it may be worth while inquiring into the causes which determine the rent paid by the cottier.

It is now generally admitted, as an elementary principle, that the value of everything is determined by the relation of its demand and supply, and that that relation is ascertained by competition. The value of labor is determined by the demand for labor as compared with the number of laborers; and that proportion is satisfactorily ascertained, and its price adjusted, by the competition between the employers on the one side and the employed on the other. The value of capital is determined by the demand for its assistance and the amount of capital existing; and this proportion, too, will be speedily adjusted where free competition is allowed. Similarly, we may infer that, in the case of land, its value depends on the relation of demand and supply, and that this relation, also, is determined by competition. We have seen that under the ordinary circumstances to which the Ricardo theory refers, there is a limit to the value of land, and that limit is discovered by competition. It appears, too, that although competition will reach that limit it will not pass it, because the demand for land will then be checked, inasmuch as capital will seek an investment elsewhere, as soon as its employment in agriculture ceases to be profitable. If, then, there is a field elsewhere for the employment of capital, rent can never pass its natural boundary, because the demand for land is limited. If, under such circumstances, the supply is also limited in any artificial manner, the only result, as far as the producers are concerned, will be, that land to the extent of that limit will be uncultivated. But, if we suppose a case where, from whatever causes, there is no field beyond the land for the employment of capital, the case will be very different. As the capital not required for agriculture cannot be invested with profit, it will disappear, but the laborers whom it has or might have employed still remain. Since there is no other means of occupation, the whole population must look to the land for their support. The laws of value and competition will still hold good. The operations of nature continue uniform, whatever the material may be. The value of land will still depend upon the demand and the supply, and the demand and supply will still be determined by competition. But the demand in the present case consists of the whole population, while in the former it consisted of monied men. In the one case the cultivation is for profit, in the other for actual subsistence. It appears, then, that although the limiting principle will still exist, the limit itself is changed; and that ultimately, the actual occupant will pay a rent which will be determined, as nearly as possible, by the difference between the produce of the land and the amount which he could elsewhere obtain for his labor.

This, then, is the difference between cottiers' rents and farmers' rents—that, in the latter case, the limit is the ordinary rate of profit, in the former, the ordinary rate of wages. Under such circumstances, any artificial limitation in the supply of land is attended with much more injurious consequences than in the former case which we noticed. As the rate of wages depends upon the amount of employment, and as rent in this instance depends upon the rate of wages, every circumstance which lessens the means of employment lowers wages and raises rents. Unfortunately, this condition of things has a tendency to perpetuate itself; the poverty of the people, whose wages are gradually reduced to the minimum of subsistence, will afford no opportunity for the rise of any trades or manufactures, except those of the rudest kind, and thus no relief will be afforded to the glutted labor market. The consumption of the great mass of the people will be of the simplest description—it will be confined almost exclusively to the actual necessaries of life. Such a state we need hardly add is eminently unfavourable to intellectual and moral progress, and these deficiencies in their turn, will be sure to re-act with terrible effect upon the physical condition of the people. It is, of course, unnecessary to point out the application of these principles to Ireland; but our country is not a solitary case—Spain, Sardinia, many of the German states at the present day, all of them up to the early part of this century, are memorable instances of the truth of these principles. In further confirmation, we must quote the words of an eminent philosophic historian, written without any view to such an application, and by one who was at least not inclined to over-estimate the teachings of Political Economy. "An agricultural country," says Dr. Arnold, "in the hands of an aristocracy, is a state at once of physical, intellectual and moral degradation, and which tends to exclude all opportunities of amendment."

If the principles we have here stated be correct, we shall find that some important practical conclusions follow from them. It will at once appear how idle it is to talk about the grasping tyranny of landlords, and to seek to check it by artificial restraints. Rent arises from and is regulated by natural causes, over which no landlord has any control. A landlord may refuse to take the rent that is offered; but, if he does, he is merely making a present of so much to the tenant. It is true that it may be wiser for him not to accept the highest offer; but it is equally true that it is his interest to take the highest offer of which there is a reasonable prospect of payment. It is no more possible to regulate the price of land than it is to regulate the price of money, or of labor, or of food. The natural demand will invariably break down all the artificial barriers that may be opposed to it. In the case of any such legislative interference, the landlord will either be obliged to let his land at a fixed price, or he will not. If he is obliged than there will be left a residue who can have no land at all; for, from the very statement of the case, it appears that the demand for land is excessive. If he is not obliged to let it at a fixed price, then those who will obey the law must go without the land, while those who are willing to evade it must, in addition to the natural price pay for the risk which such evasion would cause. There is, however, a fundamental objection to any scheme for the artificial limitation of rent, for it removes all data by which rent could be fixed. Even at present it appears that it is no easy matter to get any two experienced professional men to agree in their valuation of a farm, how much would the difficulty be increased when they no longer had the ordinary letting price of the country to guide them?

Another method which has been proposed for relieving the distress arising from the fierce competition for land is, to give the occupiers a permanent title, to convert them into owners in fee, and the present owners into rent chargers, and to prevent a recurrence of our present difficulties by rendering the new properties inalienable. We fear that this plan looks very like doing evil that good may come; there certainly appears full room for Lord Bacon's hint on such occasions, that we are certain of the evil, but very far from certain of the good. The mere change of ownership would probably prove, at best, a very trifling benefit. The laws which determine the value of land would continue in full operation, and, while the circumstances remain unchanged, the alteration of the men is of no importance. At the same time the remedy proposed to prevent the recurrence of the disease is the surest way of perpetuating it. "The magic of property" will, indeed, do much; but it must be property in its fullest sense, with all its accompanying incidents. It is not merely because they have peasant proprietors that most of the continental states are so rapidly improving in their social condition, but because those proprietors can sell their estates when they please. It is not because the fundholder is free from most of the cumbrous contrivances that clog the title of land that the funds maintain so high a price, but because he can so readily transfer his interest. It is little comfort to a Chancery suitor to know that his estate is his own, when he finds it impossible to part with it and ruinous to keep it. Mr. Kay furnishes us with remarkable evidence on this point:—"In Saxony," he says, "before the beginning of the present century, there were a number of small proprietors, who held their lands under strict settlements, and accounts published in those times represent the condition of the proprietors themselves and that of their farms to have been wretched, and to have been progressively deteriorating; and those old reports, with great discrimination and justice, declare that the cause of that state of things was not the smallness of the estates, but that the small proprietors could not dispose of their lands to men of science and capital, when they felt it to be their interest to do so."

"Cottiers," says Mr. Mill, "must cease to be." We fully agree with this dictum, although we venture widely to differ from that distinguished economist as to the means by which this object can be effected. We have already stated the grounds on which we consider the plan which he suggests of a rent limited by law or custom to be altogether objectionable. In order to state our own views, we must again refer to the principles with which we set out. The value of land is determined by the relation of its demand and supply, and that relation is ascertained by competition. To interfere with competition would be to reject our only guide. It would not alter the value of land, but would prevent us from finding out exactly what that value was. The difficulty would be only increased, and the confusion worse confounded. We must, then, look to the constituents of value—the demand and the supply. The demand is the existing population. To interfere with the progress of population, as Mr. Mill evidently desires, seems to be hopeless, even supposing that it were desirable. Emigration on such a scale as to afford present relief seems now, for several reasons, to be generally considered impracticable. The creation of other channels of industry is, indeed, most important, but it is the consequence rather than the cause of an improved social state; we must turn, then, to the other constituent of value, and examine the supply. The supply of land is evidently all the land in the country; if, then, all the land in the country is made available for the purposes of production, to the utmost extent of which it is capable, nothing more remains to be said on the subject. We need hardly say, however, that such is far indeed from being the case in Ireland. Nearly four millions of acres, all of which could be profitably reclaimed, are lying utterly waste; indeed, it is probable, as Sir Robert Kane has remarked, that there is not an acre in Ireland which is altogether incapable of cultivation. It is well known that the land that is cultivated is not nearly as productive as, with proper management, it might become. Lord Devon's Commission assures us that our agriculture is defective in the highest degree, and it would be easy to accumulate other evidence in support of a fact so generally admitted and deplored. Whatever, therefore, diminishes the productiveness of land, may be considered as diminishing its supply, as surely as, though in perhaps a less degree than those causes which keep it out of the market altogether. We have now arrived at a question of no common importance. Why, when distress is so general and so severe, is so much land suffered to remain in utter idleness, while such bad use is made of the remainder? The answer to this question has been already so fully given to this society, by one who has done more than almost any other Irishman to promote the diffusion of economic knowledge, that we need only remark that the real impediments to Irish prosperity are to be found in the state of the law of real property.

We would, however, observe, that the only sound policy in this case is a complete and total removal of the present restrictions. As long as the law allows of numerous co-existing interests in the land, the courts of justice must take cognizance of all these interests; as long as the law allows of remote and complicated titles, investigation will be expensive and conveyances lengthy. Any arbitrary alteration in these matters is as likely to work mischief as good, even supposing that it is possible to bring it into operation. There may be, and probably is, much that might be with advantage amended in the working of the Courts of Equity, and in the practice of conveyancing; all but that can be done in this way is nothing compared to the complete removal of the cause of the evil itself. The beneficial effect of the unfeudalisation of land would appear both directly and indirectly. The demand for land would be, of course, satisfied in the same proportion as the additional land brought into the market increased the supply. But, besides this, as the condition of the people improved, a demand would gradually arise for articles of luxury, and thus a continually increasing field of employment would be open for the surplus labor of the country. In this way, then, by the mutual reaction of agriculture and manufactures we should see the ignorant and miserable cottier steadily and safely disappear before the well-directed and well-paid industry and skill of the farmer.

"We may hope," says Mr. Mill, "to see from the present lazy, apathetic, reckless, improvident, and lawless Ireland a new Ireland arise, consisting of peasant proprietors with something to lose, and of hired labourers with something to gain; the former attached to peace and law through the possession of property, the latter, through the hope of it." Such a sight we may, with the blessing of God, one day witness, but it will never be brought about by tampering with rent or interfering with population. In social as well as in physical science, the only means of conquering nature is by obeying her; and in social science, too, there exist unwritten laws, not of to-day's nor of yesterday's enactment, but immutable, eternal: laws "which we did not make, which we cannot alter, and to which we must only conform." Such are the laws of value, of competition, of population; with these any interference will be probably mischievous, certainly futile. But, while we thus predict the inutility of seeking to check the demand for land—while we deprecate any interference with its price—we are fully alive to the fact, that the present system of the law of real property is one continuous interference with its supply. It is, then, to the removal of such pernicious interference that we must look; and when we shall see, as one day we most surely shall see, the last remnant disappear of a restrictive system unknown in ancient, and repudiated in modern times, legislation will have done all that it is in its power to do to promote the happiness and develope the resources of Ireland.

28

'POLITICAL ECONOMY AND THE RATE OF WAGES'[1]

Thomas Edward Cliffe Leslie

Thomas Edward Cliffe Leslie, *Land Systems and Industrial Economy of Ireland, England, and Continental Countries*, London: Longmans, Green & Co., 1870, pp. 357–79 [first published 1868].

'THE premises of the political economist,' says Mr. Senior, whose conception of the science is that of an influential school of economists, 'consist of a very few general propositions, the result of observation or consciousness, and scarcely requiring proof or even formal statement; and his inferences are, if he has reasoned correctly, as certain as his premises.' According to this view, political economy not only is purely a deductive science, but its deductions follow from premises obtained without labour of investigation, lying on the surface of the mind or of things; and they need no verification by comparison with facts; indeed Mr. Senior especially protested against its being considered by continental economists a science *avide de faits*. Considering how numerous and diverse are the things comprised under the denomination of wealth, how various the passions and motives relating to them, how numerous and complicated the conditions which control their production and distribution, it does appear to us amazing that it should ever have been thought possible to construct a science of such a subject with little or no inspection of the phenomena whose laws it aims to interpret. The shortest compass within which the ultimate problem of all science can be comprised, the fewest premises with which the investigators ought to rest satisfied as complete, Mr. Mill defines thus: 'What are the fewest and simplest assumptions, which being granted, the whole existing order of nature would result? or, What are the fewest general propositions from which all uniformities which exist might be deduced?'[2] Every great advance in the progress of science is a step, Mr. Mill adds, towards the solution of this problem; and if this be a proper definition of the general problem of scientific investigation, and political economy be a branch of it, it surely follows that its fundamental laws ought to be obtained by careful induction, that assumptions from which an unreal order of things and unreal uniformities are deduced cannot be regarded as final or adequate; and that facts, instead of being irrelevant to the economist's reasoning, are the phenomena from which he must infer his general principles, and by which he ought constantly to verify his deductions.[3] The main object of this article is to examine the conditions which govern the great department of the production and distribution of wealth, indicated by the word wages; but it is hoped that the investigation may not only elicit some information on that special subject, but also afford evidence of the necessity of studying every economic problem in conformity with the universal canons of the logic of science—of accepting no assumptions as finally established without proof, none as adequate from which conclusions untrue as matters of fact are found to result, and no chains of deduction from hypothetical premises as possessing more than hypothetical truth, until verified by observation.

The theory of wages propounded by economic writers in general, though rejected by Mr. Thornton, and subjected to important practical modifications and corrections by Mr. Mill, Mr. Fawcett, and Mr. Waley, may be said to consist of two propositions. (1.) That there is a general wages fund, the proportion of which to the number of labourers fixes the average rate of individual earnings. (2.) That competition distributes this fund among the working classes according to the nature of their work, its difficulty, severity, unpleasantness, &c., so that allowing for differences in the quality of the labour there is an equality in the rates of wages in different employments. Mr. M'Culloch's treatise *On the Circumstances which determine the Rate of Wages*, states the first of these two propositions as follows (chapter i.): 'Wages depend at any particular period on the magnitude of the fund or capital appropriated to the payment of wages, compared with the number of labourers. . . . Let us suppose that the capital of a country annually appropriated to the payment of wages amounts to 30,000,000*l*. sterling. If there were two millions of labourers in that country, it is evident that the wages of each, reducing them all to the same common standard, would be 15*l*.; and it is further evident that this rate could not be increased otherwise than by increasing the amount of capital in a greater proportion than the number of labourers, or by diminishing the number of labourers in a greater proportion than the amount of capital. Every scheme for raising wages which is not bottomed on this principle, or which has not an increase of the ratio of capital to population for its ultimate object, must be nugatory and ineffectual.'

The second proposition is stated in the same treatise thus (chapter v.): 'Were all employments equally agreeable and healthy, the labour to be performed in each of the same intensity, and did they all require the same degree of dexterity and skill on the part of the labourer, it is evident, supposing industry to be quite free, that there could be no permanent or considerable difference in the wages paid to those engaged in them. . . . Hence the discrepancies that actually obtain in the rate of wages are confined within certain limits; increasing or diminishing it only so far as may be necessary to equalise the favourable or unfavourable circumstances attending any employment.'

We maintain in opposition to these propositions that no funds are certainly appropriated by employers either collectively or individually to the hire of labourers; that the 'average rate of wages' is a phrase without practical meaning; that competition does not equalise wages; that the actual rates of wages are not determined solely by competition, or by any one general cause; and that the aggregate amount of wages is merely the arithmetical sum of the particular amounts of wages determined in each case by its own special conditions. We maintain too that the theory we controvert discredits political economy with the labouring class, and diverts the attention alike of labourers, employers, and economists from the investigation of means by which the wealth of the working classes might be increased and their relations with employers placed on a more satisfactory footing.

A remark which the first of Mr. M'Culloch's propositious might have suggested to his own mind at once is, that supposing it true that the average rate of wages depends on the proportion of an aggregate fund to the number of labourers, small light is nevertheless shed on the subject by the statement of the problem in that way. Has it ever been propounded as the theory of the rate of profit that it depends on the ratio of the aggregate amount of profit to the aggregate quantity of capital? or as the theory of rent that the average rent of an acre depends on the proportion of the total amount of rent to the total number of acres? Were M'Culloch's proposition true to the letter, the question put in a very instructive article in the *North British Review* would remain, 'How does the amount of the wages-fund happen to be what it is? What will make it rise or fall?'[4] By Mr. Dudley Baxter's estimate of the amount and distribution of the national income, 10,961,000 manual labourers have an aggregate income of 334,645,000*l.*, while 2,759,000 persons in other classes have an income of 489,364,000*l.*; but Mr. Baxter does not pretend that these statistics afford an explanation of the facts they succinctly express, namely, that there is such a total national income, such a distribution of it, and such an aggregate amount of wages received by so many labourers. How is it—it remains to be ascertained—that the many have so little while the few have so much? Why is it that both together have no more? Could any causes alter the total amount of the national income, or its distribution, or both, in favour of the labouring class; or, on the contrary, to their disadvantage? The doctrine of Mr. M'Culloch either means that the total revenue of the labouring class, 'the aggregate wages-fund,' is fixed and invariable in amount, or it does not. If it does not, if the working classes might earn more or less collectively than they actually do, the doctrine in question evidently leaves untouched the very problem it professes to solve, namely, what are the causes determining wages? If, on the other hand, it means that there is a fixed quantity of wealth appropriated exclusively and certainly to the labouring class, it must be seen in a moment to be false by any one who reflects that capital can emigrate, and that the place and manner of its employment depend on individual estimates of profit; that in husbandry there is the alternative of pasture or tillage; that in both manufactures and agriculture, machines, animals, and natural agents may be substituted for labourers; and that the amount of income, as well as of capital, expended on labour or service is as variable as the tastes and dispositions of different individuals and different periods. The successor to a large income may spend more or less than his predecessor in the hire of labourers or servants; moreover, as there will be occasion to notice more particularly hereafter, the expenditure of any given amount of income upon commodities causes a greater or less expenditure of capital upon labour according to the kind of commodities and their mode of production. Again, the same collective amount of capital and income expendible upon labour may yield very different rates of wages, according not to the number of labourers only, but to the number also of employers, and the manner in which the whole amount is divided among them. If engrossed chiefly by a few, they may fix wages by combination at a minimum; if very unequally shared among a large number of employers, the rate determined even by competition may be much lower than it would be upon an equal division, since the richer employers may get the pick of the market for a very little more than the poorer can pay. We may pass then to the second of Mr. M'Culloch's propositions, namely, that wages are equal, allowing for differences in the quantity and quality of work. So convinced was Mr. M'Culloch of the necessary truth of this proposition that he appended a note to Adam Smith's statement of the doctrine of wages, in which he affirmed that modern facilities of communication have brought the wages of labour 'much nearer to a common level than at the period of the *Wealth of Nations*;' and that they are 'nearly the same all over the country.' Now what are the facts? While Adam Smith was composing his treatise in Scotland, Arthur Young was collecting statistics of agricultural wages in England; and in the 26 counties he traversed, the lowest rate was then 6s. a week, in two counties only being so low; the highest rate was 8s. 6d., in one county only being so high; the rate varying generally between 6s. 6d. and 8s. Eighty years afterwards (in 1850 and 1851) Mr. Caird traversed the same counties and found the minimum rate still 6s., but the maximum raised to 16s. In Lancashire, again, wages had risen from 6s. 6d. to 15s.; but in Suffolk they had fallen from 7s. 11d. to 7s., though meat, butter, and milk had greatly risen, and cottage rents 100 per cent.[5] The real increase of inequality in wages in 1850, compared with 1770, was indeed considerably greater than the money rates show, for Adam Smith was altogether mistaken in supposing the prices of food to be nearly the same throughout the kingdom in his time, but they had become nearly the same in 1850. In 1860 they are still nearer a perfect equality, but the inequality in wages continues, as the following evidence proves:

'In the parish of Chester-le-Street, for example, a very large parish, with a population of more than 20,000 inhabitants, the rate of wages, whether from farmers or gentlemen, for an able-bodied agricultural labourer is at least 15s. a week, and for "hinds" about 19s. to 20s. with house free, and very often coals also. I may mention also that the rate has never varied since I recollect looking into these matters, namely, from 1843; and I may say the same rate exists in the greater part of the county of Durham and the south part of the county of Northumberland. The labourers eat meat almost every day.

'With regard to Dorsetshire, where I am now living, wages are in many places now as they have been for thirty years, namely, from 7s. to 8s. a week; and out of this they have often to pay 4l. a year for a cottage, generally a wretched one. These labourers hardly know what meat is; they have perhaps a pig, but if so have to spin out the bacon; they live chiefly on cheese, bread, and potatoes. Occasionally they may have a small patch of land near their cottage, or a piece of allotment land for which they pay a small rent. Although the price of bread, meat, &c., has risen so much in late years, the rate of labour has not varied. There are no manufactories of any kind, and the labourers are a very unenterprising race, getting through much less work than a Northumbrian who has his 15s. to 18s. a week and eats meat.'[6]

Take next an intervening county between Northumberland and Dorsetshire, with intervening rates of wages. The rector of a parish in Northamptonshire writes:[7]

'Wages in Northamptonshire ranged in 1848 from 9s. to 10s. a week, 9s. being the most common rate; in 1858 from 10s. to 12s., the latter prevailing generally near large towns. In 1868 I know of two parishes in the county where wages are only 11s. a week; generally in the richest parts of the county they are about 12s. They rise as you get near the towns; being in my parish 14s. for ordinary agricultural labourers.

'The rate is ruled in this county chiefly by two causes, the price of wheat and the amount of competition. In the neighbourhood of railway works, for example, the farmers are obliged to keep their wages in fair proportion to their profits from prices; and in such places, when a farmer gets good prices, he generally raises the wages of his men spontaneously. For instance, in 1867, the farmers about here told their men they would raise wages from 12s. to 13s.; in 1868, from 13s. to 14s. In out of the way places, where there is no competition of other employments, I fear wages are kept at old rates of 11s. and 12s.; much too little for a labouring man at present prices. One woman in this parish showed her books lately, from which it seems that she paid 13s. 4d. each week this winter for bread and flour, her husband's wages being 15s.: not much left for rent and clothing, &c.! Harvest pulls them through.'

Political economists might many years ago have reformed the poor law, improved the cottages of the rural population in many counties, and done much to raise wages in the counties where they are lowest, if, instead of assuming a fictitious equality, they had applied themselves to discover the causes of a real inequality. But it is one of 'a profound kind of fallacies in the mind of man,' says Lord Bacon, that it 'doth usually assume and feign in nature a greater equality and uniformity than is in truth.' We have seen how far agricultural wages are from that equality and uniformity which Mr. M'Culloch assumed:[8] the following evidence, given before the Trade-Unions Commission, relates to wages in towns:

'Wages all over the country vary in a most unaccountable manner, as far as any reasons arising from the circumstances either of the trade or the locality would lead one to expect. For instance, masons' wages are at Chester $6\frac{3}{4}d$. per hour, at Shrewsbury $5d$. per hour; those are two towns which of course are very similarly situated as far as expense of living is concerned, and as far as other circumstances are concerned. At Clevedon they receive only $4d$., at Penzance they receive $6d$., at Exeter $4\frac{1}{2}d$., at South Shields $7\frac{1}{4}d$., at Newcastle-on-Tyne $5\frac{7}{8}d$., at Preston $7\frac{3}{8}d$., at Lancaster $6d$..... At Blackburn bricklayers' wages are $8d$. per hour, at Liverpool $6\frac{1}{2}d$., at Stafford $6\frac{1}{2}d$., at Walsall $5\frac{1}{4}d$., at Huddersfield $8d$., at Barnsley $5\frac{3}{8}d$.; in different parts of England the wages vary from $8d$. to $4\frac{1}{2}d$. per hour. . . . Carpenters and joiners at Chester get $6d$. per hour, at Shrewsbury $4\frac{7}{8}d$., at Southport $6\frac{3}{4}d$., at Wigan $5\frac{5}{8}d$.; and wages vary from $8d$. to $4\frac{5}{8}d$. per hour. Plasterers' wages at Durham are $6\frac{1}{2}d$. per hour, at Darlington $5\frac{3}{8}d$., at Barrow-in-Furness $7\frac{1}{8}d$., at Wigan $5\frac{5}{8}d$., at Chester $5\frac{3}{4}d$., in the Staffordshire Potteries $7\frac{1}{4}d$., at Scarborough $7\frac{1}{4}d$.; and wages vary from $8d$. to $4\frac{3}{4}d$. per hour. As far as the plumbers, painters, and glaziers are concerned, it is difficult to institute a comparison; but as far as I can distinguish, they vary just as much as the other trades. Slaters' wages vary in different parts of England from $8d$. to $4\frac{5}{8}d$. per hour. Bricklayers' labourers' wages are at Chester $3\frac{1}{2}d$. per hour, at Shrewsbury $3d$., at Barrowin-Furness $5\frac{3}{8}d$., at Liverpool $4\frac{5}{8}d$., at Preston $3\frac{1}{2}d$., in London $5d$., at Hereford $3\frac{1}{4}d$., and at Gloucester $2\frac{3}{4}d$.; and wages vary from $5\frac{3}{8}d$. to $2\frac{3}{4}d$. in different parts of England.'

The secretary of the General Builders' Association, who gave the foregoing evidence, speaking on behalf of employers, attributed the striking inequality in wages he described to the disturbing influence of trade-unions. The secretary of the Amalgamated Society of Engineers, on the other hand, speaking on behalf of working men, though affirming in like manner that wages vary in quantity from town to town, maintained that the operations of the union tend to equalise them.[9] Whether this be so or not (and the information unions collect and the objects they have in view seem to tend to equalisation), the fact of great inequality remains. It is, moreover, much greater in the case of agricultural labourers, who have no unions, than of town operatives, who have; and the very existence of unionism is enough to disprove the theory that individual competition is the sole regulator of wages, and that labour naturally finds its own level, like water.

'The spirit quickeneth, but the letter killeth.' The followers of a phil-osopher owe him no literal sequence: they owe it, on the contrary, to his fame and example, and to the science or system of investigation which he estab-lishes, to give it all possible correction as well as expansion; but in political economy it has been the fate of both Adam Smith and Mr. Mill that the letter of general propositions found in their pages has been pushed with pitiless logic to the utmost extreme, without even the qualifications in those very pages, as though a *reduction ad absurdum* of the master were the object of the disciple. Adam Smith, for example, laid it down as a general principle, that 'the whole of the advantages and disadvantages of different employ-ments of labour must, *in the same neighbourhood*, be either perfectly equal or continually tending to equality, in a society *where every man was perfectly free to choose what occupation he thought proper, and to change it as often as he thought proper*.' But he was so far from treating this very limited proposition as true without exception, even within its specified limits, that he has expressly said: 'The wages of labour, it must be observed, cannot be ascer-tained very accurately anywhere, different prices being often paid at the same place and for the same sort of labour.' Yet his doctrine now commonly takes the form of an unqualified assumption that competition exactly adjusts payment in all cases to the quality and quantity of labour; that wages are equal in proportion to work all over the country; that the whole island is 'the same neighbourhood' to every man, like his parish; and that every man is able both to choose what occupation he pleases, and to change it as often as he pleases. Mr. Mill has been no less unfortunate than Adam Smith in the fate of his teaching. Instead of assuming that wages are equal, that free competition is the universal condition of the labour market, and that every disadvantage or difficulty is accordingly compensated by proportionate payment, Mr. Mill actually says, 'that wages are generally in an opposite direction to the equitable principle of compensation erroneously represented as the general law of the remuneration of labour. The really exhausting and the really repulsive labours, instead of being better paid than others, are almost invariably paid worst of all, *because performed by those who have no choice*.' In the employments of women, again, he observes that 'the remuner-ation is greatly below that of equal skill and equal disagreeableness in employments carried on by men;' the reason in some cases being, as he adds, that women's wages are not determined by competition but by custom, and, in all cases, their wages being lowered by their exclusion by men from many employments for which they are by nature eminently fitted. Speaking, on the other hand, of the effect of combination in some of the employments of men, Mr. Mill remarks that 'the journeymen typefounders are able, it is said, to keep up a rate of wages much beyond that which is usual in employments of equal hardness and skill; and even the tailors, a much more numerous class, are understood to have had to some extent a similar success.' Concurring, then, as we do with a critic of Mr. Mill's doctrine, as to the matters of fact in the following sentence, we maintain that they are matters of fact exactly analogous to those to which Mr. Mill has himself drawn pointed attention:

'How could the shoemakers compete with the tailors, or the blacksmiths with the glassblowers? . . . So far as trade and competition are concerned in the matter, the capital applicable at any particular time for the employment of additional labourers in any particular trades in this country—such, for instance, as the iron trade or the watch trade—is far more accessible to the ironworkers of Belgium or the watchmakers of Geneva, than to any unfortunate members of our own population who, not being wanted in the trades for which they are skilled, are not skilled in the trades where the demand for labour is unsatisfied.'[10]

In the case of cognate or similar trades, an interchange or migration from one to the other is not unusual. 'A man who was a ship-carpenter,' to take an example from the evidence collected by the Trade-Unions Commission, 'at the time the census was taken, very likely a month afterwards was a house carpenter, and *vice versâ*; and such is the case with certain branches of the cabinet-making trade and carpenters.' Yet even between cognate trades there is often no migration; sometimes, no doubt, because of purely artificial and indefensible obstacles,[11] yet not the less real even then; sometimes because of natural differences in the work and the men; sometimes, again, because it is by no means easy to compare the relative advantages even of trades closely related. 'Take sashes and floors,' says Lord Elcho, 'the sash requires a more skilled workman than the floor?' 'Yes,' Mr. Potter replies; 'but the floor requires a stronger man.' Sashes and floors are sometimes made by the same men; but a classification and separation of workmen is sometimes founded even on this comparatively slight difference in the work and the qualities it requires; which illustrates the principle that there are, in the nature of things, obstacles to that perfectly free choice and change of occupations which many economists have assumed. The very division of labour creates, in its natural consequence of special skill, a barrier between one trade and another. Special skill, in fact, would possess no value, and would not be acquired, if it did not limit competition. Those who possess it are nevertheless liable to changes both in demand and in the modes of production; and wages are therefore by no means uniformly proportionate to skill, or to the labourer's cost of production; a point on which we must venture to differ from the theory of wages in a new *Manual of Political Economy* by Mr. Rogers. Besides, how is the workman to estimate the real earnings in every other trade in the country? It is by no means always easy to judge what the earnings are even in another branch of his own trade at the same spot. The secretary of the Sheffield United Joiners' Toolmakers, having stated to the Outrages Inquiry Commissioners that some of the branches of the trade were over-handed, was asked:

'Which of the four is the most highly paid branch?—That is a very disputed point. If I had to decide it, I should think the grinders were the best paid branch.

'And what would a grinder make per week?—Well, 2*l.* perhaps; but not being a grinder, I cannot speak exactly. Then he has heavier expenses than other men.'

The fact is, that the workman no more has a perfectly free choice of occupations than the barrister has a power of becoming whenever he pleases an editor, or the manager of a bank or a factory, or a Queen's messenger, or a clerk in the Admiralty. The impediments to the changes of occupation and the resulting inequalities in wages are partly, no doubt, unjust and pernicious, and so far as they are so, it is by detecting and not by ignoring them that the economist will really further equality; but they are also partly inherent and natural. There is, in fact, a much freer migration between some bordering grades of capital and labour than between different departments of labour; and the doctrine that a general tax upon profits must be borne by capitalists alone requires revision accordingly—a point which we notice as an example of the manifold errors resulting from reasoning on assumptions founded, not upon facts, but upon general terms. The line of demarcation in terms between 'capitalists' and 'labourers' no more separates the two orders impassably than the term 'competition' places all the members of each order in a position to compete with each other. The number of servants who become shopkeepers and lodging-house keepers in London is very considerable—even in the country we have known the same man become a butler, a grocer, and a butler again—and a heavy tax upon profits would thus fall partly on wages, by increasing the number of servants; while a carpenter or joiner rarely becomes a bricklayer or a mason, though the pay of the latter is in some places better.

The stickler for the doctrine of labour finding its level will probably answer that the level is found, not by old hands changing their trades, but either by a greater competition for the better paid trades on the part of new hands, or by a flow of capital into employments in which labour is abnormally cheap. But the answer, like the doctrine itself, is in conflict with facts, and therefore untrue. Four generations since Adam Smith and Arthur Young have widened the actual differences of wages in England. Mr. Mill's theory of international values, it is well to observe, is entirely based on the *fact* that 'there are still extraordinary differences both of wages and of profits in different parts of the world. Between all distant places in some degree, but especially between different countries, there may exist great inequalities in the earnings of labour and capital, without causing them to move one from the other in such quantities as to level those inequalities.' But it is evident that the economist who accepts this international theory cannot reasonably or logically disregard the fact that there *are* likewise extraordinary inequalities in wages in the same country without causing a movement of labourers such as to level these inequalities.

That instead of one common cause determining and equalising wages, different causes determine them in different cases, and produce the great inequalities found in fact to exist, is easily shown. In Northumberland and Durham good wages and good food make, as we saw, the farm labourer efficient, and his efficiency, along with the good market for his produce afforded by mines, enables the farmer to pay the high price for labour which the competition of the mines on the other hand compels him to pay. In Northamptonshire, near railway works and large towns, the competition of employers in other trades compels the farmer to raise wages when his own profits are high on the one hand from the prices of produce, and when, for the same reason, food is dear to the labourer on the other hand; but in retired parts of the country old rates of farm wages continue from the absence of all other employment. In Dorsetshire the agricultural labourer's earnings are determined mainly, not by the competition of employers, but by that tacit combination on their part not to raise wages above their actual rates, which Adam Smith declared in his time to be the constant and uniform practice.[12] Not many years ago, rates of wages even lower than in Dorsetshire were current in Wiltshire from the same cause. 'The wages of labour are lower on Salisbury Plain,' Mr. Caird wrote in his *Letters on Agriculture*, 'than in Dorsetshire, and lower than in the dairy and arable districts of North Wilts. An explanation of this may partly be found in the fact that the command of wages is altogether under the control of the large farmers, some of whom employ the whole labour of a parish. Six shillings a week was the amount given for ordinary labourers by the most extensive farmer in South Wilts, who holds nearly 5,000 acres of land, great part of which is his own property. Seven shillings however is the more common rate, and out of that the labourer has to pay one shilling a week for the rent of his cottage.' The truth is that instead of competition for labour being the universal condition of trade and the universal regulator of wages, there is rarely competition for labour on the part of employers *within* a trade in a particular place unless there be competition for it from *without*. And in the absence of competition for labour from without, what competition there is on the part of employers within a trade often tends to lower wages by lowering prices and diminishing the cost of production. 'If one single employer succeed in screwing down wages below the rate previously current, his fellow employers may have no alternative but to follow suit, or to see themselves undersold in the produce market.'[13] When indeed wages are thus screwed down to a minimum, the probable consequence doubtless is minimum work, and the labourer becomes worthy of little more than his hire. The selling value of the labourer's work, it ought not to be forgotten by either employer or labourer, determines the maximum of wages; but it is seldom the sole consideration of the employer. 'How much can I give?' is his first consideration, but 'How much less can I make him take?' is generally his second. A great productiveness of labour and capital, high prices for the produce of both, security to reap a liberal profit on a liberal outlay, are the causes which enable employers to pay high rates of wages; but either competition for labour in other employments or places to which it can migrate, or the combination of labourers, is requisite for the most part to compel employers to pay labour either so as to make it highly efficient, or in proportion to its efficiency, if highly efficient. But competition for labour is not necessarily limited to competition on the part of employers. It affords an important illustration of the variety of the conditions determining wages, that in the United States land is a competitor for labour with capital because it offers the labourer an agreeable and lucrative employment, while in the United Kingdom land is not only out of the labourer's reach as an independent resource, but actually, under the system which prevails, often competes with labour instead of for it, by offering to capital employments which supersede labour, as for example, when arable land is converted into pasture or deer forest. The following evidence of an American employer respecting the influence of land upon wages in the States deserves the particular attention of the labouring classes of this kingdom:

'*Chairman*: Have you at all considered what is the reason of the fact that there is so much higher a rate in America?—Yes; it is a problem which faces us at every turn, because, in consequence of this difference in wages, you make iron in England a great deal lower than we can possibly make it. It comes into our country and undersells the iron of our manufacturers, and we are periodically ruined. And the sole cause that I know for that, is the ability of Great Britain to make iron at a less cost than we do, in consequence of the lower rates of labour in this country. You ask me the cause of this difference in the rates of labour. In the first place, there are what I should term the natural causes. We have a new country of immense extent, a very fertile soil, sparsely populated even in the populated parts, and to a very large extent unoccupied. Every enterprising man can, even near the centres of population, purchase land upon credit if he has not any capital; or he may go west and have land for nothing, by simply filing his intention to occupy it with the registrar of the land office, and he has 160 acres under the homestead law for nothing. Of course the rate of wages is regulated substantially in our country by the profits which a man can get out of the soil, which has cost him little or nothing except the labour which he himself or his family have put upon it. That is the element which in my judgment determines the standard of wages in the United States which an ordinary labourer will derive, from the fact that the man who thinks that he is not getting enough takes to the land; and if he finds that the land does not yield him so much as he could get in some other branch of industry, he goes from the land back to that industry. Therefore the governing element in our country is the annual profit which a man can derive from land which has cost him nothing beyond the labour which he himself has put upon it. In other words, what you call rent to some extent enters into the question of the value of labour in our country. You add to what would be the ordinary value of labour in this country the element of the land, and you arrive nearly at the value of a day's labour in America.

'Your theory is, that as every man in America can hold 160 acres free as the gift of the State, a man is constantly making the experiment: "How do I get my subsistence out of that 160 acres?—If I can get more by being a puddler in an iron manufactory, I will give up my 160 acres."—Yes.

'*Mr. Merivale*: I understand you to say that the natural rate of wages is fixed in America by the abundance of land, and cannot fall below that standard?—Yes; on the average it is so.'[14]

In this country, on the contrary, instead of competing for labour, land offers to capital investments, whereby the demand for labour is diminished. It is among the unfortunate results of the almost exclusive attention of trade-unions to a single, and by no means invariably successful, mode of operating upon wages by combination, that the working classes bring nothing of their great political power and intellectual influence to bear on the liberation of land from restrictions which prevent its being within the reach of the labourer, and at once a competitor with capital for the use of his powers of production, and a powerful contributor to his welfare as a consumer as regards the cost both of his dwelling and of his food. The interests of the working classes as consumers, indeed their common interests of all kinds, seem hitherto to have obtained from them scarcely any attention. The whole 110,000,000*l*. of annual profit on capital divided among the 11,000,000 labourers of the United Kingdom would add but 10*l*. a year to each labour-er's income, supposing capital to stay in the country on such terms; while money wages might be much more largely augmented, and their purchasing power perhaps doubled, by legal, financial, and administrative reforms, to which the labouring class give no heed. Among the considerations affecting their interests to which their attention seems never to be drawn, is that the aggregate amount of their revenue depends in a great measure on the modes of expenditure customary with all classes, including their own. They may, for example, spend a great part of their own earnings on things such as spirits and beer, the price of which consists chiefly of the profits of distillers, brewers, and publicans; or they may limit the bulk of their purchases to articles made mainly by labour and sold in co-operative stores. A good part of their income may thus either go back to other classes, or be redistributed among their own class, according to their own habits of consumption. An assailant of Mr. Mill's theory of wages referred to in a previous page has himself fallen into the same curious fallacy with Mr. Senior, that all the funds, expended upon commodities of whatever kind, are expended on labour.[15] Criticising Ricardo, Mr. Senior argued, 'Mr. Ricardo's theory is, that it is more beneficial to the labouring classes to be employed in the pro-duction of services than in the production of commodities; that it is better for them to be employed in standing behind chairs than in making chairs.' Mr. Longe, in like manner, ridicules the doctrine that the rich can make any addition to wages by diminishing their personal expenditure on commod-ities, and purchasing labour instead, 'a process,' Mr. Longe exclaims, 'very analogous to that of lengthening a stick by cutting off from the top a portion to be added at the bottom.' The error of both Mr. Senior and Mr. Longe lies in supposing that labourers get the whole price of all the things they contribute to produce, without any deduction for profit or rent. Take Mr. Senior's own instance of the price of a chair: part is the price of the wood, and this part is nearly all interest and rent—rent to the owner of the ground in which the tree grew, and interest to the planter, who had to wait for his money until his plantation grew up; part, and perhaps a very large part, is profit to the workman's employer; the remainder only, and it may be a very small remainder, is wages to the maker or workman himself. It is actually a very small remainder to the cabinet-maker in East London. 'The cabinet-makers at the East End, a very numerous body, are in what is called the slop trade, and are ground down by the dealers, who own what are called "slaughter houses," in which they take advantage of the small manufacturers, and compel them to sell their upholstery at little more than the cost of materials. Between dealers and want of work, I am told that numbers of the slop cabinet-makers are not earning 7s. 6d. a week.'[16]

Nearly two millions, that is, nearly one fifth of the entire number of labourers in the United Kingdom, are maintained directly as servants and labourers out of the incomes of the other classes of society, and probably their total receipts in wages and board may amount to forty millions a year. Does Mr. Longe suppose that, if these forty millions were spent by employers on commodities, instead of on labour, the labouring classes as a whole would be nothing the poorer? The difference would be that other classes instead of labourers would get a good part of the forty millions' worth of commodities which servants and labourers now buy with their wages, or receive directly in board. We may add that Mr. Senior's theory that the average rate of wages depends on the quantity and quality of commodities appropriated to the use of labourers on the one hand, and their number on the other, confounds two perfectly distinct classes of causes—those which affect the labourer as a producer, and those which affect him as a consumer; those which determine the general value of his labour, and those which determine its specific value, that is to say, its purchasing power over the particular commodities which he consumes. The sale of his labour is one exchange; the purchase of the commodities he buys with the fruits of that sale—that is to say, with his wages—is another; and these two separate exchanges are subject to quite different laws or conditions. Reductions of taxation on tea and sugar, for example, improve the quantity and quality of some of the articles labourers consume without necessarily increasing their incomes as producers, or their purchasing powers over things in general. Thus it happens that a proceeding which benefits the labouring class, considered as producers, may possibly injure them as consumers; for instance, the conversion of sheep runs into deer forests in the highlands of Scotland. More men are employed as game-keepers and gillies than would, in most cases, be employed as shepherds were the same land under sheep; but, on the other hand, labourers neither rent shooting grounds nor eat venison, while they do consume mutton, if its plenty and cheapness place it within their reach. Were the deer forests, however, restored to the spade and the plough, the labouring class would benefit both as producers and consumers; there would be both a greater demand for labour, and a greater production of the food which labourers use. We advert to such points, not only for whatever may be their special importance, but also to illustrate the great variety of the causes which affect the value of labour; and we do so, both because while employers commonly err in regarding competition as the labourer's only legitimate process, the labouring classes themselves err in laying almost exclusive stress upon combination.

Mr. Mill, Mr. Fawcett, Mr. Thornton, and Mr. Waley have demonstrated that without combination labourers would in some cases be completely at the mercy of employers. In the words of the first, 'How can they stand out for terms without organised concert? What chance would any labourer have who struck singly for an advance of wages? Associations of labourers of a nature similar to trade-unions, far from being a hindrance to a free market for labour, are the necessary instrumentality of that free market; the indispensable means of enabling the sellers of labour to take due care of their own interests under a system of competition.'[17] Accordingly when Mr. Jevons vindicates the right of labourers to combine to shorten the hours of labour, on the ground that 'the single workman, dependent for his living upon his week's wages, is utterly incompetent to enforce any concession from his wealthy employer,'[18] we think he must logically go further and admit that it may be as necessary for workmen to combine in order to get a fair price for their labour, as in order to shorten its hours. It is sometimes said that if the profits of a particular business are abnormally high, a consequent accumulation of capital resulting must raise wages in proportion; but there is nothing to compel the recipients of high profits to make that particular use of them. They may buy lands, or increase their personal expenditure, or speculate in other, it may be in foreign, investments. On the other hand, for labourers to rely exclusively on combination, seems to us a mischievous error. In many cases there is no room, in either profits or prices, for an increase of wages;[19] and in at least one case of first rate importance, combination is in practice impossible. Increased powers of competition, rather than of combination— by education, by the collection of statistics of wages, and by the reform of the land laws—are the powers the working classes should seek to confer on the agricultural labourer.

But in all cases there are two questions to which both employers and employed should attend. One is, what is the utmost that can be made by capital and labour together? The other, how is the total produce of both to be divided between them? The mistake into which both employers and labourers commonly fall is, of attention only to the latter of the two questions: neither looking to the means by which the total amount to be divided may be raised to the utmost; both looking to extort the utmost possible share of the actual total;—neither treating the problem as one of production; both treating it as one only of distribution.

In submitting such considerations we venture to propound no universal rule respecting the conditions which do or which ought to regulate wages. In place of competition being the only condition by which the value of labour is determined as a matter of fact, we find competition, combination, and co-operation all active, and each in a variety of forms; nor dare we deny that there are cases to which each is the arrangement specially appropriate at present. Sometimes we see employers alone combining, and labourers competing; sometimes it is employers who compete and labourers who combine. In some cases each of the two classes combines against the other; in some, both combine against consumers. In some cases labour is not its own sole competitor, but machinery, animals, or natural agents compete with it and diminish its value; in other cases these agencies co-operate with it or compete for it, and add to its value. In some cases, instead of a conflict between labour and capital, there is co-operation, and that in various ways: for example, sometimes by arbitration of wages and sometimes by regular partnership in profits.

So various and variable being the causes which determine the rates of wages in particular cases, it is evident that wages in many cases might be different from what they are; that the result has been mistaken for the cause; and that the aggregate amount of wages is merely the total sum of the particular amounts in particular cases taken together; and that the average rate of wages is a phrase without practical meaning or relation to the actual earnings of labour. The investigation establishes likewise, we presume to affirm, Mr. Senior's protest notwithstanding, that political economy is, or ought to be, a science *avide de faits*. It has suffered much from that tendency towards mere abstract speculation of which Lord Bacon said: 'As for the philosophers, they make imaginary laws for imaginary commonwealths; and their discourses are as the stars which give little light because they are so high.' By no means concurring with all the criticisms of a powerful censor of the science, we cannot but join in his protest against its being put forward as one 'definite, distinct, and exact, the axioms of which are as universal and demonstrable as those of astronomy; the practical rules of which are as simple and familiar as those of arithmetic.'[20] Political economy must be content to take rank as an inductive, instead of a purely deductive science; and it will gain in utility, interest, and real truth, far more than a full compensation for the forfeiture of a fictitious title to mathematical exactness and certainty.

Notes

1 Reprinted from *Fraser's Magazine*, July 1868.
2 *System of Logic*, Book iii., chaps. 4 and 13.
3 Mr. Mill's definition is: 'Writers on political economy profess to investigate the nature of wealth, and the laws of its production and distribution, including directly or remotely the operation of all the causes by which the condition of mankind or of any society of human beings in respect to this universal object of desire is made prosperous or the reverse.'—*Principles of Political Economy*; Preliminary Remarks.
4 *North British Review*. March 1868, p. 6.
5 *English Agriculture in* 1850 *and* 1851; second edition, pp. 473, 510–515.
6 Communication from a landed proprietor, April 22, 1868.
7 April 17, 1868.
8 The return of agricultural labourers' earnings for the quarter ended Michaelmas July 1869, just printed by order of the House of Commons, shows that weekly wages in the harvest quarter vary from 9*s.* to 21*s.*
9 *Earl of Lichfield*: Have the operations of your society had the effect of equalising wages in different districts where you have branches?—They have had the effect of equalising wages to a very considerable extent, but have not made a uniform rate of wages.
   Do they vary very much in different towns of the same district—say Lancashire, for instance?—Yes.
   Do you mean more than the expense of living will account for?—I believe that the cost of living is pretty near the same, go where you will, if you live upon the same diet.
10 *A Refutation of the Wage-Fund Theory of Modern Political Economy*. By Francis D. Longe.
11 In some parts of the country lathing is done by labourers, while in other parts of the country it is not. For instance, in London lathing is done by men who do nothing but lathing. I pointed out that in Liverpool plasterers and slaters went together, and in Manchester plasterers and painters. In Scarborough the plasterers tried to prevent the bricklayers from carrying on one part of that which then had been bought up to.—*Trade-Unions Commission*, 1 Rep. 3278.
12 'Whoever imagines that masters rarely combine is as ignorant of the world as of the subject. Masters are always and everywhere in a sort of tacit but constant and uniform combination not to raise wages above the actual rate. Masters, too, sometimes enter into particular combinations to sink wages below this actual rate.'
13 Thornton on the Rate of Wages. *Fortnightly Review*, May 1867, p. 562.
14 Second Report, Trade-Unions Commission, pp. 3, 5. Compare Seventh Report, p. 57.
15 *A Refutation of the Wage-Fund Theory of Modern Political Economy*. By F. D. Longe.
16 *National Expenditure*. By R. Dudley Baxter, p. 65.
17 *Principles of Political Economy*. By J. S. Mill. Book v. chap. 10, § 5.
18 *A Lecture on Trades' Societies*. By W. Stanley Jevons, M.A.
19 We cannot agree with the writer of the excellent article on Trade-Unions in the March number of the *North British Review*, before referred to, that wages may be raised by means of a reduction of interest on borrowed capital. Its owners are under no necessity to make that investment of it, and will not accept a lower interest from employers of labour than they can obtain elsewhere.
20 *The Limits of Political Economy*. By F. Harrison. *Fortnightly Review*, June 15, 1865.

29

'THE RATE OF WAGES'

John. E. Cairnes

Source: *Some Leading Principles of Political Economy: Newly Expounded*, London: Macmillan, 1874, pp. 149–88.

§ 1. IN discussing the laws of value, we have already partially solved the problems of wages and profits. For it has appeared that, where production assumes the character of a continuous operation, producers are in effect remunerated out of the values of their products, and that consequently wages and profits in each branch of production must stand, in the normal state of things and on the average, to wages and profits in every other branch, in the same relation as the values of the products from which they are derived. "Relative wages and profits" thus follow the same laws which govern the exchange value of commodities. In other words, our reasoning has involved this conclusion, that wages and profits, regarded as relative phenomena, are governed by Cost of Production, where the producers are in effective competition with one another, and, where they are not, by Reciprocal Demand. So far we were carried toward the solution of the wages and profits problem in the discussion of that value; but it is important that we should not overrate the progress that has been effected. Let me repeat: what the doctrine of value reveals to us on this subject is the causes which determine the *relative* remuneration of laborers as among themselves, and that of capitalists as among themselves. It tells us why some classes of workmen and some classes of capitalists receive the same or equivalent remuneration, while in other cases inequality in various degrees prevails; but it tells us nothing as to what determines the positive remuneration which any class of capitalists or of laborers receives, nor as to the causes on which depend the average well-being of all classes. In à word, we have ascertained what produces the ripples on the surface of the industrial stream; but of the source from which the waters are derived, and of the depth and force of the current, nothing has yet been disclosed. Why is the remuneration of industry, as a whole, such as we find it to be in the various countries of the earth? Why is it maintained at one level in England, at another on the continent of Europe, at yet another

214

in Asia, and at another still in the United States? And why again is this level progressive in some countries, stationary in others, declining in a third class? These are questions on which the doctrine of value throws no light, and it is, therefore, to this side of the general problem that we have now to direct our attention.

§ 2. I shall perhaps here be reminded that the question of the rate of wages, as well as that of the rate of profits, under whatever aspect we regard them, are, and can never be other than, problems of value; since they are simply questions of the value respectively of labor and abstinence; and that they should be dealt with in connection with that subject in the general theory of which they are implicated. I am certainly not going to dispute the allegation that wages and profits are, in a certain sense, phenomena of value. "Rate of wages" and "value of labor," "rate of profit" and "value of abstinence," are no doubt equivalent expression; and for my part I see no objection to regarding the doctrines elucidating these phenomena as constituting branches of the same general theory with that which explains the value of commodities. But I apprehend the objection, embodied in the above remark, points to something more than this. What some students of Political Economy seem to desiderate is a comprehensive formula which shall embrace in a single solution, along with the laws of the exchange relations of commodities, those of the exchange relations of labor and abstinence, and, along with these again, the laws of the exchange relations of land—that is to say, the theory of rent. Some such aim seems to have guided the speculations of Bastiat, whose work on the "Harmonies of Political Economy" is in effect an essay toward the determination of the required formula; but the result of Bastiat's attempt is not encouraging to those who would essay the same path. He produces, indeed, generalizations which seem to satisfy the needed conditions; but, closely examined, they either collapse into mere identical propositions, or are found to contain some flagrant *petitio principii*. Where not open to either of these objections, they will be found to relate to the phenomena of *comparative* remuneration—that is to say, to that portion of the theory of wages and profits which I have admitted and shown may be treated in connection with the general laws of value.

The truth is, the fundamental facts of the two problems are too essentially discrepant to admit of this mode of treatment. Verbal generalizations are of course easy. For example, nothing is easier than to say that the value of labor (I put aside abstinence and profit as not included in my present inquiry), like the value of other things, depends upon supply and demand—we may find the formula in any newspaper we take up; but what light does this throw upon the causes which govern the values either of labor or of commodities? Simply none at all, or next to none at all. What we want to know is, not whether an increase of supply will cheapen a commodity or will cheapen labor, and an increase of demand raise the price of each—every

215

coster-monger will tell you this much—but what it is which governs supply and demand in each case. Now, we can not take a step toward dealing with this question without being brought face to face with the fact that the motives which influence human beings in the production and supply of commodities are not those which influence them in the production and supply of labor; in other words, that the conditions operative in the two cases are essentially distinct. If this is not already apparent to the reader, a brief consideration will suffice to make it so.

First, then, the production of commodities is an onerous act, which will only be undertaken in the prospect of reward; whence it follows that the supply of commodities will only be secured on the condition of this prospect presenting itself. On the other hand, the production of labor, which in other words is the production of human beings, is not an onerous act, but a consequence of complying with one of the strongest instincts of humanity—an instinct which, so far from needing the stimulus of reward, can only be kept under due control by powerful restraints. In the one case, action entails self-denial; in the other, self-denial lies in abstaining from action. Prospective recompense indeed comes into requisition in both cases; but in the one it is needed to stimulate, in the other to control. Exclude the prospect of reward from productive industry, and the supply of commodities will cease; exclude the prospect of the reward which results from providence in reproducing human beings, and the supply of labor will run to excess. Nor shall we have need to modify seriously our conclusion upon this point, if, passing from the primary act of reproducing human beings, we take account of what is necessary in order to fit them, once in existence, for an industrial career. They must be fed and clothed; they must be brought up in a certain state of comfort; and they must receive a certain education—conditions which, unlike the act of originating their existence, call for, in order to their fulfillment, continuous and often arduous effort. Here, we must admit, there is an analogy between the preparation of a human being for industrial work, and the production of a commodity for the market; both processes involve cost. But there still remains this broad distinction, which effectually discriminates the two cases: The cost in the production of a commodity is undergone deliberately, and with a distinct view to industrial ends: in the preparation of human beings for their career in life—I will not say that industrial ends have no place at all in the calculation, but I will assert this, that, except in the case of technical or professional education—a mere bagatelle in the general expense of rearing a laborer—industrial considerations are entirely subordinate to considerations of a wider and altogether different character. A man, whatever be his rank of life, brings up his children—I speak of the common case—as far as he is able, according to the ideas prevailing in that rank of life. He does so mainly because he feels certain obligations of morality and affection toward them, and because it would be shameful to do otherwise. His children once arrived at maturity, no doubt his views and theirs will take a direction more distinctly governed by industrial consider-ations, or at least considerations bearing upon material success in life; but at this point the supply of labor *has been already determined*. It is now in exist-ence; and the industrial motive, now that it comes into play, operates, not upon the aggregate supply of labor, but merely upon the mode of its distri-bution. I do not deny, indeed, that, in a certain irregular way, and taking considerable periods of time, the supply of labor as a whole follows the demand for labor; but what I contend is, that it is not connected with demand by the same links which connect the supply of commodities with the demand for them. The adaptation of the supply of commodities to the demand is determined by strictly commercial motives: the adaptation of the supply of labor to the demand is not so determined. Human beings, at least out of slave countries, are not produced to meet the requirements of the market, but for entirely different reasons. Now, this being so—the conditions determining the phenomena in the two cases being essentially distinct—what can come of forcing the solutions by dint of verbal refinements into a single formula? Simply this: either our theory will be flagrantly untrue, or it will not go more than word-deep, and our show of explanation will merely serve to obscure the essential facts of the problem.

§ 3. These preliminary points being disposed of, I turn now to the proper subject of this chapter—the causes determining the general or average rate of wages. But here an objection meets me on the threshold. Are we justified in speaking of a "general" rate of wages? Are the facts expressed by wages such as may be usefully embraced in a general conception and reasoned about as an aggregate? A recent writer, Mr. Longe, has denied the existence of any facts which can warrant this expression:

> "The notion of all the laborers of a country constituting a body of general laborers capable of competing with each other, and whose "general" or "average" wage depends upon the ratio between their number and the aggregate wage-fund, is just as absurd as the notion of all the different goods existing in a country at any given time—for example, the ships, and the steam-engines, and the cloth, etc.— constituting the stock of general commodities, the general or average price of which is determined by the ratio between the supposed quantity of the whole aggregate stock and the total purchase-fund of the community . . . How could the shoe-makers compete with the tailors, or the blacksmiths with the glass-blowers? Or how should the capital which a master-shoe-maker saved by reducing the wages of his journeymen, get into the hands of the master-tailor?"[1]

To the latter questions I think I have already supplied a sufficient answer; but with regard to the objection itself, and the illustration by which it is supported, the reader will observe to what length it goes. The author of the passage just quoted is apparently unable to conceive a general or average rate where the average is not realized in each individual instance; otherwise where is the absurdity of speaking of a "general" or "average" price of commodities? If the notion of a general or average price of commodities is absurd, then what does the writer mean when he speaks of a rise or fall in the value of money? Or is that idea also beyond his conceptive power? A rise or fall in the value of money is only another name for a fall or rise of general or average prices. The idea, in short, which Mr. Longe adduces as an extreme example of absurdity, is simply one of the most familiar in the range of economic speculation. A general rate of wages is neither more nor less easy to conceive, neither more nor less absurd, than general prices. I think I know what I mean when I say that prices and wages in the United States, measured in greenbacks, have risen *generally* as compared with prices and wages, measured in gold; that the average rate is higher in the one case than in the other; and I do not think I should be very wide of the mark if I attributed this difference to the different proportions in which purchasing power measured in gold, and purchasing power measured in greenbacks, stand related to commodities and labor. Yet these familiar notions are what Mr. Longe finds it impossible to conceive.

An expression in the passage quoted would seem to imply that universal competition among laborers is an essential condition to the existence of an average rate of wages. Why it should be so (except on the supposition I have referred to, that an average rate requires that the average be realized in each particular instance) I am quite at a loss to imagine; but Mr. Longe's language seems further to imply that, as a matter of fact, the several departments of industry in this and other countries are so practically isolated from each other, that wages in any of them may rise or fall without producing any effect beyond the particular department. I have already considered the extent to which competition is really effective in our industrial life, and have endeavored to show in what way its existence or non-existence affects relative wages. To what was then said I desire now to add that, even where competition among laborers is not effective, and where consequently wages are not in proportion to sacrifices, it is very far from being true that any such industrial isolation obtains as Mr. Longe's argument would suggest. A rise of wages, let us suppose, occurs in the coal trade: does any one suppose that this could continue without affecting wages, not merely in other mining industries in full competition with coal-mining, but in industries the most remote from coal-mining, industries alike higher and lower in the industrial scale? Most undoubtedly it could not; and if any one questions the assertion, he may have his doubts resolved by what is now going on before our eyes. Nor is the explanation far to seek. Though laborers in certain departments of industry are practically cut off from competition with laborers in other departments, the competition of capitalists, as I have already pointed out, is effective over the whole field. The communication between the different sections of indus-trial life, which is not kept open by the movements of labor, is effectually maintained by the action of capital constantly moving toward the more profitable employments. In this way our entire industrial organization becomes a connected system, any change occurring in any part of which will extend itself to others and entail complementary changes. Not only, there-fore, are we justified in generalizing the various facts of wages into a single conception, and in discussing "general" or "average" wages, but we have grounds for regarding this general or average rate as constituted of elements bound together by a common connection, and forming parts of an integral whole.

§ 4. The problem of the general rate of wages, after being the occasion of perhaps more bitter controversy than any other within the field of social inquiry, seemed some years ago to have received, so far as the essentials of the matter went, its definitive solution. The great stumbling-block to its acceptance had long been the law of population, which, in spite of the over-whelming evidence adduced in its support by Malthus, provoked, as all the world knows, a violent opposition, and led to a controversy which, extending over half a century, has only died out, if indeed it has died out, within a few years. This result may be attributed partly, we may perhaps assume, to the gradual progress of sound reason getting the better of the strongest prepos-sessions; but it has of late been powerfully helped forward by the influence of Mr. Darwin's great work, in which the obnoxious principle—the tendency of human beings to increase faster than subsistence, which had been denounced as at once demoralizing to man and discreditable to the Author of the Universe—was shown to be merely a particular instance of a law pervading all organic existence. However this may be, in point of fact those attacks upon the economic doctrine of wages which were based upon objections to the Malthusian doctrines—attacks upon what we may call the *supply* side of the wages problem—have for some time come to an end. We may therefore assume that so much of the problem has been solved to the general satisfac-tion of competent thinkers, and are consequently dispensed from entering on its consideration here.

But the controversy has scarcely been closed on one side when it has been opened on another. The law of the supply of labor is no longer called in question; but several able writers have within a few years, in dissertations directed against what is known as the "Wages-fund" doctrine, challenged the view hitherto received as to the law of its demand. Foremost among these has been Mr. Thornton, who, in his book on "Labor,"[2] has made the Wages-fund doctrine the object of a special and elaborate attack; nor is it possible to deny the ability and skill with which the assault has been conducted, when we find that he can boast, as among the first-fruits of his argument, no less a result than the conversion of Mr. Mill.

Such an event, it must be frankly conceded, affords an extremely strong presumption in favor of the soundness of Mr. Thornton's view. Mr. Mill had himself been, if not the originator of the Wages-fund doctrine, certainly its most able and effective expositor; and this doctrine, supported by his argument, and implicated in his general theory, he has been led by Mr. Thornton's reasoning to discard. I say, it can not be denied that such a circumstance constitutes a weighty presumption in favor of Mr. Thornton's view; but I must also contend that it amounts to no more than a presumption. In the freedom of science, I claim for myself the right of examining the doctrine on its merits. I must own myself unconvinced by Mr. Thornton's reasonings, strengthened and enforced though these have been by the powerful comments of Mr. Mill.[3] Not indeed that I am prepared to defend all that has been written on what, for convenience, I may call the orthodox side of this question, but I believe the view maintained by those who have written on that side, and pre-eminently the view maintained by Mr. Mill himself—taking it as set forth in his original work, not as explained in his retractation—to be substantially sound, though needing, as it seems to me, at once fuller development and more accurate determination than it has yet received.

§ 5. I can not, I think, better open the examination which I propose to make of this subject, than by quoting the following statement from Mr. Mill's "Principles of Political Economy," of the nature of the Wages-fund, and its place in the industrial economy:

"Wages, then, depend mainly upon the demand and supply of labor; or, as it is often expressed, on the proportion between population and capital. By population is here meant the number only of the laboring class, or rather of those who work for hire; and by capital, only circulating capital, and not even the whole of that, but the part which is expended in the direct purchase of labor. To this, however, must be added all funds which, without forming a part of capital, are paid in exchange for labor, such as the wages of soldiers, domestic servants, and all other unproductive laborers. There is unfortunately no mode of expressing by one familiar term the aggregate of what may be called the Wages-fund of a country: and as the wages of productive labor form nearly the whole of that fund, it is usual to overlook the smaller and less important part, and to say that wages depend on population and capital. It will be convenient to employ this expression, remembering, however, to consider it as elliptical, and not as a literal statement of the entire truth."[4]

As I understand this passage, it embraces the following statements: 1st, "Wages-fund" is a general term, used in the absence of any other more familiar, to express the aggregate of all wages at any given time in possession of the laboring population; 2d, on the proportion of this fund to the number of the laboring population depends at any given time the average rate of wages; 3d, the amount of the fund is determined by the amount of the general wealth which is applied to the direct purchase of labor, whether with a view to productive or to unproductive employment. If the reader will carefully consider these several propositions, I think he will perceive that they do not contain matter which can be properly regarded as open to dispute. The first is little more than a definition; at most, it assumes that that exists in the aggregate which is admitted to exist in detail. The second merely amounts to saying that the quotient will be such as the dividend and divisor determine. The third equally contains an indisputable assertion; since, whatever be the remote causes on which the wages of hired labor depend (and the question at present is exclusively of *hired* labor) *the proximate act determining their aggregate amount must in all cases be a direct purchase of its services.* In truth, the demand for labor, thus understood, as measured by the amount of wealth applied to the direct purchase of labor, might more correctly be said to be, than to determine, the Wages-fund. It *is* the Wages-fund in its inchoate stage, differing from it only as wealth just about to pass into the hands of laborers differs from the same wealth when it has got into their hands. Our analysis thus leads us to the result, that the passage quoted from Mr. Mill can not be taken to contain controversial matter. The statements are such as may not be disputed, once their meaning is clearly understood. At the same time it must be freely confessed that it contains no solution of the wages problem: it is not a solution, but a statement of that problem—a statement, as it seems to me, at once clear, comprehensive, and succinct, presenting in clear light the two factors which constitute the phenomenon—the Wages-fund resulting from the direct demand for labor, and the laboring population forming the supply. The solution will consist in connecting these factors with those principles of human nature and facts of the external world which form the premises of economic science.[5]

§ 6. As I have already observed, it is with a portion only of this problem that we have need now to concern ourselves. The causes governing the supply of labor may be taken as sufficiently elucidated. Our business is with the causes governing the demand—governing the amount of wealth applied to the direct purchase of labor, or, as we may equally well express it, governing the Wages-fund.

It is here for the first time that room for controversy really occurs; and though the issue has not always been taken with precision, it is in effect on the point just indicated that the recent controversy turns. By the upholders of the Wages-fund doctrine the view taken is, that the amount of a nation's wealth expended in wages at any given time stands—the character of the national industries and the methods of production employed being given—in a definite relation to its general capital, while the amount of its general capital is determined by certain economic conditions resulting from the character of the people and the nature of their environment.[6] The Wagesfund, therefore, according to this view, depends, the conditions of production being given, proximately on the amount of a nation's capital, and ultimately on those more remote causes which control the growth of this fund. It is against this view of the connection of facts that the opponents of the impugned doctrine have directed their arguments. According to Mr. Thornton there is no portion of a nation's wealth "determined" toward the payment of wages. The amount which actually reaches the laborer is, I presume he would say, the result of circumstances (which, as not being "determined," must be regarded as accidental) of which the most important are those incidents in the position respectively of employer and employed which favor or restrict the capacity for bargaining. And substantially the same language is held by Mr. Longe. Rather inconsistently, however, while denying the determination of any portion of the general wealth to the payment of wages, Mr. Longe propounds a theory to explain the fact of this determination. The determining cause, he says, is not, as alleged in the Wages-fund theory, the economic conditions affecting the growth of capital, but "the demand for commodities." "The demand for commodities certainly does not directly determine the quantity of labor or number of laborers in a country, nor the quantity of corn or other things available for the maintenance of laborers, but it does determine the quantity of labor employed, and the quantity of wealth spent in the wages of laborers" (p. 46). As he elsewhere puts it, "the demand for commodities which can only be got by labor is as much a demand for labor as a demand for beef is a demand for bullocks."

§ 7. Such are the positions taken in this controversy by the disputants on either side. In proceeding to state the doctrine in question, with a view to meet the objections which have been advanced against it, it will be convenient in the first place to examine the theory put forward by Mr. Longe, and which apparently finds favor with Mr. Thornton also, as to the bearing of the demand for commodities upon the remuneration of labor; I shall then set forth the grounds on which the doctrine of the Wages-fund rests; and having done this, I shall be in a position to consider the arguments advanced by Mr. Thornton against the existence of any "determining" causes in the case.

Mr. Longe has refused to admit the existence of, and has thrown doubt upon the possibility of conceiving, "a general rate of wages." He, however, allows, at least by implication, that we may conceive an aggregate quantity of wealth as spent in wages, or what I call a Wages-fund; for in the passage just quoted he tells us the cause which determines the amount of this fund. It is, he says, "the demand for commodities." I need scarcely remark that the view here expressed is not peculiar to Mr. Longe. It is in truth about the most popular of all popular fallacies. From this root has sprung a whole cluster of maxims, such as that "the extravagance of the rich is the gain of the poor," that "profusion and waste are for the good of trade," and others of like import which have in their time done much to perplex and demoralize mankind, and are still far from being extinct. That there is much plausibility in the view here taken of the economy of industry can not indeed be denied, since otherwise how should it have obtained the almost universal vogue which it enjoys? It will therefore be worth while to sift with some care the grounds of an opinion which has certainly exercised no small amount of evil influence on modes of thinking and acting in economic affairs.

To state in its strongest form the argument for the view which I am combating: What, it may be asked, is the primary consideration that weights with a capitalist in investing his wealth? Is it not the prospect of finding a sale for his products—in other words, the demand for commodities? And, as this is that which first moves him to action, is it not also that which governs the proportions of his operations after he has entered upon action? Increase the demand for his commodities, and he will increase the amount of his investment; diminish the demand, and he will diminish the investment. But, other things being the same, the greater the investment, the greater will be the amount of his wealth spent in the wages of labor. In proportion, therefore, as the demand for his commodity is large, his expenditure in wages will be large. This is true of every capitalist and of every branch of production. From which the conclusion seems to follow that the quantity of wealth spent in the wages of labor—*i. e.*, the aggregate Wages-fund—is determined by the demand for commodities.

It seems to follow, but it does not follow; for, looking closely into the above reasoning, we find that while the conclusion is an assertion as to quantity, the premises relate to proportion. The existence of a demand, for example, for houses in a given degree of intensity will cause a certain quantity of the national capital to be directed to the building of houses; but it will not and can not determine what that quantity shall be. This will depend, in the first place, upon the amount of the total capital available for investment; and secondly, on the relative force of the demand for houses as compared with the demand for other things. What the demand for houses and for other things determines is merely the proportions in which the available capital of a country shall be distributed over the field of production. Those proportions will adapt themselves to the proportions of the various demands for commodities. Increase the demand for a given commodity, and, other things being the same, a larger proportion of the available capital will be directed toward its production; diminish the demand for it, and a contrary result will ensue: but neither in the one case nor in the other will the demand for the commodity determine how much capital shall be devoted to its production; nor for similar reasons will the demand for commodities in general determine a like result with regard to them. It is as if we argued, that because a man distributes his income in the proportion of his various needs, spending more on those articles to purchase which a larger sum is wanted to satisfy his requirements, therefore, the greater his needs the larger must be his income. Large or small, his income will be distributed in proportion to his needs; and, large or small, the Wages-fund will be distributed over the various industrial occupations in the proportions indicated by the demand for commodities. But this tells us nothing as to what determines either the amount of a man's income, or the amount of the Wages-fund. We are thus brought to Mr. Mill's conclusion, that the demand for commodities determines the direction of investment and production, but not the more or less of what the laborer on an average receives.

But it may be well perhaps to give the argument a more practical direction; and for this purpose I will ask the reader to consider some of the consequences which would follow from this theory of which Mr. Longe has made himself the expositor, in connection with the condition of labor in different countries. Supposing it to be true that the amount of wealth spent in the wages of labor is determined by the demand for commodities, then it will follow that, given the demand for commodities, we are given the amount of wealth spent in the wages of labor. The latter will vary with the former, and the Wages-fund will, on this view, bear a constant proportion to the aggregate demand for commodities. Now, as has been explained in a former chapter of this work,[7] the aggregate demand for commodities depends on the aggregate production of commodities. Speaking broadly, all commodities produced under a *régime* of division of labor are produced in order to be exchanged. The more each man produces, the more he will have to sell, and the more he will be able to buy. It results, therefore, from the theory we are considering, that the aggregate wealth appropriated to the use of the laboring population must always bear a constant proportion to the gross produce of the community. Now, how does this accord with the facts of wages as presented, let us say, in England and in the United States? According to computations made by Mr. Wells,[8] the United States Commissioner, taken in connection with some made by Mr. Dudley Baxter for this country, it would seem that the annual gross produce of the United States per head of the population bears to the annual gross produce of the United Kingdom per head of the population the proportion of $140 to $134. The United Kingdom includes Ireland, which can not but sensibly reduce the average for this country. Omitting Ireland, the annual *per capita* produce of Great Britain and of the United States would, therefore, according to these computations, be as nearly as possible the same. But the annual gross produce would determine the demand for commodities, and the demand for commodities, according to Mr. Longe, determines the quantity of wealth spent in the wages of labor. From which several positions the conclusion follows that the Wages-fund of Great Britain stands to that of the United States in the same proportion as the population of the former country to the population of the latter. Now, taking this to be so, and assuming further that the proportion of the population working for hire is the same in both countries, then the average rate of wages would for both countries be the same. In point of fact, the working population constitutes a smaller fraction of the entire population in Great Britain than in the United States: it would, therefore, according to this view, bear a less proportion to the Wages-fund here than there. In other words, we are led by "the demand for commodities" theory, applied to the results ascertained by English and American statisticians, to this singular conclusion, that the rate of wages in Great Britain should be on an average higher than in the United States!

I have taken for comparison Great Britain and the United States, because the requisite data were here easily obtainable; but any one who has followed the foregoing argument will perceive that, had the comparison been made between Great Britain and some still more recently settled country—for example, some of the Western States of North America, or one of our own Australian colonies—the *reductio ad absurdum* would have been yet more glaring. In effect, statistical details in such a comparison are superfluous. The broad facts of the case are such as can not be missed. It is evident at a glance that in such countries as our Australian colonies, or as Illinois or California, the amount of the entire annual production appropriated to the laboring population bears a far larger proportion to the whole than in old countries like Great Britain or France; that is to say, the Wages-fund in those parts of the world bears a larger proportion to the demand for commodities than in Western Europe. The demand for commodities, therefore, does not determine the Wages-fund. Observation, moreover, of the course of industrial development in such countries exhibits this fact, that, while with the progress of society the amount of wealth which goes to support hired labor pretty constantly increases, the *proportion* which this bears to the total produce of industry nearly as constantly declines—growing smaller as the realization of fortunes enables a larger proportion of the people to retire from active work, and as capital assumes more extensively a fixed form. In a word, the most prominent features in the industrial economy of new, old, and advancing countries absolutely precludes the supposition that the demand for commodities has any such connection with the interests of the laboring population as the doctrine I am now considering assumes.

§ 8. So far as to Mr. Longe's theory of Wages. I proceed now to state the doctrine of the Wages-fund, as at least I myself understand it.

It will be remembered that in the enunciation which I quoted from Mr. Mill of the wages problem, the Wages-fund is stated to consist of two distinct parts—one, the largest and by much the most important, constituting a portion of the general capital of the country; while the other is derived from that part of the nation's wealth which goes to support unproductive labor, of which Mr. Mill gives as an example the wages of soldiers and domestic servants. In proceeding to deal with the wages question, it will be convenient to omit for a time all consideration of the latter part: this will be more easily dealt with when we have ascertained the causes which govern the main phenomenon.

Restricting our view then for the present to that portion of the general Wages-fund which goes to support productive labor, we have, in the first place, to observe that the hiring of labor for productive purposes is an incident of the investment of capital. A capitalist engages and pays a workman from precisely the same motives which lead him to purchase raw material, a factory, or a machine. In searching, therefore, for the causes which govern the amount of wealth spent in the hiring of labor, we must advert to the considerations which weigh with men in devoting their means to productive investment. Why, for example, does A. B. employ his wealth in productive operations? And why does he employ so much and no more in productive operations? An adequate answer to these questions will carry us some way toward the goal we have in view.

It seems to me that the proper answer is as follows: A. B. invests his wealth productively in order to obtain a profit on the portion of his means so employed; and he invests so much and no more, because, his total means being what they are, and regard being had on the one hand to his private requirements and taste for indulgence, on the other to his desire to augment his means, coupled with the opportunities afforded him of doing so by making profit, this is the amount which it is suitable to his disposition, in the circumstances in which he is placed, so to invest. In other words, we find the amount of A. B.'s investment determined by the following circumstances: First, the amount of his total means; secondly, his character and disposition as affected by the temptation to immediate enjoyment on the one hand, and by the prospect of future aggrandizement on the other; thirdly, the opportunities of making profit. Alter any of these conditions—his total means, his character, or his opportunities of making profit, and the effect will be an alteration in the amount of his investment. Increase his means, and, other things being the same, he will invest more largely: again, increase the prospect of profit, and, other things being the same, he will invest more largely: lastly, increase the strength of the accumulative principle in his character in relation to the taste for immediate enjoyment, and once more, other things being the same, he will invest more largely: on the other hand, a change in any of these conditions in the opposite direction would lead to his investment being correspondingly contracted.

Applying these considerations to the case of a community, it seems to me that we are justified in laying down the following proposition: That, the amount of wealth in a country being given, the proportion of this wealth which shall be invested in industrial operations with a view to profit will depend, first, upon the strength of those qualities in the average character of its inhabitants which lead to productive investment—what Mr. Mill calls "the effective desire of accumulation;" and secondly, on the opportunities of industrial investment open to the community offering a rate of profit sufficient to call this principle into activity—in a word, on "the extent of the field for investment."

Such being the conditions determining the investment of capital, it is plain that, if all capital consisted in wages, or if wages bore always the same proportion to a given quantity of capital, the problem with which we are immediately concerned would here be solved; and we might refer the phenomenon in question—we may describe it as we please, the extent of the demand for labor or the amount of the Wages-fund—simply and directly to the conditions which have just been stated, viz., in a given state of the national wealth, to the strength of the effective desire for accumulation, taken in connection with the extent of the field for investment. In point of fact, however, wages constitute but a portion of capital, and, what greatly complicates the inquiry, this portion bears no constant relation to the aggregate amount. It therefore still remains for us to determine the circumstances on which depends the distribution of capital between wages and the other elements of which capital consists.

Those other elements may be summed up under the heads of "Fixed Capital" and "Raw Material." Fixed Capital, Raw Material, and Wages-fund, therefore, form the three constituents of Capital, and the problem to be solved is, What are the causes which, in a given field of industry, determine the proportion in which these three constituents combine?

Let us again suppose an individual A. B. contemplating investment; he has decided how much of his whole means he intends to employ in productive operations, but, this point having been settled, he has yet to consider in what proportions the amount shall be divided between Fixed Capital, Raw Material, and Wages. What is to prescribe the respective quotas? Manifestly, in the first place, the nature of the industry in which he proposes to embark his capital. Suppose, for example, his purpose is to engage in cotton or woolen manufacture, a very large proportion of his whole capital will assume the form of buildings, machinery, and raw wool or cotton; that is to say, of fixed capital and raw material, which would leave a correspondingly small proportion available for the payment of wages. On the other hand, if, with the same capital to invest, he had selected agriculture as the field for its employment, the bulk of his capital would take the form of wages, and fixed capital and raw material would assume a relatively unimportant place in his outlay. It is thus evident that the nature of the industry selected for investment must go a long way in determining the proportions in which the capital shall be distributed among the several instruments of production, and, therefore, must go a long way in determining the proportion which the wages element in that particular capital shall bear to its whole amount. Now the considerations which weigh with an individual capitalist are those which weigh with a community of capitalists; and we are therefore justified in concluding that the main circumstance governing the proportion which the

Wages-fund shall bear to the general capital of a nation is the nature of the national industries.

We are justified in concluding that this is the main circumstance; but a close examination will show that other circumstances also enter into the conditions which determine the final result. What the nature of the national industries really determines is the proportion in which *labor* shall be combined with the other instruments of production—fixed capital and raw material—in the general industry of a country; but what we want to know is the place which *wages* shall hold in this combination. Now the consideration of a simple example will show that, the proportion of labor to the other instruments of production being given, the proportion which wages shall bear to the total capital may vary.

Let us suppose a capitalist starting with £10,000. He finds that with £5000 he can buy fixed capital and raw material which will give full employment to 100 competent workmen; and if we suppose the rate of wages for these workmen to average £50 a year, the payment of their wages at this rate would absorb the rest of his capital, viz., £5000. His entire capital would thus be divided into £5000 for fixed capital and raw material, and £5000 for wages. But now suppose the current rate of wages for such labor as he required to have been £40 instead of £50 a year, he would have been able to procure the 100 workmen which his fixed capital and raw material required for £4000: £5000 having as before been invested in fixed capital and raw material, he would thus find himself with £1000 of capital still disposable. This we may suppose he would invest in the same business, and it would accordingly be necessary to bring together the instruments of production purchasable for £1000 in the same proportions as before—that is to say, he would have to distribute the £1000 nearly as follows: Fixed capital and raw material (let us say for the sake of round numbers) £550; wages £450. His whole capital will now be divided thus:

Fixed capital and raw material	£5,550
Wages (110 men at £40)	4,450
Total capital	£10,000

The proportion between labor, fixed capital, and raw material would here be the same as before, but whereas in the first case the Wages-fund represented 50 per cent of his whole capital, it now represents but 44 per cent. It is of course evident that, had I made the opposite supposition, and taken the current rate of wages at £60 instead of £40, it would have been necessary, in order to maintain the due proportion between labor and the other productive instruments, that the wages element should have been increased at the expense of fixed capital and raw material. The distribution of the total capital would then have stood nearly thus:

Fixed capital and raw material............................	£4,550
Wages of 90 men at £60 (nearly).........................	5,450
Total capital...........................	£10,000

In other words, the Wages-fund would now constitute 54 per cent of the total investment.

These examples show that the nature of the national industries do not determine absolutely the distribution of the national capital among the three leading instruments of production, but that the result is liable to be modified by the rate of wages which happens to be current. Now, so far as this is the case, it will perhaps strike the reader that our reasoning has conducted us into a vicious circle, inasmuch as, while seeking a solution of the rate of wages in the causes determining the Wages-fund, we have been suddenly confronted with the phenomenon itself as one of those causes. A little reflection, however, will show that the circle is apparent merely, and that the grounds of our argument are really independent and distinct. For, whatever be the causes which determine the Wages-fund, the amount of that fund being so determined, the rate of wages is merely the industrial outcome, and I might even say, the concrete expression, of the supply of labor. The modifying circumstance, therefore, in the case, though indicated by the rate of wages, is really the supply of labor; and our analysis accordingly issues in the following conditions as the determining causes of the Wages-fund, viz.: the total capital of the country (determined in the manner already explained); the nature of the national industries; and the supply of labor— facts at once distinct, and entirely independent of the subject of our investigation.

It would seem, then, that the amount of the Wages-fund (which the reader will be careful to distinguish from the *rate* of wages) is to some extent affected by the number of competent laborers offering their services, wherever those laborers are employed in conjunction with fixed capital and raw material. Now it may be worth while to point out the manner in which this influence is exerted. Reverting to our previous illustrations, it appears that, other things being the same, a rise in the current rate of wages issues in an expansion of tho Wages-fund, and, contrariwise, a fall in the current rate in its contraction. But, the rate of wages, other things being the same, varying inversely with the supply of labor, this is equivalent to saying that the Wages-fund expands as the supply of labor contracts, and contracts as the supply of labor expands. An unexpected consequence, not, so far as I know, before adverted to, results from this play of economic forces, namely, that an increase or diminution in the supply of labor, where it is of a kind to be employed in conjunction with fixed capital and raw material, acts upon the rate of wages with a force *more than proportional* to the increase or diminution in the supply; for it tells at the same time upon both the factors on which the result depends, modifying them in opposite directions—the fund undergoing diminution as the number of those who are to share it is increased; or, on the other hand, expanding as the sharers become fewer. This occurs, I say, where labor is of a kind to be employed in conjunction with fixed capital and raw material; and, it may be added, that the effect would only assume sensible dimensions where those agencies constituted a substantial proportion of the whole capital invested. Indeed it would be a mistake to regard this particular condition—the supply of labor considered as a cause affecting, not the rate of wages, but the aggregate Wages-fund—as under any circumstances more than a subordinate and modifying influence in the case. The point is one of theoretic rather than of practical importance; and, in considering the variations of the Wages-fund, it will rarely be necessary to take account of more than the two main determining conditions of that phenomenon—the growth or decline of capital, and the nature of the prevailing industries.

§ 9. It appears, then that the aggregate amount of wealth appropriated to the laboring population in any country varies, not simply with the progress of the national wealth, nor yet with the progress of the national capital, but with this latter circumstance taken in connection with the character of the national industries, the result being also, within certain narrow limits, modified by the supply of labor. In other words, it appears that the same amount of capital will yield under different circumstances Wages-funds of different dimensions, and will consequently be capable of supporting populations of different magnitudes. This position finds its illustration and verification in the industrial phenomena of different countries. For example, it is obvious at a glance that a given amount of capital invested in the Western States of North America supports a larger laboring population than the same amount invested in the New England States; and the reason is plain: the former States are more extensively agricultural than the latter, and consequently employ fixed capital and raw material less extensively in their staple industries; it follows of course that the proportion of the total investment applicable to the payment of wages is correspondingly greater in those States. Again, a comparison of an average investment in the United States—it matters not in what part of them—and in Great Britain would reveal analogous differences. Fixed capital being more largely employed in the industries of Great Britain, a given amount of capital invested in those industries would yield a smaller Wages-fund than the same capital invested in the United States, and consequently would support—allowance made for the different rates of wages in the two countries—a smaller laboring population. Similarly, if, instead of comparing different countries, the comparison were made between different epochs, we should still find the power of capital to support labor varying with the changes in the character of the industries in which it is employed. And, in connection with this, we may notice what amounts to an economic derivative law in the industrial development of progressive communities. The modifications which occur in the distribution of capital among its several departments as nations advance are by no means fortuitous, but follow on the whole a well-defined course, and move toward a determined goal. In effect, what we find is, a constant growth of the national capital, accompanied with a nearly equally constant decline in the proportion of this capital which goes to support productive labor. This is the inevitable consequence of the progress of the industrial arts, the effect of which is to cause a steady substitution of the agencies of inanimate nature for the labor of man. In making this remark it is perhaps superfluous to add that it is not to be inferred from the circumstance stated that the progress of those arts is unfavorable to the interests of labor. Even on the lowest and most materialistic view of the interests of labor the reverse is the fact; for what industrial progress under the influence of the advancing arts and sciences effects is a diminution, not in the absolute amount of the Wages-fund, but only in the *proportion* which it bears to the total capital of a country—a diminution which is perfectly compatible with a steadily progressive increase of the fund. One has only indeed to consider what the Wages-fund of such a country as Great Britain has grown to under a *régime* of advancing industrial art, and reflect on what it would probably now have been had that progress been arrested a century ago, to perceive the utter groundlessness of the notion that industrial art can, in the long run, be antagonistic to labor. Not the less, however, is it indispensable, if we would understand the most salient facts of modern industrial life, to keep constantly in view the tendency of the Wages-fund, with the progress of wealth and art, to lag behind the advances of the other factors of the national capital.[9] The fact is one of very great significance, and highly deserving the consideration of those who speculate on social subjects. For it involves this double consequence bearing on the laws of social growth—a tendency toward a relative increase of the classes not living by hired labor as compared with those who do: and again, a tendency toward increased inequality in the distribution of wealth.[10] I say it involves these consequences as tendencies; and I may add, that up to the present time those tendencies have in general been very fully realized in the actual experience of the world, and in an eminent degree in the experience of Great Britain. They exist, however, as tendencies only, and may, like other tendencies or laws of nature, be counteracted through the influence of tendencies of an opposite kind; in a word, the balance may be redressed by suitable expedients. Though the fund for the remuneration of mere labor, whether skilled or unskilled, must, so long as industry is progressive, ever bear a constantly diminishing proportion alike to the growing wealth and growing capital, there is nothing in the nature of things which restricts the laboring population to this fund for their support. In return, indeed, for their mere labor, it is to this that they must look for their sole reward; but they may help production otherwise than by their labor: they may save, and thus become themselves the owners of capital, and profits may thus be brought to aid the Wages-fund. I merely note this point at present as bearing upon the controversy respecting the future of the laboring classes, reserving the full consideration of the latter question for another place. There are those who regard it as a law of industrial development that capital should ever become more and more aggregated in a few hands, and that, as a consequence of this, the position of the laborer in the future must remain substantially what it is at present in the more advanced industrial countries—that of a recipient of wages merely. I do not pretend here to pronounce upon this question—the economic data for its determination have not yet been fully worked out; but I am justified even here in asserting this much, that the permanent maintenance of a *régime* such as is contemplated, co-existing with a progressive industry, can only issue in one result—a constant exaggeration of those features already beginning to mark so unpleasantly the aspect of our social state—namely, a harsh separation of classes, combined with those glaring inequalities in the distribution of wealth which most people will agree are among the chief elements of our social instability.

§ 10. I remarked just now, that under a progressive state of industry, though the proportion of the Wages-fund to the whole capital of a country diminishes, the positive amount of the fund for the most part undergoes increase. It must be confessed, however, that while this represents the ordinary rule, there is nothing strictly necessary in the relation of the phenomena thus presented; and that instances do occur, and sometimes on a large scale, in which the progress of wealth and industry is accompanied with a positive contraction of the Wages-fund. Such a result happens whenever that process takes place which is described by economists as a conversion of circulating capital into fixed.

As Mr. Mill has remarked, the proceeding in question is not one which in practice is frequently resorted to; the introduction and extension of fixed capital being, as a general rule, effected through the agency of fresh savings rather than by withdrawal from the support of labor of funds already thus employed. But it is beyond question that such conversions of circulating into fixed capital do sometimes occur; and, in this event, it is not less certain that the Wages-fund must, at all events for a time, be curtailed. For the most part, however, it happens that movements of this kind are on a limited scale, and, the resulting arrangements always issuing in increased efficiency of production (for this is the motive for adopting them), the gaps made in the Wages-fund are quickly filled up; so that the consequences which ensue, though perhaps serious enough, are rarely of large dimensions. I say this is what usually happens when circulating capital is converted into fixed; but there are times when the process is conducted on something like a national scale, and then it may be productive of even disastrous results. An occasion of this kind, for example, occurred in the industrial history of England during the sixteenth century, when the exchange of a very rude and primitive agriculture for one that might by comparison be called scientific, and more particularly an extensive conversion of tillage-lands to pasture, under the influence of causes then affecting her general trade, issued in the remarkable phenomenon of a rapidly growing national capital, with improved industrial processes and extending trade, accompanied by a sudden and portentous development of pauperism. No doubt the recuperative power of progressive industry told in the long run; and perhaps before the century was over, or the new Poor Law had well come into operation, the encroachment made on the laborers' division of the national wealth had been more than repaid: but it is nevertheless true that the event amounted to a crisis in the national industry, and was, for a large portion of the people, fraught with disaster and ruin. Something of the same kind has been in progress in our own day in Ireland. A protective Corn Law, combined with the demoralization of the people from political and social causes, had generated an industrial system which could not be permanently sustained. Under the combined influence of free trade and the potato disease this system suddenly collapsed, and it became necessary to pass from a crude *régime* of tillage to one in which capital was extensively converted into fixed and permanent forms. The result has been the introduction of an agriculture suited to the country, and largely carried on by improved modern processes, and a rapid increase in general wealth; but simultaneously with this a sudden contraction of the Wages-fund, of which the unequivocal evidence is found in a population reduced in a few years from eight to five and a half millions. Occurrences of this kind place it beyond doubt that extensive changes in the character of the industry of a country, even though they be all in the direction of scientific progress, improved processes, and ultimately and even immediately augmented wealth, may nevertheless effect a reduction in the means for supporting productive labor, and may for a time act disastrously on its interests.

§ 11. I have now stated the doctrine of the Wages-fund as I understand it, in connection with the general problem of the rate of wages; but before proceeding to trace its bearing upon the relations of capital and labor, and the various practical questions arising therefrom, it will be convenient to pause here for a short time in our development of the general theory, in order to consider the objections which have been urged against the doctrine by Mr. Thornton—objections which, as I have already informed the reader, have been powerful enough to effect the conversion of Mr. Mill. Mr. Thornton's argument ranges over a considerable portion of his volume, but the gist of it will be found in the following passage:

> "If there really were a national fund, the whole of which must necessarily be applied to the payment of wages, that fund could be no other than an aggregate of smaller similar funds possessed by the

several individuals who composed the employing part of the nation. Does, then, any individual employer possess any such fund? Is there any specific portion of any individual's capital which the owner must necessarily expend upon labor? Of course every employer possesses a certain amount of money, whether his own or borrowed, out of which all his expenses must be met, if met at all. With so much of this amount as remains after deduction of what he takes for family and personal expenses, he carries on his business—with one portion of that balance providing or keeping in repair buildings and machinery, with a second portion procuring materials, with a third hiring labor. But is there any law fixing the amount of his domestic expenditure, and thereby fixing likewise the balance available for his industrial operations? May he not spend more or less on his family and himself, according to his fancy—in the one case having more, in the other less, left for the conduct of his business? And of what is left, does he or can he determine beforehand how much shall be laid out on buildings, how much on materials, how much on labor? May not his outlay on repairs be unexpectedly increased by fire or other accident? will not his outlay on materials vary with their dearness or cheapness, or with the varying demand for the finished article? and must not the amount available for wages vary accordingly? And even though the latter amount were exactly ascertained beforehand, even though he did know to a farthing how much he would be able to spend on labor, would he be bound so to spend the utmost he could afford to spend? If he could get as much labor as he wanted at a cheap rate, would he voluntarily pay as much for it as he would be compelled to pay if it were dearer? It sounds like mockery or childishness to ask these questions, so obvious are the only answers that can possibly be given to them; yet it is only on the assumption that directly opposite answers must be given that the Wages-fund can for one moment stand. For if in the case of individual employers there be no Wages-funds—no definite or definable portions of their capitals which, and neither more nor less than which, they must severally apply to the hiring of labor— clearly there can be no aggregate of such funds, clearly there can be no national Wages-fund. And be it observed, fixity or definiteness is the very essence of the supposed Wages-fund. No one denies that some amount or other must within any given period be disbursed in the form of wages. The only question is, whether that amount be determinate or indeterminate. If indeterminate, it can not of course be divided, and might as well not exist for any power it possesses of performing the sole function of a Wages-fund, that, viz., of yielding a quotient that would indicate the average rate of wages."[11]

Mr. Thornton, the reader will perceive from this passage, does not deny the existence of a Wages-fund: he admits the legitimacy of contemplating in the aggregate those funds—the wages of individual workmen—of which we know the existence in detail; but he contends that neither the particular sums in detail, nor therefore the aggregate which they compose, are "determinate"—an expression under which he includes at once their "pre-determination" toward the destination they afterward receive, and their "limitation" within their actual bounds. It must at once be conceded that, in the sense in which (as appears from this passage as well as from the whole tenor of his argument) Mr. Thornton understands the "predetermination" and "limitation" of the Wages-fund, his position is unassailable. Undoubt-edly "there is no specific portion of any individual's capital which the owner must necessarily expend upon wages." "There is no law fixing the amount" of any man's "domestic expenditure, and thereby fixing likewise the balance available for industrial operations." Nor is any man "bound to spend," in the payment of labor, "the utmost he can afford to spend." I should have con-fidently asserted, I will not say that no economist, but that no reasonable being had ever advanced the theory of a Wages-fund in this sense, if it had not been that Mr. Mill had accepted the reasoning I have quoted as a refuta-tion of that theory.[12] As it is, I can only say that this is not the sense in which I have myself understood the doctrine (and I first learned it from Mr. Mill's pages); and further, I must add, that if economic doctrines in general are to be understood in the sense here assigned to the Wages-fund doctrine—namely, as expressing principles which compel human beings to the adoption of certain courses of conduct in despite of their own inclination and will, there is not a single one within the range of economic science that could endure ten minutes' criticism. The doctrine, for example, that the supply of a commodity tends to conform to the quantity demanded at the normal price, is as well established as any principle of Political Economy. How is it proved? By showing that, if the supply of the commodity falls short of this quantity, the market price will rise above the normal price, profits on the production will be exceptionally high, and, as a consequence, a larger amount of capital and labor will be "determined" toward the production; while in the contrary case the "determination" of capital and labor would be in the opposite direc-tion. But if by "determination" of capital is to be understood some force which compels the capitalist irrespective of his own wishes and views of his own interest, the reasoning is manifestly groundless. Mr. Thornton might say here, quite as truly as in his argument against the Wages-fund, there is no law, physical or legal, there is no moral principle, which compels any capital-ist to employ his capital in a branch of production simply because profits in that branch are rising. Again, take the law of rent: how is that law estab-lished? By some such reasoning as this, namely, by showing that the competi-tion of farmers for land will "determine" to the possession of landlords all that profit upon land which is in excess of the ordinary profits upon industry;

while the competition of other occupations with agriculture will prevent the amount so determined from rising beyond the limits of the exceptional profit. But what is to prevent Mr. Thornton form interposing here the same series of objections he has urged against the Wages-fund? "Rent," he might exclaim, "determined by the law of exceptional profit! Is there any specific portion of a farmer's capital which the owner *must* necessarily expend upon rent? And who can tell beforehand what the amount of his exceptional profit will be? May not his outlay on repairs be unexpectedly increased by flood or other accident? Will not his outlay on materials vary with their dearness or cheapness, or with the varying demand for the produce? and must not the amount available for rent very accordingly? And even though the amount of exceptional profit were exactly ascertained beforehand, even though the farmer did know to a earthing how much he would be able to pay to the landlord, while reserving average profit to himself, would he be bound so spend the utmost he could so afford to spend?" And so the theory of rent would collapse, and Mr. Thornton might enjoy an easy triumph over Ricardo and all who have since followed in his wake. In short, it is evident that, if this style of reasoning be legitimate, the whole structure of economic doctrine must inevitably go down.

What then is the answer to Mr. Thornton? Why, I take it, this: that his reasoning conception of the nature of an economic law—of what is meant by "pre-determination" and "limitation" in the sphere of economic action. A "law" in Political Economy does not mean either legal coercion or physical compulsion, or yet moral obligation; nor does the "determination" expressed in an economic law mean the necessary realization of certain results independently of the human will. What an economic law asserts is, not that men must do so and so whether they like it or not, but that in given circumstances they will like to do so and so; that their self-interest or other feelings will lead them to this result. The predetermination in question is of that sort which leads a hungry man to eat his dinner, or an honest man to pay his debts, and depends for its fulfillment, not upon external compulsion of any sort, but upon the influence of certain inducements of the will, our knowledge of which enables us to say how in given circumstances a man will act. It is in this sense that, speaking for myself, I understand the "predetermination" of a certain portion of the wealth of a country to the payment of wages. I believe that, in the existing state of the national wealth, the character of Englishmen being what it is, a certain prospect of profit will "determine" a certain proportion of this wealth to productive investment; that the amount thus "determined" will increase as the field for investment is extended, and that it will not increase beyond what this field can find employment for at that rate of profit which satisfies English commercial expectation. Further, I believe that, investment thus taking place, the form which it shall assume will be "determined" by the nature of the national industries—"determined," not under acts of Parliament, or in virtue of any physical law, but through the influence of the investor's interests; while this, the form of the investment, will again "determine" the proportion of the whole capital which shall be paid as wages to laborers. It is in this sense I say that I understand the "predetermination" implied in the Wages-fund doctrine; and against the doctrine so understood I can not find that there is any thing very formidable in Mr. Thornton's criticisms. They are simply beside the mark—at all events, beside my mark. "Capitalists put aside a portion of their means with a determination that, whatever happens, they shall be spent in wages!"—The doctrine, as I understand it, makes no such assumption; nor am I, in holding it, bound to maintain any such absurdity. "Employers are anxious to buy their labor as cheap as they can, to spend as little as possible in wages."—No doubt they are; but while they are anxious to get their labor cheap, they are also anxious to place certain amounts of their wealth at profitable investment; and, to do this in the most advantageous way, a certain proportion of the sums so invested *must* go to the payment of wages.

I say deliberately "*must*" go to the payment of wages, for this is the consequence involved in the doctrine I have endeavored to expound. Assuming a certain field for investment, and the prospect of profit in this such as to attract a certain aggregate capital, and assuming the national industries to be of a certain kind, the proportion of this aggregate capital which shall be invested in wages is not a matter within the discretion of capitalists, always supposing they desire to obtain the largest practical return upon their outlay. To accomplish this, the instruments of production, labor, fixed capital, and raw material must be brought together in certain proportions—a condition which requires, as I have shown—the supply of labor being given—a distribution of the aggregate capital in certain proportions among those instruments. Supposing, now, capitalists to succeed in forcing down the rate of wages below the point at which, having regard to the number of the laboring population, the amount, which the fulfillment of this condition would assign to the payment of wages, was absorbed—either the capital thus withdrawn from the Wages-fund must remain uninvested and therefore unproductive, or if invested, and not invested in wages, it would take the form of fixed capital or raw material. But by hypothesis the fixed capital and raw material were already in due proportion to the labor force, and they would consequently now be in excess of it. A competition among capitalists for labor would consequently ensue; and what could this end in but a restoration to the Wages-fund of the amount withdrawn from it? Mr. Thornton probably would tell me that the amount saved from the payment of wages might, and probably would, be turned to swell the private expenditure of capitalists, who, taking out the results in this form, would simply continue to receive larger profits at the expense of their workmen. No doubt this is a possible contingency in particular cases, but, the character of the wealthy classes remaining on the whole what it is, increased accumulations in other quarters would neutralize exceptional extravagance in some; and larger profits would not be less powerful than before to attract increased investment. In a word, my argument brings me back to the position from which I started, that, the aggregate investment being determined by certain mental and physical conditions, and the national industries being such as they are, there is but one distribution of the capital invested which is consistent with the greatest advantage to the investors. That distribution involves a certain proportion spent in the payment of wages, and it is to this result that capitalists, if true to their own interest, *must* conform their conduct.[13]

So far as to one leading objection urged against the Wages-fund doctrine. It is further contended that the doctrine assumes the existence of a limitation to the amount of that fund for which there is no warrant in facts. As Mr. Thornton puts it, "may not the capitalist spend more or less on his family and himself according to his fancy—in the one case having more, in the other less, left for the conduct of his business?" The aspect of the question here brought into view involves considerations of so much importance that it will be best discussed in a separate chapter.

Notes

1 "A Refutation of the Wage-fund Theory of Modern Political Economy," by F. D. Longe, pp. 55, 56.

2 "On Labor: its Wrongful Claims and Rightful Dues," etc., by W.T. Thornton. Second Edition, 1870.

3 See *Fortnightly Review* for May 1, 1869.

4 "Principles of Political Economy," book ii., chap. xi.

5 "The political economy of the wages question," says Mr. Brassey (p. 251), "is simple enough." Certainly it is, if it consists in showing that every rise or fall of wages is traceable to a change in the relation of supply and demand. But it seems to me that Mr. Brassey has mistaken the statement of the problem for its solution. It needs no proof surely to see that if £10,000,000 be added to the existing capital of a country, and the greater portion applied to the direct purchase of labor (the supply of labor and other things continuing the same), wages must rise; or that the withdrawal of a great sum from the payment of wages, as on the occasion of a commercial collapse, must on the other hand, *cæteris paribus*, involve a fall of wages. To tell us this is not to solve the wages question, but to state it. What we want to know is what determines the relation of supply and demand—of the Wages-fund to the laboring population. Why is that relation such as to yield one rate of wages in the United States, another rate in Great Britain, and a third rate on the continent of Europe? If Mr. Brassey would fairly address himself to this problem, I think he would find that the political economy of the wages question is not quite so "simple" as he supposes.

6 As set forth, for example, in Mill's "Principles of Political Economy," book 1., chap. xi.

7 See *ante*, pp. 23–26.

8 Wells's Report, 1869, p. 13.

9 These remarks receive a practical illustration from the important and suggestive article by Professor Fawcett in the *Fortnightly Review* (January, 1874), in which he calls attention to the slight increase which has occurred in the rate of wages in

Grent Britain contemporaneously with the large additions recently made to our national wealth.

10   This latter result can not indeed be said to be necessary; since it is conceivable that laborers by limiting their numbers might keep the rate of their remuneration on a level with the growing incomes of other classes. To do this, however, two conditions would have to be fulfilled: the productiveness of industry would have to increase in a degree sufficient to permit of this high rate of remuneration consistently with yielding also a rate of profit high enough to attract capital toward investment; and secondly, the result would imply such a degree of self-control on the part of the laboring population as, I fear, experience gives us no warrant for expecting.

11   "Labor, etc.," pp. 84, 85.

12   Mr. Mill's acceptance of Mr. Thornton's argument on this point is the more perplexing as he has himself, in more than one passage of his work, strenuously disclaimed that notion of an economic law against which Mr. Thornton's reasoning is directed, and, on the other hand, asserted the view for which I contend in the text; for example, in the following: "Demand and supply are not physical agencies, which thrust a given amount of wages into a laborer's hand *without the participation of his own will and actions.* The market rate is not fixed for him by some self-acting instrument, but is the result of bargaining between human beings—of what Adam Smith calls 'the higgling of the market.'" (Book v., chap. x., § 5.)

13   The notion that any portion of the wealth of the country should be "determined" to the payment of wages would seem also to shock Mr. Longe's sense of economic propriety; which is strange, seeing that his own doctrine that it is "the demand for commodities which determines the quantity of wealth spend in the payment of wages" plainly involves this consequence. He puts the case of a capitalist who, by taking advantage of the necessities of his workmen, effects a reduction in their wages, and succeeds in withdrawing so much, call it £1000, from the Wages-fund; and asks how is the sum, thus withdrawn, to be restored to the fund? On Mr. Longe's principles the answer is simple—"by being spent on commodities;" for it may be assumed that the sum so withdrawn will, in any case, not be hoarded. "But," urges Mr. Louge, "it might be spent on foreign wines, or on a trip to Switzerland;" the suggestion of course being that in this case the expenditure could do no good to English labor. If so, then we seem to have made a mistake in repealing our protective laws; nor were projectionists, after all, so very wrong in seeking to encourage native industry by compelling expenditure toward domestic productions. May I venture to remind Mr. Longe that expenditure on foreign wines and in Swiss travel must and can only be paid for by an export of British productions, and that it therefore creates a demand for such productions, though more circuitously, quite as certainly as if it took a more direct form. The answer, therefore, to the case put by Mr. Longe is easy on his own principles; and I am disposed to flatter myself that the reader who has gone with me in the foregoing discussion will not have much difficulty in replying to it upon mine.

30

'WORK AND THE WORKMAN

An address to the Trades' Union Congress'

John Kells Ingram

Source: *Journal of the Statistical and Social Inquiry Society of Ireland* 8 (1879–80): 106–23

I BELIEVE I am indebted for the privilege of addressing you to-day to the impression produced on the minds of some of your leaders by a discourse which I delivered at a recent meeting of the British Association for the Advancement of Science. What I proposed to myself in that discourse was to show that certain prevailing ideas as to the constitution and method of Economic science required revision and amendment. Whilst recognizing the valuable work done by economists, and notably by Adam Smith, I endeavoured to show that many of them, by taking abstractions for realities, by drawing unverified deductions from *a priori* assumptions, and by giving to their conclusions, even when in a certain sense just, too absolute a character, missed the truth, and set up figments of their own imagination for laws of social life.

But the most important proposition I sought to establish was this—that the Economic phenomena of society cannot, in our researches, be isolated, except provisionally, from the rest,—its material aspect from its intellectual, moral, and political aspects,—without our being thus led into grave error. Or, to state the same thing in other words, I asserted that in the study of society, regarded as a subject of theoretic contemplation, the attempt to constitute the investigation of its Economic laws into a separate science is a philosophically vicious procedure, and that such inquiries must be regarded as forming *one* branch, to be kept in constant and close relation with the others, of the general Science of Sociology.

The views of method which I thus put forward met with a remarkable degree of attention, and even of acceptance, both in these countries and abroad. This arose, as I have always felt and said, not from any originality in the conceptions, for they were not new, nor from any special merit in my exposition of them, but from the fact that they fell in with a spontaneous movement of mind which had been everywhere taking place. I was only the spokesman of convictions which had been gradually forming, and were now pretty well matured.

Some of those who possess your confidence were attracted by these views. They believed, as I have reason to think, that the method of investigation which I advocated mainly on philosophical grounds, would tend to the formation of juster and more humane conceptions of social practice. And thus it has happened, that I have now an opportunity of laying before you some considerations respecting the conduct of life and the actual dealings of men, to which the larger and less one-sided mode of study I recommended appears to lead us. I have naturally chosen as the special department of human affairs, to which I should address myself on an occasion like the present, the position, the requirements, and the future of the working-classes. To fix our ideas—though most of what I shall say would admit of wider application—I shall keep before me, as a definite type of the workman's life, the form which it assumes in the great centres of manufacturing industry.

Every particular social problem is only a case of this general one, how to subordinate all social forces to the highest permanent well-being of the entire community. Now, the more we study this great question, the more we shall find that no material expedients—however useful in their proper place—will suffice for its solution. That solution must be essentially moral. The end in view can be attained only by means of a generally accepted code of social duties, continuously applied and brought to bear on practice by the systematic solicitude of society. The essential basis of this action is the establishment of stable intellectual convictions respecting the conditions of healthy social life—in other words, a scientific Sociology. Duties, in fact, are social functions freely performed, and they cannot be fixed with the degree of definiteness necessary for practical discipline, without a study of the functions as they arise out of the natural constitution and historical development of the social body. The ideas appropriate to each function must thus be elaborated, in order to determine the corresponding duties. This is the high practical destination which lies before Sociology, and which gives it an importance and interest transcending that of every other department of human knowledge.

What then are the general conceptions we ought to form of the industrial functions? What are the relations which have here to be regulated, and what the moral ideas which ought to preside over that regulation?

The whole modern organization of labour in its advanced forms rests on a fundamental fact which has spontaneously and increasingly developed itself, namely, the definite separation between the functions of the capitalist and the workman, or, in other words, between the direction of industrial operations and their execution in detail. Appearing at the close of the Middle Ages, when industry began to take the place of military activity, this separation has become more and more pronounced with the growing expansion of productive enterprise. The active rich have thus tended to assume the position of practical chiefs of modern society; the determination and conduct of all industrial operations, the government of the world of labour, has more and more passed into their hands. This ascendancy of wealth is deplored by some, and, if it necessarily meant what is properly known as plutocracy—the absolute domination of wealth, the prospects of society would be gloomy enough. But the use of wealth, as of every other social force, must be regulated and moralized, a task which ought to be easier than that of controlling the rude preponderance of military force, which was its historical predecessor.

The active rich, if they would develop in themselves the sentiments which befit their position, must rise above the purely private point of view, and regard themselves as discharging a true public function—that, namely, of administrators of human capital. They cannot claim to be creators of this capital; the largest part of it is the fruit of the labours, economies, discoveries, inventions, and institutions of many generations. The office it fulfils is that of rendering possible the continuation, under equitable conditions, of the common work of society; and the active rich are by their position morally charged with its preservation and management for this end, and its transmission, with increase, to our posterity. The institution of individual property guarantees to them the security of possession and independence of action which are necessary for the efficient discharge of this function. Without such personal appropriation, there could be neither vigorous initiative, nor persistent activity, nor vigilant economy. There can be no army without officers as well as soldiers, and this principle is just as true of industrial as of military organization. No important operation could be effectively conducted, if every one who took part in the execution of it had a voice in its conception and general direction. Great improvements could with difficulty be introduced, if their adoption had to be submitted to a vote, which would often be ignorant, timid, or prejudiced. But whilst the security and independence of the capitalist class are thus guaranteed, its members are subject to the moral responsibilities which attend on every social function, and which are not in their case the less real because society for good reasons renounces, except in extreme cases, their enforcement by material means. This conception of the capitalist as a social administrator heightens his dignity, entitling him to respect by virtue of what is really a public office—a respect which can, on that ground, be shown by his inferiors without hypocrisy or servility, even when his private character is entitled to little esteem. At the same time the ideal thus presented must on good natures have an elevating effect: must tend to raise them above the vulgar abuses of wealth, and to make them regard as the greatest advantage it confers, the power of more largely and effectually benefiting their fellow-men.

Our views of the office of the workman must also be transformed and elevated. The way in which his position is habitually contemplated by the economists, and indeed by the public, is a very narrow, and therefore a false one. Labour is spoken of as if it were an independent entity, separable from the personality of the workman. It is treated as a commodity like corn or cotton—the human agent, his human needs, human nature, and human feelings, being kept almost completely out of view. Now there are, no doubt, if we carry our abstractions far enough, certain resemblances between the contract of employer and employed, and the sale of a commodity. But by fixing exclusive, or even predominant attention on these, we miss the deepest and truly characteristic features of the relation of master and workman—a relation with which moral conditions are inseparably associated. As in science it is the method we pursue on which the value of our investigations will in the long run depend, so in matters of conduct the point of view at which we place ourselves tends to determine the character of our whole procedure. And by viewing labour as a commodity, we at once get rid of the moral basis on which the relation of employer and employed should stand, and make the so-called law of the market the sole regulator of that relation.

Such a perverted conception arises from the individualistic way of looking at the relation in question, as if it were purely a matter of private concernment. But the entire case receives a different complexion when we place ourselves at the social point of view, from which alone these subjects can be rightly studied. Labour, in the widest sense of the word, is then seen to be the continuous and combined effort of our race for the improvement of its condition and its nature; the present using the acquired knowledge and transmitted resources of the past, and handing down an augmented inheritance to the future. All forms of labour, from the loftiest intellectual achievement down to the humblest share in material production, come to be viewed as elements in this great human movement. The lowest genuine exertion of strength or skill—the endeavour to do any piece of work honestly and thoroughly, is thus ennobled and consecrated. Master and workman fulfil different, but equally necessary parts in a joint social enterprise; the one supplying the instruments and provisions needed for its prosecution, and having the general direction of the operations, the other contributing the hand, eye, brain requisite for their execution in detail. This is the only really human conception of labour—the only one which puts employer and employed each in his right place. It presents the workman, not as a semi-slave selling himself or part of himself for purely private ends, but as a free man co-operating according to his ability in the service of humanity, under the guidance of an associate in the same service, who differs from him only as captain from private soldier.

The highest ideal of the moral obligation incumbent on all of us, is that of living for others. Now it requires no sentimental exaggeration, but a simple appreciation of facts as they are, to show the working-man that this is what, by his industrial vocation, he is called to do. For all that goes to the material sustenance of his contemporaries, for all of material treasure or accommodation that is by them transmitted to their successors, his co-operation is indispensable. He is privileged to see more clearly than workers of a higher order the direct effects of his exertions in the promotion of the common good. For the elevation of his sentiments it is only necessary for him to keep before him these realities of his social function, and to do consciously and with loyal willingness what he is in fact, by the necessities of his position, doing every day.

The first effect of a thorough appropriation of this conception of the workman as a social functionary will be to supply a foundation for his just dignity. It will place on a solid basis his claim to a respect and courtesy on the part of his superiors in rank, which are far from being yet sufficiently wrought into our modern manners. It will also profoundly modify our way of viewing his remuneration. His faithful service is now too often regarded as obtaining in his wages a full equivalent return, dispensing us of all further obligation towards him. But, as Carlyle has said, "Cash never yet paid one man fully his deserts to another; nor could it, nor can it, now or henceforth to the end of the world." This coarse view is not in fact applied in the case of the higher social offices; there the idea of a functionary who serves the public well having got his complete requital by receiving his salary would be recognized as a vulgar one. The salary is in such cases regarded only as furnishing the means of continuing the function under such conditions as the due preparation for it, and the fitting discharge of it, require in the interest of the community. Now from the social point of view the separation hitherto set up in our conceptions between public and private functions, as well as between the higher and the humbler offices, must be given up. Public and private offices are equally departments of the service of Humanity, which differ only in the manner of their retribution. The wages of the working-man are to be regarded as the indispensable means of keeping him in such a state of physical health, material security, and moral quietude that he may be able to continue his service to society, and to prepare a new generation for the same service. The only true recompence of the right performance of his functions, lies in the conscious fulfilment of social duty, and in the approbation and esteem which this justly earns from such of his fellow-men as have the opportunity and the capacity for appreciating his work.

The twofold conception I have presented of the capitalist and the workman brings out distinctly their duties to each other. Those duties are such as spring from their relation as mutually indispensable associates in the execution of a great social function. This implies, along with the cultivation of habits of mutual respect, a spirit of mutual help and furtherance, and a loyal interest in each other's prosperity. These obligations are binding on both sides. On the part of the workman they call for faithful work as opposed to eye-service, and for abstinence from all unreasonable demands. In the master, as the higher and more powerful of the associates, they involve a larger responsibility and duties of a wider range. As the appropriate motto of the feudal ages was *Noblesse oblige*, so that of modern industrial society must be *Richesse oblige*. The masters must subdue in themselves the base inclinations which prompt too many, while accumulating personal gain and lavishing it on their own pleasures and ostentations, to neglect their co-workers who

ought to share in equitable measure the benefits arising from their joint operations. Wealth can never be what a man should "seek first;" no spurious
economic doctrines can shut out the moral obligation which accompanies us
into all our enterprises, that, namely, of finding our happiness in loving and
helping our fellow-men rather than in selfish pursuit of our own advantage.
The masters ought to be, as some of them have nobly shown themselves, the
friends of their workmen, interested in their welfare and that of their families, and actively studying that welfare—giving them opportunities of intellectual improvement; striving to make all the conditions of their labour as
favourable as possible to their health, comfort, and morality; keeping them
together and assisting them to maintain their homes when they are innocently suffering from any public calamity. The master who succeeds, as it is
called, without caring for his men and helping them to succeed along with
him, has attained no true success; in spite of the wealth he has accumulated,
tried by every real standard, his life has been a failure.

In what I have been saying I have assumed the continued existence of the
separation between the functions of the capitalist and the workman which
has increasingly prevailed in the constitution of modern industry. The social-
istic schemes which would forcibly abolish this separation by taking all the
wealth of the community into the management of the State have found little
welcome amongst English working-men, who have been hitherto distinguished by their freedom from the subversive utopian notions which have
attracted popular favour in other countries. Deeply feeling the evils of industrial life, as it now is, they yet have not aimed at the overthrow of its present
organization. Whilst resisting special movements and tendencies on the part
of the employers, they have not attacked them as a class or institution. The
so-called co-operative system, if extended to the fullest conceivable development, would indeed have the effect of supplanting the masters, without compromising the principle of property. But I think this system has not, as yet,
won much cordial approbation from our working-men, or largely coloured
their ideas of the social future. It has been much more warmly taken up by
philanthropic writers on their behalf. The co-operative stores, or societies of
supply, indeed, appear to have been a genuine effort of the people to escape
from the abuses of the retail traffic, and obtain good articles at reasonable
prices for their daily consumption. These have, I believe, been really successful, and have done much to correct the evils of adulteration, and the
enhancement of prices arising from credit dealings. When these results have
been thoroughly attained, such societies will most probably disappear. In any
case they are not true co-operative societies—they are merely joint stock
companies. But the co-operative societies of production have far more
widely-reaching objects, at least in the conceptions of the social speculators
who have most strongly advocated them. To these they present themselves as
the true solution of the labour problem. Professor Cairnes believed that in
this new organization of industry lay the one hope of the working-classes,

and Mr. Thornton preached it as a panacea for the evils of the world of labour. I ought to speak with caution and modesty in opposition to such men; but I am compelled to say that in my opinion the proposed solution is an impracticable one, and that the material and moral results of any attempt to realize it on the large scale would disappoint the expectations that have been entertained respecting it. Such attempts are, of course, and ought to be, perfectly open to the working-classes, and it is possible that many trials of the system may be made before the disillusion comes. But I believe it is sure to come. The whole of the commercial and trading classes, as Mr. Howell has said, would not quietly submit to be "shouldered out of the way" by the new industrial system, and the sustained vigour of management and concentration of skill and energy which arise from the ownership of one or a very few, would be more than a match for the looser and less compact organization of these societies. Their operations will at least be always exposed to risk of failure, and I cannot think that the all-important object of the stability of working-men's homes can be furthered by subjecting their scanty means to the vicissitudes of commercial success, which large capitals may bear without fatal strain, but to which small resources should not be exposed. The breakdown of a co-operative factory, as has been well observed, is in its results fraught with far greater evils, both of material disaster and of moral discouragement, than can attend the collapse of a private firm. Our recent policy has been to give the security of the State for the deposits of the savings of the working-classes—a policy founded on the just idea that for them not gain, but the prevention of loss, is the first object. The natural destination of such savings is not industrial investment, but the formation of a modest reserve to meet special domestic exigencies, or to make possible the performance of special domestic duties. The suggestion has sometimes been made that the capital of the trades-unions should be embarked in co-operative enterprise, but such a step must surely be deprecated by all friends of those bodies, whose efficiency essentially depends on their funds being at once available for any emergency.

Much stress has been laid by the advocates of the co-operative system on the enlightenment and the moral benefits which must arise from its practice. It is said that it will bring the working-men to understand the grave difficulties with which employers have to contend in the conduct of their business, and will make them more reasonable in their dealings with their employers by showing them in a practical way the bearing on production and prices of the regulations they desire to enforce on the masters. It will be observed that this implies only a partial or temporary trial of the system, and looks to the organization of employer and employed as the really permanent and normal one. The instruction so received might be useful enough, but it would be dearly purchased by extensive and repeated failures, and I believe the same lessons can be sufficiently inculcated through study and observation without seriously compromising the interests of families. It is also alleged that the working of the co-operative system, regarded in its reaction on character, will call forth many of the highest qualities of our nature. All combined action of men for honest ends doubtless develops some useful elements of character; but the degree of elevation of these elements depends on the nature and objects of the combination, which may be of a kind of starve other nobler traits. I believe in no moral regeneration founded on appeals to private interest: social motives alone can truly moralize; and I cannot help thinking that upon the whole the tendency of the co-operative system would be to spoil the best qualities of the working-man. His characteristic type would tend to be transformed into that of the small capitalist. For the absence of habitual money-making cares, and the disengagement of mind when his daily work is over,—which are amongst the best compensations of a workman's laborious life—would be substituted the fretting anxieties of the trader. The large sympathies and generous impulses which are natural to the one would be supplanted by the comparative deadness to social interests, and the constant gain-regarding attitude of the other. The enjoyment of domestic life and the cultivation of the intellect would tend to be subordinated to the pursuit of profit. The workman would be likely to prolong unduly the hours of labour on the plea that he was working for himself. Instead of the frank and warm-hearted friend of the fellow-workers with whom he was daily associated, he would be tempted to become their spy and the controller of their actions, not on the basis of general morality, but on that of his private interest. I have spoken strongly, because I wish to emphasize my dissent from propositions on this matter which are sometimes quietly taken for granted. I do not of course say that the system would in every case produce the moral consequences here indicated, but I am convinced that its general tendency would be to affect injuriously the peace of the working-man, his freedom of mind, his openness to elevated ideas, and his real independence.

I believe that the immense majority of working-men must remain to the end working-men, and that only. I further believe that this necessity admits of being fully reconciled with their happiness and their dignity. They would, in my opinion, best consult their real interests by recognizing these truths as soon as may be, and sincerely renouncing the pursuit of a different position. What they ought to aim at is the elevation of their class as such, without seeking to alter the basis of the existing organization of industry. In this work they will find not only an abundant but a fruitful field for all their public spirit, energy, and sagacity.

The interest of the Trades' Union movement seems to me to lie precisely in this, that it follows the practical and hopeful line I have just indicated. Assuming the permanent existence of the relation of master and workman, it for the first time practically asserted the necessity of systematically regulating that relation, and set on foot an effort, however inadequate and often mistaken, towards realizing such a regulation. Attacked and denounced as scarcely any other institutions ever have been, the unions have thriven and grown in the face of opposition. This healthy vitality has been due to the fact that they were a genuine product of social needs—indispensable as a protest and a struggle against the abuses of industrial government, and inevitable as a consequence of that consciousness of strength inspired by the concentration of numbers under the new conditions of industry. They have gradually purged themselves of many abuses which appeared in their earlier proceedings—abuses which were in some degree explained, if not palliated, by the gross injustice with which they were treated by the law. From that injustice they have completely liberated themselves by steady, moderate, and well-considered action. They have been, as is now admitted by almost all candid minds, instruments of progress. Not to speak of the material advantages they have gained for working-men, they have developed powerful sympathies among them, and taught them the lesson of self-sacrifice in the interest of their brethren, and, still more, of their successors. They have infused a new spirit of independence and self-respect. They have brought some of the best men to the front, and given them the ascendancy due to their personal qualities and desirable in the interests of society. According to the testimony of all who have the best means of knowing, the most influential members of these bodies, instead of multiplying and encouraging strikes, have diminished their frequency and mitigated their violence, and have fostered the habit of recurring to milder methods for the adjustment of disputes.

It would be an impertinence on my part to advise working-men to maintain the unions. They can appreciate their value far better than I could do, and nothing is clearer than their fixed resolve, not only to maintain those institutions, but to develop and extend them. What I would urge is the importance of introducing more and more of moral elements into their action. They have already recognized that violence and menace are forbidden to them as means of effecting their objects, and this has immensely strengthened them in public estimation. They should proceed further in the same path. If there be any thing remaining in their rules which cannot be defended on principles of the highest social morality, they ought to expunge it. They should put forward no claims that are not rigorously just. They should seek to give effect to these claims by conciliatory methods, regarding strikes as a last resource, sometimes indeed necessary, but always deplorable as intensifying evil passions and compromising many innocent existences. They should discuss all the questions that concern them—such as those of wages, hours of labour, piecework, apprenticeship—on higher grounds than those of material class interests. They should invite the attention of the thinking public to these questions, and look to the best disinterested opinion as the judge and controller of their operations. The action of the trades' unions cannot solve the problem of the regulation of industrial life; essentially based on antagonism and the assertion of rights, they cannot work a reconciliation which depends on the acknowledgement and application of rules of duty.

The real and radical solution of this problem, as of the general social problem which includes it, can be effected only by such a reorganization of ideas and renovation of sentiments, as will rise to the dimensions of an intellectual and moral reform. But the unions may be powerful agencies in keeping alive a sense of the need of that true solution, in impelling society towards it, and in preparing the public mind for it. For these ends, even apart from their immediate services, their action will long be indispensable, and will be more and more valuable, as it relies increasingly on moral means.

For the direction of the efforts of the working classes towards the amelioration of their position, it is necessary that they should decide on the answer to the question—what are their real requirements? What are the objects which, though not at once fully attainable, they ought to keep before them, and towards which they ought steadily to march? These requirements—omitting minor points, and looking only at the broader elements of their condition—appear to me to be three in number; and I proceed to consider them in succession.

The first is—*Adequate wages.*

Adam Smith, placing himself at the point of view from which the working-man is regarded as a social functionary, says—"It is but equity that they who feed, clothe, and lodge the whole body of the people, should have such a share of the produce of their labour as to be themselves tolerably well fed, clothed, and lodged." "Tolerably well"—that is his expression—which is dictated by a same appreciation of realities—of the limits imposed by the unalterable conditions of human life. But this expression plainly has relation not to a fixed, but to a movable standard of living. The "tolerably well" of one period or one state of society might be the "scandalously ill" of another. If I were asked to give precision to Smith's sentence by introducing this element, I should say that in a normal state of things, wages at a given time and place should not fall below what is necessary to enable a working-man and his family (supposed of average number) to live in a manner, the most economical indeed, but still consistent with whatever the contemporary local civilization recognizes as indispensable for physical and mental health, or required by the rational self-respect of human beings. I fear we are in many instances far enough removed from this measure; but I do not see how we can evade the necessity of reaching it, if the highest ends of society are to be attained.

The idea of the relation of wages to a social standard of living has an important bearing on a view now often put forward. It is said that the unions have forced up wages so as to make it impossible to compete with foreigners, a statement strangely at variance with what is at the same time alleged by others, that wages would stand at the present rates if the unions had never existed. We are told that the working-classes ought to submit to reduction of wages, in order that our capitalists may undersell and paralyse their foreign rivals, and that so wages, temporarily depressed, may afterwards rise to a higher level than the present one. Curiously enough, the same appeal is made in the continental countries, where workmen are similarly counselled to deny themselves with a view to defeat British capitalists; and there would be more foundation for the demand there than here, wages having risen in late years much more rapidly abroad than at home, if it were true that rising wages necessarily imply more costly production. To judge by the language used by capitalists and their spokesmen, it might seem that the great question of industrial life at the present time was this—what working population among civilized nations would be content to live the most miserably in order to drive the others out of the markets of the world? I hope our working-people will follow no such *ignis fatuus*. The political economists, in discussing the question of population, justly insist on the value to the working-classes of maintaining the standard of living they have reached. The English workman has, as a result of the whole past, attained a standard superior to that which prevails in general in continental countries; and it is most important that the ground gained in this direction should not be endangered. What is really to be desired is that the foreign workman's standard of living may also rise, and that he may maintain every increase of wages which he has once secured. This will doubly promote your interests, for he will then be a better customer for English products generally, and he will be less likely to be transferred from his own country to England for the purpose of keeping down your wages.

Not only must our workmen refuse to fall in with the narrow and short-sighted policy of which I have been speaking; they must take care not to let their sentiments be perverted by the cry of foreign competition. The tendency of this headlong chase after English industrial supremacy, as it is called, is to renew something of the old jealous hostility to "the foreigner" which used to be fostered in the interests of military ascendancy. But, however the capitalist may feel, the sentiment of the workman at home towards the workman abroad, should be one of sincere fraternity. They have the same hopes and aspirations, and the problems in which they are interested must receive identical solutions. Let us not blind ourselves to plain truths. Our patriotic partialities must not, any more than our domestic preferences, make us unjust to others, or false to the general weal. The industrial populations of the west are all co-workers for the universal good. It is desirable in the interest of humanity that they should all increase in skill, in energy, and in perseverance, and that they should adopt the most improved methods of production. If any foreign country has peculiar facilities for any form of production, it is desirable that those facilities should be brought into effective operation. It is the happy prerogative of industry, in which it contrasts with military activity, that it admits of the simultaneous prosperity of all. Economists have expounded an important idea which tends to reconcile the antagonistic interests of nations as rival producers. They have pointed out that to the division of occupations which in each separate nation facilitates production and increases wealth, corresponds the natural distribution of different kinds of production between different communities, according as local circumstances or national aptitudes prescribe. If each nation withdrew from branches of industry for which its native bent or its circumstances disqualify it, choosing those for which it has a special advantage, the common harmony would be greatly promoted, while the general wealth would be augmented. It is one of the great evils of the protective system that it stands in the way of these adjustments which would reconcile conflicting claims and turn competition into co-operation.

English workmen cannot be the best in every department of skilled industry; there are some kinds of it for which they have not a natural genius. But they will always hold the foremost place in some departments. It seems established by competent testimony that they are now the most energetic and persevering workers in the world; and that the quality of their work is still, on the whole, the most enduring and trustworthy. That it can retain its entire superiority in these characters over foreign work, is not to be expected. But it is alike the interest and the duty of our capitalists, by offering really good wares—not sham and shoddy ones, made only to sell,—and of our workmen, by honest careful labour, to keep as high as they can the reputation of British industry, and make as valuable a contribution as possible to the wealth of mankind.

The second requirement of the workman is *A Well-regulated Home.*

I have hitherto generally spoken of the working-man as an individual; but no study of his position is complete which overlooks the fact that he is ordinarily the head of a family. The principal solace of a life of labour—nay the principal source of human happiness generally, lies in the exercise of the domestic affections. It is the duty of the chiefs of the industrial world to do all that in them lies towards securing to the working-man the enjoyment of so great a blessing. This involves in it the regulation of his labour in such a way that he may have the opportunity of sufficient intercourse with the members of his family, and may return to them fatigued, perhaps, but not exhausted in body or broken in spirit by too prolonged or excessive exertion. A life of work and nothing but work is no life for a man, who must not be degraded into a mere instrument of production. An Irish poet has claimed for the working-classes—

"Leisure to live, leisure to love, leisure to taste their freedom."

and the demand is a just one. Work of some kind, honestly and faithfully done, is incumbent on all men, from the highest to the lowest; it is unworthy of us to shirk our fair share in the common service of Humanity. Work with the hands is the necessary, and, in my judgment, under right conditions not the unhappy destiny of the great majority of our race. But the best, the most effective work is not the most prolonged. "It will be found, I believe." says

Adam Smith, "in every sort of trade that the man who works so moderately as to be able to work constantly, not only preserves his health the longest, but, in the course of the year, executes the greatest quantity of work." It is surely no insoluble question for physiology, what is the average time during which the powers of attention and effort can be kept in full exercise with the best results for the health and permanent efficiency of the human agent. It is doubtful whether even this limit should be reached in a civilized community. And this for several reasons, of which one only is now insisted on, namely, that the workman needs both in his own highest interests, and in those of society, an habitual expansion of his domestic affections. For family life is not merely the source of the purest happiness; it is also the best school of the heart. The hardness and selfishness which the pressure of practical life too often produces is best tempered by the atmosphere of the domestic hearth, where we learn, in the most elementary and attractive form, the lesson of living for others. It has always been recognized that in the practice of the domestic virtues is laid the surest foundation of civic and social worth. This is a consideration which has perhaps not sufficiently attracted the attention of the Malthusians, usually blind to all but the material side of the subject they discuss.

Now woman, first as wife, secondly as mother, is the centre of a home. It is in her action, whether unconscious or voluntary, on the nature of the man—if she be a worthy representative of her sex—that the chief moral efficacy of the domestic union lies. She presents a model and exemplar of the qualities in which he is most likely to be deficient—gentleness, tenderness, unselfishness. As mother, she exercises a real moral providence over her children. She has in her hands the first development of the natures of the young and the formation of their habits, and how ineffaceable these earliest impressions are, is the lesson of all experience. Happy results of this kind are often attained in a large degree by the mere ministry of love, when the woman is far from approaching the ideal of her sex, and when she wants the intellectual cultivation which would so much aid and elevate her endeavours.

In order to enable her really to discharge these sacred offices, the neglect of which is a fatal waste of all that is most precious, the woman must be freed from the necessity of non-domestic labour which is now too often imposed upon her. This is a step in the upward movement of the working-classes which cannot be suddenly effected, but it is an essential one, and they must set their faces towards it. Those classes are now justly demanding that they should be in the fullest sense incorporated into modern society, that the gains which advancing civilization has brought to the superior ranks, such as intellectual cultivation, and political and civic recognition, should be extended in the utmost practicable degree to them. This social benefit too, the consecration of woman to her domestic office, which is enjoyed by the ranks above them, must become theirs also; for the moral motives which dictate it apply as strongly in their case. Some of the coarser forms of labour which were positively degrading to women have been rightly interdicted by law; the change of which I speak will have to be carried out by the spontaneous action of the working-classes themselves, as the increasing amount and better employment of their wages will make it possible.

It will easily be understood that the object is not that women should be maintained in idleness. Those of us who are happy enough to have the opportunity of making such observations know that a good woman works as constantly as the most industrious husband, though in a different sphere. On the practical side she is the economist, utilizing to the utmost the resources of the home and studying incessantly the health and comfort of its inmates. But the office for which she is most indispensable is the moral one, the cultivation of the affections and the regulation of the habits of a new generation; and this requires the restoration of woman to the domestic hearth. Beginning with mothers, as the most urgent case, that restoration must be extended afterwards to the younger women, who should be trained not for material production (except so far as that is possible within a family), but for the regulation of homes and the physical care and moral formation of human beings. I know how vast this programme is, and I do not overlook the difficulties which beset some portions of it from the necessity of material guarantees for women who are not either wives or inmates of a father's home. But those difficulties are not insurmountable, and I am convinced that there is no social reform which would tend more powerfully than the one I have been advocating to the happiness of women and the elevation of the working-man.

Other considerations connected with the right constitution of the workman's domestic life can here be no more than glanced at. The modern solicitude for the sanitary improvement of dwellings will modify his habits for good, by making home more attractive, whilst it will tend to the production of a healthier and more energetic industrial population. The acquisition, too, of the dwelling as his property will have the most important reactions on the sentiments and habits of the family; and those persons deserve the gratitude of the community who are labouring to make this acquisition easier by modifications of the law.

The third requirement of the working classes is *Education*.

Their elementary instruction has, until quite of late, occupied most of the public attention, and absorbed the largest share of individual effort; and justly so, for it is the necessary foundation of all else. But contemporary opinion seems to be altogether in favour of the gradual provision of a higher and wider instruction for working people; of opening to them a larger access to scientific and æsthetic culture. This opinion, however, in many minds rests on a very narrow basis. The demand for the scientific instruction of the workman has generally been urged on the ground of its technical value as likely to make his labour more intelligent and more effective. Now on this consideration, which is true as far as it goes, might rest the necessity of giving him some notions of the truths of those physical sciences by which the processes of industry are dictated or explained. But the higher ends of science in the formation of the man and the member of society are thus left altogether out of account. Again, æsthetic culture for the workman is encouraged on the ground that it will give greater elegance and finish to the products of his skill, which also is a just conception in itself. But this view, exclusively followed out, would lead to a very undue limitation of art as an element of education, and would shut out poetry and music, because their value lies, not in their technical utility, but in their general mental and moral influences.

The principles which should guide us in determining the right general education of working-men are identical with those which should be applied to the solution of the same question for other classes. There may be special difficulties in applying the solution in the case of the workman; but that consideration cannot affect the rational basis of the solution. Now the general aim of education, so far as it is scientific, is to give a man a right general conception of the world in which he lives, of the permanent conditions, whether absolutely fixed or modifiable, to which his whole existence is subjected, and with which all his efforts, in order to be successful, must be kept in harmony. These conditions are of three kinds, as embodied in the laws of inorganic, vital, and social phenomena. No education is complete which does not embrace the essential ideas relating to these several classes of facts. Even by the upper and middle ranks this large culture has not been attained. Our courses of instruction are so overlaid with exaggerated specialities and superfluous refinements, that the materials for an intelligent appreciation of our life on all its sides are seldom, if ever, furnished by our modes of training, and the defects of official systems have to be supplied, if at all, by further individual self-cultivation. But I am convinced that, even for the working-classes, by due condensation of the intellectual treasures at our disposal, a comprehensive education of this kind might be provided, if they on their part were willing to make the necessary effort to obtain it. In other classes parents postpone for their children the entrance on professional work, in order to secure for them a more liberal general culture. The working-classes should consider how something similar might be effected for them. Of the practical way to this great acquisition, I ought to speak with reserve; but it will probably be found to lie in a reorganized system of apprenticeship. I believe there is a very general impression that that old institution has been somewhat inconsiderately dealt with in the modern development of collective industry, and that it required rather to be adapted and improved than to be undermined and largely broken down as it has been. It is while a youth is learning his handicraft that a portion of his time might be taken from work for his scientific instruction; and if the latter were made as important an object as the former, the ancient term of seven years, from fourteen to twenty-one, might still be found not too much for the combined technical and educational preparations. The æsthetic capabilities also might be concurrently trained, not alone, as I have said, to improve art workmanship, but also for the higher purpose of humanizing and sweetening life—of giving it grace, refinement, and charm.

It is evident that of all the sciences the most important are those which have to do with the determination of duties. But, as I showed at the outset, social duties cannot be rationally established without a study of the constitution and development of society. Hence the necessity of a scientific social doctrine, which ought to form a universal element of our system of education. Its importance is two-fold; first, as a foundation of individual discipline, and secondly, as a basis of public opinion. As to its operation on individual conduct, by establishing the laws which regulate social phenomena, it sobers and tranquillizes the mind, showing that the fundamental constitution of practical life is beyond our control, and that no popular sovereignty, ever so unanimous, can alter the essential nature of things. At the same time, proving that social phenomena are, by virtue of this very subjection to natural laws, largely modifiable in their secondary dispositions by wise human intervention, it teaches, along with the lesson of submission, that of hopeful effort. It brings out the consequences of every line of conduct as affecting the welfare of others and of the whole community with such clearness as to defy sophistry or evasion. It enables each to see and feel his personal share in the daily civic co-operation, in the great work of maintaining and developing the material and moral life of the race, and to understand the normal relations of his own office with the other social functions; and thus, while heightening his sense of dignity, it deepens his consciousness of responsibility. Such a basis of discipline ought not to be restricted to any class, but extended to all. The object of giving such instruction to working-men is not to make them savants or philosophers, but to assist in training them as enlightened, courageous, and conscientious citizens, acknowledging and practising their duties to their families, their country, and their kind.

But further, such a social doctrine is necessary as a basis for public opinion. The direct action of truth on the individual intellect and conscience will not suffice for the regulation of conduct. The strong reaction of all upon each must be brought to bear, both to control selfishness and to stimulate sympathy. Fixed principles respecting the social relations and social duties, once freely adopted by competent minds, and then systematically diffused by education, would form an opinion strong enough to support the good inclinations and to resist the vicious tendencies of individuals. Public opinion is evidently destined to exercise in the future an action in the regulation of social life of which we have yet had but little conception. The healthy and effective exercise of this power will depend on its due guidance and concentration, a subject of which much may be said into which I cannot enter now. One thing is plain, that the working-classes will more and more become the great laboratory of public opinion. This would be inevitable from the fact that they compose the mass of society, and suffer most from the imperfections of the social system, even if they were not, as they now are, invested with political power. Hence the importance to other classes as well as to themselves of their being directed in their judgments by a true social doctrine—which, discountenancing all violence and oppression, will at the same time furnish just standards founded on rational ideas, by which the mode of discharge of every social function, whether public or private, can be tried and estimated.

I have not, you will observe, presented the view that the intellectual improvement of the workman will assist him in rising out of his class into a higher sphere of life. I do not either for him or for his employer contemplate what is called "getting on in the world" as the great end of existence. In much of the popular literature of self-help, the hero held up to our admiration is the man who, beginning as workman, scales the ladder of social elevation, and closes his career as a master; and it is almost implied that the great question is not how to improve and ennoble the workman's life, but how to enable the ambitious and energetic to escape from it. I think current ideas on this matter require a good deal of correction. The causes which determine the rise of some to the rank of directors of industry, whilst others remain in the position of workmen, are not always easy to trace; most frequently, accidental elements of situation or opportunity are involved. But so far as personal qualities are operative, it would be a great mistake to suppose, as is too often taken for granted, that a rise of this kind is always or ordinarily connected with superiority of nature. A man who remains a workman all his life, may be, and often is, in all the essential qualities of manhood, of far greater intrinsic value than another who raises himself to wealth and rank. The practical qualities which most lead to what is called success—toughness, dexterity, and caution, valuable no doubt in themselves, may be combined with a poor intellect and a narrow heart. The very processes by which industrial ascendancy is reached, even when the means used are strictly legitimate, involve grave dangers to men's natures. The constant habit of self-regard, the temptation to put aside the claims of others, the intense pre-occupation with possibilities of profit, have a tendency to produce on the intellectual side limitation of views, and on the moral side, hardness and want of sympathy. These qualities have often been observed in self-made men, and particularly in the smaller capitalists who are still suffering from the deteriorating effects of the struggle. It is only just, however, to add, that in natures fundamentally good, when the strain of acquisition is relaxed, the possession of wealth and the power it bestows often develops the better elements and brings out the noble instincts of the genuine chief. More frequently, perhaps, social fruit is not derived from these elevations before the second generation, and then only where it does not happen that vanity and a weak imitation of the old aristocracy lead to a life of luxury and ostentation, and a contemptuous neglect of industrial duties.

But, be this as it may, there is no reason why we should think less of a man because ambition and the desire to be rich are weak in his nature. They are weak, I believe, in most healthy natures, and it is well that it should be so; morality and religion have always deprecated any intense degree of them. We cannot indeed dispense with a strong dose of them in some members of the industrial world; for they are necessary to bring about the formation of large capitals and to provide efficient directors of industry. But the development of these elements of character is required only for the actual or destined capitalist; they are foreign to the vocation of the ordinary working-man, and if indulged, produce, from the necessary limitation of his circumstances, a miserable restlessness and spirit of revolt. What is really important for working-men, is not that a few should rise out of their class—this sometimes rather injures the class, by depriving it of its more energetic members. The truly vital interest is that the whole class should rise in material comfort and security, and still more in intellectual and moral attainments.

I have now concluded the remarks which I thought would usefully occupy the time we were to spend together. Little conversant with details, I have dealt mainly with general principles, and I have perhaps somewhat tasked your attention by the lines of thought I have followed. But what I have given you was the best I had to offer; and I trust it may be of some use in helping you to avoid false paths, and in fixing your attention on the true means of achieving the end of all your efforts—a better and nobler life for the workman of the future.

31

THE RICARDIAN THEORY OF RENT
Sections I–III

Hutcheson Macaulay Posnett

Source: Hutcheson Macaulay Posnett, *The Ricardian Theory of Rent*, London: Longmans, Green & Co., 1884, pp. 9–53.

§I.—The Ricardian rent theory

Nature of Theory.—What is a theory? It is a condensed yet exact note of facts. But it is something more than such a portable compendium. It is also an explanation of the facts, a statement of their causes, if possible a reduction of these to one supreme cause. Moreover, this problem of causation is intimately connected with other great problems—the effect of the facts on social and individual life, and, in accordance with the nature of the effect, their proper treatment by man if his power can reach them. We call the definition and explanation of fact *science*, and the suggestion of human conduct we call *art*; and some, like the late Professor Cairnes, would go so far as to confine economic studies to the definition and explanation of the phenomena of wealth, leaving what we may call the art of economics to statesmen. If we were at present concerned with such fanciful limitations, we might show that the constancy of social growth and decay renders the severance of science and art impossible in any branch of social study, such as political economy and jurisprudence, and that economists and jurists who have attempted such a distinction have signally failed to carry it out. At present, however, we merely employ the triple division—definition, causation, suggestion of conduct—as a convenient method of briefly stating the Ricardian theory of rent.

Ricardian Definition of Rent.—The definition of Ricardo should be sufficient to show that whatever he is undertaking to explain, it is not that fact which men commonly call 'rent.' According to Ricardo, 'rent' is 'that portion of the produce of the earth which is paid to the landlord for the use of the original and indestructible powers of the soil.' This portion of the produce of the earth is often confounded with the interest and profit of capital; and the term 'rent' in popular usage is even 'applied to whatever is annually paid by a farmer to his landlord.' But 'rent,' as commonly used in English, denotes, as Mr. Sidgwick observes, 'the payment made for the use of immovables' *i.e.* either of the surface of land, as used in agriculture or pasturage, or of buildings erected on land, or of the minerals it contains, and the right of removing and selling them; while the French 'rente' is used more widely to denote 'any income that accrues without labour on the part of the person to whom it is paid'—a sense in which the English term was sometimes used in the days of Charles II. Thus the Ricardian definition contains three points of essential difference from the modern usage of the English word 'rent.' The popular sense of payment for a loan of immovables fails to notice—(*a*) the source from which the payment is made—whether it is a 'portion of the produce of the earth' or wealth otherwise obtained; (*β*) the uses to which the object of the loan is intended to be applied—agricultural, pastoral, manufacturing, or otherwise; and (*γ*) whether the object of the loan is the natural or improved fertility of the soil, or land of any fertility whatever.

To contrast the various meanings attached to the word 'rent' by English and Continental authorities is a duty which the minute economist can perform for himself. But we may here conveniently distinguish three prominent senses in which the word has been used. 1. The *popular* sense, in which returns due to capital expended in improving the productive power of land, returns due to natural fertility, payments for pleasure residences, business houses, factories, and the like, are lumped together. 2. The *peculiar economic* sense—Ricardian—which not only confines 'rent' to the consideration paid for the loan of the natural fertility of land, but confines the source of payment for such loan to the products of land industry or their price. The peculiar narrowness of this definition may be illustrated by three out of the many difficulties it raises. (*a*). Can we, with Ricardo, *include* situation in the natural fertility of land? Professor Bonamy Price says we cannot, and, observing that 'rent is the result of many forces and not of one,' condemns the Ricardian theory as logically excluding accessibility to markets and similar considerations. (*β*). Can we, as Ricardo takes it for granted we can, distinguish natural from improved fertility? Mr. Sidgwick maintains that in a country which has long been cultivated it is impossible to accurately distinguish returns which are due to natural fertility alone; whereas according to Ricardo it is in such a country that economic rent is of the utmost importance: and so far as rent depends on situation, Mr. Sidgwick declares that 'it is plainly due not to the original qualities of the land, but to the development of the human community inhabiting it, and the manner in which this community has disposed itself over the surface of the country'. (*γ*). If there are returns due to the natural fertility of the soil, and if they can be separated from all other returns to land, labour, and capital, are they so important as to be the true basis of rent and its definition? M. Leroy-Beaulieu in his recent work 'La Repartition des Richesses,' Paris, 1882, answers in the negative; and Mr.

Sidgwick, while admitting the importance of distinguishing two elements in rent—interest on the present value of labour previously expended and another element due the appropriation of land—does not believe that any practical advantage is gained by following Ricardo in his deviation from common usage. A little examination will show that the Ricardian definition bristles with such difficulties. We therefore need not pause to raise such minor points as whether it properly includes the rent of pasture land or not. 8. But besides the *popular* and the *peculiarly* economic or Ricardian sense of rent, there is a *general* economic usage which extends the term beyond the Ricardian meaning, so as to include returns due to capital sunk in the improvement of land for productive purposes, but falls short of the vague popular meaning in excluding the 'rent' of business-houses and building sites in towns, that of factories, workshops, and the like.

Ricardian Causation of Rent.—The idea of *natural fertility* forms the pivot of the Ricardian rent theory—the centre towards which all its explanatory causation of rent gravitates. This we discover on proceeding from the definition to the causes of Ricardian rent. These are twofold—social and physical. The *social causes* are the existence of free individual landowners, free farmers, and free labourers. Ricardo does not pause to ask whether these three social 'freedoms' mean the same social fact; or whether the social 'freedom' of one class excludes that of another; or in what sense such class and individual 'freedoms' can coexist; or if in any sense they coexist in England, how this modified coexistence has come about, and in what other countries and ages it is present or absent. His social classes and individuals are simply assumed to be 'free' to compete, and to be moved by no motive save self-interest in the race of competition. Such freedom of competition—which we shall hereafter examine—results, according to Ricardo, in average wages and average profits as between farmer and labourer; and such average wages and profits eventuate in the payment of such a rent to the landowner as represents the 'original and indestructible powers of the soil.' Adam Smith had said that 'rent'—meaning in his own vague language 'the price paid for the use of land'—is 'proportioned not at all to what the landlord has laid out upon the improvement of land, but to what the farmer can afford to give.' Ricardo, calling to the aid of the social factors utilised by Smith—average wages and profits—the physical factors of natural fertility and its degrees, sought to found his rent theory upon conditions of nature as underlying those of man's social life. The question of rent from Smith's point of view had been, What can the farmer afford? But this is to allow, as Smith allows, that the price paid for the use of land 'is naturally a monopoly price'; whereas Ricardo purposes to show that rent, just like profits and wages, has its natural limits. Where are these natural limits? In the degrees of fertility greater than that degree which is just sufficient to allow of average wages and average profits: all returns beyond these averages must, in the presence of 'free competition,' pass to the landowner. Thus the causation of Ricardian rent consists of social causes cooperating with physical facts. The *social causes* are—(1) Individual ownership, unshackled by State interference, custom, or moral obligation; (2) individual occupancy by a farming class, likewise unshackled; and, (3) the existence of labourers perfectly free to compete. The physical causes are—(1) The limited quantity of land; and (2) the varying degrees of its fertility. The effect of the ideally 'free' social conditions is to give the farmer his average profit and the labourer his average wage; and the three social, *plus* the two physical causes just mentioned, result in *natural* or Ricardian rent.

Ricardian Effects of Rent.—But these five causes of rent have as yet enabled us only to deal with the phenomenon *statically*. We must next trace the effects of natural rent so caused on the economic motion, development, of social life, and the effects of such social development on natural rent. The effect of social progress on rent Ricardo thus explains:—'On the first settling of a country in which there is an abundance of rich and fertile land, a very small proportion of which is required to be cultivated for the support of the actual population—or, indeed, can be cultivated with the capital which the population can command—there will be no rent. . . . If all land had the same properties, if it were unlimited in quantity and uniform in quality, no charge could be made for its use, unless where it possessed peculiar advantages of situation. It is only, then, because land is not unlimited in quantity and uniform in quality, and because, in the progress of population, land of an inferior quality, or less advantageously situated, is called into cultivation, that rent is ever paid for the use of it. When, in the progress of society, land of the second degree of fertility is taken into cultivation, rent commences on that of the first quality, and the amount of that rent will depend on the difference in the quality of these two portions of land.' The rise and progress of rent are thus admitted to depend on social development closely linked with physical facts. Social progress means increasing population, as well as increasing wealth; and an increasing population means an increasing demand for food; and an increasing demand for food means the necessity of taking lands of inferior fertility or situation into cultivation, or, what amounts to the same thing, more expensive cultivation of lands already tilled. In this way social progress not only brings rent into existence, but tends to increase it, by expanding the difference between the best and worst soils under cultivation. The same process increases rent and necessitates additional labour, with proportionally less return, *i.e.* diminishes wages and profits. 'If good land existed in a quantity much more abundant than the production of food for an increasing population required, or if capital could be indefinitely employed without a diminished return, there could be no rise of rent; for rent invariably proceeds from the employment of an additional quantity of labour with a proportionately less return.'

Now, if the effects of social progress are thus to raise rent, while the returns to labour and capital decrease, it might seem that the landowner gains by the loss of labourer and capitalist. But the effects of rent on social development are not regarded by Ricardo in this light. A principle which he declares to be 'of the utmost importance in political economy' is introduced as a veritable *deus ex machina* by whom the conflicting interests of land-owner and community may be harmonised. This is the principle that rent does not form an element in the price or cost of food, and the implication that the landowning class consequently costs the community nothing. The following is Ricardo's proof of this principle: 'The value of all commodities is always regulated, not by the less quantity of labour that will suffice for their production under circumstances highly favourable, but by the greater quantity of labour bestowed by those who continue to produce them under the most unfavourable circumstances; that is, the most unfavourable under which the quantity of produce required renders it necessary to carry on the production.' Hence the price of food depends on the cost of that part which is raised at the greatest cost. Now this part is raised on the worst lands in cultivation; and these lands on the margin of cultivation only just suffice to afford average profit and wage *without* rent. Rent, therefore, does not enter into the price of food, which depends upon the non-rent-paying margin of cultivation. We shall hereafter examine the true purport of this reasoning. At present we need only add that in the attempt to prove that the landowning class costs the community nothing there lurks this practical suggestion of human conduct, viz., that any interference with the landowners' 'freedom' can do the community no good. 'It has been justly observed,' says Ricardo, 'that no reduction would take place in the price of corn although landlords should forego the whole of their rent. Such a measure would only enable some farmers to live like gentlemen, but would not diminish the quantity of labour necessary to raise raw produce on the least productive land in cultivation.' Taken with the assumptions of free competition between farmer, labourer, and landowner—which are also implied recommendations to leave these classes uninterfered with by the State—this inference that the land-owners cost the community nothing may be said to form the *art* of the Ricardian theory—the suggestion of human conduct which it contains—which, like all truly Ricardian art, is *laisser-faire*.

Such is a brief outline of the Ricardian rent theory—(1) the peculiar defin-ition of the phenomenon to be explained; (2) the three social and two phys-ical causes of the phenomenon; and (3) the two corollaries of the theory, viz., that social progress tends to increase rent and to lower wages and profit, and that rent does not enter into the price or cost of food. We need not here discuss the sources from which Ricardo put together this theory—the connexion of the physiocratic 'produit net' with his natural fertility, his indebtedness to Smith for average wage and profit, and to Anderson, Malthus, and West, for the notions of degrees of fertility and their diminish-ing return. We may be sure that a doctrine which saw the light in 1777 was not unearthed in 1817 for no purpose, and that the defence of the landowning class as deriving their wealth, not from labour, but from the natural fertility of the soil, is not unconnected with fears for the labour-economics of Adam Smith, and the revolutionary spirit abroad in Europe when Ricardo wrote his treatise. But all such historical disquisition our space compels us to forego. We have stated the definition, causation, and effects of rent according to Ricardian theory. In opposition to believers in this theory, we venture to maintain that its definition is a *petitio principii* assuming the existence of physical or natural rent, as well as the possibility and practical advantage of distinguishing such rent from returns to capital and labour; that the social causes upon which the theory rests cannot co-exist, and are linked with the physical by a chain of fallacies; that the corollaries to which the theory leads are mutually destructive; and that the *laissez-faire* which is tacitly its practical outcome is not only a huge scientific blunder, but is the most certain provocative of extreme revolutionary action. In establishing these conclusions we shall treat the social and physical aspects of the Ricardian doctrine apart: we shall consider the defence of Ricardo which Dr. Walker has been pleased to offer; finally, we shall offer some remarks upon the problem of rent in its connexion with the economics of the future.[1]

§ II.—Social aspect of the Ricardian rent theory

'Free' Landlords.—It is an old observation that a problem correctly put is half a problem correctly solved. If we ask what is the cause of rent, we should possess some definite notion of the phenomenon to be explained. What is 'rent'? We look back to the clan communities out of which nations have everywhere been developed, and we miss the phenomenon. We look to the days of feudal serfage, and their customary dues are not what we mean by rent. The metayer paying his customary quota of the land's produce to the owner is not a payer of 'rent' as we understand the term. The Indian village-community pays its dues to Government, but we call them taxes. Our eyes traverse the countless grades of living civilization and barbarism, and while we trace our own social development repeated in living forms, the distinctions of past and present insensibly disappear: the spirit of history and comparison is at work: slowly we become conscious that our orthodox idea of rent has grown with the growth of our social conditions, and assumes a triple freedom of landowner, farmer, and labourer. The ideal freedom of the landowner to dispose of his land without public or private control recalls, at least, three great chapters in the comparative history of European institutions—chapters in which the ruin of communal by individual ownership, the centralization of individual ownership in the Sovereign, and the growth of hereditary tenures, are detailed. Even then we have by no means exhausted the full meaning of true landowning freedom. Feudal obligations

must decay, laws of settlement and inheritance must cease to impede, debt incumbrances must be relegated to some convenient limbo of economic speculation, before our assumed freedom can be realized. Adam Smith had enough honesty to observe *en passant* that his theories of equal wages and equal profits would require for their practical realization a state of perfect freedom. Ricardo might, with advantage, have imitated his candour. As it is, we are surprised to find that 'free trade' in English land is a desideratum of 1884, but a jaunty assumption of 1817, an assumption without which Ricardo's very idea of rent—the phenomena he undertakes to explain—is false. On this count we must, therefore, charge the 'majestic argument' of Ricardo with undertaking to explain a mythical phenomenon. A question like that with which the voluptuous Stuart fooled the wise men is propounded. We imitate the folly of the latter. We pause not to ask whether the question of cause is founded on a basis of fact. We start by assuming the absolute freedom of land-ownership as our *point d'appui* in explaining the cause of rent. Truly, he were but a poor theorist who would fail to build up a 'majestic' social theory if at liberty to bind his cloud-euckoo-town so lightly to the things of earth.

'Free' Farmers.—But if the landlords of the economic cloud-cuckoo-town are to be cloud-cuckoo landlords, their compatriots are to be cloud-cuckoo farmers and labourers. Adam Smith had traced the rise of the comparatively free farmers of his day out of medieval serfage, and had noted the slow progress of those remedies which had secured the farmer's leasehold rights against the owners, his heirs, and the community at large. Common sense would imagine it to be tolerably evident that if the farmer has no lease, then, in the absence of State interference or customary tenancy, he is, as a farmer, simply the serf-at-will of the landlord. But State interference and customary tenancy are both expressly excluded by the Ricardian hypothesis of free competition. The farmer without lease is, therefore, so far from being 'free,' a veritable serf. It may be said that the landlord will deal kindly with his serf; but this is to introduce moral considerations into the science of self-interest—a desecration to be ordinarily regarded as scientifically impious, but, in Ricardian economies, nothing short of the abomination of desolation. Again, it may be said that the non-leaseholding farmer may have alternative employments to which he can turn his capital and labour, and so rise above serfage. But these must be employments other than farming, and therefore do not affect the *farmer's* status. Hence we may lay down the principle, that from the Ricardian standpoint—excluding custom, moral consideration, and State interference—the non-leaseholding farmer, so far from being free to compete, is a mere serf, upon whom any conditions short of starvation can be forced, and even starvation itself, if the hope of larger profits should make it economically advantageous to clear the land for cattle-raising. And yet, under such conditions of tenancy-at-will alone can a true 'competition-rent' exist; for that leasehold interest, which raises the farmer

above a serf competing against other serfs for the only kind of subsistence within his reach, ties up the hands of both farmer and landlord, and during its term of continuance banishes altogether the pretended 'freedom' of both. The 'free trade' in land, which Ricardo unconsciously postulates, is, in fact, a contradiction in terms, because it is an assumed freedom of hostile interests—a conflict in which not freedom but compromise is the possibility to be achieved. In order that the landlord should possess this freedom, he must be shackled by no lease; and tillage upon such condition—State interference, moral consideration, and custom, being, by Ricardian hypothesis, excluded—implies the absence of freedom in the farmer. Contrariwise, the freedom of the farmer implies the absence of restriction, even by lease, of State interference, custom, and moral consideration, *plus* the presence of alternative employments to which he may turn his capital. It is this very possession of capital that prevents the quondam serf-farmer from accepting his old serf-conditions, and enables him to demand and obtain that leasehold interest which limits the hitherto unlimited freedom of the landowner.

But it will be said that the economist may discount the leasehold limitation of freedom and competition as *temporary*. As the economic cloud-cuckoo-town is peopled by economic men, whose actions, directed by self-interest alone, are performed in an imaginary vacuum of perfect freedom, which human nature, as it is found, 'doth strangely abhor'; so imagination, in the unconscious handling of the most unimaginative of men, performs the part of an Ariel for a Caliban, and creates, with due propriety, an economic cloud-cuckoo time and space. With economic space we are not at present concerned. Time the economist measures by no paltry days, or weeks, or years. Decades, or fractions of centuries, or centuries, are the proper time-standards for the average economic man, though the real economic changes which the real men undergo during the same decades and centuries may be conveniently ignored as friction or historical disquisition—to the indefinite extension of the statical average man, like an obscuring shadow, over the world-wide field of varied social growth. We are accustomed now-a-days to the sight of materialist astronomers measuring the distances and ages of worlds with Titanic standards of space and time, compared with which those of a Jove or Saturn were Lilliputian; and the sight of earth-born pigmies—as they declare themselves to be—wielding the measuring-rods of everlasting giant-gods is too common to be ridiculous. Our cloud-cuckoo economists seem to have imitated this practice in miniature. Twenty or thirty years of leasehold, here or there, are of course no impediment to the freedom and self-interest of the *economic* landlord or farmer. For the abstraction and classification 'landlord' and 'farmer' have got so far removed from their earthly and individual re-presentatives, that thirty years of individual life are as nothing to those gigantic abstract personages in whose august company the Malthusian insect moves with the air of a modern Methuselah. But with all due deference to the modern Methuselah, we venture to hint that his rather flippant averages, and his self-contradictory endowment of impersonal abstractions with personal freedom, are very seriously affected by thirty-year leases and sundry other vulgarly human considerations, which he would do well to descend from the Titanic company and survey. In fine, we again charge Ricardo with mistaking the problem to be solved, by dealing with a rent paid, not by or to *men*, but by and to beings at once free and unfree, to whom time, except in giant measures, is of no concern, and who, in search of their natural profit, can apparently range the bounds of space with an agility and freedom worthy of that 'wondrous horse of brass on which the Tartar king did ride.'

'Free' Labourers.—Thus of the social factors in the Ricardian theory two have been observed to possess qualities in which the living factors of living society are singularly deficient. Strictly speaking, the Ricardian social group is composed of five entities. These are the landlord, farmer, labourer, interest-receiver, and 'general community.' But the interest-receiving species had, even by Adam Smith, been assimilated with the profit-receiving; and the farmer, as being really a profit-receiver, had been treated as belonging to the same economic species. As for the 'general community'—which economists with free logic treat at one moment as the whole nation, or even the world, and at another as the same nation or world *minus* one or other of the above species, and, yet again, as something opposed to all the above species, and consequently implying that the economic social classification is imperfect—this wonderful 'general community' is so palpably artificial that economists keep him in the back ground, save where his appearance is absolutely necessary. We shall have something to say presently about this economic personage, so studiously placed in the back ground of the economists' social picture, and his bearing on the rent question. At present we reserve our attention for the third prominent figure of the economic group—the abstraction 'labourer.'

If, as we have found, it is absurd to speak of the real landlord and farmer as possessing a *co-existent freedom*, it is still more absurd to pile contradiction on contradiction by assuming a like co-existence of freedom in the relations of farmer and labourer. In order that the labourer should be really 'free,' he must be a small capitalist, capable of subsisting without work so long as his employer's terms are unfair—a moral consideration which 'average wage' undertakes to conceal by the vagne phrase 'standard of comfort'; or he must have alternative employments and that small capital which may be needed to tide him over the expenses of changing his employment. In either case he is a small capitalist, and so far removed from the tacit labourer-conception of Smith and Ricardo—the conception of a being earning subsistence *plus* the means of replenishing his race. Now, if the labourer is also a capitalist, however small, he is no longer a labourer in the Ricardian sense, for Ricardo's social classes pretend to be at least abstractedly separate. The freedom of the labourer, therefore, where it results from the possession

266

of small capital, is not *labourer's* freedom but *capitalist's* freedom, from the Ricardian standpoint. But if the labourer is *not* a small capitalist, then he is on his knees before the farmer or employer—an industrial suppliant, not a free industrial competitor.

You say that the labourers are free to compete amongst themselves for any employment in a given neighbourhood or nation. Well, let us discount as nothing difficulties in the transference of labour, in the want of skilled in preference to unskilled labour, and the numerous considerations to which Cliffe Leslie has called attention. Let us suppose that the individual members of the labouring group, no matter what its extent, are free in their competition *against one another*. Is this the industrial 'freedom' upon which the Ricardian economy is based? If it is, then is it perfectly compatible with serf-relations between the labouring *class* and any other economic group, farmer or landlord, or manufacturing capitalist. But this serf condition on the Ricardian hypothesis is no mere matter of contingency. We have seen that, unless he is a small capitalist, the labourer *must* be a serf, the be-all and end-all of whose existence is subsistence and the replenishment of his race. It may be said that we are neglecting the element of population-progress or population-decay. If, for example, the agricultural labouring population should be too few for the work which the farming population requires to be done, will not the wants of the farmer raise the labourer above the subsistence-receiving and race-conserving serf into a comparatively free competitor? But in what sense will he be 'free'? Simply in the sense that he cannot be *made* work without higher wages, and that these higher wages give him some small *capital*, by the aid of which he can resist reduction to the old serf-level.

The freedom from compulsory work at such a wage as some other social class may think fit to fix is no very ancient freedom, as the Statute Books of England, for example, would prove. But this 'freedom' to work or not—if that is all that the Ricardian free competition of labourers is meant to convey—contrasts remarkably with the 'freedom' which the Ricardian theory assumes in the other abstract social units with which it deals. The freedom of the landlord is freedom to obtain by his monopoly of land the highest rent he can; that of farmer or capitalist is to obtain by capital the highest profit possible, which involves the lowest possible rent and the lowest possible wage—a freedom which manifestly conflicts with the former. In these conflicting 'freedoms' there is no reference to bare subsistence and replenishment of race. Why? Because both farmer and landlord are—the former openly, the latter tacitly—assumed to possess that *capital*, the tacit denial of which to the labourer makes him logically a serf. This capital-less labourer possesses two kinds of freedom, viz., his individual freedom to work or not—under the lash of hunger if he does not work—and his individual freedom to compete against fellow-labourers, likewise capital-less, for such employment as is forthcoming.

267

There is a third possible freedom which Ricardian economy does not contemplate—the individual and collective freedom of the labourers to compete against capitalist and landlord for a share in the distribution of wealth exceeding that which suffices to give them individual and collective subsistence and replenishment of race. But this—the only kind of free competition which can raise him above a serf-like position—is excluded by the Ricardian theory. Why? Because that theory draws a hard and fast line between the 'labourer' and the 'capitalist'—actually going so far as to maintain that any rise in wages must be at the capitalist's loss. This is the reason why a logical economist like Cairnes foresees that, arguing within economic lines, the probable future of the working classes *as such* cannot be bettered, and that their only mode of rising in the scale of wealth-distribution is to become participators in profits. It is strange that Cairnes did not apply his own reasoning to the Ricardian assumption of freely competing labour. Had he done so he must have seen that this theory is based not on free but on serf-labour, and that the very conception of ideal freedom between the economist's social classes is absolutely a contradiction in terms. Nay, more, at the hazard of an apparent paradox, we shall go so far as to say that the real freedom of the labourer, which increases with his command of capital and consequent ability to resist a mere subsistence-and-race-replenishment wage, may conceivably bring with it a decrease in his power to shift freely from place to place. Let the labourer acquire an interest in land or capital, just as the leaseholding farmer acquires his interest in land; and, while this interest limits the freedom of capitalist or farmer to drive the hardest bargain with him, it may affect the labourer himself much in the same way as the leaseholding farmer is affected by capital sunk in soil or fixtures. The farmer cannot be called free to emigrate or migrate his capital so sunk. Neither is the labourer free to emigrate or migrate his labour if he possess capitalised interests which cannot be readily and without loss turned into cash. They who doubt this will do well to read the recent correspondence between Mr. Davitt and Mr. E. D. Gray, in the *Freeman's Journal*, dealing with the effects of labourers' cottages on the freedom of the labourer to migrate whithersoever his labour may be required.

But the apparent paradox can be readily explained. Among the various meanings of which economic 'freedom' is capable there are two peculiarly likely to be confused; the power to do what we like with property not human, and the power to do what we like with ourselves—without taking into consideration whether this latter may mean the pseudo-freedom of being able to commit suicide rather than suffer starvation. Such confusion is the effect of treating human labour as if it were a mere *commodity*, and being afterwards compelled to bring in by a side door the excluded moral element of *humanity*. Hence 'labour' is, as a commodity, nominally free when the *human* labourer is receiving starvation wages. Let the human labourer put together a little capital; let him be able to refuse the starvation wage, and what is the consequence? The pretended freedom of the impersonal commodity gives place to some restricted freedom of the human being. The labour-commodity, which has been previously treated as freely passing from place to place, and only connected with time by the number of years it will take to be raised, is now a human being connected by human ties with this or that locality, in spite of all pretended economic freedoms, and enjoying no unhuman prerogative of averages extending over decades or quarter-centuries.

Thus, if the Ricardian theory mistakes the farmer and landlord, by whom and to whom rent is paid, for mere impersonal abstractions gifted with conflicting freedoms, and moving in ideal conditions of space and time, the same may be said of the *average labourer* whom the theory affects to regard as typifying if not the moral at least the economic conditions of the human labourer. As a matter of fact, these social classes with their imaginary freedoms fail to express the economic conditions of any past or present human society. As a comparative and historical exercise the reader might inquire whether it expresses the past or present social life of England, France, Germany, Russia, of Hindostan or China; in short, of any civilised or barbarous people with existing institutions or a written past. When he has thus satisfied himself by the test of experience, he may with more confidence deny the self-contradictory implications of the theory, in the full assurance that its ideal society can never even 'tend' to be realised until human reason 'tends' to allow the truth of contradictories.

Ricardian Individualism.—Social classifications are indeed no modern invention. The Code of Manu has its fourfold classification based upon the social bond of religion, and, though Orientalists know how ideal is this classification, we may safely affirm that it could not have been further removed from social realities than the boasted system through which our modern *doctrinaires* affect to rule the destiny of nations with masterly inactivity. Hebrew and Arab, Greek and Italian, Teuton and Celt, have had their social classifications based on ties of social kinship and closely bound with their religious sympathies. But never until modern days have men classified their social communion on the distinct understanding that if they have any social creed at all, that creed at least for economic purposes may be displaced by the negation of all creeds—individual self-interest supposed to work under impossible conditions of unrestricted social freedom. It is no purpose of ours to sentimentally bewail the effects of teaching this unworkable assumption, for we believe that the mere idea of founding any branch of social science on the negation of all social creed could not have arisen, much less have attracted confident belief, save in the minds of men whose moral currency had been already long debased. But among men whose social morals are corrupted, to imitate the Greek's mythical town-makers, and 'to build out the gods' is the only method of avoiding a blasphemy. Even so have we avoided a blasphemy, and, while pretending for economic purposes to exclude moral considerations, have in the ideal character of our economic society given a fair picture of that anti-social selfishness which the rule of propertied force unbased on social creed is certain to produce among the propertied classes. When, therefore, we find that the mythical personages of the Ricardian social drama are puppets worked by the sole influence of self-interest, we do not say that human beings worked by such a motive alone are nowhere to be met with in the flesh. We only say that the moral vacuum of propertied force has been somewhat unduly extended to men in whom plutocracy has not yet subordinated all social sympathies to self-interest. We need ask no question as to the relative *numbers* of those who do, and those who do not act from this motive, nor need we inquire the *degree* in which the anti-social motive influences our social life. The solution of these problems has never been reached save by one method of crucial experiment—the disruption of social life. What we are concerned with in the Ricardian motive is not the extent to which it may prevail, but the propriety of making it the sole test of *economic* action.

Let us observe the galaxy of fallacies which the union of self-interest with imaginary social freedom is found to involve. 'Let not government, or custom, or moral consideration interfere with the free play of individual and collective self-interest.' Upon this motive and this freedom we found our economic ideal. Remove any obstacles to their perfect attainment, and then '*laissez aller, laissez passer.*' Such is the gospel of the Ricardian economy, with the falsity of which the falsity of the rent theory is bound up. But this economic gospel depends for its truth upon an implied assumption, viz., that the free play of individual self-interest is not only possible, but produces the greatest national wealth—the economic measure of national prosperity. It is this *economic* gospel which we affirm to be a perfect galaxy of fallacies: with moral or social considerations, we admit, it has no connexion.

Wherein consist the fallacies? In the first place, it has been already shown that the assumed freedoms of individuals and classes are not only never realised in existing, but are actually impossible in *any*, social life. In the second place, the economic measure of national prosperity, while affecting to merge individual into social existence for purely economic purposes, is by the very nature of 'wealth' compelled to desert the economic for moral considerations. For 'the greatest possible wealth' cannot be formulated as the *economic* end of social life until a definition of 'wealth,' irrespective of national and individual moral character, is forthcoming; and such a definition must be regarded as impossible. Why? Because the 'possession of exchange value'—which in the flippancy of orthodox economics passes for a definition of 'wealth'—ignores the fact that the human character, with all the individual and social wants of civilization, is the primary creator of such value—a character without which five-sixths of our modern 'wealth' were but so much dust and ashes.

But, in the third place, the gospel of greatest wealth must either declare the fair distribution of wealth to be no concern of economics, or prove that free individual self-interest results in the fairest distribution practicable. If fair distribution is no concern of economics, then what are average wages and average profits? Not fair distribution, but that distribution which would prevail under the greatest production of wealth—an economic ideal distribution. Be it so. Now, it is a well-known corollary of the Ricardian rent theory that the landlord, 'in the absence of counteracting causes,' obtains an ever-increasing share of national wealth. Does *this* distribution tend to 'the greatest possible production of wealth'? The landlord is the owner of 'the inherent and indestructible' fertilities of the soil; his increasing wealth represents these fertilities. If he lays out capital on the improvement of his land, he is a *capitalist plus* a landlord; and any returns upon this score are his, not as landlord, but as capitalist. As landlord, therefore, he cannot possibly increase the fertility of the soil. Let us give him the benefit of supposing that he does not diminish it. Still, by the very hypothesis of Ricardo is he excluded from *increasing* the national production. This labour and capital may do; but this landlord, as distinct from capitalist and labourer, *cannot* do. But the principle of diminishing returns from land involves a tendency of profits to a minimum; and wages, as we have lately seen, are, by Ricardian reasoning, either bare subsistence wages, or participate in these diminishing profits. National wealth, therefore, on Ricardo's own showing, tends to be absorbed by that social class which cannot *increase* wealth. It therefore follows that the economic gospel of greatest wealth cannot mean the production of the greatest possible wealth.

Now, if it is not for the greatest production of wealth that the ideal Ricardian distribution prevails, what *economic* good can it bring? If, then, it produces no economic good, let us even allow the economist a self-contradictory excursion into morals, and let us suppose that the ideal distribution which he imagines to result from the free play of self-interest is *morally* the fairest practicable. What does this remarkable harmony of anti-social economics with social morality imply? It implies that individual self-interest and corporate self-interest—national, less than national, greater than national, universal—are identical—an identity in virtue of which a millennium of self-contradictory freedoms is to be established by the policy of *laissez faire*. To the paradise of fools that millennium may be safely consigned: let us attend to the supposed identity of individual and corporate interests. We say nothing of the involved identity of interests between every form and grade of social life—the most civilized and the most barbarous—in the past and in the present. We confine our comparison to the relations of the individual with any social group. On the hypothesis of an individual future existence of infinite duration it may be that an identity of individual and corporate interests is not inconceivable. On that assumption the individual, like the corporation, never dies. But if the life of the individual be limited in its relations to space and time, as it is actually in this life found to be limited, then not only do we affirm that individual and social interests cannot be identical either in time or space, but that they are absolutely incommensurate. It follows that the relations of the individual to the group admit not of identical interests in an ideal of impossible freedom, but only of compromise, adjusted by social or state control. But the Ricardian economists have often enough declared or implied their repugnance to support material on spiritual considerations. We may, therefore, conclude that the economic harmonies of social with individual self-interests are the mistaken echo of a life-theory, which the Ricardian economists, of all men, would be the last to invoke. *Ils ont pris les souvenirs pour les espérances.*

We have inferred that the assumed identity of individual and social self-interests is economically unworkable—an inference which involves the further inference that compromise, not identity, is alone achievable. But this very necessity of compromise, to which our review of the pretended freedoms of competition had by another route conducted us, is fatal to the ideal theory of competitive freedom and the superimposed doctrine of *laissez faire*. We have thus linked together, as chains of the same fallacy, the impossible economic identity of social and individual interests, and the self-contradictory assumptions of competitive freedom. We now pass from the social to the physical aspect of the rent problem. If Ricardo has mistaken the social aspect—the human individuals and groups, and their characters—has he also mistaken the physical? We shall see.

§ III.—Physical aspect of the Ricardian Rent Theory

Social Life and Physical Facts.—So far as physical nature is concerned, the Ricardian theory affects to rest on solid facts, which are indeed irrefutable, but, without the aid of the social classification and the assumptions we have just criticised, as closely related with the Vaishya or Shudra of Manu as with landlord of English social life. These physical facts are the existence of natural fertility (fertility in the soil naturally, unmade by man) and of different degrees of that fertility + the naturally limited quantity of land. It is not to be supposed that the discovery of these facts was reserved for the 18th, or any century of the Christian era. It may be presumed that the Assyrians, whose lease-contracts are still extant on cuneiform inscriptions, knew the difference between good and bad arable, and that the ancient rules of communal agriculture were at least partially dictated by fears of deteriorating the natural powers of the soil. If we were to discover on some sarcophagus or papyrus an account of an attempt made by a land-owning class to attach their social existence to such physical facts, the originality of Anderson and West, of Malthus and Ricardo, might be in jeopardy. Even as it is, the autochthons of Hellas bear such striking resemblances to the economists' heroic mythology that, were it not for their altogether unique economic men, we should be inclined to abate the claims of the moderns, or at least to advise a new book-battle of rival autochthonisms. But we shall forego the wager of battle. We shall allow, without controversy, that nature has her fertilities and her degrees of fertility. Our real interest is to discover the landlord's genealogy and the kind of logical 'tree' by which his eponymous ancestry is traced back to the soil. At first sight it might seem that each and all the personages of the Ricardian group might with equal propriety or impropriety advance a claim of kinship with old mother Earth. But economists have clarified so many of our old-world notions, moral or otherwise, that the true key to the Adam-legend is no doubt found in their theory. An elaborate system of gradual elimination has enabled them to discover the sole and rightful claimant to the honours and, be it added, emoluments of autochthonism. The capitalist has his natural profit; the labourer his natural wage; the interest-receiver his natural interest; but in none of these classes can we find any connexion with the natural fertility of the soil. The sole remaining claimant is the landlord; to him accordingly shall the divine rights of autochthonism be decreed.

It may be asserted that our impiety has risen to such a pitch as to positively caricature the 'majestic argument' of Ricardo; and it may be sapiently added, that the most majestic argument is apt, when caricatured, to look ridiculous. It might be replied, that caricature is not always the enemy of truth. But we forego any such defence. We emphatically deny the charge of caricature. We assert in sober earnest that such a process of elimination as we have briefly sketched is positively the sole method by which Ricardo, or any other economist, can link the economic existence of a social class with the facts of physical nature. We assert that, without his ideal economic men and his ideal average of wages and profit. Ricardo's attempt to connect natural fertility and its degrees with a certain group of human beings could never have been made. And we also assert, that the irrefutable truth of these physical facts, unlinked by chains of reasoning with social classification, could not make either Ricardo's or any other rent theory. Let us prove our assertions.

Natural Rent and 'Free' Competition.—The difference between the production-returns of the best and worst natural soils in cultivation is the quota of national wealth which, according to Ricardian logic, must go to the landlord. It may be that the landlord class, as capitalists, have contributed to create the improved fertility of the soil; but we propose to treat the landlord proper and the landlord capitalist as distinct—a distinction not only warranted by, but even essential to, Ricardian theory. Deferring, therefore, our consideration of the landlord capitalist, we direct our first attentions to the nature-made landlord. We ask, What are the causes which prevent the differences between the highest and lowest natural-fertility-returns from passing into the pocket of some other than the landlord class? The answer is brief—free competition and self-interest. We need not rehearse the contradictions of this self-interested freedom. Either the landlord is a force-backed monopolist of land, crushing out with his despotic freedom all social freedoms but his own, or, whether controlled by custom or State interference, he is not the *free* landlord postulated by Ricardo.

But overlooking the mass of contradiction involved in the free competition theory, and consequently in the doctrine of average wage and profit, let us ask, How does the free competition assumed force the rest of the community to leave at the landlord's disposal the wealth due to natural fertility in its different degrees? Ricardo was not so foolish as to say that this quota could be artificially fixed by land-valuers, or the apparatus of a Court. It is the outcome, as he conceives, of certain social facts. What are these facts? Competition is going on for the farm of Whiteacre, and the farmers competing for the holding are determined to yield to one another from no consideration other than self-interest. The landlord of Whiteacre is a man likewise constituted: the elements of which his nature is composed are economic only; he wants the highest rent he can get, and he is shackled by no Government restrictions, by no customary or moral considerations. What invisible influences cause the competition between the farmers themselves and that between the farmers and the landlord to be so adjusted as only to give the latter his natural rent and no more? Self-interest and free competition. If the landlord, by some oversight, lets his land at less than the natural rent, the lessee gains more than the average profit of his class, and his class—the question of lease or no lease being conveniently disregarded—offers an increased rent. If the rent happens to include more than what is due to the degrees of natural fertility above the lowest in cultivation, the lessee gives up the holding—the element of leasehold contract being again disregarded. There is, in fact, a three-cornered competition of self-interest between the individual landlords to get their lands let, a kind of competition which economists find but little necessity to consider, between the individual farmers for holdings, and finally, between the class landlord and the class farmer; and the free play of this three-cornered self-interest is supposed to result in the natural rent of the landlord class. But even granting this free play of self-interest, and granting its imaginary result so far as the two classes in question are concerned, why may not some other class of the community participate in the natural rent? If the capitalists are excluded by their average profits, does it follow that the labourers are also excluded? Here again it is the function of an imaginary 'freedom' to conserve from violation the natural emoluments of the landlord. Here again there is a three-cornered competition—between individual capitalists for labourers, between individual labourers for work, and between the class capitalist and the class labourer—and the free play of these self-interests is supposed to result in an average profit and average wage which cannot touch the *natural* rent. Average wages are in fact, according to Ricardian theory, either subsistence-and-race-reproduction wages, or so much taken from the profits of capital—in either case no inroad upon natural rent. And interest, in like manner, being regarded as a deduction from profits, we reach the Ricardian belief, that no social class, save the landlord, can be regarded as the residuary proprietors of natural rent.

The Corollaries of 'Natural' Rent. 1. Rent and Price or Cost.—We have shown that the landlord's *peculium* in the Ricardian distribution of national wealth rests upon an assumption of imaginary and impossible freedoms. We need not be surprised to find the most contradictory corollaries deduced from such a theory. While anxious to vindicate for the landlord a kind of physical *naturrecht*, Ricardo wished to show that the sacred emoluments of the favoured class were borrowed from no losses to the community, and, though admittedly not the fruits of their own labour, possessed the mysterious virtue of coming from the labour or pocket of no man. It is the nemesis of unreason that its logic is suicidal; and never was logic more desperately suicidal than that of the Ricardian apology for the landlord class. Two mutually destructive corollaries are the outcome of the Ricardian natural-rent theory. According to the first, the wealth which goes to the landlord in the shape of rent is no element in the cost of production. Why? Because the price of agricultural produce depends upon the demand of population compared with that last degree of natural fertility which must be taken into cultivation in order to satisfy this demand. Now this marginal point of cultivation is assumed to be the minimum of natural fertility incapable of paying rent and only affording average wage and profit. Hence the price of agricultural produce depends upon a cause—margin-of-cultivation-cost—which only begins to operate where rent ceases to be paid. It is generally forgotten that this margin-of-cultivation-cost depends, not on the mere existence of the lowest point of natural fertility taken into cultivation in order to supply the existing demand of population, but on these facts of population and natural fertility *plus* the doctrines of average wages and average profits. Moreover, even admitting such a margin-of-cultivation-cost—which the self-contradictory character of free competition negatives—it does not follow, as Ricardo infers, that rent is no element in the *general* price of agricultural products, but only that rent is not an element in the price of that particular *part* which happens to be raised under the worst conditions of natural fertility. Either the landlords are paid no rent at all, or they are paid it out of wealth due to the produce of the soil or to some other source. But if they are paid from some other source, the payment must come from capital, or wages, or interest—all of which the Ricardian definition affects to sever from rent. From the produce of the soil they, therefore, must be paid either in kind or in the price such produce will fetch.

In fact, the principle that 'rent forms no part in the price of agricultural produce' may either be a harmless truism or a gigantic fallacy. If we concede the Ricardian position—that the cost of that part of produce which is raised at the highest cost fixes the price for all produce—we of course imply that rent is not the cause of price, for the produce raised at highest cost cannot afford to pay rent. But the propositions, 'Rent is not the *cause* of the price of agricultural produce,' and 'Rent forms *no part* of this price,' are widely different. The ambiguity which has deceived so many economists lies in the word *cause*. If rent is not the *cause* but the *effect* of price, it would seem at first glance that rent does not 'enter into'—'is no part of'—price. But the mere fact that rent, on Ricardo's own showing, is the *result* of price should suffice to warn the student against a latent ambiguity. The proposition, 'Rent is not the cause of agricultural price,' simply means that the prices of agricultural produce do not depend on the private ownership of land. It has no bearing whatever on the advisability, or non-advisability of allowing national wealth to be appropriated by individual ownership. It merely asserts the truism that, if we define rent as the return due to degrees of natural fertility greater than the least in cultivation, and if we allow price to be caused by the cost of raising agricultural produce on this margin of cultivation where rent is not paid, then rent is not the *cause* of price. Desert the truism, pretend that rent is not an element in the general price of agricultural produce, and we perpetrate the most gigantic of economic fallacies, logically implying that rent is altogether unconnected with the distribution of wealth. The fallacy is sometimes expressed in another form. 'Rent,' it is said, 'is no element in the *cost* of production.' If this proposition means by 'cost of production' the cost of producing to the producer, *i. e.* the farmer, then the farmer's 'cost of production' from the Ricardian standpoint being average wages and average profit, Ricardian rent, *i.e.* the return due to natural fertility superior to that which just yields average profits and wages, of course is excluded from such 'cost of production.' But something much more practical than this truism is intended to be conveyed by most of those who use the phrase. The implication conveyed is, that because rent does not enter into the *particular* cost which forms the market standard of price, it therefore does not enter into *any* cost, into *any* price. This implication that individual ownership costs the community nothing is, it is needless to say, an astonishing example of an *argumentum à particulari ad universale.*

Fallacious relations between 'rent' and 'price,' or 'cost,' have been variously expressed. For Ricardo 'rent is not a component part of price.' For J. S. Mill 'rent does not really form any part of the expenses of production or of the advances of the capitalist'—a proposition on which his own 'Papers on Land Tenure' were destined to throw remarkable lights. For Mr. Fawcett 'rent is not an element in the *cost* of producing food,' or as he elsewhere says, 'rent is not an element in the *price* of agricultural produce'—propositions which the Right Honourable Gentleman's advocacy of the Land Act of 1881 has probably forced him to mentally modify. Finally, Mr. Marshall accepts the teaching of Ricardo as meaning that 'rent does not enter into the expenses of production,' which is further defined as meaning that 'rent does not determine the normal value of produce.' Mr. Marshall, whose conception of rent is singularly loose, goes so far as to imply that the 'rent' of factories, workshops, and such like—so carefully excluded from the definition of rent by Professor Price and other economists—likewise does not 'enter into the cost of production.' This variety of opinions shows what very different meanings have been attached to the propositions '*rent* does not enter into *cost*' or '*price*'—differences manifestly due to the variety of ideas attached to the three terms. 'Cost' and 'price' are at one moment 'cost' and 'price' to the community as distinct from owners of land and from producers: again 'cost' means the expenses of production to the producer, *i.e.* the farmer, and is, therefore, viewed apart from the price the community pays; and yet again the very idea of 'rent' is arbitrarily narrowed or widened.

Still we may select for criticism two prominent modes of expressing the fallacy under discussion, viz., 'rent is not an element of *price*,' 'rent is not an element of *cost*.' The former proposition can bear two meanings, viz., either that rent is not the *cause* of price, or that rent is not contained in the general prices of agricultural produce, and so absorbs none of the wealth of the community. The first of these meanings is, from the Ricardian standpoint, a mere truism—'rent' by the very definition of Ricardo being excluded from the domain of average wages and profits, and the relation of this domain of average profit and wage with the community's demand for food being laid down as the *cause* of prices. The second of these meanings is simply a confusion of particular with general price, and amounts to a declaration that Ricardian 'rent' is a mere abstraction without any tangible connexion with either the production or distribution of wealth. The proposition that 'rent is not an element in *cost*' is also capable of two meanings, viz., that rent is not an element in the producer's (*i.e.* farmer's) cost of production, and that rent is not an element in the cost of food-production to the community as distinct from owners of land and producers of food. The first of these meanings is, from the Ricardian standpoint, a mere truism; for, assuming that the impossible freedoms of competition result in an exact correspondence of natural rent with degrees of fertility above the lowest in cultivation, and an exact correspondence of this lowest degree with average wage and profits, rent cannot enter into the farmer's cost of production unless it invade average profits and wages—and any such invasion is expressly excluded by the hypothesis of competitive freedom. The truism, of course, is reduced to fallacy by exposing the impossibility of the freedom upon which it rests. The second of these meanings confuses the ideas of cost and price—just as Adam Smith repeatedly confuses them—and combined with the first, as it often is, implies that the wealth which the landlord receives in the shape of 'rent,' while costing the farmer and labourer nothing, costs the community nothing also. This form of the fallacy, while contradicting the Ricardian admission that rent is the *effect* of price and depends on the social development of

277

wealth, reduces the Ricardian doctrine to an absurdity, by cutting off every source of wealth from which rent can be derived. It may be said that degrees of natural fertility superior to the lowest in cultivation are intended by Ricardo to be the sole remaining source. But it must never be forgotten that the Ricardian landlord *produces nothing*, and that consequently the wealth which comes to him as rent, whether it represents degrees of natural fertility or not, must be received from some other social class.

We thus conclude that the first corollary of the Ricardian theory, however differently expressed, is either a truism within the range of its own false assumptions, and therefore reducible to a fallacy by the disproof of these assumptions; or a fallacy irrespective of such assumptions.

Second Corollary: Conflict of Interest between Landlords and Community.—But unfortunately for this strange vindication of a costless class of air-and-water consumers, the Ricardian rent theory has another corollary to boast of. As the degrees of natural fertility shade off into that minimum which only just supports average profit and wage, so also do the profits of capital tend to decrease, and so also do wages tend to be reduced to bare subsistence and race-replenishment rate. While the increasing distance between the best and the worst natural fertility gives the landlord class an increasing share of national wealth, the same process of recourse to inferior soils increases the cost of production and lowers profits and wages. Still, that rents gain at the loss of capital is of course an intolerable fallacy, when we have once grasped with becoming facility the idea that rent has nothing whatever to do with cost *particular*, and *therefore* with price *general*. Are not the landlords' gains due to natural fertility, and how can that be any loss to the community? But, O wise economic sophist, in what do these gains consist, and how is it that the growing national indebtedness to natural fertility benefits the exchequer of one social class and drains that of the rest of the community? The gains consist not in abstractions economic, or ponderous measurements of space and time, but in something much more tangible—in the command of national wealth. Now, if the rest of the community lose its command of wealth while the landlord gains, is it not somewhat a stretch of even economic imagination to declare the landlord's gains nobody's loss?

We confess that our homespun idea of wealth is a relative idea; that a rich class in a community means for us a poor class co-existing with it; and that the increasing wealth of any class accompanied by the decreasing or stationary wealth of the rest of the community means for that class a greater over-lordship which will require nothing but political power to make itself unassailable. To pluck the heart out of the fallacy, the progress of national wealth, being limited by the natural resources which the nation can command, proprietors of these natural resources, if left to their monopoly of freedom—*as Ricardo assumes they are to be left*—not only can but must acquire an increasing share of national wealth, not in virtue of any closer bonds with nature or her fertility than those of other men, but because the growth of wealth and population gives to the owners of land the power of refusing the means of living, save on constantly severer terms to those who compete with one another for livelihood dependent on the use of the soil. It will be said that the progress of national wealth, independent of the use of land, staves off the results of this monopoly. It does. But at the same time it raises the value of land-monopoly. Without men and the accumulation of wealth land can have little but prairie value. It is the growth of population and wealth, operating upon individual ownership, that raises the prairie into monopoly value. In the natural fertilities of uncleared lands there are, no doubt, very considerable differences. But until human beings come into existence and are possessed of wealth, whereby to sell and purchase, these fertilities are economically worthless. In other words, natural fertility and degrees of natural fertility present no relations with any social class, until, individual ownership of land having been first developed, the growth of population and wealth gives to landowners monopoly value which, in the weakening of their political influence, they find it convenient to theoretically defend.

In dealing with this conflict between unrestrained individual landowner-ship and the interests of the community we have employed a term which Professor Bonamy Price earnestly deprecates—the term 'monopoly.' Protest-ing against so invidious an epithet, as associated with restrictions condemned so vigorously by the Parliament of Elizabeth, Professor Price holds it 'most unfair to insinuate, by the use of the word "monopoly," that the possession of land has any affinity with these artificial preferences.' We regret to dis-agree with Professor Price, whose unvarying candour and appeal to facts are refreshing contrasts with the stereotyped English political economy. But the Ricardian doctrine of rent-natural, basing the landlord's status on nature's fertility as if it were the *peculium* of a social class, really forces Mill and every upholder of the Ricardian theory to admit that individual landownership, on Ricardo's hypothesis, is a 'natural monopoly.' Nay, whoever maintains Ricardianism in its entirety cannot even adopt the modification of Mill, but must admit that Ricardian landownership is an artificial as well as a natural monopoly; for the unshackled freedom of the landlord, postulated by Ricardo, must be either created or allowed by the State. We may seek to avoid this admission by treating the landlord as a capitalist, or by attempting to base his status directly or indirectly on the efficiency of labour. But to do so we must surrender that theory within whose charmed domain of natural fertilities the landlord, powerless *as landlord* to increase the well-being of the nation, can only act as a sponge, passively absorbing national wealth.

'Natural' Rent and the Efficiency of Labour.—The defence of the land-lord's economic status by an appeal to the efficiency of labour is an idea which the Ricardian economist cannot logically propound. He is precluded from doing so by the fact that his theory has deprived the *landlord* as such from contributing in any way to the increase of production. Landlord and

capitalist are not only distinct, according to Ricardian logic, but, under penalty of confusing the very idea of natural fertility, must remain so. Hereafter we shall examine the nature of this distinction. At present we suppose it to be true. If the landlord be also a capitalist, it is easy to imagine that we are defending the status of *landlord* when we are really maintaining the superiority of large over small cultivation—a mistake aptly illustrated by Sir James Caird's book on the 'Landed Interest and the Supply of Food.'[2] The causes which have of recent years tended to put out of sight the Ricardian idea of *natural* rent are peculiarly deserving of study, because they have affected the theories of very able economists (such as Mill and Cairnes) apparently without awakening any serious misgivings of unorthodoxy. We shall therefore briefly note these causes, and then trace the effects of treating the landlord as a capitalist on the Ricardian theory.

Many causes have recently contributed to raise the importance of capital in the improvement and cultivation of the soil, and to consequently reduce to increasing insignificance any theoretical pretensions of *natural* fertility. Among these causes might be mentioned the increased agricultural competition consequent on free trade, and the elaborate cultivation by improved machinery, needed, invented and used in consequence; the enormous growth of town-made capital, and the spread of its ideas to agricultural relations; and the increasing political powers of the middle classes, which tend to man the legislature with exponents of their own ideas. But, above all, the economic conditions of Ireland have contributed to expose the fallacies of the Ricardian theory. While the ideas of town-made capital have exploded the natural rent idea in England, the miseries of a tenancy left to the ideal freedom or serfage of Ricardo were in Ireland exposing the true nature of private monopoly in land. It is unnecessary to do more than recapitulate the causes which in Ireland produced such disastrous effects; failure of crops; decreased efficiency of agricultural labour, consequent upon the English markets being thrown open to the foreigner; the increasing advantages of pasturage narrowing the range of agricultural employment; the absence of alternative employments, save in one small district of Ulster; incumbered landlordism unable, save at the risk of ruin, to reduce rents; and political power in the hands of the small farming class. On the one hand, absurd fallacies of free competition and free contract could not live in the atmosphere of a country in which incumbered landlords and rackrented tenants-at-will, farming for subsistence, gave them the lie direct. On the other, the great town-populations of England and Scotland were growing familiar with the spectacle of rents prodigiously raised by the mere growth of manufacturing capital, railway development, and like causes. Thus, while continental economists, living in agricultural and manufacturing conditions very different from those which suggested his false ideals to Ricardo, were exposing the social fallacies of free competition and self-interest, the very progress of those conditions which he had falsely idealised were in Great Britain and Ireland exposing the physical fallacies of natural rent. By tracing the relations of the Ricardian landlord to the Ricardian capitalist, we shall understand the nature of this interesting exposure.

If we venture to ask how the natural fertility of the soil, with its varying degrees, can be ascertained, we must not suppose that Ricardo in 1817 had solved the problems which in 1881 distracted the wits of our august Witenagemôt. Where natural fertility begins and where improved fertility ends, or where natural fertility ends and improved fertility begins, are problems which, however closely connected with the 'inherent and indestructible fertility of the soil,' the Ricardian economist finds himself relieved from discussing. How? By the free play of self-interested competitions which, while creating average wages and average profits, mark off the domain of natural fertility by an imaginary boundary-line. Now, in the first place, these conflicting competitions have been already shown to exclude the Ricardian ideal of social freedom; and, in the second place, even if such impossible free competitions could be realized, it can be shown that they are no index to the natural rent postulated by Ricardo. Let a practical necessity for distinguishing between such natural rent and returns due to capital arise, and the economic mirage of Ricardo vanishes. This is exactly what is happening in Ireland and Great Britain. It has become of the utmost practical importance to distinguish the capital expended by the landlord in permanent improvements from that expended by the farmer likewise; and, at the same time, causes which have improved the value of land without the aid of either landlords' or farmers' capital have brought into prominence a wealth-monopolizing capacity in land, which, under the name of *unearned increment*, is emphatically denied to be the outcome of *natural* fertility.

Now, what aid can the Ricardian rent theory offer to those who wish to distinguish natural rent from—(α) the earned increment of the landlord-capitalist; (β) the earned increment of the farmer; and (γ) all of these from the *unearned* increment? Absolutely none. Rent, Ricardo had defined as 'that portion of the produce of the earth which is paid to the landlord for the use of the original and indestructible powers of the soil,' and he had expressly endeavoured to distinguish between such economic rent and payments to the landlord 'for the use of the capital which had been employed in ameliorating the quality of the land.' But who will undertake to show that payments 'for the use of the original and indestructible powers of the soil' are not a *past* unearned increment? The very idea of unearned increment is fatal to the pretended connexion between natural fertility and any social class. Why? Because it directly denies the right of any class to appropriate, by the mere possession of land, wealth which others have created. But natural fertility, from the fact of its being *natural*, or unmade by man, must derive its value from the wealth which others have created, unless the owner is himself a producer—and to be such he must be more than the landlord proper of Ricardo. Hence the advocate of the unearned-increment idea must either assimilate the landlord's status with that of capitalist, and throw the natural-rent element altogether overboard, or must be ready to admit that the economic landlord is nothing but a land-monopolist, whose rent is *always* unearned increment, greater in the neighbourhood of towns, less elsewhere. In either of these alternatives he must give up the Ricardian apology for landlordism as based on nature, either by admitting that the landlord has no social status but that of a capitalist, or by denying the landlord class any domain of natural fertility distinct from that of the unearned natural increment which is claimed for the social community in general. Ricardian logic fails to distinguish the earned increment of capitalists from the natural rent of the landlord, because the freedoms of competition, which it supposes to work out the distinction, are impossible. The same logic is rationally outlawed by the conception of unearned increment, which implies an assertion of national claims to the future natural increase of land values, and therefore an implicit denial of any real distinction between the natural domain of the nation and the natural domain of the landlord class.

It would seem that the ideas of earned and unearned increment were embraced even by able economists, like Mill and Cairnes, without a suspicion of their unorthodox implications. To sequestrate for the good of the community the future unearned increment, as these economists propose, is an idea fatal to the pretended freedoms of competition, on which Ricardian theory so pretentiously reposes. Why? Because the pillars of Ricardian theory are free demand of land produce and free competition, between land-owners and landcultivators. Obtrude the idea that so much rent, *i.e.* according to Ricardo, wealth resulting to the landlord from the forces of free competition, is due to other causes than free competition, viz. the general growth of national wealth, and you spring a mine on the entire Ricardian theory—a mine which must explode not only the idea of natural rent, but also that of a natural margin due to the free action of self-interested competition. Mill, in spite of having formerly maintained the assumption that rent due to 'natural causes' can be distinguished from rent due to capital expended by the landlord—*i.e.* that the economic landlord proper can be distinguished from the landlord-capitalist—must, if we may judge from his 'Papers on Land Tenure,' have soon followed up his surrender of the Wage-Fund by a second surrender of Ricardian fallacies. Contrast, likewise, the views of Cairnes, in his chapter on the Ricardian Rent Theory, in his early essay on the 'Logical Method of Political Economy' (1857), with his later essay on the 'Unearned Increment of Land' (1873), and we have a similar conflict of theory. Both economists, in fact, reflect the transitional ideas of political economy which the conflict of new and old social conditions is creating among us. On the other hand, Continental economists, whose different social conditions led them from the first to distrust the imagination of Ricardo, need no doctrine of unearned increment to explode the natural rent. 'La terra non è in nessuna parte una ricchezza gratuita. La distinzione di *agenti naturali appropriati e non appropriati* non ha senso.' Such, for example, are the forcible conclusions of G. E. Garelli. In fact, the attempt to distinguish natural from improved fertility, in countries long settled, has been as miserable a failure as the attempt to connect the landlord's status with such fertility.

Summary of Ricardian Rent Fallacies.—We may now sum up the fallacies, physical and social, upon which Ricardo's economic theory was erected; and in doing so we shall sum up the arguments against its further retention in social science—1. The free competitions upon which it rests are self-contradictory. 2. The physical facts to which it appeals derive their social significance from these self-contradictions. 3. It is essential to the theory to distinguish natural fertility or value from the fertility or value due to—(α) owner's capital; (β) farmer's capital; and (γ) the influences of neighbouring town-growth, manufacturing progress, railway development, and the host of causes which create *unearned increment*. But the Ricardian theory, having no means of measuring natural rent save so-called free competition, cannot separate these various elements of land-value, and, in its so-called natural rent, is consequently dealing with an unknowable quantity. 4. The corollary, that rent does not enter into cost of production, or price, is either a Ricardian truism reducible to fallacy, or a fallacy direct. The price of agricultural produce = the amount of wealth given by the community in exchange for such produce: and the *national* cost of such produce is this entire price, not merely that part of the price which represents that part of the cost which is highest. 5. The second corollary of the rent theory, viz. that the same natural force operates to increase landlord-wealth, and to reduce all other national wealth, contradicts the first by admitting that hostility of landlord to national interests which it is the object of the first corollary to deny.

It would be easy to select other specimens from the galaxy of fallacies of which the Ricardian rent theory is composed: *e.g.* the assumption that the 'free' farmers cultivate their average-profit-producing land *with equal capitals*—an assumption which Mr. Marshall, with landable candour, inserts into his statement of 'the law of rent.' But in dealing with Ricardo, we must alter the schoolman's rule into '*fallaciæ* non multiplicandæ præter necessitatem.'

Notes

1 Quotations from Ricardo cited throughout this section will be found in his 'Principles of Political Economy and Taxation,' chap. iii.
2 See chapter on 'Landowner, Farmer, and Labourer,' especially pp. 68, *sqq.* where the English triple system—and therefore the *landlord* as one of its factors—is defended as yielding, in comparison with other countries, 'larger returns at less cost.'

32

'THE HISTORY AND FUTURE OF INTEREST AND PROFIT' [1]

Thomas Edward Cliffe Leslie

Source: Thomas Edward Cliffe Leslie, *Essays on Political Economy*, 2nd edition, Dublin: Hodges, Figgis; London: Longmans, Green & Co., 1888, pp. 243–68 [first published 1881].

THE history of interest, which involves that of profit, is connected with fundamental changes in human society, and in the ideas and feelings on which it rests. It raises, too, economic and social problems of no little importance for the future of the civilized world. Once it was a question wholly of moral and religious sentiment, at length embodied in positive law, whether interest were permissible, and, if so, what rate should subsist. A generation ago in this country all restraint of its rate, together with all other interference on the part of society at large, or the State, with pecuniary dealings between adult men, seemed definitely abandoned. But on the Continent of Europe the legitimacy of interest is vehemently disputed by the adherents of Socialism; a feeling against it is growing up in the United States; and even in England, although no special question about interest has been raised, there are indications of a tendency to revert to ancient ideas on kindred subjects.

The mediæval reprobation of interest under the name of usury has often been ascribed to the Christian Church, but its origin may be traced to a much earlier stage of society. Churchmen and canonists, doubtless, appealed to Christian doctrine, as well as to Aristotle's doctrine, that interest is unnatural, because money, unlike corn and cattle, is barren and cannot beget money; and since nothing is lost by the loan of an unproductive commodity, they argued that the lender was in equity entitled to no recompense. But Aristotle himself unconsciously sought to justify a notion inherited from prehistoric times, when the members of each community still recognized each other as kinsmen; when communism in property existed, at least in practice, and no one who had more than he needed could refuse to share his superfluous wealth with a fellow-tribesman in want. Tacitus, who remarks that usury was unknown to the ancient Germans, tells also that anyone might enter the house of a German, and ask for what he pleased: receiving it as a matter of course, and placed under no obligation by the gift. Describing, in like manner, the ancient customs of the Eskimo, Dr. Rink says that if anyone had anything to spare, it was ranked among goods that were possessed in common; and if a man borrowed the boats or weapons of another, he was not bound to give the owner any compensation for damage or loss. The usages and sentiments of archaic communism survived in various forms long after private property, even in land, had grown up. Far down in the middle ages, the rich man who closed his hall-door, and dined in a private room with his family, was a byword for extraordinary selfishness and meanness. Many other mediæval customs and opinions had their original source in pre-historic tribal and family ideas, and in the practices of a stage of social evolution when each little community deemed itself one in blood and ancestral gods, and individual proprietary rights were most imperfectly developed. The maxim 'Natura non facit saltum' is true of the social as of the physical world. The structure of English mediæval society, especially on its economic side, had throughout a foundation of which the original type must be looked for in archaic kinship. The guild was a brotherhood bearing all the marks of deriving its organization and fundamental ideas from the ancient joint family. The township or village community had been constituted either by actual kinsmen or by a body of men organized as such. The typical town was an expansion of the township. The nation was an amalgamation of tribes whose tribal ideas survived in various forms. On all sides social structures, practices, and notions existed, descending from a time when neighbourhood was scarcely possible without blood relationship or formal adoption, unless in the case of the conquered serf. The feeling of actual kinship might have disappeared in that of membership of a local community bound together by ancient customs, rights, and obligations, but neither townsmen nor countrymen could have conceived individuals dwelling in the same place, without bond, connexion or reciprocal duties, each pursuing what life and occupation he thought fit, controlled neither by his neighbours, nor by ancient local usage. The theory of mediæval prices had grown out of the archaic idea that the vendor of a commodity or the labourer for hire in a neighbourhood was either a member by descent or adoption of the local community, or its servant, and in either case bound to conform to its usages, to render to it honest and loyal service, and to accept customary or equitable remuneration. And the connexion is close between the prohibition of interest and the penalties in the early statutes against forestalling, engrossing, and regrating. The forestaller was regarded as seeking an exorbitant profit, not by honest work, but simply out of the necessities of a neighbour, who stood in the shoes of the ancient kinsman, and had inherited, as it were, the moral rights of one. A man was held entitled to a fair price, determined commonly by custom or authority, for work or produce, but not to a profit on buying or storing up things of which his fellow-townsmen stood in need. Dr. W. von

Ochenkowski, in a recent work of merit, 'Englands wirthschaftliche Ent-wickelung im Ausgange des Mittelalters,' lays too exclusive a stress on the duty which the mediæval citizen owed to the State. That duty plays an important part in mediæval economy; but Dr. von Ochenkowski overlooks the nearer duty which the burgher owed to the civic body, and the inhabitant of a township or manor to the little village community and its lord.

The fundamental idea of modern English economy—that every man should be free to follow his own pecuniary interest as he thinks fit without fraud—does not distinctly emerge until the sixteenth century, in which Shakespeare deplored the decline of the loyalty of the antique world, 'when service sweat for duty, not for mead.' Yet we may detect in commercial towns an earlier break with antiquity in respect of dealings between lenders and borrowers. Two opposite practices in relation to the payment of interest co-existed in the fourteenth century, one descending from social infancy, the other developed in the progress of intercourse between mercantile people—among whom, moreover, the clergy were in no great esteem—by experience of the needs of trade. There were ordinances of the Mayor of London against usury, but they were rarely enforced, and seem to have been chiefly aimed against foreigners and the high rate of interest they exacted. The civic authorities formally sanctioned in the case of citizens what would now be regarded as an enormous rate of interest, and passed accounts in which it was charged, as in accordance with 'the custom of the city.' The city records show that the fortune of a ward was customarily intrusted to his guardian to employ in his own business, paying interest at ten per cent. Thus, in 1374, the account of a mercer was duly presented respecting '£300 belonging to a minor, son of a late citizen, and delivered to the mercer to trade with.' The mercer 'charges himself with £300 so received, and with the increase by way of profit, four shillings being paid yearly for the use of every pound accord-ing to the custom of the city, of which he asks that he may be allowed two shillings in the pound for his trouble, according to the custom of the city.'[2] The customary rate of profit is here computed at twenty per cent., the cus-tomary interest at ten per cent., or half profit; the rate of profit being 'double interest,' as Adam Smith says it was in his time, four hundred years after-wards. The Act 37 Edward III., c. xi., which puts merchants, citizens, and burgesses with a capital of £1000 on the same footing in point of expendible income as landowners with £200 a-year, proves that twenty per cent. was then considered the customary rate of profit in the commercial towns of the kingdom. It is observable, too, that ten per cent., the customary rate of interest among the tradespeople of London in Edward III.'s reign, is the rate permitted by the Act of Henry VIII. in A.D. 1546, which first legalized inter-est, so that it seems to have been still regarded at the latter period not only as the traditional rate, but also as moderate and reasonable.

We must not, indeed, take the profit and interest customary in commercial towns in the reign of Edward III. as representing rates current throughout the country. The profits of agriculture after the pestilence in the middle of the fourteenth century, lowered as they were by the rise of wages consequent on depopulation, could not have borne a rate of interest approaching to ten per cent. on the capital engaged in ordinary farming. Outside of the region of town trade no regular or customary rate prevailed. Unless among townspeople, money in the Middle Ages was usually borrowed not to make profit, but because the borrower was in need, and the interest was often extortionate. In many cases the penalties on usury prevented loans altogether. The amount of accumulation, moreover, in the Middle Ages was small, and but little of it took the form of coin, the only loanable form of capital, even townspeople commonly investing their savings in land, cattle, sheep, plate, household stuff, and clothing. The amount of capital that could be put into trade was limited in various ways, and, save in trade, loans for interest were surrounded with danger, discredit, and trouble. Money, too, that is to say coin, was scarce. The English silver mines had become exhausted in the four-teenth century:[3] the Papal See caused a constant drain of treasure; foreign war was another source of pecuniary loss; and base money from abroad supplanted the sterling coin of the realm. Monasteries and great landowners not unfrequently raised loans, but there was so little lending throughout the country, that we may confine our attention to the towns.

Several questions arise with respect to interest and profit in the towns. How did so high a rate of interest as ten per cent. come to subsist in medi-æval trade? Why did it continue at the same rate, neither fluctuating from time to time, nor declining on the whole, as it has done in modern times? How was a customary profit of twenty per cent. established? The high rate of interest in the Middle Ages has often been ascribed to the insecurity of cap-ital. But unless in foreign commerce—which as yet was chiefly in foreign hands, and in which there was danger of both piracy and shipwreck, and great gains and great losses were made—trade risks were less in the Middle Ages than they are now. Trade, in general, was carried on in a small, custom-ary, circumspect way, regulated by guilds and civic authority; demand and prices could generally be estimated beforehand; and there was little or no speculation. The rate of commercial interest was not determined by the demand for, and supply of, money; had it been so, it would have varied from time to time, instead of remaining steady at ten per cent. Its explanation must be sought, first of all, in the rate of profit. Modern economists have for the most part assumed that competition proportions prices to cost of pro-duction and equalizes profits. Mediæval economy was based on very differ-ent principles, yet it brought about a much closer approximation of profits to equality, and a much closer correspondence of prices with outlay, labour, and sacrifice. The mediæval theory was, that the trader owed to the com-munity to which he belonged good articles for reasonable and moderate remuneration, and should not seek his own 'singular profit;' while he was, on the other hand, entitled to such profit and prices as yielded a sufficient livelihood to himself and his family—the family forming an important unit in the social economy. In Elfric's 'Colloquy of the Eleventh Century,' the Merchant says, 'I say that I am useful to the King and to ealdormen and to the rich and to all people. I ascend my ship with my merchandise and sail over the sealike places, and sell my things, and buy things which are not produced in this land.' To the question, 'Will you sell your things here as you bought them there?' he answers, 'I will not, because what would my labour benefit me? I will sell them dearer here than I bought them there, that I may get some profit to feed me, my wife and children.' Anything above a fair profit was regarded, like extortionate interest, as usurious, because out of proportion to labour and cost. Thus the 'Ordinances of the Plumbers,' approved by the Mayor and Aldermen of London in the thirtieth year of Edward III., ordain 'that everyone of the trade shall do his work well and lawfully, and that for working a clove of lead for gutters or for roofs of houses, he shall take only one half-penny, and for working a clove for furnaces, belfrys and conduit pipes, one penny. Also that no one for any singular profit shall engross lead coming to the said city for sale, to the damage of the commonality, but that all persons of the said trade, as well poor as rich, shall be partners therein at their desire.' There were many ordinances, both royal and municipal, in the fourteenth century for the sale of various commodities 'at reasonable prices.' The general standard of 'reasonable' or fair price and profit was custom. Where the seasons, as in the case of food, or other circumstances made a customary price impossible, the local authorities or the central government itself intervened to prevent sellers from taking advantage of the necessities of buyers. There was abundance of self-seeking and greed of lucre, as well as of hypocrisy, in the mediæval world, but they worked not through competition, but through combination; towns, guilds, companies, classes, grasping at exclusive privileges, monopolies, and gains. Men pursued their prey, as it were, in troops and packs. What was sought was not the gain of individuals as such, but of communities, corporations, fraternities, and orders.

The causes determining mediæval profit may then be easily understood. Its high rate was not the result, as in new countries in modern times, of a great productiveness of labour and capital, aided by prolific natural agents. In a small, and, compared with our own, a nearly stationary commercial world—where the number of persons engaged in each trade was limited by guild ordinances, or by the governing body of the town; where every business was carried on in accordance with usage or rule, even the amount of capital or work being often restricted; where prices were controlled by custom, public opinion, authority, or positive law—the ordinary rate of profit might be without difficulty measured, indirectly regulated, and kept at a high level. Twenty per cent. came accordingly to be the customary rate of profit in the fourteenth century, and seems to have continued so long afterwards. Again, the customary rate of interest in mediæval trade was half profit, or ten per cent., not because the competition of lenders and borrowers resulted in such a rate—for competition would have produced a fluctuating, not a stable or customary rate—but, it may be reasonably conjectured, on the same principle that prevailed in the common European tenure of metayage, that the person furnishing the capital should get half of the produce, and the person performing the labour the other half. Throughout the greater part of Europe down to the sixteenth century the prevailing rate of interest was ten per cent., and twenty per cent., or double interest, appears to have been the customary profit, at least in common opinion.

The statute of Henry VIII.'s reign (37 Henry VIII., A.D. 1546), which legalized interest at ten per cent., though prohibiting higher rates as usurious, opens a new epoch in the history of the subject. Interest was now distinguished from usury. The same cause that had led the civic authorities of London two centuries earlier to sanction trade loans at that rate, now acted on the Legislature with respect to all loans. Economic considerations prevailed over early moral ideas and later theological dogmas. The extension of manufactures and commerce called for an extension of credit, and interest was the foundation or *raison d' être* of credit. The change was connected, too, with the Reformation and the decline of ecclesiastical authority, while the position and influence of merchants and citizens had risen. There was, at the same time, a general tendency of legislation towards a relaxation of restraints on the disposition and use of property, of which the Statutes of Fines and of Wills are instances; commercial policy and the dictates of experience superseding the notions of both archaic and feudal society respecting the inalienability of family property. Theology recovered ground for the moment in Edward VI.'s reign, when 'a Bill against Usury,' in 1552, enacted that the late statute sanctioning interest should be 'utterly abrogate, void, and repealed.' But in 1571, an Act of Elizabeth, following that of Henry VIII., again legalized interest at ten per cent. Thenceforward the Legislature intervened only to lower the legal rate, which early in the seventeenth century was reduced to eight, afterwards to six, and in the middle of the eighteenth century to five per cent. These reductions might appear at first sight like attempts to tighten restrictions on dealings between lender and borrower; but they simply followed at a distance a fall in the market rate, which always averaged below the legal maximum. During Elizabeth's reign, though the Queen herself, at her accession, had borrowed at twelve per cent. on account of the supposed insecurity of her throne, the market rate sank far below the lawful ten per cent. Throughout the seventeenth century the usual rate was five per cent. In the eighteenth century the interest on the National Debt stood at one time so low as three per cent. The immense loans contracted by the Government during the long war with France afterwards caused a considerable rise; but the permanent tendency of the rate in modern times, amid frequent fluctuations, has been to decline. In the later Middle Ages it stood, as we have seen, at ten per cent.; while in the present year, according to the price of the Funds, it has kept close to three per cent. What have been the causes of this fall? What conditions now govern the rate of interest? How are its incessant fluctuations on the one hand, and its decline in the long run, on the other hand, in contrast with its stationary rate in former years, to be explained? Is a continuous fall to be looked for in the future?

Many eminent writers before Adam Smith supposed that the fall in the rate of interest after the middle of the sixteenth century had been caused by the change in the purchasing power of money, consequent on the influx of silver from America. Money, they said, was worth less, and therefore less was given for the use of it. But, as Adam Smith has replied, the change in the purchasing power of money affected both interest and principal alike, and could not alter the proportion. Yet the writers referred to were not wrong in ascribing the reduction of interest mainly to the increase of money, though mistaken in their view of its mode of operation. It was by augmenting, not the sums of money in the market for commodities, but the stocks of money entering the loan market, that the new silver lowered interest. The sudden descent in the market rate in Elizabeth's reign, already alluded to, may be traced mainly to two causes—the increase of silver in Europe after 1545, when the mines of Potosi were discovered, and the new coinage under the great queen. In 1523, it had been computed in Parliament that the total amount of money in the kingdom did not exceed a million. Elizabeth's mint coined more than five millions. Old men, says Harrison, in his description of England in her reign, could remember when it was rare for a farmer to have so much as six shillings in hand; whereas, when he wrote, it was common for one to have as much as six or seven years' rent by him, though rents had enormously risen. Little of the coin thus accumulated in the country was put out at interest; but in London and other commercial towns stores of money did not lie idle.

The steadiness of the mediæval rate of commercial interest has already been accounted for by the steadiness of the rate of profit on the one hand, and the fact that half profit was accounted fair interest on the other, in conformity with the principle commonly followed in farm tenures through-out Europe—that the person advancing the capital was entitled to half the produce. According to Adam Smith, interest in his time bore the same pro-portion to profit. 'Double interest,' he says, 'is in Great Britain what the merchants call a good, moderate, reasonable profit—terms which, I appre-hend, mean no more than a common and usual profit.' Whether this estimate was strictly accurate may be questioned. The rate of profit was no longer as certain as it had been under the mediæval system. Nevertheless, the phil-osopher lived in an age in which custom was still 'the principal magistrate of man's life.' Trade was carried on in the main by customary methods. In old and well-known employments, to which he limited the doctrine of the equal-ity of profits, the rate may have been tolerably well ascertained and uniform;

and the steadiness of profit tended to make interest steady. Some of Adam Smith's fundamental ideas—such as the correspondence of price with cost of production, the equality of profits, and that ordinary profit was double interest—had come down from an earlier economic world, many of whose usages and traditions survived. He referred phenomena, which were really vestiges of an old stationary economy, to a new and progressive one slowly emerging, under which free competition was about to supersede custom, law, and official control, and to transform a standstill and uniform world into one of infinite diversity, and change, and incessant movement. His own observations show that industrial and commercial progress was already creating wide divergence of prices, profits, and interest from old standards. The period was one of transition, which at length brought the old economic *régime* to a close, and established one of which production on a large scale, speculation, unlimited competition, and ceaseless fluctuations of prices, profits, and interest are essential features. We are thus brought back to the questions, What are the modern conditions determining the rate of interest, and whether its continuous decline is an inevitable consequence of social progress? These inquiries involve topics transcending the province of economics; but even those that are strictly within it deeply concern the future of the civilized world.

Why, then, is the rate of interest on the best security only three per cent. in Great Britain, while it is higher in the United States, and even in Holland, formerly the stock example of low interest? The answer which a chapter of Mr. Mill's 'Political Economy' suggests, and which is true so far as it goes, though inadequate, is that the desire and the means of accumulation have led in this country to the existence of a quantity of capital which its owners are led by the preference of other pursuits, or of ease and leisure, above commercial business, to lend instead of personally employing; while there is, on the other hand, a demand on the part of people engaged in trade for loans. The consequent equation of demand and supply results in a rate of commercial interest which indirectly governs the price of the funds and the income from such investments, trade being the chief competitor with Government stock and similar securities for loanable capital. In connexion with this explanation, it should be borne in mind that the increasing accumulation is not the only cause that has vastly augmented the supply of loanable capital. The greater part of the movable and immovable property accumulated in a country, in goods, machines, materials, cattle, buildings, and soforth, never directly enters the loan market; and in former times such accumulations would not have affected the rate of interest even indirectly. But banking and credit have rendered the intervention of money no longer necessary to effect loans, unless in a panic. A vast quantity of wealth, not itself directly loanable, is practically converted by credit into productive capital, of which borrowers get the command. The manufacturer and the merchant obtain, through the intervention of banks, advances of the fixed or circulating stock they stand in need of. In former times they must first have obtained a loan of money in sterling coin. Credit, though unfortunately called money in city phraseology, is neither money nor capital, but it acts as the representative of both in the loan market, and has virtually multiplied beyond calculation the supply of loans. Yet, vastly as it has augmented the supply, it has not tended only to lower interest, for it has also vastly augmented the demand. The holder of goods can get advances on his stock, and is often a borrower. The operation and activity of modern credit are, moreover, connected with a system of industrial and commercial enterprise which creates a prodigious need of the loan of capital to carry it on. It is impossible, accordingly, to lay down any general proposition respecting the effect of credit on the rate of interest. At one time it augments chiefly the demand for loanable capital, and at another time the supply. The difficulty is thickened by the close connexion between the action of credit on capital on the one hand, and on the circulation and prices on the other. When credit expands in the loan market, it is active also in the market for commodities, and prices rise, giving promise of profit; when it collapses in the former, it contracts in the latter, and prices fall, to the discouragement of enterprise. The chief fluctuations of both interest and prices thus find their explanation in credit, which is not, like coin, a given quantity, but subject to sudden expansion and contraction.

When all this has been said, we are still far from an adequate view of the movements of interest. The supply of capital and the demand for it determine the shares of lenders and borrowers in the revenue derived from its employment in business, but do not determine the revenue to be shared. The price of stock and the rate of interest on such securities are governed by the competition of investments, of which trade is the chief; and the terms which trade can offer must depend on the expected profit. If the rate of profit anticipated in business be twenty per cent. at the least, a much higher rate of interest will evidently follow a given state of supply and demand in the loan market, than if no higher profit than ten per cent. could be looked for. Interest fluctuates from causes independent of the rate of profit, and bears no fixed proportion to it—sometimes varying in an opposite direction when the immediate need of loans is urgent. But only high profit can permanently support high interest, and low profit can afford only a low recompense to the lender of capital. The rate of profit determines in general both the maximum and the minimum of interest; the maximum must be below it, or the borrower would make nothing, and the minimum must not be so low as to drive the owners of capital to employ it themselves, instead of lending it, or to spend it. Thus before we can adequately explain the causes governing interest, we must ascertain those determining profit. For the like reason we can make no answer to the inquiry whether interest tends to rise or to fall in the progress of society, until we have learned the tendency of profit in that respect. In speaking of profit, however, it is not meant here that there is in modern trade any customary, equal, or average rate, such as is talked of in text-books. The mediæval rate of profit was a customary one, and the commercial rate of interest was then a customary one likewise. Now profit is uncertain, variable, and speculative; nevertheless, interest still bears an essential relation, though not a fixed proportion to it, being higher when and where high profits are frequent and probable, than where the returns are commonly small. The rate of profit can no longer be described as 'double interest,' but unless the returns to capital ordinarily exceeded bare interest, and afforded remuneration for its active employment, borrowing in business would cease.

The inquiry whether the rate of profit necessarily declines as the world grows older has a double claim to attention, possessing an intrinsic importance apart from its relation to the future of interest. Historical and surrounding facts seem at the first view to support the doctrines of those economists who regard a tendency of profit to a minimum as an inevitable consequence of social progress and an established economic law. The actual fall of interest from ten to three per cent. seems presumptive evidence of a fall of profit on the whole hitherto, since interest bears always a relation to profit. And though individual traders now sometimes make more than the ordinary mediæval profit of four shillings in the pound, no one supposes that, gains and losses together, profit approaches an average of twenty per cent. on all the capital in trade. In Adam Smith's time the market rate of interest was generally below five per cent., yet merchants thought double interest good profit. The economic world of his day, it is true, resembled the mediæval more than the modern world in the narrow dimensions of trade, the lack of movement and change, and the influence of custom. Yet there were essential differences. Prices and profits were not artificially kept to a certain standard by guilds, civic authorities, and laws. A natural tendency of profit to decline from age to age could hardly, therefore, be inferred from its lower level in the eighteenth century than in the fourteenth. *A fortiori* no such inference can be drawn from a comparison of mediæval profit with its rate under the industrial and commercial system of our own time. In the middle ages each trade was in the hands of a limited and organized body; capital, competition, and production were subject to various restrictions; prices were customary, or regulated; the total amount of profit was accordingly small, but the rate was high. Under unlimited competition, unrestricted production, and uncontrolled prices, had the state of society permitted of such a system, profit would have varied much in individual cases and in different employments; its aggregate amount might have been much greater, because the amount of capital would have been so, but the mean rate would in all probability have been considerably lower.

If from historical we turn to surrounding facts, the state of trade and agriculture in this country during recent years is regarded by many as indicating more than a temporary fall in the profit of British capital. The novel feature of reduced assessments to the income-tax, especially under Schedule

D, and diminished proceeds of the legacy and succession duties, exhibit a retrogression only partially accounted for by diminished incomes, expenditure, and savings of landlords and farmers. But the most prosperous countries, the United States and France for example, have their unprosperous periods. The tendency towards more stringent protection abroad is not to be regarded without anxiety; yet our trade statistics prove that an immense market is still open to our productions, and that British energy hitherto has surmounted opposition. A falling-off in the foreign demand for British produce, such as is sometimes argued from the small proportion of exports, would have the opposite effect of diminishing the proportion of imports, by altering the equation of international demand to the disadvantage of Great Britain. A diminution of exports might result from hostile tariffs, but imports would fall off more. A good market abroad for our exports raises their value measured in foreign commodities, and swells the amount of goods given for them; while a declining demand in foreign countries would compel us to give more for our imports; the ratio of exports would increase, exporters would sell at ever-increasing disadvantage and diminishing profits. Yet even in such an event it could not be inferred that the advance of society lowers the returns to capital, but only that national ignorance and international jealousy may do so in commerce as well as in war. The chief unsoundness in the actual state of matters, and the most threatening indication for the immediate future, lie in two circumstances independent of foreign countries, namely, that our trade is carried on in uncircumspect, over-speculative, and haphazard manner, and that the immense fabric of our system of credit rests on so narrow and precarious a basis that it might suddenly be overthrown altogether. The gradual and spontaneous growth, however, with better communication and commercial information, of a better organization of our industrial economy, is not to be despaired of. With respect to agriculture, on the other hand, it is not enough to say with Mr. Bright that adverse seasons have caused the depression of the profits of British farming and the ruin of many farmers. Farming that pays only in fine seasons must be a losing business in such a climate as ours. It is no mere question of sunshine; nor will five thousand or more miles, at which engineers will smile in spite even of Lord Derby, protect the British corn-grower from loss in competition with American produce under present conditions. Cereals, however, play a minor and diminishing part in British rural economy, and even as regards them, the exhaustion of virgin soil and the increase of population may alter the terms at which the Transatlantic grower can hereafter sell. On the whole, the present situation forebodes no lasting depression of the profits of British capital.

But the question as to the tendency of profit to fall is not to be answered by reference to the particular case of Great Britain, still less its state at this moment. It involves a consideration of the general causes on which profit depends, and the conditions under which they will operate as ages advance and capital accumulates. Adam Smith thought that the mere growth of capital necessarily entailed a fall of profit. 'When,' in his words, 'the stocks of many rich merchants are turned into the same trade, their mutual competition tends to lower profit; and when there is a like increase of stock in all the different trades carried on in the same society, the same competition must produce the same effect in them all.' Were this reasoning correct, profit must inevitably decline in every prosperous country. But there is a flaw in the argument. When in a single trade alone the goods for sale increase, the competition of the sellers may force them to accept reduced prices and lower profits, because the general produce and revenue of the country may not have increased in proportion. But when capital and production take larger dimensions in all businesses alike, all producers have more to exchange, the general revenue is greater, and no class need get less for its goods in the market. It might even be that no increase of capital or production in any pre-existing employment would follow an augmentation of the total amount. A new trade was a rare thing in Adam Smith's days; now scores grow up every year, and new trades may both absorb much new capital and create new markets for the produce of old trades. If the growth of capital lower profit, it must be either by raising wages or by forcing resort to inferior or more costly instruments of production.

A later theory of a tendency of profits to a minimum is that an increased cost of subsistence follows the advance of population; so that, to obtain a sufficient supply of labour when capital is increasing, employers must raise wages and submit to a decrease of profit until a stationary state is reached, at which the further increase of capital is arrested. This theory is defective in two opposite ways. On the one hand, it omits all but one of the causes tending to a depression of profit; on the other, it overlooks both counteracting agencies, and the possibility of a change in the fundamental conditions determining the movement of population. The soil, in the first place, is not the only natural agent whose productiveness diminishes. Mines of all kinds would be exhausted even by a stationary population, whereas the productiveness of agriculture would increase with agricultural skill, were the number of consumers to remain constant. The cost of land, too, rises for all purposes of production, and not in agriculture alone. Many employments again besides agriculture yield diminishing returns to successive applications of capital, because the best places are taken by the first-comers, and those who come later must work in worse situations. The first roads, canals, and railways in a country are usually those, as M. Leroy-Beaulieu has observed, between the chief centres of population, wealth, and business, and traverse the districts where traffic and movement are greatest, later lines of communication running through poorer and less populous localities. The best sites for docks, wharves, warehouses, shops, and other places of business are, for the most part, the first occupied. When any new and lucrative enterprise is started, or any invention or novel production is introduced, a crowd of competitors follow, and profits fall off. Nor is an increased cost of food the only cause tending to raise wages; it is not the cause that has raised them in England during the last twenty years. Facilities for migration, emigration, and combination, together with greater intelligence, knowledge, and self-respect on the part of the working classes, have produced the rise.

Yet there is another side to the subject. The rate of profit depends on the ratio of the gross returns to the total outgoings—on the cost and efficiency of all the instruments of production, not of labour alone. Given the entire produce of the capital, labour, and natural resources of a country, in order to ascertain how much is profit, we should know not only how much falls to the share of human labourers, but also how much must be applied to the main-tenance of fixed and circulating capital, including animals, seed, materials, fuel, machinery, buildings; how much, too, must be paid as rent for the use of natural agents; and how much is to be deducted in taxation and legal expenses, or what is the cost of protection and of the other advantages of government. In a country whose natural resources are abundant and prolific, efficiently co-operating with capital and labour at small cost, and whose gov-ernment and legal system are inexpensive, both wages and profit may be high. If the soil and climate be favourable, mines of all kinds rich and easily worked, the structure of the country lending itself to cheap and rapid loco-motion, taxes and law costs small, it is plain that the return to capital, alike in agriculture, manufactures, and commerce, may give a large surplus in profit, although at the same time the reward of labour is abundant. And what the bounty of nature may effect may be effected by the art of man. Better machinery may be applied at once to the factory, the farm, and the locomotive: while chemistry cheapens and improves the cultivation of the ground, it may do like service in every branch of manufacture. Less costly and more efficient means of heating and lighting every place of production and business may be discovered. The general rate of profit might thus be sustained by the progress of science, though population were advancing. No speculation respecting the economic future of the civilized world which does not take account of the inexhaustible resources of science, and of the pro-gressive development of the human faculties for discovery and invention, has now much claim to attention. Labour, in the narrow sense, is not, as political economists as well as 'social democrats' have assumed, the sole cause of profit. There might be production and profit without the employment of a single human labourer, and profit in that case would be greater or less, according to the qualities of the other agents, and the manner in which they were used. A company in a new colony, where hired labour was not to be had, might carry on a great business by the aid of animals, machines, and natural agents; the profit depending partly on the cost, partly on the powers of these animate and inanimate coadjutors. And the progress of industrial art constantly augments the number and efficiency, and diminishes the expense, of some of these auxiliaries. The fact that the best steam-engines still waste the greater part of the fuel is enough to show that the field for economic invention in mechanics is immense. Again, if it be true that the first railways are the best situated, and bring in the largest returns, it is true also that commerce and industrial movement have a constant tendency to spread, and to create markets and traffic where there had been stagnation. The tendency of many great enterprises, like the Suez Canal, is to become more remunerative. Fifty years ago the farthest-seeing mind could not have formed a conception of the profitable occupations that steam would provide for fresh accumulations of capital, and steam is perhaps a feeble agent compared with some future sources of power. The facilities for the migration and emigration of labour may tend to raise wages at the expense of profit; but they are connected with causes which constantly enlarge the sphere for capital in the application of neglected or imperfectly developed resources, both in old and new regions. The overflow of British capital to foreign countries has two aspects. Mr. Mill has contemplated it as a sign of the fall of profit in old countries; but it may be regarded also as an example of the tendency of social progress to find fresh fields of employment for their accumulations. Students of Mr. Herbert Spencer's works know, moreover, that there is reason to question the undiminished fecundity of the population of the civilized world, which the theory of a decline of profit assumes. Civilization makes constantly greater demands on the nervous system, enlarges the brain, and multiplies its expenditure of physical power, thereby diminishing the quantity expendible on the increase of the race, while at the same time raising the standard of wants, and augmenting prudence. One and the same cause—the increase of cerebral force and activity, and therewith of science, foresight, and adaptation of means to ends—tends to add to the industrial productiveness of the people of the West, and to slacken the growth of their numbers, although a different future may be before the people of the East. The time must indeed come, after countless ages, when the decline of solar and terrestrial heat shall arrest the mental advancement of the human race, and make the returns to capital and industry dwindle. But within economic as distinguished from astronomical and geological periods, there seems no ground for concluding that in the more civilized parts of the globe man must press constantly closer and closer on the means of subsistence, and thrift and enterprise consequently obtain a decreasing reward. Were population stationary, it may perhaps be argued, the price of labour would rise to such a pitch from the accumulation of capital as to leave little or no profit. The answer is, that the accumulation would not take the form of wages, but of new mechanical and other agencies for aiding production, which would benefit the labourer as a consumer without raising the cost of his services. One remote difficulty, indeed, raises a formidable, and at present insoluble problem, namely, What is to be done for coal and iron when the mines become exhausted? Yet the men of a former age might have regarded the disappearance of forests, and the consequent rise in the cost of wood, with equal embarrassment. It is at least certain that the earth contains resources now undreamt of, which science is sure to reveal; or, rather, which the mind of man, the real cause of all wealth and profit, is sure to discover. Some of the chief sources of modern profit must ultimately fall short; but food is not likely to be among the number, because the number of human beings can be kept within bounds—as it is already in France and among the old American families in the States of New England—and substitutes for those which must fail may be in the womb of time. No certain conclusion respecting the future of profit can be reached, but the theory of its tendency to a minimum has no claim to the character of a law of social progress, ignoring, as it does, some of the chief results of that progress, and its chief cause—the constant improvement of human faculties. Profit may uniformly fall from its first high level in new countries like the Western States of America, yet may not continuously decline in old countries. The rate will probably vary from time to time in the future as it has done in the past.

If profit, then, be subject to no law of inevitable decline, can interest be so? It is almost needless to say that no inference can be drawn from its lower level in modern times than in the Middle Ages, since the mediæval rate of profit was fixed, and interest bore a fixed proportion to it. Now, profit is indeterminate and fluctuating; interest, too, fluctuates from causes independent of profit, affecting the loan market, such as the state of credit, the foreign exchanges, the movements of bullion actual or anticipated, the harvests, Government and foreign loans, and political events and prospects. The movement of interest in trade may consequently be different from, and even opposite for the moment to, its movement in respect of other investments. The price of Government stock might be high, and interest on such securities falling, while the rate of discount showed that men of business were eager for loans, either because credit had been shaken, or because a shock to it or a scarcity of money was apprehended, or, on the other hand, because a speculative mania had arisen. Or again, people in trade might be slow to accept short loans on very favourable terms, because waiting for a turn in commercial affairs, while stable and permanent investments like the funds or land mortgages returned a high interest. Yet the main cause determining, throughout the whole field open to capital, the general tenor of the movement of interest, is the rate of commercial profit. Let new channels of trade offer bountiful returns for a series of years, and the savings of the country would flow into them, the price of Consols would fall, and mortgagors would pay dearly for loans. The main reason why the rate of interest has been constantly higher in the United States than in England is that the prolific natural resources of America have afforded a richer field for the employment of capital than was found in this island. The chief cause of the rise of interest in Holland is that Dutch capital has found in colonial undertakings, American investments, foreign commerce, and husbandry at home, more profitable employment than lay open to it a century ago. And the stationary state ultimately reached by the whole civilized world may possibly be that of a stationary population, whose savings are more productively employed than those of the present generation, and yield a higher interest.

We have yet to consider how profit is distributed between lenders and borrowers of capital, and what proportion falls to the share of the former. Gross profit, according to Mr. Mill, is made up of three elements:—interest, or the reward of simple abstinence; insurance, or the compensation for risk; and the remuneration for superintendence or management. This analysis however, errs in treating insurance as a constituent of profit. The sum spent in insuring the goods of a manufacturer or merchant against fire or ship-wreck forms part of his outgoings, not of his profit upon them. He may spend what he receives both as interest and as recompense for management, but what comes to him as insurance should be laid by to provide against accident or loss, and is not expendible income. It is true, since losses and accidents may be escaped, that men in a trade exposed to them who do not insure may get a higher profit from the higher prices caused by the risk. They have played double or quits, and have won. But if all risk in trade, and therefore insurance, could be extinguished, the total amount of profit would not be diminished, as it would be by the extinction of interest, or of the earnings of management. On the contrary, were the same amount of insur-ance required in all trades alike, its elimination would be a saving, and a source of additional profit all round. The mistaken classification of insur-ance with the elements of profit, instead of with those of cost of production, is connected with the common inaccuracy of treating interest as higher in proportion to risk. Interest proper is not income, and safely expendible as such; the provision against loss of the principal is not so. As in the case of profit, however, particular lenders may be gainers by the risk of losses which do not actually befall them, though nothing may be gained from it by lenders all round. How far risk attracts or repels capital depends indeed partly on national character and the temper of the age. But the presumptuous trust in their own good fortune, which Adam Smith imputes to the greater part of mankind, tends to make the losses resulting from risk exceed, on the whole, the indemnity.

Profit, then, includes two elements only—interest for the mere loan of capital, or an equivalent where the capital is the employer's own, and the additional return resulting from its active employment in production. This second element is not happily called wages of superintendence or earnings of management. Regarding it in that light, Mr. Alfred Marshall and some emi-nent foreign economists consider it simply as a species of wages, determined by the same causes that govern the recompense of skilled labour in general, such as the rarity of the faculties and acquisitions required, and the amount of toil undergone. Were there no other constituent than this, in addition to interest, in gross profit, interest would absorb a greater share of profit than it does, and therefore be higher than it actually is. The surplus above interest arising from the active employment of capital is in proportion, not to the difficulty and trouble of management, but to the amount of the capital. If two companies, one employing twice as much capital as the other, can make a good profit by selling at a particular time or place, the gain of each will be in proportion to the business done and the amount of the sales; and one will make twice as much as the other, although the skill and exertion required to conduct the operations in the two cases may be the same. There may be a manager of each company who gets a fixed salary, and this, doubtless, is wages; but the profit on the transaction will be so much per cent. on each company's capital, and may far exceed the manager's pay. The shares of interest on the one hand, and of the return for the employment of the capital on the other hand, are determined by the supply of and demand for it in the loan market. The proportions will vary in different countries and ages, according, in a great measure, to the attraction or repulsion that active trade has for the owners of capital. The rate of interest, in short, is determined by no invariable rule; but, like that of profit, seems subject to no law of inevitable decline—at least until great astronomical and geological changes supervene, and the whole solar system begins to approach the end of its career.

So far the future of interest and profit has been considered with reference to economic conditions alone. But is it certain that economic conditions exclusively will henceforth control them? The policy of society in reference to both has been determined by various conceptions. Archaic notions and feelings founded on kinship, Greek philosophy, Roman law, Christianity, Catholic theology, commercial ideas, the modern regard for individual liberty, political economy, have all played a part in their history. Other sources and modes of thought have yet to be reckoned with—democracy, the views of the working classes, German and French Socialism, the subtler shapes of Socialism which ostensibly seek only to enlarge the intervention of the State in the economical sphere, and new conceptions of moral and social duty. The authority of the economic theory hitherto dominant with respect to individualism, competition, and non-interference, is visibly shaken even in England. The notion that all capital should belong to the State for the benefit of the working classes has many strenuous adherents in Germany and France, notwithstanding the wide distribution of property in those countries, but for which it would have already overcome all opposition. The favour with which Mr. Henry George's 'Progress and Poverty' has been received in the United States makes a curious revelation of the tendencies of educated thought in a country where individual energy has worked under the most propitious conditions. Mr. George, indeed, proposes to confiscate land-rent only without compensation; but rent in a vast number of cases is virtually a form of interest, being the return to an investment by purchase or outlay. Protection, again, is a revival of the mediæval regulation by law or authority of trade, prices, and profit; and the policy of most civilized countries is protective. In

England, a generation ago, when at length Bentham's 'Defence of Usury' had led to the abolition of a legal limit to interest, much more seemed to be swept away. The change apparently formed part of a wider and deeper change in social opinion and legislative policy, and belonged to a general movement of thought, emancipating human conduct from a multitude of ancient restraints in the name of morality or religion. Yet, little as people are dreaming of it at present, there are indications of a tendency on the part of English society to slide back to the mediæval system of regulating contracts, bargains, pecuniary dealings, and prices by authority. Fair wages, fair profits, and fair rents are now objects more or less distinctly conceived by many who, ten years ago, regarded buying in the cheapest and selling in the dearest market as the sole rule in all questions of contract. No one, perhaps, in England at this moment thinks of controlling interest; yet propositions are now often put forward respecting wages and profit involving the regulation of both, and indirectly, therefore, of interest, which follows the movement of profit. Ten years ago no English statesman would have listened to a proposal to regulate rent in any part of the United Kingdom by statute or judicial decision. Yet the principle of the Act by which judicial rents are now introduced into Ireland is no other than that of the mediæval law against usury, that the owner of property should not be permitted to take advantage of his neighbour's necessity to extort a high price for the loan of it. The establishment of rings and corners, and of bulling and bearing in English trade, might considerably alter public opinion with regard to the mediæval laws against forestalling and engrossing. Democratic legislation will assuredly intervene in directions not in accordance with the doctrines that have commended themselves hitherto to the minds of great capitalists or landowners. Ideas of moral and social obligations, too, seem likely to play a greater part in the commercial sphere than they have ever done since Adam Smith based a complete economic code on the desire of every man to better his own condition, and some of these ideas may make light of that code.

The misfortune is that great general principles, like that of the freedom of contract, are now abandoned in a moment to promote a particular measure, perhaps expedient or necessary in itself and defensible on special grounds, like the Irish Land Act. Mediæval economy has been ignorantly decried; there was much in it that was good in design and suited to the time; yet let us not ignorantly go back to it from a notion that we are following new and advanced guides. Let us look steadily before us; and if we are to revert to an ancient system which tolerated no individual liberty in production or exchange, let us, at least, do so advisedly and deliberately, not sliding back into it unconsciously.

Notes

1 *Fortnightly Review*, November 1st, 1881.
2 Riley's *Memorials of London*, p. 378. Compare a fishmonger's account, *ibid.*, pp. 446, 447.
3 See Dr. Georg Schanz's excellent work, *Englische Handelspolitik, gegen Ende des Mittelalters*, i. pp. 492–494.

33

'THE WAGES-FUND THEORY' AND 'VIEW OF LONGFIELD'

William D. McDonnell

William D. McDonnell, *A History and Criticism of the Various Theories of Wages: Being the Whately Memorial Prize Essay for 1887*, Dublin: William McGee; London: Simpkin, Marshall, 1888, pp. 2–19, 31–4.

§ 2. The wages-fund theory

At the close of the last, and the commencement of the present, century both the state of the industrial world in England, and the method of economic speculation then coming into fashion, were peculiarly favourable to the rise of a doctrine which treats the rate of wages as depending on the ratio of a supposed wages-fund to the number of the labouring population. A large accumulated capital existed in the hands of employers, population was increasing rapidly, the working classes were too poor to maintain themselves until the completion and sale of the product, and the national industries were chiefly of a kind which required that a considerable interval should elapse between the execution of the labour and the time when the value of the product could be realized. The labouring classes were, for all practical purposes, excluded from becoming owners or occupiers of land, and the country had long reached the stage of diminishing returns in agriculture, so that any addition to the population was generally attended by a decline in the efficiency of labour, and a consequent fall of wages.

Under an industrial regime of this kind, it is evident that wages were, as a rule, advanced out of capital, and the capitalist reimbursed himself upon selling the product just as a bill discounter does on a bill becoming due. The conditions were, as Professor Walker expresses it, financially more favourable, and industrially less favourable, for the payment of wages, than in new countries in which capital is scarce, in which labour is skilful and intelligent, and natural agents highly productive. Economic speculation, at the time to which I refer, was carried on mainly from the capitalist's point of view, and it was natural that an individual employer, who saw that he advanced a certain sum to his men in the shape of wages during the period required to fit a particular article for the market, and then received himself the whole price for which it sold, should accept, as universally true, a doctrine which seemed to be in harmony with the facts which fell within his own narrow experience—a doctrine which assumes that wages are not only advanced, but also paid, out of capital, and measured by it, and that the efficiency of labour and the productiveness of natural agents can only affect wages so far as they lead to increased accumulation. Not only was economic speculation carried on too much from the stand-point of the capitalist, but the economists of the earlier Ricardian school lived too exclusively in a world of abstractions; they wanted that "strong instinct for realities" for which Adam Smith was remarkable, and were too little in the habit of verifying their *a priori* deductions by comparing them with the actual facts of life. They bestowed little observation on the industrial system of their own age and country, and seldom looked to former times or other countries to see how far their theories possessed the universality which was claimed for them.

Such was the general character of the economic world in which the wages fund theory was first distinctly formulated by James Mill. Indistinct foreshadowings of the doctrine may indeed be found in earlier writers, but I think I am correct in saying that James Mill was the first writer who gave clear expression to it. It was restated and insisted on as an almost self-evident truth by nearly every English economist of the *a priori* school—by McCulloch, and Senior, by John Mill, and Fawcett, and Cairnes—the last of whom was, perhaps, its clearest exponent and its ablest defender.

No direct attack seems to have been made upon it during the first half of the century, although some doubts were thrown upon it, and theories inconsistent with it were advanced. The note of dissent was, however, clearly sounded by Mr. F. D. Longe in 1866, and two years later the objections to it were set forth with much greater ability by Professor Leslie, in an article in *Frazer's Magazine*. The year 1869, however, is the one which has became memorable in the history of the controversy by the conversion of Mr. Mill. In that year Mr. Thornton published his work *On Labour, its Wrongful Claims and Rightful Dues*, and the immediate effect of his performance is described by Professor Walker (*North American Review*, January, 1875) in the following words:—"No sportsman who had fired at a squirrel, to hear, a minute after, the crashing of boughs above him, and to see a bear come tumbling out of the tree, could have been more astonished than Mr. Thornton must have been, when, promptly on the publication of his work, John Stuart Mill, without a reservation, and even without a parley, surrendered the whole territory covered by the wages-fund flag, with all the materials and properties complete, and marched out without even the honours of war." How far Mr. Mill's conversion was due to Mr. Longe and Professor Leslie we are without the means of judging. He himself seems to have attributed it entirely to the impression produced upon him by Mr. Thornton's book. However this may be, his recantation was unconditional and complete, both as to the theory itself and its corollaries. He declared that Mr. Thornton had deprived of all scientific foundation the doctrine that combinations cannot raise wages, and that the wages-fund theory, which had been a barrier closing the entrance to an important province of economic enquiry, was merely "a shadow that will vanish if we go boldly up to it."

The last chapter in the history of the wages-fund theory is that contributed to it by Professor Cairnes, in *Some Leading Principles of Political Economy Newly Expounded*, which contains a masterly restatement and analysis of it, although he at the same time confesses, strangely enough, that it is not a solution, but merely a statement, of the wages problem—the problem being, in his opinion, to ascertain the causes which lead to an increased demand for labour (that is, to an increased wages-fund) on the one hand, and to an increased supply of it on the other.

America is the only country except England in which the wages-fund theory has made many converts, and even there the conditions were so unfavourable to its growth that it would probably never have taken root if it had not been transplanted from a more congenial soil. Except in the New England States the practice of advancing wages out of capital is not universally followed even at the present day, and fifty years ago wages were seldom so advanced in any part of the Union. The national industries were chiefly of an extractive kind. The product was capable of being quickly harvested and brought to market; the labourer was usually well off, and able to maintain himself during the interval required for the realization of the value of the product, and where he was unable to do so his wages were partly advanced to him and partly paid when the product was sold. The stage of diminishing returns had not yet been reached, and an addition to the number of the labouring population was accompanied by an increase of the *per capita* product owing to the concentration of labour and a more effective combination among the men. It is evident that in such a state of things the economic atmosphere was as unfavourable, as in England it had been favourable, to the growth of the wages-fund theory. In America the facts which came into collision with the theory lay on the surface of the social system. In England they were buried deep beneath the surface, and were only brought to light after a close analysis and a careful comparison of the English social system with those of other countries.

Such being the history of the wages-fund theory, I have next to inquire how far it satisfies the test by which every scientific theory must be tried—the test of explaining the facts. I shall first state the theory; I shall then state the facts; and I shall then consider to what extent it harmonizes with and explains them. The wages-fund has sometimes been understood to mean the sum actually paid in wages, and it has been supposed that the teachers of the theory meant to assert that wages depend on the ratio of this fund to the number of the labouring population; and that all you had to do to find the average rate of wages was to divide the sum actually paid by the number of actual recipients. It is in this sense that Professor Perry appears to understand it when he says:—"There is no arguing against any of the four fundamental rules of arithmetic. The question of wages is a question of division. It is complained that the quotient is too small. Well then, how many ways are there to make a quotient larger? Two ways. Enlarge your dividend, the divisor remaining the same, and the quotient will be larger; lessen your divisor, the dividend remaining the same, and the quotient will be larger."—(Perry's *Elements*, p. 123.) If this is the wages-fund theory, it is no doubt perfectly true, but at the same time perfectly worthless; it is a mere statement of an arithmetical fact which contains, as Dr. Ingram has observed, no economic element whatever; and it seems to me that it would be an insult to the memory of those great men who held and taught it as an important economic truth, to suppose that they meant anything so puerile as this. I therefore assume that they meant by the wages-fund, not the sum actually paid in wages, but the sum pre-determined and destined by certain fixed economic causes to be paid, and that the doctrine which they taught was that wages depend on the proportion borne by the amount of capital so destined and determined to the number of the labouring population. If the wages-fund, in this latter sense, is capable of being ascertained, and if the facts do not conflict with the theory, then the doctrine as last stated must contain an important economic truth. Let us now, therefore, enquire whether the facts do conflict with it or not. We find two countries, such as England and America were fifty years ago, the former possessed of a large accumulated capital—large, not only absolutely, but large compared to the labouring population—the latter with a small capital, both absolutely and relatively. What would the theory lead us to predict with regard to the rate of wages in these two countries? Surely, that it was high in England and low in America. And yet the fact was just the reverse; and why? For this plain reason, that labour was far more productive in America than in England, partly on account of its own efficiency, and partly on account of the fertility of the natural agents upon which it operated. Can anything more than this one example be required to show that a large wages-fund (in the second of the two senses in which, as I have shown, that term is capable of being understood) is not the *only* thing upon which, the number of the labouring population remaining the same, the rate of wages depends, but that it also depends, and that in a still greater degree, on the efficiency of labour. Wherever you have a body of skilful, industrious, energetic men, and natural agents of a high productive power, there the reward of labour will be high, even though capital be scarce and the wages-fund small, because it is the product, and not capital, which is the real and ultimate source from which wages are paid. Wherever you have a similar body of men, and similar natural agents, and, in addition to these, a large capital and a large wages-fund, there the position of the labourer will be still better, because the conditions will be *financially*, as well as *industrially*, in his favour, and because the competition of capital for the aid of labour will be keen.

Let us now consider the wages-fund theory as applied to a country in which the stage of diminishing returns has not been reached, and in which an addition to the labouring population will cause an increase in the produce of industry, not merely in proportion to the increase of labourers, but in a greater proportion. What will the effect be upon wages? The product has increased, not only absolutely, but relatively to the number of labourers, and is it not both "morally just and economically possible" that the labourer should obtain a share of the increase? It certainly seems so to me, and the evidence goes to show that he *does* obtain it—not merely ultimately, after the increased production has had time to cause fresh accumulations, *but at once.* So also, by a parity of reasoning, in an old country in which natural agents yield a diminishing return to each additional application of capital, a fall of wages will take place as a consequence of an influx of labourers, because employers in estimating the price at which they can afford to employ the new labour will take into account, prospectively, the diminished return which will be received upon each successive application of capital. So too, if we take a case in which the increased or diminished productive power is due, not to an increase or diminution of the fertility of natural agents, but to a change in the industrial qualities of the labourer, we get a precisely similar result. It is supposed that the labour of an average Bengalee is from five to eight times less efficient, according to the sort of work you put him to, than that of an average Englishman. If then a body of Bengalee workmen were suddenly substituted for the existing body of English workmen, a great fall in wages would take place. The advocate of the wages-fund theory would explain this by saying that it was caused by the reduction in the wages-fund, consequent on reduced production. But this explanation ignores the fact that the fall in wages will take place *at once*, that is, immediately on the substitution of the less efficient labour of the Bengalees for that of Englishmen, because the employers of labour will foresee a diminution of the product, and will make their calculations accordingly. They will see that because the new men produce less they must be paid less, or else profits will vanish or be converted into a loss.

The wages-fund theory assumes that an employer, in calculating what he can afford to pay his men, thinks only of how much capital he will have after having provided himself with machinery, materials, etc., and it is supposed that he will expend the whole of this residuary capital in the purchase of labour. It assumes that he cannot spend more and that he will not spend less. But will he not also take into account the prospective value of the product? In the western states of America an employer often commences the industrial year with only a quarter the amount of capital necessary to pay his men. He accordingly agrees to pay them only quarter wages until the product

307

comes to market, and they then receive their share of it minus the quarter which has been already paid to them. Here it is plain that it is to the product that the employer looks as the source from which he is to pay his men, and it is evidently the product, and not the employer's capital, that measures their wages. If, in the following year, the employer has reason to expect that the product will be unmarketable, he will probably suspend operations and employ no labour that year, because the source is dried up from which he had previously paid his men three-fourths of their wages and from which he had repaid himself the fourth which he had advanced. I say that he will probably suspend operations, not that he will certainly do so, for he may continue to produce at no profit, or even at a loss, in order to keep his men together in hope of better times, and because he cannot extricate his fixed capital from the business. But however this may be, it is certain that an anticipated decline in the value or amount of the product will *tend* to make him employ less labour or to employ it at lower rates.

If we leave out of account that share of the produce which goes to the landlord as rent and to the State as taxes, the whole of what remains must be either wages or profit; and it seems to me impossible to adduce a single argument to show that the share of this residue which the labourer obtains depends upon the ratio of the wages-fund to the number of labourers, which could not also be used to prove that the share of the capitalist depends upon the ratio of a supposed profit-fund to the amount of capital. And yet this has never been put forward as a theory of profits; and why? Because during the period of abstinence the capitalist has always maintained himself, just as the labourer did in America when wages were not paid till the close of the industrial year, and hence it was obvious that his profit came from the product. In England the capitalist did so maintain himself; the labourer did not; and so it seemed as if wages and profits came each from a different source, when in truth the difference was only in the time and manner of payment. The labourer was, as it were, paid by a bill which reached maturity on the day the product was sold; the capitalist was paid by a similar bill; but the labourer had his bill discounted at once by the capitalist, whereas the capitalist waited until his became due and then received the the whole price of the product in liquidation of both bills.

I have already indicated the circumstances which favoured the growth of the theory of the wages-fund. The reason of its having so long retained a hold on men's minds is obvious. It seemed to afford a logical resting place to the weary enquirer, and to provide him with a compact and portable formula for the solution of a multitude of perplexing questions. It satisfied that craving for simplicity and uniformity which is the last infirmity of the philosophic mind, and which makes it, as Bacon said, "assume and feign in nature a greater uniformity and equality than is in truth." It was popular with employers of labour, because it supplied them with a ready answer to the complaints of their men, and with social optimists because it enabled them to justify the existing industrial regime. With the working classes, on the contrary, it never was popular, and it did much to discredit in their eyes economic teaching in general. It was natural that they should regard with suspicion and dislike a doctrine which "deprived such agencies as strikes and trades-unions of even a standing in a court of Political Economy" (Walker, *North American Review*, 120, p. 85), and which told them that all their efforts to affect wages were useless which did not either check population or promote accumulation—or at least that the utmost they could accomplish was to accelerate a rise of wages which was already "in the air," and which would equally occur a little later on if they remained passive and avoided the expense of a strike. It was evident that as soon as Political Economy came to be written more from the point of view of the artisan, and less from that of the employer, the wages-fund theory would be placed upon its trial before no very lenient tribunal, and it probably owes its downfall more to this change in the general spirit of economic speculation than to the attacks of Mr. Thornton and Mr. Longe. Opinions which have enjoyed a long popularity are often silently undermined by moral and economic causes, and it is only when these have accomplished their work that the men appear who get the credit of having killed them. If the attack on the theory of the wages-fund had been made twenty years earlier it would in all probability have failed.

The wages-fund theory as taught by some writers, especially by Mr. McCulloch, professed to furnish a formula, not only for ascertaining the general or average rate of wages, but also for fixing the particular rates prevailing in different employments. These rates, it was maintained, are always such as to distribute the total wages-fund among the various industries, in exact proportion to the severity, duration, and disagreeableness of the labour in each, as well as the time and expense required to learn, and the skill required to exercise it. "Hence the discrepancies," says Mr. McCulloch, "that actually obtain in the rate of wages are confined within certain limits; increasing or diminishing it only so far as may be necessary to equalize the favourable or unfavourable circumstances attending any employment." Mr. McCulloch, and those writers who have followed in his wake, seem to have supposed that in teaching that the level of wages in any trader must be such as to make its "net advantages" (to use Professor Marshall's convenient expression) exactly equal to those of other trades, they were preaching a doctrine of Adam Smith's. Now in no part of Adam Smith's book do we feel "that abiding sense of being in contact with the realities of life," of which, as Dr. Ingram remarks, the reader of that book is always conscious, so much as in the chapter on the rates of wages and profits in different employments; while, on the other hand, in the writings of most of his successors of the English school, we nowhere feel ourselves so far removed from realities as in those parts of their works which deal with this very subject. Adam Smith has shown even more than his usual caution in stating the numerous qualifications and conditions which limit the proposition that competition equalizes the net advantages of different employments. He has shown that it is only true in the same neighbourhood, and when the labourer is perfectly free to choose and change his occupation, and even in the same neighbourhood, and upon the hypothesis of perfect freedom, he shows that the proposition is only true as regards old established industries, those which are in their normal state, and those which form the main occupation of the men engaged in them. Although Mill has been represented as teaching that competition raises wages to the exact point required to compensate the labourer for the hardships and disadvantages of the business, yet, the doctrine can in reality only claim the sanction of his authority in the same sense in which it can claim the support of Adam Smith's. Indeed, as Professor Leslie observes, it has been the fate of both of these great men to have had some of their views reproduced in such a shape as almost to make one think that the *reductio ad absurdum* of the master was the object of the disciple. Mr. Mill, so far from assuming that the net advantages of different employments are equalized by competition, tells us "that wages are generally in an opposite direction to the equitable principle of compensation, erroneously represented as the general law of the remuneration of labour. The really exhausting and really repulsive labours, instead of being better paid than others, are almost invariably paid worst of all, because performed by those who have no choice." Again, he maintains that women's wages are not determined by competition, and "that the remuneration is greatly below that of equal skill, and equal disagreeableness in employments carried on by men." He also admits that combinations have been successful in securing net advantages in some trades far superior to those enjoyed by others. McCulloch states that wages in his time were nearer a common level than when the *Wealth of Nations* was written, and were "nearly the same all over the country" (note to his edition of the *Wealth of Nations*, p. 34). But the latter part of this statement is certainly untrue, and the truth of the first part of it, although the evidence is not quite decisive, is very doubtful. Improved communication has, no doubt, done much to facilitate the migration of labour from place to place. Newspapers and advertisements teach the workman where his services are most wanted, and railways and steamers enable him to go there. But can labour migrate from employment to employment much more easily than it could do in Adam Smith's day! I do not say that it cannot do so; I say that it is far from certain that it can, and that many impediments to its movement still exist. Just as improved: communications and the influx of gold between 1850 and 1870 destroyed old inequalities of prices and created new ones, so the introduction of machinery and the extent to which the division of labour has been carried have raised up new inequalities in wages, by creating new obstacles which impede the movement of labour from employment to employment in place of old obstacles which have been swept away. "Whatever Ricardo's hypothesis may lead to," says Professor. Leslie, "the real economic conditions of production and distribution have nowhere equalized wages, profits, or rents; they have in fact, in recent times, produced new inequalities through the different rates at which industrial development has proceeded in different localities, the different natural advantages of different localities, and the rise of such a multitude of special industries, and such continual change in the conditions, that omni-science only could estimate their prospects, or enable competition to equalize them."

I am aware that Professor Marshall has pointed out some cases in which the division of labour has formed a kind of bridge between two trades that were formerly distinct, enabling labour to pass more freely between them. "A country watchmaker," he says, "could not easily become a gunmaker or *vice versa*; but many men in a large watch factory could easily find employment in a large rifle factory. When the late American war came to a close, a famous rifle factory devoted itself to making sewing machines." Such cases as these are, however, the exception and not the rule, and the great number of specialized industrial qualities to which the division of labour has given birth impede the migration of labour more frequently than they promote it. Professor Marshall himself admits that skilled labour migrates from employment to employment much less freely than unskilled labour; while Mr. Giffen has shown that the proportion which the number of skilled labourers bears both to the number of unskilled and to the whole community has enormously increased during the last fifty years, and he tells us that not only has a substitution taken place of artizan labour for rude labour, but "the proportion to the whole community of the higher paid artizan and professional workers and clerks who are economically members of the working classes, has greatly increased." So that that section of the working class, the members of which, according to Professor Marshall, find it most difficult to change their employments, is on the increase, both absolutely and relatively. It is no uncommon thing to see thousands of skilled workmen unable to obtain employment, while much machinery is standing idle for want of hands, because the skill of the unemployed men is not of the kind required to work it. The factory inspectors reported in 1860, that in London above 90,000 men were out of employment in one set of industries, while in another set a large demand existed for labour to work machinery then idle.

Thus we find that, even as applied to highly civilized communities, the assumption that competition equalizes the net advantages in different employments is only a rough approximation to the truth. How much further then must it be from it in those countries where custom, to a greater or less extent, excludes competition—in which wages are often paid in kind, or in different currencies, and in which the most skilful statistician or actuary would sometimes find it difficult, as between different industries, to determine which of them possessed net advantages superior to the others. It is difficult for an Englishman or an American of the present day to form an idea of the degree to which, in some parts of the world, the social organism is, as it were encased in a crust of custom which makes it impossible for the workman to seek the best market. And, even if nothing prevented him from seeking it, the knowledge that would enable him to find it may lie far beyond his reach.

These considerations lead me to the conclusion that that branch of the wages fund theory which deals with the problem of particular wages rests upon assumptions which are only true of a small part of the world, and even of that small part they are only true when taken subject to a number of limitations which have been ignored—not indeed by all—but by a great number of English economists. It is impossible not to join with Professor Leslie in lamenting that the earlier disciples of Ricardo, instead of assuming an equality of wages which had no real existence, did not search out the causes of existing inequalities so as to pave the way for their removal. Even granting that the scientific economist is going beyond his province when he gives advice, or proposes remedies, he is certainly well within it when he points out the causes of evils, leaving it to others to suggest the cure.

§ 6. View of Longfield

Neither Professor Jevons nor any of his critics seem to have been aware that a theory of wages, not indeed identical with, but still closely resembling his had been put forward by Judge Longfield, in his lectures delivered before the University of Dublin in 1833–4. Professor Jevons has, in speaking of Professor Hearn's admirable work, *Plutology*, attributed the fact of its having received less attention than its merit deserves to its singular title and the distant residence of its author. The fact that he himself seems never to have heard of Longfield's lectures, proves that for practical purposes, and so far as the commerce of ideas is concerned, Ireland is even a more "distant residence" than Australia. Judge Longfield "extends" (to use his own words) "to the profits of capital that principle of an equality between the supply and the effectual demand which in all cases regulates value. . . . In the case of capital and profits this equality between supply and the effective demand is produced by such a rate of profit, as is equal to the assistance given to labour by that portion of capital which is employed with least efficiency, which I shall call the last portion of capital brought into operation, and for the reasons already mentioned, the rate of profit cannot be much higher or lower than this." (Lecture ix. p. 193.) The rate of profit having been thus determined, he tells us in the following lecture (x. p. 215) that "the wages of labour depend upon the rate of profit and the productiveness of labour employed in the fabrication of those commodities in which the wages of labour are paid, and therefore the comforts of the labourer will depend on the rate of profits and the relative value of his labour and the productiveness of that labour which is employed in fabricating those commodities on which he wishes to expend his wages."

With the soundness of Longfield's theory of profits I am not here concerned. What I wish to point out is the close resemblance between his theory of wages and that of Jevons, and to call attention to the fact that it was published twelve years after the wages-fund theory had been formulated by James Mill, and while McCulloch and Senior were preaching it. It is certainly a singular fact in the history of the wages controversy, that such a theory should have been advanced at such a time, and that it should never have been noticed by any English economist. It will be seen from the extracts which I have given, that it is the rate of profit, and not merely the rate of interest, as in Jevons' theory, that Longfield treats as being determined by the utility of the last increment of capital.

Professor Jevons' *Theory of Political Economy* appeared in 1871. In the following year Mr. L. Shadwell, independently of Jevons, published an article in the *Westminster Review*, in which he explained a theory of wages of which, in a subsequent work, entitled *A System of Political Economy*, he speaks as being identical with that of Jevons. It does not seem, however, that there is any other point of contact between the views of these two writers, than the great stress laid by both of them on the connection between the efficiency of labour and the reward of the labourer. The views of Professor Hearn, whose *Plutology* was published about ten years before Professor Jevons' book, approach more closely to those of Longfield and Jevons. Unfortunately the value of the excellent chapter of the *Plutology* on the adjustment of the terms of co-operation, is diminished by the author's refusal to treat the question of real wages as one which lies within the province of the economist. He considers that it belongs to the economist to ascertain the amount of money which labour realizes, but to "follow the purchase-money of labour into the labourer's hands, and to make inquiries as to its application, belongs rather to the practical statesman" (*Plutology*, p. 330). This seems to me to amount to an admission, that the material welfare of the majority of the community is a subject with which political economy does not concern itself, since it only gives us, in terms of money, the labourer's share of the product, without telling us what amount of the "necessaries, conveniences, and amusements of life" that share will command.